American Benedictine Academy

HISTORICAL STUDIES · MONASTERIES AND CONVENTS

4. CONVENT OF SAINT BENEDICT

WITH LAMPS BURNING

WITH LAMPS

LET THEM JOIN THE NUMBER OF
THE WISE VIRGINS WHO AWAIT
THE CELESTIAL BRIDEGROOM
WITH LAMPS BURNING, TRIMMED
WITH THE OIL OF PREPARATION.

Ceremonial: Consecration of Virgins

BURNING

Sister M. Grace McDonald, O. S. B.

SAINT BENEDICT'S CONVENT

SAINT JOSEPH, MINNESOTA

NIHIL OBSTAT   Colman J. Barry, O.S.B., *Censor Deputatus*

IMPRIMATUR   † Peter W. Bartholome, D.D.
Bishop of Saint Cloud

April 2, 1957

The *Nihil Obstat* and the *Imprimatur* are ecclesiastical declarations that a publication is free of doctrinal or moral error, not a statement of the positive worth, nor an implication that the contents have the Bishop's approval or recommendation.

57–13066   Library of Congress Catalogue Card Number

1957
SOFTCOVER EDITION, 1980
PRINTED BY   The North Central Publishing Company
Saint Paul, Minnesota

St. Benedict in his Rule established a school of the Lord's service with prayer, reading, and manual labor as the occupation of his monks. But the spirit behind the directives of St. Benedict taught that his followers should adjust themselves to changing conditions and new opportunities. Prayer and work would go hand in hand, but the specific program of any given convent would depend upon prevailing conditions. The general aim would remain constant, but the particular work for each group would be altered by existing circumstances. It was a rule of life which could be followed in the cold north or in the torrid south, as well in the sixth century as in the twentieth. Adaptation to time and place was to be the particular characteristic of the Benedictine houses.

It is the purpose of this book to trace the growth of the Convent of St. Benedict in St. Joseph, Minnesota, from its establishment to the present time. In doing so, the author has attempted to show how a frontier country modified the character of an Old World Benedictine convent with its centuries of tradition, and how at the same time this religious community influenced in its turn the cultural and religious life of Minnesota and the Midwest. She has found it necessary, therefore, to describe the environment — national, political, and religious — into which the sisters ventured. After 1900 it was the lot of the community and its superiors to continue and to perfect the pattern of Benedictine life worked out by their pioneer predecessors. Each succeeding prioress was to direct the community toward one or the other facet of this Minnesota Benedictine pattern.

Mindful of the words of Pope Leo XIII admonishing historians to be fearless in telling the truth, the author has endeavored to draw a true picture of St. Benedict's Convent. But the whole story can never be told. The story evades the telling. It is a hidden one of love and sacrifice poured forth tirelessly within the confines of school rooms, hospitals, and orphanages. This ardent spirit is the breath of life to the entire organism. It actuates the whole. But it works in secret. It has been said, indeed, that the flames women fan do not become the roaring fires that lay low whole continents for Christ. Women perhaps are skilled in tending tiny sparks, the feeble flames that glow and glimmer again only in the warmth of encouragement. Many of the actions of women are great only in the light of eternity.

The history of St. Benedict's Convent would give a totally inadequate idea of the convent's labors if some space were not devoted to the development of the charitable institutions under its care. Separate histories of the Benedictine charitable institutions appear in Part Four of this work. No attempt has been made to write the histories of the Benedictine priories and foundations at Atchison, Duluth, Bismarck, Tacoma, St. Paul, and Eau Claire, which are daughter houses of St. Benedict's Convent.

Sister M. Grace McDonald, O.S.B.

FEAST OF THE ASSUMPTION OF THE BLESSED VIRGIN MARY
1957

TABLE OF CONTENTS

PART FOUR

CONVENT OF ST. BENEDICT'S INSTITUTES

LIST OF ILLUSTRATIONS

Parochial school teachers at
St. Cloud, 1889.

Chapel at St. Benedict's Convent,
1890.

The Reverend Henry Borgerding,
O.S.B., chaplain.

The Reverend Henry after thirty
years of chaplain service.

Mother Cecilia Kapsner.

Rear view of convent, 1910.

Mother Rosamond Pratschner.

The 1917 meeting of heads of Benedictine convents.

St. Bede's Priory erected.

The Most Reverend John Treacy blesses priory of St. Bede.

St. Paul's Priory erected.

St. Placid's Priory, Olympia, Washington.

The superiors of St. Benedict's Congregation meet.

St. Bede's Priory, Eau Claire, Wisconsin.

St. Mary's Priory, Nauvoo, Illinois.

Abbot Primate Bernard, O.S.B., visits St. Benedict's.

St. Paul's Priory, St. Paul, Minnesota.

Campus.

St. Benedict's Hospital and St. Raphael's Hospital, St. Cloud.

Second hospital in St. Cloud.

St. Cloud tornado, 1886.

Operating room, 1908.

Patient's room, 1912.

Graduate nurses, 1911.

The orphanage in St. Paul, 1879.

Sister Benedicta Klein, superior of orphanage.

Sister Juliana Venne and orphans.

Abbess Augustina of Eichstätt.

BETWEEN PAGES TWO HUNDRED FORTY-FOUR AND TWO HUNDRED FORTY-FIVE

Laborers in the Diocese of St. Cloud.

The Reverend Aloysius Hermanutz, O.S.B.

White Earth Indian Mission.

Mission school at White Earth.

Sister Philomene.

Sister Philomene's Indians at Calloway.

Interior of mission school at White Earth.

Log church at Red Lake.

Benedictines at Red Lake, 1889.

Red Lake Indian school.

Little Flower Indian Mission.

Reverend Francis Clougherty and

Benedictine sisters leave for China mission.

Benedictine sisters in their Peking convent.

Sister Rachel Loulan buried in Kaifeng.

Sisters nurse soldiers in Kaifeng, 1938.

Chinese missionaries work in refugee camps.

Formosa Middle School students.

Benedictine sisters in Tokyo.

Mission school in Tokyo.

Puerto Ricans, Japanese and Chinese enter St. Benedict's.

Mission school in Tokyo.

Puerto Rican missionaries.

A Puerto Rican scene.

The school at Humacao, Puerto Rico.

Hospitals at Ogden, New Prague and St. Cloud.

Dedication of St. Cloud Nurses' Home.

BETWEEN PAGES TWO HUNDRED NINETY-ONE AND
TWO HUNDRED NINETY-FIVE

Map of St. Benedict's field of work at home and abroad.

Map of St. Benedict's work in Minnesota.

PART ONE

OLD LAMPS IN A NEW WORLD

1 EICHSTÄTT AND THE CALL TO AMERICA

Eichstätt — Pennsylvania — Minnesota! The combination of place names seems to have been thrown together at random. Eichstätt is as far away as Bavaria and as long ago as nine hundred years. It is still a diocesan seat and the home of a convent of Benedictine nuns which was established in the eleventh century.

The Diocese of Eichstätt has an ancient and honorable history. It was founded by the great St. Boniface himself who made St. Willibald its first bishop. At the nearby town of Heidenheim, St. Boniface established a religious house of nuns which would follow the Benedictine rule, and he appointed St. Walburga its first superior. Such was the planting.

Ninety years after the death of St. Walburga her relics were transferred to Eichstätt. Local tradition tells us that one of St. Willibald's successors, a Bishop Otkar, was responsible for this transfer. According to the story this Bishop Otkar wished to rebuild and enlarge the small church and convent in Heidenheim. He set laborers to work around the place, but through carelessness these men disturbed the relics of Walburga.

Perhaps on the same night the bishop had a vision of St. Walburga who reproached him for the carelessness of his workers and threatened him with dire consequences should any further desecrations occur. Following this and several other events of a supernatural character the bishop decided to take action. He announced that to make full reparation for his earlier neglect he would transfer the relics of the saint to the more important town Eichstätt itself and reinter her body in the Church of the Holy Cross on the Romerberg.[1]

Some of the nuns of Heidenheim followed the relics of their foundress to Eichstätt and established a little convent in connection with the church. In time both became known as St. Walburga. Little is known of the history of this convent except that the number of nuns seems to have dwindled in the course of time. In the eleventh century Loedegar von Lechsgemund-Greifsbach decided to rebuild the church and cloister. Bishop Heriburt, then occupying the seat of Eichstätt, willingly gave consent and invited Benedictine nuns from St. Erentraud Shrine in Nonnberg, Salzburg, to make the foundation.[2]

For the next four hundred years the story is completely lost to the historian. But when the thread is again picked up in the fifteenth century, the pattern is not a pleasant one. Four hundred years of material well-being, liberal endowments, and membership drawn from the nobility had produced a blighting effect. Reform was needed, and it came when in 1445 the zealous and active Bishop John of Eich was appointed bishop of Eichstätt. With the sanction of Pope Callixtus he called in nuns from Marienberg near Boppart on the Rhine and appointed one of their number abbess. With these nuns to act as leaven the reform went ahead rapidly. Within a short time discipline and zeal again motivated the convent.[3] This new spirit proved so strong that the convent passed through the storm of the Protestant Revolution without a lessening of fervor.

Having passed through this crisis the convent was immediately faced with another. The famine and terror of the Thirty Years' War burst upon St. Walburga. At the beginning of the war, the front was so far from Eichstätt that the reigning Bishop George Rosch even undertook to build a new St. Walburga Church and renovate the cloister. But before the building was completed the conquering Swedes entered the town in 1634 and plundered the cloister.[4] Abbess Helen von Trokon-Zeulenreuth, who was too ill to flee, was taken prisoner along with six nuns who had refused to leave her bedside. The town was forced to raise a huge ransom to get the nuns released. The parting act of the Swedes was to set fire to the cloister.[5]

The end of the war saw the convent so poor that the nuns were forced to leave their enclosure to beg for food. In their search for aid some of the nuns even went as far as Vienna.

The nuns knew they would have to rebuild, but it seemed a hopeless task. Through war, famine, and pestilence, the population of the German states had been reduced fifty per cent. The treaty of peace had not improved the spirit of the people to any great extent because of its terms. To compensate the German secular princes for losses of lands to France, the religious princes, known as prince-bishops, were deprived of their holdings, both territorially and judicially. These lands were in turn given to the secular rulers. The new religious principle forced upon most of Europe by irreligious rulers that the religion of the sovereign would determine that of his people also helped to confuse the common man of the day.

Because of these two social upheavals the people rapidly developed a spirit of apathy in religion and anarchy in government while their leaders eagerly embraced rationalism. High and low alike drifted into religious indifferentism and antagonism toward the Catholic Church.[6] With the Church thus crippled the absolutism of prince and state grew without hindrance. All of this in turn paved the way for the French Revolution and the upheavals of the early nineteenth century.

For the sisters of Eichstätt, however, the French Revolution brought no change in the orderly life of peace, prayer, and penance for the sins of mankind. There were by this time forty choir nuns to carry out the liturgy with appropriate solemnity, and sufficient funds had finally been found to beautify again the Convent of St. Walburga with works of art. The convent also enjoyed the good will of nobility and royalty. In return for the interest taken by the convent in his daughters, the Emperor Charles VII presented the abbess with a costly pectoral cross hung with a broad blue ribbon. He granted her the right to wear this cross and to use it with her coat of arms.

The zeal of the convent had carried it safely past the perils of the French Revolution, but the community was again threatened when the new policy of secularization of Church property was instituted. As a reward to the Bavarian princes for their cooperation with Napoleon, the Treaty of Luneville in 1801 raised the Bavarian Prince Maximilian to the dignity of a king and forcibly annexed the Diocese of Eichstätt to Bavaria. Eichstätt had been one of the few religious territories which had escaped secularization after the Thirty Years' War. This act not only deprived the bishop of Eichstätt of his temporal power, but it also turned over the property of the diocese, including the convent, to the new kingdom of Bavaria.

The new king promised to provide for the expenses of the expro-
priated convents and religious houses, but it is a matter of history
that many of these houses were immediately closed and their inhabitants expelled in a heartless manner. St. Walburga's was allowed to
remain in existence, but the government refused to let it accept new
members and sent the younger nuns back to their homes. The older
nuns were given meager pensions and allowed to remain in the
convent until death.[7] These nuns were permitted to live in common,
but were forbidden to recite the Divine Office on the pretext that
it disturbed devotion. At the death of the last nun the state planned
to take over the property and put it to other use.

Upon the death of Maximilian in 1825 relief again came to the
Church. King Ludwig, his successor, was interested in re-establishing peace and reviving the Church. He early decided to restore some
of the convents and monasteries, particularly those of the Benedictine
Order. Fortunately for St. Walburga's its old nuns had survived King
Maximilian. It had not yet passed into the hands of the government.
In spite of the king's announced intention to renovate the convent
building, it took nine years before he could overcome opposition
within his own government and fulfill his promise. Even then, the
building still lacked means of support; the lands from which the
convent had formerly received rent and food had not been returned.
To make amends for this loss and to give the convent a means of
livelihood, King Ludwig presented a new building to the nuns and
decreed that they should open a school for the young girls of Eichstätt in October, 1836.

Material rehabilitation alone did not suffice in re-establishing
religious fervor. Thirty years of governmental interference in prayer,
religious services, and conventual life had deadened the spirit of this
convent as of all others. Fortunately for St. Walburga's the new
head of the diocese, Bishop Reisach, was a reformer; and under him
a new spirit was inaugurated. To enable this group of nine aged nuns
to carry out their liturgical prayer and other exercises, as well as to
undertake the new teaching program, the bishop brought into their
ranks some members from another Benedictine institution. The spirit
of St. Benedict was revitalized and St. Walburga's began a new
chapter of its history. Membership increased rapidly. Within sixteen
years the convent could respond to the need of the Church in the
United States and send religious to labor there.

During its nine hundred years of existence St. Walburga's has passed through vicissitudes of fire, war, famine, and secularization. It has survived them all while witnessing the rise and fall of empires, kingdoms, and dynasties. Though old in years, it has always retained that spirit of St. Benedict which makes for perennial youth. Sometimes this spirit wavered, but it was never completely extinguished. Fortunately for America, when the call came to plant a branch house in the new soil of the New World, the religious spirit of St. Walburga's was at its height.

One day in April of the year 1851 the peace of St. Walburga's in Eichstätt was disturbed when a traveler from America knocked at its portals. But his loud and determined knock could not have disturbed the conventual silence as much as did his message. Father Boniface Wimmer, O.S.B., the stranger at the door, had come to apply for sisters to teach the German immigrants in Pennsylvania.

This priest had been working among the German Catholics in Pennsylvania since 1846. Ordained a priest in 1831, he had entered the Benedictine Order at Metten, Bavaria, a few years later. Stories of the loss of faith among the German immigrants seeped back into Germany; and Father Wimmer, convinced that the loss was due mainly to the lack of German-speaking priests, started a movement within his monastery to stop this leakage. Of indomitable will and excellent organizing ability, he soon obtained permission to lead a small band of missionaries to the backwoods of Pennsylvania and there to set up a Benedictine priory. King Ludwig of Bavaria, interested in the Germans in America and always a friend of the Benedictine Order, aided the venture with a gift of money. Father Wimmer, with fifteen lay brothers and four students established the Priory of St. Vincent in Pennsylvania in 1846. After five years of work there, he saw the need for sisters to conduct the local school. He decided finally on Benedictines.[8] Characteristically, he did not make the appeal in writing but called in person at the historic old convent of St. Walburga.

At first the nuns were filled with consternation at a proposition so foreign to their life of strict enclosure and to their educational work which was still limited to girls. But when Father Wimmer pictured to the nuns the great loss of faith among children of German immigrants and the urgent need for Catholic schools, they soon became very enthusiastic about missionary work in the Lord's vineyard in

America. When the missionary promised that their enclosure could be kept, that they would be given only girls to teach, and that the American convent would be a dependency or a branch house of St. Walburga's, they gladly accepted his invitation. Father Wimmer remarked to a friend that the sisters were more enthusiastic than he had expected and without much ado promised him whatever help he needed. The bishop of Eichstätt gave his approval at once.[9]

The year following Father Wimmer's visit to St. Walburga's was one of raising funds for the expense of the journey, plans to equip the venture with the things they hoped would be most practical, plans concerning the personnel of the new community. Mother Edwarda Schnitzer, the abbess, petitioned the *Ludwig-Missionsverein* for passage money and for help in establishing the new American dependency. This *Missionsverein,* or Propagation of the Faith Society, had been founded in Bavaria in 1838 mainly to care for Germans who had migrated to America. The *Annalen der Verbreitung des Glaubens,* published by the Society, printed the yearly reports and letters of missionaries working in America, together with a report of all the money received and disbursed by the Society. Because of King Ludwig's interest in its cause, the Society was officially named the *Ludwig-Missionsverein.* The king himself answered Mother Edwarda's petition and granted her 8000 florins.[10]

But the question uppermost in the mind of each nun was who would be the fortunate ones chosen for this new field of work. This problem was not so quickly settled. Only after months of deep thought and prayer for guidance did Mother Edwarda announce her choice. The lot fell to the nuns Benedicta Riepp, Walburga Dietrich, and to the lay sister, Maura Flieger. Sister Benedicta Riepp, who was to be the superior of this small band, was only twenty-seven years of age and of slight and delicate build. Though the new climate and the hardships of mission life were to affect her health severely, she was destined to establish several religious houses in America. She had entered the Eichstätt convent from her home in Waal, Suabia, in 1844, and had spent some time there as teacher and novice mistress. The second member of this small group, Sister Walburga Dietrich, was an older woman who had acted as instructor of needlework at the convent. She was the daughter of a business man. The lay sister, Maura Flieger, was the daughter of a farmer in Heilig

Kreuz. She had also taught needlework after her entrance into the convent in 1847.[11]

In the absence of records and letters, details of the preparation for the new venture and the journey are meager. But a few facts may be gathered from reports and letters to the *Ludwig-Missionsverein*. No doubt the courage of these women did not falter up to the time of saying farewell to their convent home on June 11, 1852. Even then they did not feel completely cut off from St. Walburga's, for they were accompanied as far as Pleinfeld by Mother Edwarda and four companions. Full realization of their step came to them on June 18 when they stepped on board their steamer, the *Washington*, in the port of Bremen. The gang plank was drawn up and the ship pulled out of port. The three valiant women bravely choked back a sob; and better to gain control of their feelings, they started to pray the rosary. The presence of two Premonstratensian priests from Tyrol and two Servite priests from Innsbruck cheered those on board and made bearable the days that followed, for Mass was said and devotions were held in common every day when the weather permitted. One of the priests was Father Max Gardiner, a noted Indian missionary who was returning to his work in the Mississippi River region. He delighted his listeners with stories of Indian life.[12]

The ship reached New York safely on July 3, and the sisters disembarked the next day amid the celebration of the Fourth of July. Father Boniface Wimmer had failed to have someone at the port to meet them. Arrival in New York City is a bewildering thing at any time; arrival for foreigners in the midst of confetti, fire crackers, and shooting cannon was worse. For the timid cloistered nuns the experience must have been terrifying. To add to their distress, there was no one to guide them to Pennsylvania. Some kind person, perhaps Father Gardiner, must have befriended them, for they reached St. Vincent's Priory at Latrobe, Pennsylvania, a few days later. Here they rested a week before undertaking the 116-mile overland journey to St. Marys. Father Wimmer told them this stop was made to prepare them for the rough country surrounding their field of labor. There was another reason. He had failed to make a formal and regular application to Bishop Michael O'Connor of Pittsburgh for permission to establish the nuns there. Only now was he conscious of this neglect. He thought it better to detain the nuns until that document was procured. As soon as the permission was received the nuns joyfully started for St. Marys, their American foundation.[13]

Their journey came to an end on July 24 when they reached St. Marys Town, or St. Mary.[14] But what a contrast it was to the picture painted in such glorious colors by Father Wimmer on his visit to Eichstätt! Here they saw a stretch of country situated between steep and wooded hills, completely isolated from the rest of the world. The nearest railway was some days' travel away. Wagon roads were mere trails winding in and around the hills. Because of difficulties in transportation and in clearing the heavily-timbered land there were few cultivated farms. The country did not produce wheat; and little could be shipped to the place, for trains and steamboats were far away and the wagon roads were mere ruts.

Their second disappointment came when they were shown the building which was to be their cloister. It was an old frame building of many colors, located at the edge of a forest a hundred paces from the church then being constructed. This house had been used originally by Mother Caroline and the Notre Dame sisters, who had withdrawn from this field of labor in 1849 because of the hardships and the lack of promise of either growth or permanency. When the Benedictine nuns arrived they found that part of this dilapidated building was being used for parish services. They found, too, that the part used as church could be entered only by the public door and therefore was a public place, outside of their enclosure. In time this was remedied by putting a grille in the wall between the chapel and the enclosure. When winter came, the nuns discovered that the house was so poorly constructed that the wind blowing through the many crevices made it impossible at times to keep warm even in bed.[15] This was the unpromising place in which the women's branch of the Benedictine Order was planted in the United States.

As the history of the Benedictine nuns unfolds it will be seen that this first planting of the order in the United States is typical of many of its later foundations. There will be repeated the same generous response to the pressing needs of the Church in a particular locality at a particular era. The following chapters will tell the story of that response.

2 THE PENNSYLVANIA PLANTING

The school opened soon after the arrival of the nuns with an enrollment of approximately sixty girls. Sister Benedicta Riepp taught German, and Sister Walburga Dietrich gave instructions in needlework. As the nuns could speak only German, a lay woman was employed to teach English. Realizing their language handicap Father Wimmer arranged for English instructions, and every morning each nun had to recite five verses of Holy Scripture by heart as a practice in pronunciation and vocabulary. The school was a public school, and the salaries of the teachers were paid by public taxes. Nevertheless the combined salaries of the two nuns amounted to only $25.00 a month. Though this salary was assured and regular, it was hardly sufficient to support three persons. But the settlers were poor and could afford no more. Sister Benedicta Riepp, or Mother Benedicta, as she will hereafter be referred to, pitied the young children who "came to school half clothed and stiff from the cold, forced to sit all day with nothing to eat but a piece of black bread." [1]

The nuns fared hardly better than the little girls. Bread was portioned out to each nun daily, and potatoes and buckwheat cakes constituted the bulk of the meal. An extra plum or a few dried berries or a full bowl of mush was sufficient to make a red-letter day. One Christmas a large kettle of mush was cooked, and the nuns were told they might on this occasion eat until their hunger was satisfied. As one chronicler remarked, "The great treat was to be able to get filled up." [2]

The teaching staff was increased the second year when St. Walburga's sent over a contingent of one choir nun, two lay sisters, and one candidate. This group left Germany from the port of Bremen where they boarded the *Herman* on December 2, 1853. It was a luxurious ship, a thing of great wonder to these cloistered women. A fellow-passenger wrote of the wonderful life-saving devices in the cabins, of the brilliantly lighted rooms, and the hustle and bustle of the waiters in the dining room.

A second reinforcement for America arrived in 1855 after Father Boniface, recently made abbot, again visited Eichstätt and offered to take with him on his return to America all who offered themselves.

Despite their knowledge of the hardships of missionary life the nuns, Willibalda Scherbauer, Emmerama Bader, Philomena Spiegel, and two candidates offered themselves. Sister Willibalda, the daughter of a government official, was a music teacher as was also one of the candidates, Aloysia Knapp.[3] This group sailed from Bremen on November 1, 1855, on the *Washington* — the same ship that had carried the foundress and her two companions three years previously. It was a rough crossing that included a 24-hour storm. All became seasick, but most had recovered by the time the ship reached Southampton.[4]

This addition of five members from the mother house at Eichstätt still did not provide enough religious to accomplish the work Abbot Boniface Wimmer had planned for them. Further, his belief in the necessity of vocations from the area in which a religious house is established resulted in his urging Mother Benedicta to receive twelve novices on October 16, 1853, when the community had been established but fifteen months. Mother Benedicta felt this act to be premature. Her house was but a dependency of St. Walburga's and therefore it had no right to open a novitiate. She was upheld in this by Mother Edwarda Schnitzer at Eichstätt. In a letter dated July 4, 1853, Boniface Wimmer admitted:

> Those at St. Walburga's are not pleased that the Superioress at St. Marys opened a novitiate here. The prevailing opinion seems to be that St. Marys is only a subject house and is to be governed by St. Walburga's as a dependency. . . . I hope that my alleged reasons for independence from Eichstätt will be honored.[5]

Despite this recognition of the disapproval of Eichstätt Abbot Boniface inducted two new classes of novices in the following year and another in the spring of 1855.

Mother Benedicta found herself between the two authorities. She wanted to be loyal to St. Walburga's but she was under the jurisdiction of Abbot Wimmer who considered the convent at St. Marys a foundation which he had made and for which he was responsible. So there commenced between these two strong characters that great struggle which was to last until Mother Benedicta's death. Mother Benedicta, not yet thirty-two years of age, but a former mistress of novices, acknowledged that the circumstances of a new country, new type of work, and the poverty of the place prevented the Rule and

Constitutions from being followed in all details at all times. She acknowledged that some changes would have to be made. She had the same young American spirit as Abbot Boniface; but she would not make those changes without the consent of Mother Edwarda as long as the American convent was a dependency of St. Walburga's. She could see as well as Abbot Boniface that a complete separation from the European house would make the problem of adaptation to this new country an easier matter, but until St. Walburga's and the bishop of Eichstätt had declared the separation, she would not go ahead with changes. Abbot Boniface, on the other hand, in true American frontier fashion, could not wait while golden opportunities were passing by. This separation could have been an actuality in 1855. When Bishop Ottl of Eichstätt sent the third group of nuns to the United States he, at the same time, sent the following letter to the bishop in Erie.

George, by divine commiseration and grace of the Apostolic See, Bishop of Eichstätt. Greetings in the Lord.

When our beloved daughters in Christ, Willibalda Scherbauer and Emmerama Bader, professed, Aloysia Knapp and Catherine Schoenhofer, novices, and Philomena Spiegel, lay sister of the monastery of St. Walburga, made known to us their plan of emigrating to North America in order that there they may be associated to the convent of nuns of St. Benedict in Marytown, lately instituted as an aid for the education of girls, and when they supplicated earnestly that we send them for this purpose: we, granting their petitions, having held a council with the Prioress and Conventuals of our monastery, and after proper examination of the above-named religious, are sending them in the Lord, nevertheless on these conditions that they cease not to observe their sacred vows of religion strictly and that they fulfill chiefly their vow of obedience most religiously to the new superior, which they had vowed to the prioress. We earnestly commend these religious whose excellent fervor for the promotion of the honor of God and the salvation of souls we have acknowledged to the Most Reverend and Illustrious Lord Ordinary of that diocese, to whose jurisdiction they have been transferred, asking that he vouchsafe to receive them with apostolic charity. Given at Eichstätt in the Kingdom of Bavaria, October 6, 1855.[6]

However, this letter had no effect on the daily life of the nuns nor, as later developments will show, was the independence of the American house fully understood at St. Walburga's.

Bound up with this question of independence was the question of jurisdiction. Abbot Wimmer claimed that when Rome gave him jurisdiction over Bavarian Benedictine monks in the United States, the nuns were included, and that this jurisdiction was even recognized by the American hierarchy.[7] But two years later, in 1857, he was to attempt to have this claim confirmed by Rome.

Considering himself the founder and superior of the Benedictine nuns, Abbot Wimmer gave special care to their spiritual and financial needs. He controlled all income and the donations which the king of Bavaria allocated to them. At times some of these funds were diverted, temporarily, to the needs of his monks, and this caused misunderstanding. For example, a donation of 8000 florins intended for the building of a convent was used instead to complete some buildings at St. Vincent's. Some hint of this misdirection of funds must have reached the king, for in a letter to His Majesty on July 4, 1853, the abbot explained his act:

The actual process of building a convent could not be started immediately since the necessary plans and preparations were not and could not be made — due to the fact that the entire colony was working toward the completion of a new church. . . . Since the sisters could not make use of your Majesty's donation at the time they consented to lend me the money on condition that I use part of it toward defraying their immediate housing expenses.

He concluded the letter by promising that a convent would be built the following year.[8]

In other matters, too, Mother Benedicta and her nuns found themselves subject to the abbot's direction. He changed their daily *horarium* requiring them to adopt the order of spiritual exercises at St. Vincent's and rise at 3:30 A.M. to recite Matins and Lauds. Meditation, Prime, and Holy Mass followed. He it was, and not the community, who chose new members and judged their fitness to live a religious life.

That Mother Benedicta was desirous of escaping such authority is not surprising. Moreover, four years of residence at St. Marys had convinced her, as it had the Notre Dame sisters before her, that the location was not the best place for a foundation. The country was too hilly and marketing of the meager crops was impossible, for there was neither railway nor river within several miles of the settlement. At the same time several bishops had asked Mother

Benedicta to establish her sisters in their episcopal cities. She was particularly desirous to accept the offer of the Bishop of Erie, for she considered him her immediate ecclesiastical superior. The abbot would not hear of it. Finally in 1856 she did succeed in sending six sisters to take over a parish school in Erie. Matters became critical, and the abbot, according to his own words, "desired to end this feminine tyranny by deposing Mother Benedicta as superior and to put another in her place." [9] It was then that Mother Benedicta begged him to allow her to migrate to Minnesota with thirteen sisters.

The details of the migration to Minnesota are difficult to determine because of the contradictory statements made by the interested parties. In statements made some time later, the abbot claimed that the Minnesota house was established without his permission, in defiance of him, and without a formal invitation of the ecclesiastical authorities in St. Paul, Minnesota. The whole thing, he said, was undertaken in a spirit of revolt and contradiction, with the most flagrant violation of the Holy Rule and of the canons of the Church, and under these circumstances it could not be sanctioned.

However, a few facts can be ascertained. The Benedictine priests of St. Cloud and St. Joseph had written to the abbot in the spring of 1857, begging for nuns for their parishes. [10] On May 3 Mother Benedicta wrote to the abbot pleading to go to Minnesota:

I beg to leave St. Marys and go West lest my health be seriously impaired here. I feel that in the West I shall give better satisfaction than here. It is impossible for me to remain here where I have found neither contentment nor peace. Eight to ten sisters are willing to accompany me . . . in fact they are most anxious to do so. [11]

Sister Willibalda Scherbauer, too, had written to him of her desire to join the new foundation. In early summer the abbot capitulated and promised that after Profession Day in July he would release five or six sisters and eventually send them to the West. But in the meantime he would take them with him to Indiana, Pennsylvania, where they could be prepared for the western mission. He stipulated, however, that the sisters should not migrate to Minnesota until a decent house was prepared for them there. [12]

Mother Benedicta may have questioned his reason for taking the group to the settlement of Indiana, Pennsylvania, as a preparation for Minnesota. Early in June she wrote to Father Demetrius di

Marogna at St. Cloud that the Lord Abbot had given her permission to go to Minnesota and said that she should notify the Minnesota priest that she and her sisters would reach the area at the end of June or the beginning of July.[13] When a gift of money arrived from Europe, Mother Benedicta sent a band of six missionaries on their way to Minnesota. She accompanied them as far as Erie. Understandably, this hasty independence irritated the abbot, but he might well have remained only temporarily irritated had Mother Benedicta merely sent the nuns West. However, she herself left Erie for Eichstätt and Rome to seek clarification of her position in relation to Abbot Wimmer. When the news of both these events reached the abbot, he immediately requested Bishop Josue Young of Erie to detain two of the group who were still in Erie waiting for passage to Minnesota. Then began his own long wait for news from either Eichstätt or Rome.

Of this trip to Europe there is no record from the pen of Mother Benedicta or from her traveling companion, Sister Augustine Short. The letters extant were written by those opposing her action. But even from them the story can be constructed. Some months previous to this journey Mother Benedicta had asked Bishop George von Ottl, of Eichstätt, and Mother Edwarda Schnitzer of St. Walburga's for permission to come to Germany to seek counsel in the many problems that were facing her as a result of Abbot Wimmer's relation with her community. This was done at the suggestion, or at least with the consent, of the bishop of Erie. The bishop of Eichstätt replied that instead of making the journey she should send him a written report on her complaints and petitions and that he would then direct her. This Mother Benedicta did not do but departed for Europe as soon as she had sent the little band of nuns to Minnesota.[14]

Her arrival at St. Walburga's in Eichstätt was not a pleasant home-coming. Her reception was one of shocked surprise and of coldness — surprise because she had been advised not to come, coldness because the American convent had without proper authority received twelve novices into its ranks. Mother Benedicta was placed in an isolated part of the convent and throughout her ten-month stay she was "seldom permitted communication with its members." [15] Repulsed by Mother Edwarda, she appealed to Bishop von Ottl of Eichstätt to bring her cause to Rome. He, too, was cold and unsympathetic and he commanded her to put in writing a conscientious, short, and articulate account of her petitions, grievances, and questions. Help from the Eichstätt officials seemed hopeless and Mother Benedicta decided to seek aid from Archbishop Carl August, of Munich. In August she succeeded in getting to Munich where the archbishop and King Ludwig resided. Bishop von Ottl of Eichstätt had not been willing to listen to her; neither did he want her to present her case to these important men. On August 31 Bishop von Ottl wrote to the Court Chaplain at Munich:

One fine morning I was told that Mother Benedicta had left St. Walburga's and had gone to Ettal, Ulm, and Munich. I beg you, dear friend, to see to it that Benedicta does not present herself to His Majesty, King Ludwig. It would distress me unspeakably to have her annoy him with her groundless and unjustifiable complaints. I am very sure she will not dare to go to Rome — at least not while I am there.

To explain his own inactivity in settling the matter he added:

This problem of jurisdiction and dependence of the American convent should be settled by ecclesiastical jurisdiction in Rome. Possibly the Archbishop of Munich will refer this to the Holy See.[16]

He also wrote to the archbishop of Munich to express the wish that the archbishop himself bring the matter to Rome.

When Bishop Young of Erie learned of Mother Benedicta's difficulties in getting her cause brought before the Holy See, he wrote to the bishop of Eichstätt who then with the archbishop of Munich laid her petitions before the Holy See. One petition concerned the reception of candidates and novices. The second applied to the admittance of sisters to final profession. Mother Benedicta complained that the abbot admitted to profession "all novices whom he has invested with the habit without allowing the superior or the community to say a word. Whenever the choir nuns proceed according to ecclesiastical tradition and the novices fail to receive the required votes, then he takes them away by force and has them pronounce their vows in another house." [17] The third problem concerned the enclosure and therefore the vows. Solemn vows to which the nuns were accustomed were compatible only with a strict enclosure, and Mother Benedicta stated that the enclosure was impossible at St. Marys because the abbot sent his monks to the convent to work on certain projects with the lay sisters, and also because he refused to designate a room outside of the enclosure for the reception of visitors. Simply crossing the doorstep brought one into the cloister. Her next question pertained to the choice of superiors of the various American Benedictine houses: were they to be appointed by Abbot Wimmer or were they to be chosen by the religious members of those houses? Her last petition was that the convent and not the abbot have the control of the convent finances. Underlying all of the petitions was the question: how much authority did the abbot have in the management of the American Benedictine convent.

Six months of loneliness and isolation and criticism had now been spent by Mother Benedicta in trying to get her case brought to Rome. Early in the next year, 1858, the affair had progressed so far that it had been put into the hands of Cardinal Barnabo, Secretary of the Sacred Congregation of the Propagation of the Faith. In March Abbot Wimmer was notified of the charges and given a chance to present his case. At the same time Bishop Josue Young of Erie and Bishop Michael O'Connor of Pittsburgh were canvassed for their views.

Abbot Wimmer replied in a few months with six counterpetitions. He requested that the convents at St. Marys, Erie, and Newark be recognized as priories, be incorporated into the American congregation of monks, and be "placed under the complete jurisdiction of the abbot president of the congregation." [18] He requested that the Benedictines in America be allowed to make solemn vows without being held to the customary enclosure, and that they be permitted to teach in the public schools. Then finally, because of their heavy teaching duties, he asked that the nuns be permitted to substitute the recitation of the Little Office of the Blessed Virgin for that of the Divine Office. The abbot had previously dispensed them from praying Matins and he now asked, "Ought it to be done in this way, or the whole be said, or ought the Little Office be recited in its place?" [19]

These proposals were made in July of 1858. Abbot Wimmer was in the meantime quite confident of his standing in Rome, but he did not know that the American bishops Young and O'Connor would support Mother Benedicta's cause. Through a combination of circumstances the dispute was ultimately handled not by the Congregation of Propaganda but by the Sacred Congregation of Bishops and Regulars. Cardinal Barnabo, prefect of the former group, explained that the Congregation of Bishops and Regulars was at that time working on the question of the quality of vows which might be pronounced by the nuns in the United States. Since one question put forth by the abbot was about vows, the whole matter of dispute between Abbot Wimmer and Mother Benedicta would be given to the Congregation of Bishops. In a letter to Abbot Wimmer the cardinal said:

I also asked the Bishops of Pittsburgh and Erie to take care to relate to me whatever they know that pertains to this controversy. Furthermore, very recently, the replies of the Bishops, whom I highly approve of, have come to me, and since the question concerning the quality of the vows which may be pronounced by nuns in the United States of North America is now pending, having been brought up in the business before the Sacred Congregation of Bishops and Regulars, for that reason I thought that the controversy, which has arisen between you and Sister Riepp, should not be separated from that weighty matter of vows. Since this is the situation, I have passed on the petition of the aforesaid nun, your reply, and also the replies of the Bishops to this Congregation, from which, therefore, an opportune decision is to be expected.[20]

Long before the trial reached this point Mother Benedicta had returned to the United States. She returned apparently a loser — Abbot Wimmer's attitude toward her was one of condemnation and of severe ostracism. She found the convent doors practically closed to her. During her absence in Europe Abbot Wimmer had appointed another nun as superior in the convent at St. Marys and had confirmed Sister Willibalda as superior in far-away Minnesota. Not only had Mother Benedicta lost her place as superior, but no house could invite her to live with them. When she came to the convent at Erie she soon discovered that though she lived with the nuns she was not one of them and that she was carefully watched.[21] From Erie she wrote to the abbot, explaining her action in Rome and telling him of her present position.

Broken in health because of these problems and the ravages of tuberculosis, Mother Benedicta looked about for a place of rest. She had originally intended to join the Minnesota group on her return from Europe, and she still longed to do so. Mother Willibalda Scherbauer, whom Mother Benedicta had appointed temporary superior before leaving for Europe, was only too pleased to receive her, and made her request to Abbot Wimmer.[22] Some time during the summer months of the year 1858 Mother Benedicta and a companion left for Minnesota.

3 THE TRIP WEST

While Mother Benedicta was braving storms and seasickness on her way to Bavaria, her nuns were following the tortuous windings of the Ohio and Mississippi Rivers on a river steamer. As little as Mother Benedicta foresaw the humiliations and trials awaiting her on her arrival in Europe, so little, too, did these western missionaries dream of the trouble in store for them in Minnesota. Neither could they have dreamed of the great results which were ultimately to come from this venture.

Four nuns and two candidates made up this group of Benedictines setting out to plant the spirit of St. Benedict in the Midwest. It was a group of young nuns ranging in age from eighteen to twenty-seven. Sister Willibalda Scherbauer, the oldest of the group and superior by appointment of Mother Benedicta, seems to have been of a dominating personality, more forcible than gentle or sweet in character. The daughter of Graf Scherbauer, an assessor in Castel, Bavaria, she had been placed at an early age under the care of the Benedictine nuns at Eichstätt.[1] There she had often met King Ludwig I, the generous friend of German missionaries in America. There, too, she received the habit of St. Benedict and, only four years after her profession, volunteered to join her sisters already in the United States. She was an accomplished musician and tradition has it that she once played before King Ludwig. Though of Bavarian birth, Sister Evangelista Kremeter held the distinction of being one of the first women to make vows in a Benedictine convent in the United States. Sister Gertrude Kapser was born in Bavaria and, like Sister Evangelista, had come to this country with her relatives. She later entered the convent at St. Marys, Pennsylvania. She was destined to live an active mission life for fifty years in Minnesota and Kansas. The fourth religious, Sister Gregoria Moser, twenty-three years of age, and the candidate, Miss Mary Wolters, were Americans by birth. The other candidate, Miss Prisca Meier, was of Prussian origin.

The customary route of travel to the West for those encumbered by luggage was by rail and wagon to Pittsburgh and thence by boat down the Ohio River to the Mississippi. Although records are lacking, one can assume that the nuns followed the same route as did the Benedictine monks the previous summer, for it was the common one of that day. Railroads were still in their primitive form, very uncomfortable even for a short trip. Small holes in the ceiling of the coach gave sufficient ventilation during the winter. When the heat of summer became too oppressive, the wooden panels between the windows could be dropped for fresh air, but only at risk of being covered with flying sparks from the engine. Because of the great cost and inconvenience, the nuns traveled in a day coach in preference to the primitive sleepers. The sleeping cars were "rattlers" crudely fitted up with three tiers of shelves. With three tiers of bunks or berths in these low cars the traveler was compelled to slide into the berth and lie on his back. The pillows and mattresses for his berth were piled at one end of the car and were carried or dragged by him to his allotted place.

At Pittsburgh the passengers changed for the Ohio River boat. Traveling down the Ohio they passed Steubenville, Coal Port, and Cincinnati, where Bishop Purcell had his cathedral. Louisville was the next place of importance and a short stop was made here. This was a city boasting of twelve gas-lighted streets.

Snags, sunken boats, and reckless engineers made travel on the Ohio River dangerous. There were enough marks of former accidents along the way to keep the passengers apprehensive. Four miles from Pittsburgh could be seen the wreckage of a boat sunk in mid-channel. Forty miles farther on, the traveler saw a burned and abandoned steamer. Near St. Louis the captain of the boat could point out the spot where a part of a boat lay submerged. Nor was it encouraging for passengers to know that engineers had speed records to maintain or break, and that in their eagerness they often threw salt pork and grease into the fire box to create extra pressure. Too generous amounts of this fuel sometimes caused the boilers to explode. That meant death for all on board.

If no accident occurred, the boat reached St. Louis in twelve or thirteen days. Here the passengers disembarked and waited for a Mississippi River boat destined for St. Paul. The wait varied from a few hours to several days, for the hour of arrival and departure of boats was always an uncertain thing. Only packet boats attempted to make schedules. Irregularity was not due to carelessness, but to factors over which the boatmen had, at times, no control. Running into floating trees could cause a tie-up for repairs; a boat stuck on a sandbar might use up all its firewood in working itself off. Then it would be forced to send ashore for more fuel. Such were the every-day accidents that worked havoc with any printed time-table. But a few days' delay in St. Louis could be profitably used by the nuns to get a much needed rest and to refresh their souls by the reception of the sacraments.

The four-day trip from St. Louis to St. Paul was more pleasant than the trip down the Ohio. The Mississippi River boats were mar-vels of splendor because of the sharp competition between the various lines, not only for the immigrants but also for tourists and pleasure-seeking travelers. The cabins, the airy upper decks, the promenades, the gilded ballroom, were reserved for the pleasure-seekers. The immigrants and the nuns were crowded in the lower decks. But the Mississippi captains were noted for their courtesy to all, especially to the few nuns who came their way. The view along the route was one of ever-changing beauty. All these things lightened the journey. As they steamed up the river hour after hour, they were traveling the way of the early French explorers a century and a half earlier. Along this river had paddled LaSalle and Father Hennepin. There on Lake Pepin was the spot where, in what was later to be Minnesota, the first Catholic mission had been established by Father Guignas and Father Nicholas de Gonnor. Up this river in 1700 had journeyed LeSueur with a sailing vessel, two canoes, and nineteen men. Indeed, these intrepid Frenchmen were busy mapping the far interior of the country while their English contemporaries were still clinging to the Atlantic shore.[2]

To those early French explorers how everlasting must have seemed the tree-lined waterside. The endless monotony of trees and water, water and trees must have been depressing — especially when one recalls that muscular energy alone propelled the skiffs against the current of the stream. Now, a century and a half later, the Benedic-tine nuns who were traveling up this same stream could sit on the deck of a steamer and enjoy the windings of this river between its forested banks, broken here and there by small river towns.

The arrival of a steamer at the river towns was a matter of great importance to the inhabitants, and the usual large crowd was at the landing at St. Paul when the boat arrived that late June day in 1857. The whistle of the boat had announced the arrival while the steamer was still far down river. The nuns thought the whole town was out to welcome some noted guest, but learned that the crowd was the usual one eagerly awaiting mail or news from the outside world. When that small group of black-garbed women disembarked at St. Paul, few people noted their arrival, for they were in secular dress, wearing the shawls and poke bonnets of the period. But they must have made a pitiable appearance, travel-worn, bewildered, not knowing where to stay for the night. No one saw in this group the tiny flame of sanctity and culture that was being carried to the Midwest, nor the nucleus of an organization of over a thousand members, who in course of time were to educate and mold the minds and hearts of thousands in the upper Mississippi River valley.

In their predicament a kind citizen came to their rescue and directed them to the convent of the Sisters of St. Joseph. There they were hospitably received. The lodgings were primitive, but the joy of the nuns was supreme for they were once again within cloistered walls with the privilege of attending divine services. But their joy was somewhat dimmed when they learned that the ordinary of the diocese, Bishop Joseph Cretin, had died some months before and that Father Augustine Ravoux, the administrator, had received no notice of the coming of nuns into the diocese.[3] In this situation the nuns awaited the decision of the diocesan administrator, for they had no papers from Abbot Wimmer nor from Mother Benedicta. Fortunately for them, Prior Demetrius di Marogna of St. Cloud arrived in St. Paul on the third day of their stop-over. He was irritated, for the abbot had sent no letter announcing their coming and no place of residence had been procured for them in St. Cloud. But he was a gentleman of nobility with too much reverence for religious women to show his irritation in their presence, though he did express his chagrin when he wrote the following letter to Abbot Wimmer on July 14, 1857.

Most Reverend Father Abbot,

When I arrived with Father Cornelius at midnight on June 28th at St. Paul, where we went to get the citizenship papers for P. Cornelius, we were welcomed and not a little surprised with the announcement "the Sisters have arrived and are lodged at the hospital." I was surprised and embarrassed, and I could not suppress the cry of "over hasty." Moreover, the whole affair is enveloped in a mysterious obscurity, and I hardly know what to do with these women. . . . They have no letters or papers from you nor from their Superioress. I spoke with the Administrator of the diocese and he was annoyed. Finally it was decided that I was to take them with me and to care for them. This I then did. . . . There are four Sisters and two candidates besides Fini Leshall, an orphan. . . . All appeared pale, emaciated, and ailing.[4]

So the tired, disheartened nuns began the last lap of their journey on July 2 aboard the steamer *North Star*.

They must have sensed Prior Demetrius' annoyance, and once they learned that there was no convent awaiting them, the journey probably was not pleasant. But the fifteen stops along the way to load and unload cargo and passengers may have aided in distracting them from their gloomy anticipations. At last, on July 3, they were told they were nearing St. Cloud. But theirs was not to be a landing in the "grand manner" at the regular landing and up the sixty-foot ascent into the town. Two miles below the town, the boat was stranded for two days. Prior Demetrius and most of the passengers went ashore in small boats. The next day, July 4, the nuns did the same. Sister Willibalda seems to have enjoyed the episode for in a letter to Abbot Wimmer she wrote:

Father Prior and almost all the other people got out of the boat into a smaller one. We did likewise the next day since there was no expectation of getting immediate help, and we moved to land. We are all very happy to have had this unexpected experience; otherwise we would not have been able to see the Benedictine college because Father Prior said nothing to us about it, nor did he point it out. However, after this experience we were forced not only to pass by the little monastery, but also to enter it and to enjoy some refreshment, since we had been on the boat for three days without food, because the price of a meal came to half of a dollar. We were all very much pleased with monastic fare. We left [the boat] on the Fourth of July about three o'clock in the afternoon and were accompanied by the Rev. Fathers Demetrius, Benedict, and Bruno to St. Cloud.[5]

The history of the west bank of the Mississippi River, the side on which St. Cloud was tucked away, goes back to the days of French and Spanish sovereignty. The French flag flew over this territory from the time the explorers took possession of the land down to the year 1762 when France ceded it to Spain. When in 1803 it was learned that this land was to return to French sovereignty, the United States purchased the territory west of the Mississippi River known as Louisiana Territory. Included at its upper end was the site of the future St. Cloud.

Despite this early Americanization, St. Cloud remained Indian land until 1853, four years before the arrival of the Benedictine nuns. In that year the settlers put in their first crop of corn, but they could not acquire legal title to the land for it was still in the hands of the national government and had not as yet been surveyed. The white men found here previous to this date were not settlers, but fur traders, Indian agents, or Indian missionaries. Among the latter were Canon Francis de Vivaldi, who worked among the Winnebago Indians as early as 1851, and Father Francis Pierz, who came the following year to work with the Chippewa Indians.[6]

Father Pierz was a tireless worker traveling from one band of Chippewa Indians to another, converting them and strengthening them in their new-found faith. When at last he found that the white man could not be kept from encroaching on Indian land, and that he would inevitably force the Indian to share the land, if not to give it up, Father Pierz started a campaign for settling north central Minnesota with the type of white man who would not ruin his dear Indians. This campaign he carried on through German newspapers both in the United States and abroad, for it was to German Catholics that he particularly appealed. As a result of his enthusiastic, at times exaggerated, advertising of Minnesota, the upper Mississippi and Sauk River valleys were soon settled with German Catholics either from abroad or from the eastern and older sections of the United States. By the spring of 1854 at least fifty families had arrived in Minnesota in answer to his call.

Father Pierz sought to attend to the spiritual needs of the Catholic settlers in this section of Minnesota as well as to care for his various Indian missions. But, as he himself said, he found the work too heavy for his "seventy-year-old bones." At his request, Bishop Cretin of St. Paul appealed to Abbot Wimmer in Pennsylvania for priests to attend to the spiritual needs of the German settlers in Minnesota. Upon their arrival, Father Pierz handed over to them the site and building materials for a church in St. Cloud.[7]

St. Cloud in 1857 was a frontier town at a point where the Red River trail crossed the Mississippi River on its way to St. Paul from Pembina near the Canadian border. But it was not a typical river town, as it had been built not on the levee or very edge of the river, but upon its high banks. Neither did the village face the river. It looked toward the farms of the plains, suggesting that its prosperity would be agricultural rather than commercial. In St. Cloud the English-speaking pioneers had settled at what was called the Lower

Landing or lower St. Cloud. Here lived the professional men and government officials. Some of the inhabitants boasted of close connection with prominent people. There was Henry C. Fillmore, a nephew of President Fillmore; and Reverend Thomas Calhoun, whose father was a cousin of John C. Calhoun. Another, prominent in his own right, was C. C. Andrews, an author who was later to become United States minister to Norway. Here also lived Jane Swisshelm, the editor of the local newspaper.

Lower St. Cloud had but one main street, dusty, with here and there a wooden sidewalk before some pretentious log house of business. In fact, there were not more than a dozen houses in the settlement. The homes on the side streets were reached by grassy paths along the roadside. The Germans settled in what was called middle St. Cloud — in and around St. Germain Street where some of their countrymen opened places of business as early as 1854. Many of the names over the doors of those establishments in middle St. Cloud are well known in St. Cloud today. There Joseph Edelbrock and Balthasar Rosenberger had general stores. John Tenvoorde and Barney Overbeck conducted hotels for the numerous German immigrants, and John Metzroth was the tailor.

The spiritual shepherd of these German Catholic settlers was Prior Demetrius di Marogna. This man was a native of Lagarina in the Diocese of Trent and a member of the noble family of the Counts di Marogna. He had migrated to the United States where he had joined the Benedictine monks, and had led the first band of Benedictine priests to Minnesota.

Herds of deer and elk roamed within a few miles of St. Cloud and a few adventurous ones even strayed through the village occasionally. Bands of Chippewa Indians ten miles back from the village annoyed the settler with their untimely visits; and when their number reached five hundred, the settlers were worried and angry. Such a crowd of good marksmen left little wild meat for the white man, while their constant scalping parties kept the outlying farmers on the alert. Children could be hushed into obedience by threats of an Indian visit.[8]

But a touch of the "western fever" could change this frontier town of the plains into a thing of beauty. And most of the people coming west had that fever. One of them, Jane Swisshelm, the editor of the *St. Cloud Democrat* wrote:

At this time you may imagine the stage has been crossing the ferry and winding up and around a steep wooded bluff sixty feet high, so that we are in St. Cloud. . . . On one side of the principal street and on the bank of the river commanding a fine view of miles of river and green islands, woodland and prairie, stands the Stearns House. . . . On the other side of the street stands the office of the *St. Cloud Democrat*. . . . Up street stands the first church going bell on the march of civilization. . . . As you go on up street you come to a deep ravine which separates lower and middle St. Cloud and over which there is a bridge. . . . At the other end is Jones' blacksmith shop . . . Wearing's carriage shop, and Powell's hardware establishment.

Back from the Democrat office, in a beautiful grove of oak trees, stands a handsome building with cupola and bell. As you go on up the street past tasteful residences you pass the residence of Dr. Simonton. . . . There is a famous St. Cloud sulphur spring, the waters of which are imbibed by invalids as a cure for everything but secession. There is a magnificent but unimproved water power here; and "thousand islands" and Catholic school for boys lies just below. The site of St. Cloud is the most beautiful that can be conceived, and the best adapted for building a large city.[9]

But in this midsummer of 1857, the season of the nuns' arrival, there was no shade in the settlement but that cast by its buildings, for the district had been ravaged by a grasshopper plague just before the nuns arrived. An eye-witness of the tragedy wrote that within two days the fields presented the appearance of having been plowed, and the entire harvest was a dead loss for the settlers.[10]

4 FIRST DAYS IN ST. CLOUD

Even more distressing than the desolate scene in St. Cloud was the ever more vivid understanding of what it meant to arrive there with no home, no convent in which to resume normal religious life. Vacant houses to let were, of course, unheard-of. Even the generosity of people who offered the hospitality of their small two-room log cabins to one or the other nun emphasized their predicament and had to be refused. They knew that unless they established themselves so that they could chant the Divine Office together, eat together, work together, live together as a family under Sister Willibalda, they would not really be carrying the Benedictine flame from Pennsylvania to Minnesota. In the end, Mrs. Wendeline Merz offered the use of her large unplastered, unfurnished garret. Garrets in log houses were not spacious places. Even the largest and best were so low that it was possible to stand erect only in the middle under the apex of the room. Unbearably hot and crowded as such a place must have been, it at least promised the nuns some privacy and the possibility of living together and maintaining the routine of the convent life. Here they lived for eight days without beds or furniture of any kind, while Prior Demetrius di Marogna and his priests wrestled with the problem of what to do with them. Would they send them on to the St. Joseph parish eight miles away where a teacher was needed in the local school but where no house was to be had for a convent, or would they keep them in St. Cloud where they might find a house but where no teachers were needed? Father Bruno Riess, O.S.B., of St. Joseph, proposed that they come to that place and occupy the rectory which he would vacate. He even offered to give the nuns an 80-acre timber claim. But to teach in the district school they would have to take teachers' examinations and acquire teachers' certificates.[1]

In St. Cloud the German Catholics were divided on the school question. Among those who favored a public school there was division over the teaching staff. Some favored Catholic laymen of their choice, others were willing to accept religious. Prior Demetrius expressed his opinion of the plans when he informed Abbot Wimmer:

One group wants to hire a German teacher from Cumberland. . . . He is to be the head of the so-called free school which at the same time is to remain Catholic. Two incompatible ideas. Moreover, this school would not be under my supervision and direction — a thing I can never subscribe to.[2]

But before the nuns' arrival, the public school faction favoring lay teachers had been victorious, and a layman was already under contract for the school in St. Cloud. There was consequently no parochial school in which the nuns could teach. Nevertheless, Prior Demetrius decided to keep them in St. Cloud. He reasoned that until the lay teacher's contract ran out in spring the nuns could support themselves by giving lessons in music and fancy needlework, for the group of English speaking people which formed the professional and government class in St. Cloud would be good patrons. He declared: "There is no want of work for the Sisters . . . and the Americans pay better than the Germans."[3] Finally, Mr. John Tenvoorde, who was conducting an "entertainment hall" and a boarding house on what is now St. Germain Street near Fifth Avenue, was persuaded to let his boarders go and to rent the place to the nuns for $250 a year.

This house, the first Benedictine convent in the upper Midwest, was the plain frame and log structure common in pioneer settlements. The prior described it thus to his abbot:

In St. Cloud I had to rent a house, which was vacated for me. This included a garden. The house has two rooms and a spacious refectory with a built-on kitchen. On the second floor there are a large room, a small one, and above the refectory, a long attic room where ten or twelve school children's beds can easily be placed. Well, garden, and cellar are there in the enclosure. But the rent for the year is $250.00. . . . That price is cheap for here. The garden and yard are to be enclosed with a high board fence and will serve as enclosure. Should the remainder of the Sisters come to Minnesota we should have to transplant them to St. Joseph where a house could be rented. However, we would be obliged to remodel it at the cost of no less than $300.00.[4]

With what eagerness the nuns scrubbed and scoured the entertainment hall to make it serviceable as a convent! Furnishing the house took little time, for besides some clothes their trunks contained mainly books, sheet music, and religious articles. The windows were neatly covered with paper in lieu of curtains; a grille was made across the door of the room facing the street; a few treasured religious pictures were hung on the walls; and these religious women were again within a convent. When certain parts of the house were declared to be within the enclosure and a regular schedule followed, Benedictine conventual life for women was planted on Minnesota soil.

Though the community was now settled within cloister walls, it was still in a precarious position. Something more than insufficient means of livelihood threatened its existence. Since Abbot Wimmer felt the nuns had left for Minnesota before the time set by him, he intended to make them realize the gravity of what he considered an act of utter disobedience. Accordingly, he forbade Prior Demetrius to allow them a chapel and the services of a chaplain or to recognize them as regular religious.[5] Their constitutions held them to an enclosure, and the church was several blocks away. To hear Mass on Sunday they would now be compelled to break their enclosure. Such orders placed the nuns, as well as the prior, in a serious dilemma.

The abbot then demanded, through Prior Demetrius, a letter of submission to himself from the nuns. He further insisted that Sister Willibalda resign her position as superior and leave the convent, and that Sister Evangelista take her place as superior. Only when these conditions were complied with, would he appoint the prior as their chaplain and allow his priests to recognize them as religious. In this he was acting within his rights if he had jurisdiction over all Benedictine nuns in the United States. After reading Abbot Wimmer's conditions to the nuns, the prior sensed their ready desire for obedience and regularity. On August 12 he wrote the following letter:

I have read to Sister Willibalda the conditions mentioned in your letter. She assured me that the Mother Superior [Benedicta Riepp] as well as herself and the other sisters are agreed that they had no one else in mind as superior for their Minnesota foundation than myself in the first place, or if need be, yourself. . . . The Mother Superior and the sisters are very willing to have a superior in accordance with the prescriptions of the statutes. . . . The other points or conditions have so far been observed and complied with by Sister Willibalda and the sisters.[6]

Prior Demetrius, however, must have suspected that these nuns were not as culpable as the irate abbot made out. He wrote: "At present I have myself taken over the direction of the sisters because one cannot leave them to themselves. Nearly destitute, to whom should these poor children turn in this distant and strange country? What I did till now I did because I regard it as a Christian duty." [7]

Meanwhile, these orders of the abbot threw the little convent into consternation. Not to be recognized as a legitimate community, Sister Willibalda to be put out of the convent, Sister Evangelista Kremeter to be superior, and to have no relations whatsoever with Sister Willibalda or with Mother Benedicta on her return — all this produced tremendous confusion. Their troubled state of mind is reflected in Sister Willibalda's letter to the abbot when she wrote:

This morning after Mass Father Prior informed me that you, Father Abbot, are quite worked up against me personally and absolutely do not want to recognize me as a member of a religious community. Fr. Abbot, can you imagine that I am able to remain emotionally insensible at such a report? I was speechless and have wept continually. . . . I have much to accuse myself of before God and do so, but I know nothing to accuse myself of in this case. I ask you to tell me what I did wrong. Punish me as you wish, but do not dismiss me from the order. . . . Would you want to expel a poor nun from the cloister? No, I do not think you would want to do this. . . . Perhaps you are under the impression I came here in order to be the superioress. By no means. Mother Benedicta told me that the Bishop of Erie suggested that I should act as superioress until she returned from Europe. However, you may appoint any one in my place. I readily submit.

Nine days later she wrote again to Abbot Wimmer:

Father Prior tells me that you expressly forbade me to come to the West and that, after I had asked you in writing. It is true that I asked you to come here and you, Reverend Father, gave me a reply neither orally nor verbally. You did not say the least thing . . . so I thought the Father Abbot did not want to have anything to do with me. . . . Please grant me your pardon and set my mind at peace. I promise amendment and fidelity.[8]

For Sister Evangelista Kremeter, too, there was soul searching and heartache. To her appointment as superior of the Minnesota house, she protested her incapacity, and to the abbot's orders that she must have nothing whatsoever to do with either Mother Willibalda or Mother Benedicta, she answered: "How could I treat my own sisters thus? If your orders must be complied with, I will feel constrained to leave and seek to secure salvation in a stricter order. . . . With all the other points of your ultimatum it will be our endeavor to comply."[9]

A letter on August 27 showed that Prior Demetrius believed the action was harsh. He asked that Sister Willibalda be pardoned, given a penance, and be allowed to stay in the convent. He even ventured to add that in this Minnesota undertaking the "sisters had been in the wrong but there may have been fault and mistakes on the other side too." It seemed to him that "humanly speaking, the overhasty coming of the sisters to Minnesota was in reality by special permission and providence of God, which likes to transcend and cross the ideas and plans of man. The sisters are very necessary in St. Cloud. They are respected and loved." [10]

Despite the fact that his priests in St. Cloud had from time to time mentioned to Abbot Wimmer the esteem and honor in which the nuns were held by the people and the way in which monastic discipline was observed, he decided to see their way of life and to assure himself that they accepted him as their superior. The time was due for him to visit his monks in Minnesota and the two visitations could be combined. This was no sooner conceived than it was acted upon, and he started for Minnesota. He arrived one day in mid-October, unexpected and unannounced. His visit was cold and formal. He took Sister Willibalda to task and, according to his own account, she cried, and in tears begged for forgiveness. When he was convinced that the nuns were completely humbled and were not plotting disobedience to him and that Mother Benedicta Riepp had gone to Europe not to undermine his position but to have hers defined, he gave in and recognized the community as a part of the Benedictine family. He admitted that the nuns were doing a great good among Catholics and Protestants, and he appointed Sister Willibalda superior for three years. A few days later he wrote the following account of the meeting to Mother Scholastica Burkhardt at Erie, Pennsylvania.

Naturally we spoke of the existing conditions. Sister Willibalda cleared herself as well as she could and where she could not do so she acknowledged herself guilty and begged with tears for forgiveness. . . . She begged earnestly for recognition for her convent such as I gave the others and to treat her convent like the rest. I did not want to give in. After I convinced myself that they could get along, I gave in and recognized her as prioress and vested Prisca and Marianne, and allowed the new prior, Cornelius, to read Mass (in the convent) on Sundays and Communion days. I also allowed the brothers to bring the fuel to them and asked the prior to do what he could to help them get a house of their own. [11]

When he recognized the convent as one of the Benedictine family and appointed Sister Willibalda as superior, he stipulated that neither she nor the convent was permitted to receive novices; only he or his delegate, the prior, had that power. This was one of the things that Mother Benedicta was at that very time questioning in Rome. Little did either Abbot Wimmer or Mother Willibalda know that the Holy See would reject the abbot's claim of jurisdiction over the Benedictine convents and place them under the bishop's care.

It was well that the St. Cloud foundation was to be cut off from the house in Pennsylvania, for it would then be following a Benedictine tradition. According to the Holy Rule of St. Benedict, a Benedictine convent is an autonomous family group and down through the centuries Benedictine convents and monasteries had severed organic connection with the founding house as soon as they were self-supporting. The reason for this rending of ties was that, cut off from all dependent ties, the new convent became more readily a part of the region in which it was established. The new foundation thus more readily lost its foreign character, identified itself with the people, and recruited its new members from the people in whose midst it worked.

The ten months spent in their temporary abode showed the Benedictines' adaptability to any new situation. Crowded as they were in this place, they took in six boarding pupils. One of these was a six-year-old French-Indian girl, sent by the great missionary, Father Pierz, to be prepared for Baptism. She had learned her catechism in English. When the sacrament was to be administered to her, she answered the usual questions as instructed, but when the priest began to recite the Latin prayers she interrupted him with "What are you saying now? It is neither French, English, nor Chippewa. How can I answer you?" [12]

To others than boarding pupils the sisters gave religious instructions. This was apparently a very necessary work, for Sister Evangelista declared, "There are girls here fifteen years old who still do not know the alphabet nor the Ten Commandments, much less the Our Father. . . . In this land where everything is still primitive and the people unlearned, much good can be done." [13] Mother Willibalda gave instructions in singing, drawing and painting. Mary Wolters, a candidate, taught English and music. Sister Evangelista taught German. Sisters Gregoria and Gertrude taught needlework and sewing. The tuition for German or English lessons was one dollar per month, as also for sewing and knitting lessons. For finer needlework two dollars per month was charged. The non-Catholic members of the settlement asked for instruction in art and needlework. These were the people, too, who were clamoring for music lessons. So, at the suggestion of the prior, and in spite of their poverty, the sisters sent for a piano. The prior wrote on that occasion that the piano cost $330 including the cost of shipping it from Pittsburgh.[14] Except for their care of six or more boarding pupils, the nuns' work was mainly with the non-Catholics of the village. In contrast with the Catholic immigrants struggling to make payments on frontier farms, the non-Catholic and English-speaking settlers were likely to be professional men or government officials with a regular salary and ready cash for such luxuries as music and art. Many of this group had been prominent in social and political life in Washington. There was, too, a group of Southerners with their colored slaves living in the leisurely, aristocratic way of open hospitality in homes reminiscent of the South — low, one-story buildings with wide verandas more suited to southern temperatures than to Minnesota blizzards. Among the Southerners were Reverend David Lowery, the author of several books and the Tennessee friend of President Jackson and of Zachary Taylor; and L. S. Hayes, the man who was responsible for getting young Thomas Jackson, later known as Stonewall Jackson, an appointment at West Point.[15] This bit of transplanted South with its grace, leisureliness, and its chivalry did tend to keep St. Cloud from being overwhelmed by the struggle for existence or carried away by the desire for wealth. Within six months after the arrival of the first English-speaking settlers four pianos had been brought to the settlement. But the German settlers had brought with them their traditional love of music, even though they were without money to procure instruments or lessons. Because of these economic factors the sisters found their first music pupils among the English-speaking and non-Catholic groups. But if there was not much money among the German settlers nor many provisions, there was charity. These good Catholic frontier people did not let the nuns starve and often brought food from their own scanty stores. Sometimes it was vegetables, and sometimes it was that very scarce article, milk. One morning, on opening the kitchen door, they found that someone had presented them with a young pig. Once in a while they received wild pigeons.

Such gifts in the year 1857 were precious, coming as they did from settlers whose fields and gardens had been stripped by grasshoppers so completely that there was not even seed for the coming spring. Some potatoes and a bit of corn had been saved from the grasshoppers, but the half dozen cows left without proper forage did not give their usual supply of milk. Almost all of the chickens had died. Never having met with such an abundance of grasshoppers before, the chickens did not know when to stop eating, and death was the result. The following incident comes from the memoirs of one of the Benedictine priests.

Father Clement, although a powerful man, succumbed under the pressure of hard times. He was seized by typhoid as physicians call it, but was probably the result of endurance and starvation. . . . Light but nutritious diet was prescribed for him, but we had no eggs in the house, moreover no means to obtain them. The hens enjoyed the grasshopper banquet and perished in great numbers. The physicians prescribed chicken soup and eggs. I canvassed the farms of the vicinity and finally succeeded in finding at St. James one old hen and one egg. For the hen I paid $1.00, for the egg 25 cents; and after this I had no more materials for chicken soup. . . . God helped me in the emergency and my patient recovered.[16]

The settlers that winter lived mainly on potatoes and corn. Potatoes, cooked in their jackets so that nothing would be wasted, alternated regularly with corn-meal mush served without milk or butter. The small box-shaped coffee mills common in homes of that period ground no coffee that year but were used instead to grind the precious kernels of corn for mush and bread. Roasted corn took the place of the coffee bean. The settlers could add to their meat diet by hunting wild game, but to cloistered nuns this means was not open.

The Benedictines no doubt fared more poorly than did the settlers. But they were also probably better fitted to stand the shortage of food than were the other inhabitants, for these religious women were accustomed to a life of frugal abstinence. Their rules and statutes as brought from Bavaria did not permit breakfast, and meat was allowed them but three times a week. Even in times of plenty their noon meal was not to consist of more than soup, bread, and one other dish. The evening meal was about the same. They were accustomed to cold rooms in winter, for by the same statutes stoves and fire places were allowed only in the workroom and classrooms.[17]

For the nuns as well as for the other settlers, procuring clothing was also a problem, demanding not only a trip to St. Paul, but money as well. And money was scarce throughout the United States for the country was caught in the throes of a financial depression. To save their woolen habits, the nuns wore them only for their morning chapel services. For the manual labor of the day, they wore calico dresses.[18]

In these privations which the nuns shared with early settlers they not only endeared themselves to the people but learned to understand their needs. At the same time the Bavarian culture of these Benedictines was to be gradually transmuted to one suitable to nineteenth century America. After several months of adaptation to western life they were better prepared to undertake work in the parochial schools of Minnesota — schools quite different from the Bavarian convent schools where the daughters of noble families were educated.

5 EARLY CONVENT AND SCHOOL

During the nine months the Benedictines lived in the rented Tenvoorde house, they had no opportunity to take part in parochial activities or to widen their influence among the people. Their contact with the people of the settlement in 1857 came only through private lessons in music, needlework, and religion. But Father Demetrius di Marogna, O.S.B., and Abbot Wimmer had decided that as soon as the lay teachers' contract expired, they would insist that the parishioners accept the nuns as teachers. Both nuns and priests counted the days until they could put the new plan into operation.

In preparation for the event, the parish plastered the church and the classroom and laid a floor. The upper floor of this 40 by 24-foot church was made habitable as a home for the sisters by the erection of a partition or two and a bit of plaster. But the building was poorly constructed. It gave the appearance of being "sided" but the siding was nothing more than the clapboards nailed on the skeleton framework or naked studding. This, faced on the inside by a coat of plaster, was the only thing between the interior and the cold winter winds. No system of ventilation was needed: every joint and seam admitted the cold prairie winds. The floors, of rough planks with wide cracks, were to prove a sore trial to the nuns during the winter months. Soon their feet were so frostbitten and swollen that they could not wear shoes and were forced to bind their feet in straw, a measure originally adopted to prevent frostbite. A highboard fence was erected enclosing the yard and buildings. In this enclosure was a pyramidal shed in which was hung the church bell — the first church bell in St. Cloud and in Stearns County.[1]

There was excitement in St. Cloud in the early spring of 1858 when it was announced that the Benedictines were ready to open school. Parents called to inquire about textbooks, slates, and tuition. Those opposed to putting nuns in charge and those preferring a district school went about gossiping and trying to defend their position. Although they did not register their children, approximately twenty pupils were enrolled the first days. The records of students have long been destroyed, but the names of some are known. Among these were Mary Edelbrock, Lizzie Rosenberger, Catherine Felders, and Mary Brown. Among the boys were Anton, Barney, and Joseph Edelbrock, Henry Rosenberger, John Niebler, Joseph Reichert, and Louis Emmel. Among the pupils taking private music lessons were Jennie and Mary Mitchell, Mary and Jennie Cramsie, Sophia and Cecilia Corbett, and Nettie Swisshelm, children of non-Catholic parents.[2] The non-Catholics were generous in their patronage, and Jane Swisshelm, the editor of the local newspaper wrote: "There is a school kept by a company of Benedictine nuns where is taught, in addition to the common branches, German, drawing, music, and needlework. The subjects are taught by ladies of polished manners and unusual proficiency. The school is in much favor with our citizens and is in a flourishing condition." [3]

Teaching in a frontier school was anything but monotonous. Rumors of Indian outbreaks, the arrival of river boats, and the passing of the noisy Red River caravans all broke the routine. During this first school term a band of Sioux Indians took advantage of the absence of the Chippewa warriors from their camp and killed eleven of the old and defenseless Chippewa Indians left behind in their village. In retaliation the Chippewa chief, Hole-in-the-Day, and two attendants started out in pursuit of the Sioux. They returned triumphantly with several Sioux scalps which they proudly showed in the streets of St. Cloud. A little later a band of Indians camping south of the convent paid the Benedictines an unceremonious visit. They sent the nuns into spasms of fear as they danced their war dance to the pounding of drums and the noise of their own voices. They would wander about the village peering through the windows and even into the school room. One hideously painted Indian made the rounds of the houses to appear suddenly in the kitchen doorways.

One day in late July a band of Indians came down the Mississippi River in their canoes and camped on the islands near the settlement. The whole village turned out to see them as they crossed the river. According to the news reporter, the most conspicuous member of the group was a squaw, a tall striking figure, dressed in red leggings and a blue blanket "which she wore wrapped straight around her from the neck to within six inches of her ankles." These periodic visits of the Indians not only enticed the white children away from school, but they frightened the nuns — until the veteran Indian missionary, Father Pierz, told them that the Indians would never harm the sisters or the Blackrobes.[4]

The teachers had difficulty in keeping the children quiet and attentive when a distinctive creaking, squeaking sound announced the coming of a train of Red River oxcarts. These two-wheeled carts, carrying from eight hundred to one thousand pounds of furs and meats, were drawn by oxen in a single harness of untanned hide. The carts were made without iron. Wooden pins took the place of bolts and nails. The sound made by the oaken axle in the ungreased wooden hub could be heard a mile or two away. As soon as that creaking sound was heard, the pupils in the classroom became restless and found excuses to walk across the room to the blackboard or to the drinking-water pail. The drivers of these carts, usually metis from Pembina, would be taking the products of the Red River district to St. Paul. In the summer of 1858 a caravan of one hundred and forty carts made its way across the prairie to St. Cloud. Late in the week it camped on the prairie nearby to wait till Sunday so that the men and women could attend Mass in the little church. In the afternoon the whole caravan traveled along the main street and passed the convent on its way to the ferry which was to bring them over the river. The sight was picturesque. Everyone, young and old, turned out to see the train and probably to transact a bit of business with the drivers of the carts. The following incident was described by an eyewitness:

Some of the carts had metal boxes for axles to turn in. Most of them were drawn by oxen in single harness of untanned hides joined together with the same material. . . . There were several women in the group and each drove her own cart. Their carts were painted and covered. One woman stopped her cart before going down the incline to the river and handed her child of six months to me. The baby was dressed Indian fashion. She smiled, then took the baby on one arm and the bridle in the other and down to the river she went.[5]

One of these caravans carried three bears, two black and one cinnamon. What stories the children had to tell their teachers the following day!

. All schools of that day deemed it necessary to put on a heavy program at the close of the term of school. In fact, the public judged a teacher by her ability in "putting on programs," and the Benedictines willingly or unwillingly adapted themselves to that custom. Because it was customary to give each child in the school a chance to appear on the program these "exhibitions" were lengthy affairs. The public's willingness to sit through long demonstrations may be ascribed not only to parental pride, but to the scarcity of other cultural entertainment. Perhaps the fact that the superior, Mother Willibalda, played three musical numbers with accompaniment by two prominent citizens was itself an attraction. The *St. Cloud Democrat*, June 30, 1859, carried this announcement of what was probably their first recital:

The school under the charge of the Sisters will give an exhibition on Thursday evening the 7th. at 8 o'clock. They will be assisted by members of the Young American Literary Society. . . . There will likely be a small admission fee for the benefit of the school. It will be in the chapel and those who want seats will have to go early.[6]

On July 21, appeared the following frank appraisal of the program:

On Thursday evening the 7th, the school under their charge, assisted by a number of the other young folks, gave an exhibition which gave great satisfaction to a large audience, notwithstanding the performance was long.

The exhibition was opened with piano music, "The Vienna March," played by Miss Cramsie. Then followed "The Portress," a comic dialogue by Sophia Corbett, Jennie Cramsie, and Mary Mitchell. . . . Declamation by Jessie Garlington. "Lala Mendi," played and sung by five voices. "The Egg Thief," (German) a comic dialogue, by Katherine Fielders, Henry Rosenberger, and John Niebler. This piece was capitally performed and exceedingly amusing.

Next we had the "Old Playground," played and sung by Sophia and

Cecilia Corbett. Always good. "The Swiss Air" by Hunten, played by the Lady Superior and Mrs. Palmer. . . . "Phantasm" played by the Lady Superior in masterly style. . . . "School Committee" a dialogue by Misses Cramsie, Leaschell, Mitchell, and Monti. "Overture" on the piano by the Lady Superior accompanied on violins by Mr. Edelbert, and Josephine Leaschell. Very fine. "Ezekiel Stubbins," by Stephen Miller, Jr., J. B. Marvin, William and J. Mitchell, and W. F. Miller, not well done, as the performers were weary, having walked from Grand Lake that day. . . . "The Chimney Sweep," a dialogue by Mary and Jeannie Cramsie, Mary and Jennie Mitchell, Cecilia Corbett, Josephine Leaschell, and Nettie Swisshelm.[7]

In the audience that evening were the proud parents of the pupils and many of the leading personages of the village. The pastor of the parish would consider it his duty to be present at the closing exercises of this new school. Another prominent figure was Mrs. Jane Swisshelm, the editor of the *St. Cloud Democrat,* who was present to watch her daughter. Mrs. Swisshelm was an abolitionist and a woman suffragist who was soon to arouse the locality by her personal and caustic remarks about local and national celebrities whose political views differed from hers. Abolition of slavery was her constant battle cry. When one or other of that group of Southerners who had settled in upper St. Cloud and in Sauk Rapids drove through the dusty streets of St. Cloud and past her newspaper office with a Negro slave coachman, this wielder of the pen would go into a frenzy and publish in the next issue of her paper an article about slave holding on free soil.[8] The partisanship of her press is well illustrated by the following editorial published in an issue in 1861 when President Lincoln had asked for a day of fasting and prayer throughout the land:

Fast day! No one paid any attention to it here. The people have an idea that this is a time for work; that work is prayer and that the President had better be doing his duty relieving the forts and protecting the public property than sniffling and asking an insulted God to suspend the working of his inimitable laws to cover up his treachery.[9]

Similar caustic statements made about prominent men and women of St. Cloud soon brought their wrath upon her, and one night her press room was broken into and the type thrown into the nearby Mississippi River. Scathing as were her remarks about the local and national leaders, she was generous with praise where she thought it was due, and never printed anything even slightly derogatory about the Benedictines and their work. In one issue of her paper she wrote:

The Lady Abbess is small, slight, delicate, graceful, and as accomplished a lady as you could meet in any circle. From her waking the first echoes of those broad prairies in a call to bow regularly at an altar of Christian worship and my wielding the advance press, I am inclined to dispute with the lords of creation the palm of always holding the flagstaff as westward the star of empire takes its way.[10]

The friendship of this fiery woman suffragist and abolitionist, who was, moreover, a strong Calvinist, with the cloistered nuns is hard to explain. On the surface they had nothing in common except their sex and a Pennsylvania German background. But perhaps courageous loyalty to ideals was the bond of mutual admiration.

Despite the satisfactory work performed by the nuns, the income from this small school was not sufficient to keep them in clothing and food, for the tuition of $2 per child per semester — which the parish paid — brought them only $60. Nor was even this meager sum always paid regularly. A line in the old parish Sunday Announcement Book of St. Mary's Parish reads: "Nothing has been paid for the last five months. Since the Sisters opened the school, almost nothing has been paid." A fair or bazaar, the nuns decided, would be the best means of raising the necessary funds; and they immediately got out their needles — crochet needles, knitting needles, fillet needles — as well as tatting bobbins. The bazaar proved a success, and these bazaars became an annual affair. One advertisement informed the residents that the fancywork for sale and for raffle would be on display at Grandelmyer's store and at the convent; that every one of the three hundred twenty-five articles was worth the $1 entrance ticket. In the list of articles were such things as "men's embroidered linen bosoms, gentlemen's stitched shoes, ladies' white embroidered pantalettes, crocheted suspenders, crocheted lamp nets, fancy feather flower baskets and snuffer plates." [11] From the proceeds of the fair a few improvements were made in the school and convent building, and a few debts paid.

But there was more to the lives of the nuns than teaching and programs and debts, paid and unpaid. There were, for instance, the visitors. In 1859 a group of Grey Nuns, traveling by oxcart on their way to St. Boniface, Canada, stopped three days with the sisters in

St. Cloud.[12] Mother McMullen, one of the group, confided in her diary that despite the poverty of the place she and her companions were showered with care. She regretted that they could not converse fluently with the Benedictines, only one of whom spoke any English.

Bishop Thomas Grace of St. Paul visited the Benedictines when he came to St. Cloud in 1859 to administer the sacrament of confirmation. A more interesting visit by Bishop Grace occurred in 1861 when he stopped on his way from Pembina to receive some new members into the convent and to give the nuns the opportunity of caring for his companion, the crippled Indian missionary, Father Joseph Goiffon. It is not hard to imagine the sympathetic questions that drew from the good priest and Bishop Grace the story of the sufferings that explained his crutches and wooden leg.

It was on a return trip to Pembina, after an official visit with his bishop in St. Paul in October, 1860, that disaster struck Father Goiffon. Within one day's journey from his mission and anxious to reach his destination in order that he might say Mass the next day, November 1, the Feast of All Saints, he left his slow-moving caravan of Indians and metis and pushed on ahead alone. He had but twelve more miles to travel when rain, snow, and hail set in. Soon all trails were wiped out and he lost his way. Dismounting, he rolled himself up in a blanket and turned the horse loose to find its way home. On the second day he found his horse not far away, stuck fast in the mire. Seeing that the caravan had not passed that way but had taken another route, he gave himself up as lost and began to prepare for death. On the fifth day two men passed and heard his moans. They found the missionary in a condition bordering on insanity. His clothes were frozen to his body and his cassock had literally to be chopped off. A kind settler cared for him in his house, but when gangrene set in he was moved to the bishop's house at St. Boniface across the Canadian border. There a double amputation of one leg and one foot was made in order to save his life. Finally, the last sacraments were administered to him and preparations were made for his funeral. The sisters in the kitchen busy making candles for Christmas thought they might as well make those for the probable funeral as well.

Father Goiffon no doubt smiled as this part of the story was told to the St. Cloud nuns. The Canadian sisters nearly finished the story of his life when they accidentally turned over a pot of candle grease into the fire and set the whole house ablaze. He was hastily picked up and deposited in a nearby shed. "Neither did this kill me," and he might be excused if he said this with a bit of bravado. Proudly he could point to the crutches and the wooden leg which he had made while convalescing in the hospital at St. Boniface.[13]

But the most exciting event was the arrival of Mother Benedicta Riepp. It will be recalled that on her return to the United States in the fall of 1858 she had found no room in the convents in the East; she stayed there only long enough to notify Abbot Wimmer of her desire to go to Minnesota where she planned to go from the first. Though she was broken in health and though Rome had not yet settled her problems, she was confident that justice would prevail; and she encouraged her sisters in patience and endurance. When she arrived at St. Cloud she quietly took the position of a subject member of the community while Mother Willibalda completed the three-year term to which Abbot Wimmer had appointed her.[14]

Mother Benedicta's presence and influence tended to strengthen the spirit and the observance of Benedictine customs. Though the nuns had always wished to chant the Divine Office with the dignity they remembered, circumstances in pioneer Minnesota had made this impossible. However, by 1860 their number had increased to twelve and then it was possible to recite the Office with the liturgical solemnity to which the older members had been accustomed in St. Walburga's. In many other things, such as food and enclosure, the Rule and statutes could not be observed. Yet the ideal was always kept in mind.

The community soon realized that the rule of strict enclosure brought with them from Bavaria was hardly compatible with teaching in a frontier parochial school. Playground supervision from the window or doorway was understandably a failure. Neither was proper prefecting of the pupils possible during religious services. Because the chapel was public and outside of the enclosure, Mother Willibalda and her nuns could not attend services with the pupils in the body of the chapel. It is true that in St. Walburga's the nuns attended Holy Mass in a public chapel, but their choir stalls were so placed that the nuns could neither see nor be seen by the parishioners, and their choir was entered only from the convent. Here in St. Cloud the religious tried to follow the same idea by having a grille made in the wall between the church and convent. This allowed them to participate in services without leaving their convent enclosure. Mother Willibalda, who was church organist, presided at the organ from her side of the grille, and the choir sang from the parish side. This aloofness from the people of the settlement was so alien to the western frontier spirit of neighborliness, to that close spirit of unity that made everyone's joys and sorrows the concern of the whole settlement, that it tended to alienate some of the parishioners.

Hovering over this period of struggle to establish and to adapt cloistered Benedictine life to the Minnesota frontier, was a cloud of uncertainty. What was the status of the nuns? What would Rome say to Mother Benedicta? To Abbot Wimmer?

6 MISUNDERSTANDINGS, INDIAN WARS, DEATH

While the nuns in the convent at St. Cloud were awaiting Rome's decision in the matter of the abbot's jurisdiction, their general peace and routine were broken one day by startling news. Parishioners called to congratulate the nuns on receiving a munificent gift of money from the King of Bavaria. Others came to congratulate them and to collect bills. They were soon harassed by the creditors who refused to believe that the nuns knew nothing of the gift. They had not received the money nor had they received any notice that they were to be recipients of a kingly donation. On questioning the pastor, they learned that in the fall of 1858 the King of Bavaria and the Ludwig Missionsverein had donated $1,280.00 to them; that the royal gift had been sent to Abbot Wimmer, earmarked for the sisters; and that the abbot had used the money to purchase land four miles beyond the settlement of St. Joseph to which the Minnesota monks had squatters' claims.

The situation which gave rise to this appropriation of money was one common on the American frontier. The monks in St. Cloud, like the other early settlers, had squatted on land owned by the government and not yet offered for sale. According to law, after the government surveyed the land and put it up for sale, the squatters — if they had the money on hand — could purchase the land. If not, the land and all improvements went to the man who had the cash. This required ready cash; cash was scarce and interest high in that year of continuing financial depression. With the king's gift at hand, the abbot saw the chance of a lifetime to procure those beautiful acres some twelve miles from St. Cloud. It must also be remembered that in 1858 the abbot's claim of jurisdiction over the Benedictine sisters in America had not as yet been settled by Rome and he still claimed he was protector and head of all Benedictine convents. Besides, he was sure the king would appreciate his good business sense in grasping every opportunity to establish a strong monastery in the West. He felt that procuring land for the establishment of a strong monastery far outweighed the needs of the nuns at the time, and so he had acted.

Knowing nothing of this reasoning and realizing that the money was lost to her, Mother Willibalda let no time elapse in notifying King Ludwig of what she thought was a misapplication of funds, and the abbot was questioned by Court Chaplain Mueller in a letter of March, 1859:

Did you have the right to withhold the money from the sisters? I consider it wrong. This is the third time you have done this. The first time to the sisters in St. Marys, Pennsylvania, the second time to the sisters in Newark, where they received only half the sum designated for them. And now complaint from St. Cloud. You are losing your credit with His Majesty. I succeeded in excusing your action to His Majesty but you must pay back to the sisters the 3000 florin [$1280.00] by September 1859. I have informed Sister Willibalda of this decision. The Mission Society will withhold its designated 3000 florin from your allotment in case you do not pay back. That is the situation. I advise you therefore not to do again in the future what you have done in the past. The women are making strong representations against you. I believe of course that you need money and could gain great advantages with it, but then this does not give you any right to take for your use money that has been designated and destined for others, no matter how honestly you mean it.[1]

On April 9, the abbot wrote to King Ludwig:

Gracious King and Protector, it grieves me deeply if I have lost your respect in this case of the 3000 florin because of Sister Willibalda's letter.

I am sorry if I have done anything not in accordance with the general rules. It matters little to me what worldly men think of me but I am in no way unmindful of how good men esteem me. As I place Your Majesty in that class let me put my case before you so as to regain your esteem. . . . First, I must acknowledge that I have made a mistake. I should have left the gift untouched and to have begged Your Highness to give further directions. Under ordinary circumstances I would have done that, but this was not an ordinary circumstance, for here I was prompted to act only for the love of Your Majesty. I wanted to found a monastery — not a simple priory but a potential abbey — under the title of St. Ludwig in remembrance of our debt to you. . . . A good piece of land was claimed by the brothers but this was to be lost if I could not pay for it . . . and then came the 3000 florin just at the right time when we had either to buy the land or to give it up. The decision was easily made. We must have it for the honor of our king. To obtain the land was to obtain the monastery; the money for it was here; it is the king's own money and his present. It was named for the sisters to be sure, but only with the understanding that the sisters would use it to advantage — which was not the case. Surely Your Majesty would not object to my using it for a Ludwig monastery when to wait for word from Munich would mean that the date for buying would be past and the land lost. Surely it was not wrong then if I acted according to the mind and the spirit of Your Highness and bought the land. It was my love for Your Highness that caused me to reason thus. The temptation was great. I consented and made the mistake of buying in Your Majesty's honor. I regret that I can not be sorry; rather I am glad, glad from my heart because otherwise we would not have gotten a monastery in honor of St. Louis.[2]

The letter continues with statements that Mother Benedicta had gone to Rome to slander him and that the Minnesota nuns were a restless group of women who had established themselves without his permission. Claiming that his title of "Superior of the Order in America" gave him jurisdiction over the women's branch of the order and that his claim was recognized both by Rome and by the American hierarchy, he declared that he would not recognize the Minnesota convent as a religious house in good standing until the sisters had submitted to his jurisdiction. Neither would he allow his monks to give them spiritual or material aid. He further declared that the "St. Cloud group has been reported to the Apostolic See and the decision in regard to their future is pending." He concluded the last part of his letter by saying, "I hate evil gossip but I cannot help doing a little of it in my own defense." [3]

But four months after Abbot Wimmer's accusations were sent to the king, Bishop Grace of St. Paul visited St. Cloud and admitted two young women to the community. That act indicates that its reputation could not have been in question, for no bishop would have admitted new members to a convent of dubious standing or of a precarious future.

In 1861 Bishop Grace again showed his approbation of the Benedictine foundation. In company with the veteran missionary, Father Ravoux, he stopped at the St. Cloud convent on a trip to the Red River valley and he received the vows of four other members of the Community.[4] The spirit and religious fervor of this convent must have been admirable. Of it Bishop Grace wrote in his diary, speaking of himself in the third person:

The Bishop remained in St. Cloud till after Sunday when he received the profession of four sisters of St. Benedict and gave the habit to two other novices. The Bishop's stay among these good sisters which gave him an occasion to witness their piety, their innocence, their heavenly mindedness and real spiritual happiness was one of the brief periods granted but seldom to men in which a foretaste is had and a conception obtained of the felicity of Heaven. He will never forget it or the dispositions of soul at the time which made him very susceptible of such enjoyment for which he will be ever thankful to God and will ever regard it as a special grace intended for some purpose of His Providence which it is hoped will meet its due fulfillment through His most Holy will.[5]

In June, 1859, the Court Chaplain of the Ludwig Missionsverein wrote to Abbot Wimmer stating that the king had stated he need not pay the 3000 florins to Mother Willibalda until Rome decided whether the St. Cloud convent and the other Benedictine convents were under the jurisdiction of the abbot or not.[6]

That decision was rendered in December, 1859. On the sixth of that month the Sacred Congregation of Bishops and Regulars in Rome issued a decree in regard to the 1858 proposals and counter proposals of Mother Benedicta and Abbot Wimmer. By it, the Congregation denied the abbot's petition that the nuns be allowed to make solemn vows as was customary in Europe, but it was silent on the matter of substituting the recitation of the Little Office of the Blessed Virgin for that of the Divine Office. In regard to the more basic problem of jurisdiction, the decree rejected the abbot's petition to bring the convents into union with the American Cassinese Congregation under the rule of the abbot-president. Instead, the Benedictine convents were placed under the jurisdiction of the bishops of the dioceses in which they were established.[7]

Until now, the abbot had acted as protector of the Benedictine sisters and controlled the gifts of money received from the King Ludwig Missionsverein. Now the funds would pass through the hands of the bishop. On learning the contents of the decree, Abbot Wimmer wrote to King Ludwig that he did not know what was to become of the convent at St. Cloud since he no longer had supervision of the sisters. He stated that their future was precarious and added:

I am announcing this most respectfully to Your highest Majesty, that Your Highness may arrange the disposal of the 3000 florin in accordance with the situation. My most humble request would be . . . to let the sum be given to the Priory of St. Louis in St. Cloud, because this is of much greater importance than a convent of sisters, because there are now eight priests and the priory is the only support of the bishop and of the Catholic population of Minnesota . . ." [8]

In the course of time the monks received the money, and the sisters of St. Cloud learned of their final loss of the 3000 florins. But they had the American frontier spirit of that day, and undaunted they kept on with their life of prayer and service. Besides, Abbot Wimmer promised to reimburse them as soon as they were ready to buy a home of their own. This promise was kept. Repeatedly through the years when the sisters have been in need of financial help, the monks at St. John's Abbey have come to their aid. So, for instance, in 1883 the abbey cancelled the $12,647.00 debt which the sisters owed them. The monks have continued to prove themselves loyal friends and advisers in matters temporal and spiritual, and in the course of years the Abbey has repaid the sisters a hundred fold. In the course of the solemn opening of the Centennial celebration, January 1, 1957, Abbot Baldwin Dworschak could say:

The communities of St. Benedict's and St. John's have been associated for one hundred years in many ways that have brought blessings to this part of the world, to the Church, to the diocese of St. Cloud, and to our own holy Order. We at St. John's are particularly happy that this co-operation has existed and that it has increased during the recent years and I think it is most fitting that I take this occasion to thank Mother Richarda and the members of the Community who have contributed towards this co-operation. In proportion to the manner in which we have co-operated many of our blessings have been received.

In the same month that the jurisdiction of the Benedictine convents was placed in the hands of the bishops, Bishop Young received a mandate from Rome, to be executed at his discretion. This was to see to it that Mother Benedicta Riepp return to St. Walburga's in Eichstätt. Issued in the interests of peace, this decree need not be interpreted as a complete condemnation of Mother Benedicta.[9] Perhaps that was why Bishop Young wrote to Abbot Wimmer on January 28, 1861, asking him to ask the Congregation of Bishops and Regulars to permit Mother Benedicta to "finish her days in Minnesota." Bishop Grace of St. Paul also asked the Abbot to intercede for her and stated that he himself intended to write to Rome in her favor.[10] With two bishops advocating her cause, she was allowed to remain in this country.

Encouraged by the knowledge that they could keep their American foundress with them and that under diocesan authority they were now established in the local school, the Minnesota Benedictines looked forward to a period of peace and growth.

As long as their ranks remained unbroken and they were bound by the closest ties of religious charity, each sister was a bulwark of strength to the others, and hardships were borne with a joyous spirit. The year of 1862 was to see this solid phalanx broken. Mother Benedicta Riepp, who had been in poor health since her return, died on Sunday morning, March 16. The only record of the death of the American foundress is that published in the local newspaper. It is pitifully brief:

The Mother Superior of the Sisters of the St. Benedict Order died at the convent in this place last Sabbath morning. She was buried the next forenoon with the usual services and rites of the Roman Catholic Church. The funeral was largely attended.[11]

Nothing better than a rough wooden coffin made by the village carpenter could be procured for Mother Benedicta, for the nearest undertaker was in St. Paul eighty miles away. The sisters did their best to cover the roughness and the bareness of the box with some black cloth.

The same year brought them another reminder of their insecurity. On August 21, 1862, the sisters and the citizens of the surrounding country were thrown into a panic when Johnson, a Christian Chippewa Indian, brought news to St. Cloud that Chief Hole-in-the-Day was holding a council with his Chippewa Indians in response to a call for help sent to him by the Sioux Indians who were on the war path in southern Minnesota. This latter tribe, feeling keenly the injustice of the white man and goaded on by agitators, had started to pillage and murder the settlers of southern Minnesota, not waiting for the Chippewa Indians to strike in the north. Johnson, who had heard of this call for co-operation and the proposed council meeting, hastily left to find Father Pierz, the missionary, knowing well that only he could dissuade Chief Hole-in-the-Day from joining the Sioux

Father Pierz was found in St. Cloud, having a brief soul-refreshing visit with his brother priests, while the sisters were laundering and remodeling his altar linens. On receipt of the bad news he grabbed several bags of tobacco and left immediately with the runner. The news that the Chippewa Indians were going to make St. Cloud their base for their attacks on the surrounding country soon spread through the settlement. As it passed from mouth to mouth, the story grew and soon the whole county was thrown into wild excitement. Quick action was taken by some of the more levelheaded men. A meeting of the settlers was called and a home protection committee formed. Men joined the home guard but guns and ammunition had to be sent from St. Paul. Four days later this poorly-equipped home guard with its chaplain, Father Eberhard Gahr, O.S.B., was called to protect a settlement some thirty miles away, leaving the women and children of St. Cloud area unprotected. The women were frantic; they left house and cattle, and with their children fled to town to Broker's Building, the only large brick building in town. Others fled to the sisters' school and convent. In their haste they did not even take a blanket. Fortunately for them, Mr. Burbank of the transportation company of that name, kept part of his stores in Broker's Building and was able to supply these refugees as far as his stock allowed. The sisters shared what they had with those who gathered under their roof. Forty-two women and children of lower St. Cloud gathered in Mrs. Swisshelm's house and newspaper shop. This group kept large kettles of hot water ready for assault against the enemy and spent spare moments practising firing a gun.

In the meantime the men who remained in the settlement worked frantically at the construction of log forts — one in middle town near the convent; the other, Fort Holes, in lower St. Cloud. Fort Holes was described by Mrs. Swisshelm as a stockade circular in shape and forty-five feet in diameter. The walls were made of two rows of deep-set posts with boards nailed on the inside. The space between the two walls was filled with dirt and then covered with sod. In the center of this structure was a tower with loopholes for twelve "sharp shooters." [12] All of this structure was enclosed by a wall ten feet high sloping outward.

What the sisters did under these circumstances we know only by inference. We do know that they were not forced to leave their convent walls and take refuge in the fort, and so their daily routine of prayer could be maintained. They must have worried about the three sisters who had been sent a short time previously to care for the school at St. Joseph, the nearby settlement.

In St. Joseph eighty families gathered from farms within a radius of thirty miles. As there were but five houses in the village, the Benedictine priests opened the church, school, and even the stables to the refugees, and the place was used as a fort. The three sisters remained in their room attached to the school and church. One of the defenders of the town recorded the excitement, hardships, and mental anguish of the besieged. He wrote:

We expected an attack any day. . . . We planned that every one in the district should gather in one place and build a sort of fort. We decided that St. Joseph was the best place, and people for thirty miles around came and everybody got busy. The Benedictines had a great barn there and Mr. Linneman had a shed, so we packed them in, our families, as many as there was room for. They were packed like sheep. . . . The women took care of the children and moulded bullets. In those days we did not buy any shells already made or leaded; we loaded the guns and also had guards thrown all around St. Joseph. . . . There was no shirking for every one knew what it meant if the Indians once broke through.

One night as one of the guards was going to relieve the other, the one got so scared that he shot his gun which was to have been the signal that the Indians were coming. That started the excitement. The church bell was rung and everybody who could lift a gun had to get out. . . . As we were getting ready to give the Indians a reception, a guide came running in and said that it was all a mistake and the shot was an accident. What a relief. Every one was so happy. But we kept on with our work getting out timbers for the fort. . . . After we had completed the fort and had moved in, word came that the Indian uprising had been crushed. How happy we were. Some prayed, some sang, and some cried for joy. But we wasted no time for each man gathered his family together and started back home.[13]

The Chippewa Indian uprising never did get beyond the first stages because of the speedy and fearless action of the missionary who persuaded Chief Hole-in-the-Day not to join the Sioux Indians in their massacre. In a letter to the Leopoldine Society written April 15, 1863, Father Pierz related the part he played in suppressing this revolt. It is worth quoting for it gives a version not generally known.

When through a friendly Indian, news of this evil plot was brought to me, I started out . . . with but a large supply of tobacco. . . . I soon met . . . about thirty men who surrounded me and asked: "Father, where are you going?" "I wish to speak with the chief men," was my answer. . . . They showed me a line on the road over which no white man might pass. I laughed at that and stuck out my foot saying, "I do not fear your death," and started to cross the line. At that same instant four stalwart fellows lifted me bodily and carried me some ten paces across the line. "Now you did not walk across the forbidden line; we carried you, and you are not then under the death penalty."

A short distance ahead I was shown by the second patrol another mark which they assured me I must not cross at the risk of my life. Then I said, "In that case your chief and men must come to me." Thereupon they all came. I greeted them and offered them tobacco as a sign of friendship and asked them what this all meant. They hung their heads. . . . Fully half an hour I spoke to them explaining how foolish was their rebellion against the white race and how great a crime is murder. . . . In a friendly way I pointed out to them the fatal outcome of a contest with the well drilled and well armed white soldiers. . . . The Head chief, Hole-in-the-Day, gave me his hand and said, "Father, today we will go to Crow Wing and make peace." The other chiefs concurred.[14]

There was, however, a far greater threat to the existence and continued growth of the Benedictine foundation than the death of Mother Benedicta or the Indian uprising. This was the spirit of many of the Catholics themselves — a hostility that was evident in the desire of laymen to control the school. It was, in part, a matter of money. But even more it was a state of mind characteristic of many mid-century immigrants.

ST. WALBURGA CONVENT IN BAVARIA
WHERE MOTHER BENEDICTA
AND MOTHER WILLIBALDA
BEGAN THEIR RELIGIOUS LIFE.

ABBOT BONIFACE WIMMER, FOUNDER OF
THE AMERICAN CASSINESE BENEDICTINE

FATHER FRANCIS PIERZ, MINNESOTA
INDIAN MISSIONARY.

FIRST PRIOR OF MINNESOTA
BENEDICTINE MONASTERY,
DEMETRIUS DI MAROGNA.

FIRST SUPERIOR OF THE MINNESOTA
BENEDICTINE NUNS, MOTHER
WILLIBALDA SCHERBAUER.

T. JOHN'S FIRST ABBOT,
RUPERT SEIDENBUSCH.

MOTHER ANTONIA HERMAN, SECOND
SUPERIOR OF THE MINNESOTA BENEDICTINES.

OLDEST CONSECRATED CHURCH
IN MINNESOTA AT ST. JOSEPH.

ST. CLOUD CONVENT, CHURCH AND SCHOOL ON CORNER
OF ST. GERMAIN AND EIGHTH AVENUE, 1858.

OLD ST. MARY'S, FIRST CATHOLIC CHURCH AND ACADEMY IN
BISMARCK, 1880.

AN EARLY PAROCHIAL SCHOOL, PIERZ, 1872.

THE NORTH STAR BROUGHT THE SISTERS TO ST. CLOUD, 1857.

SUPERIOR OF THE MINNESOTA CONVENT,
MOTHER ALOYSIA BATH, 1877-1880
AND 1889-1901.

SISTER EVANGELISTA KREMETER,
ONE OF THE FOUNDERS OF THE
ST. CLOUD CONVENT.

MOTHER RICHARDA AT THE
GRAVE OF MOTHER BENE-
DICTA RIEPP AT ST. JOSEPH

HEADDRESS WORN IN 1857.

GROUP WHO LEFT ST. CLOUD TO FOUND A CONVENT AT
ATCHISON, KANSAS.

THE FIRST CONVENT AT ST. JOSEPH, 1869, FROM AN OLD DRAWING.

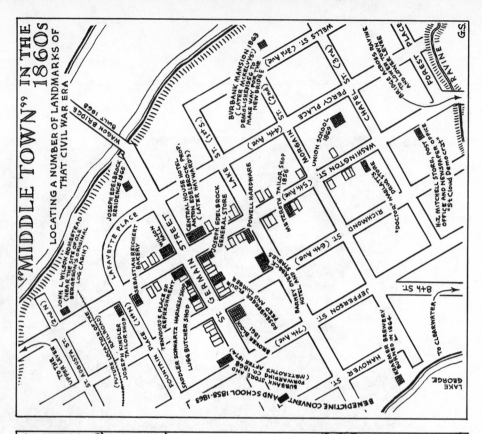

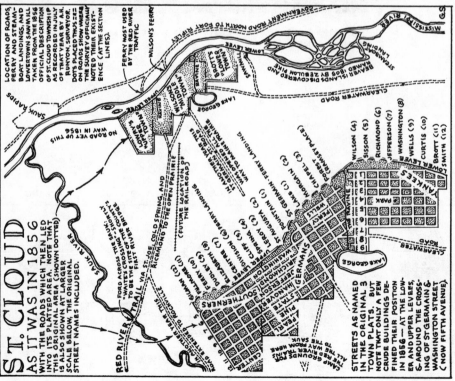

EARLY ST. CLOUD, MAPS BY GLANVILLE SMITH.

The German settlers of St. Cloud and its environs were indeed practising Catholics, but they had come to this country with an economic distrust of religious congregations and were tinged with the anti-clericalism rampant in Europe at the time. They had come to this country unaccustomed to giving financial support to the schools of their Faith. In many of the European states, church property had become secularized during or after the period of the French Revolution. In the 1840's and 1850's some of this property had been handed back to the Church for use but not for ownership. The state issued rules controlling the use of the property, sometimes going so far as to designate the days and hours of holding services in the churches, the admittance of new members into the convent or abbey, and the subjects to be taught in the schools under Church care. The state cared for the maintenance of the buildings and paid the salaries of the clergy, in recompense for its confiscation of the Church's property. Accustomed to such state and lay control of church affairs, the European settlers were predisposed to look for a similar situation in America. They saw nothing out of order in the claim that they, and not the pastor, were to decide whether the parish would have a parochial school or not. But in the United States they found that the ecclesiastical authority and neither the laity nor state, was in complete charge of parish affairs.

Moreover, these immigrants, intoxicated with their new-found political freedom and with the right to rule through their vote, wanted to exercise this new power in parish matters as well. They could run their settlements as they chose and could be elected to the local school board. In order to exert this new power and to have the kind of parochial organization they knew in Europe, they worked for the establishment of district public schools instead of parochial schools. Sometimes, it is true, they would give in to the pastor's wishes by hiring sisters to teach in their district school. In so doing they forestalled the pastor's complaint that the children were not getting a Catholic education. However, they still had the school under their own control to the extent of engaging and dismissing the teachers. At the same time, they did not have to support a parish school.

Early in 1863, after the sisters had spent four years in parochial school work, a group of Catholics in middle St. Cloud decided to erect a district school for their part of town. They realized that their school tax money went to the support of the public school in the lower end of town, from which their children were practically excluded because of distance and differences in language and nationality. Support of the Catholic school in middle town was an added burden. Besides this economic motive, there was the old anti-clerical one just described. Toward the end of the spring term this group demanded the lease of a portion of the church property as a site for the new school building. The pastor asked the advice of Bishop Thomas Grace of St. Paul. From Bishop Grace's letter to Prior Othmar it is evident that the people had demanded the property as their right. It is apparent, too, that they were erecting this school not in competition with the parochial school, but as a substitute for it. The bishop wrote:

Father Demetrius has already spoken to me in regard to the proposition for leasing a portion of the church ground in St. Cloud for a public school edifice. We cannot be too cautious in yielding to other claims and privileges over the property of the church, especially in such cases as the one in question in which there is reason to suspect that the congregation demands as a kind of right that such lease shall be made. The probability that a Catholic teacher may be appointed does not change the character of the school which remains essentially a school in which no religion is allowed to be recognized; and it would seem strange that a school system which the church has denounced as God-less should have a local habitation on ground dedicated to church purposes. I am sorry to hear that the congregation are giving the good Sisters more trouble. These people are not worthy of having Sisters to draw down blessing upon them.[15]

But in justice to these people of St. Cloud, it must be stated that some of their complaints against the sisters were justifiable. For one thing the sisters had not mastered the English language well enough to satisfy the demands of the state government. In the matter of school discipline there may also have been good cause for complaint. Proper supervision of the playground was, of course, impossible for teachers who were cloistered and not permitted to go out on the playgrounds or sidewalk. Maintaining discipline would be a problem for women unaccustomed to teaching boys. Another handicap under which the teachers worked was the old Eichstätt tradition of changing the classroom teacher every hour. This type of management no doubt worked well in a girls' boarding school in Bavaria but it was not the system in vogue in the United States at the time. The custom has its good points and its bad points, but because it differed from the American mode, it gave the group opposed to religious teachers an opportunity for unfavorable criticism.

This trouble with the people of St. Cloud caused the sisters to look about for a more congenial settlement. Late in the summer of 1863 the Catholic parish at Clinton, later called St. Joseph, Minnesota, the largest and most prosperous parish in Stearns County, offered the sisters a home if they would give up St. Cloud and move to St. Joseph. About the same time the Benedictine priests in Atchison, Kansas, asked for sisters for their school. The convent in St. Cloud now numbered fourteen members — too many for the needs of St. Joseph, and it was decided to accept the Kansas offer. Most of the sisters wanted to leave Minnesota, for after six years of struggle they felt they had not yet taken root. There seemed nothing to lose in the move and probably much to gain.

During the early part of this summer of 1863, Mother Willibalda had made a visit to the Chicago Benedictines and there inquired about the Kansas mission. Shortly after her return to St. Cloud the exodus to Kansas took place.[16] Exodus it was, for when Sister Evangelista Kremeter left she took with her six companions, or one-half of the community. Those remaining were Mother Willibalda, Sisters Antonia Streitz, Gertrude Kapser, Bernarda Augé, Johanna Reser, Boniface Bantle, Theresa Marthaler, and the two candidates. These, with the exception of Mother Willibalda and Sister Antonia Streitz, were very young, having entered the religious life in St. Cloud during the previous five years. With the exception of Mother Willibalda and Sister Antonia, none had in any way been connected with the older convents in Pennsylvania or in Bavaria. This was the group that was left to make the new foundation in the village of St. Joseph. There this small community of Benedictines was to strike deep, permanent roots and in time develop into a religious community numbering over one thousand members. For the first fifty years most of the members would come from the rural Catholic families of central Minnesota. But their apostolic work in time was to extend from the Mississippi to the Pacific coast and the Far East.

7 NEW STRUGGLE FOR EXISTENCE

On October 21, 1854, nine years before the sisters accepted the invitation to establish themselves in St. Joseph, a solitary traveler could have been seen trudging over the prairie toward the settlement of St. Joseph, or Clinton as it was then called. He was short and slightly bent under the weight of his seventy years. He carried a heavy pack on his back. The pale eyes of the rider squinted as though he had spent years in smoke-filled Indian tents. These eyes were made still less conspicuous by his habit of keeping them partly closed, mute testimony to the long journeys he had made in the glare of the prairie sun. His clothes were wrinkled and worn, and a yellow wig showed at the edge of his close-fitting cap. The pack on his back was carefully wrapped and strapped. Much care was taken of this luggage, for it contained Mass kit, Breviary, and articles of devotion.

This lonely traveler was the great missionary of the Chippewa Indians, Father Francis Pierz, making his first visit to the future village of Clinton, then a settlement of only a couple of houses eight miles west of St. Cloud. The few settlers had arrived scarcely five months before, and they were lonely without the religious services to which they had been accustomed in Germany and in the more eastern part of the United States. Father Pierz knew of their need and he was on his way to pay them a visit. Because his coming was expected, the people of the immediate settlement were gathered to hear a sermon and to receive the sacrament of penance. Among these pioneer Catholics were Peter Loso, Martin Fiedler, and Balthasar Fuchs. On the following morning an attentive group of men and women who knew the meaning of life without the consolation of the Holy Sacrifice and the sacraments participated in the Mass offered in the home of Martin Fiedler. The inconvenience of kneeling on the rough sod floor without support went unnoticed as did the fact that they had been fasting for long hours. Nor were they aware that the altar linens needed ironing. After the Mass Father Pierz gave a long, stirring sermon on sin and hell — a sermon that only he could give who had lived so many years with pagan converts and half-breed trappers. In the afternoon baby Suzanne Meisenburg was baptized. No doubt the missionary thought this white baby was far noisier than the Indian babies he had baptized on the edge of a lake or in a temporary church made of leafy boughs. The ceremony performed and recorded on the flyleaf of his Breviary, the missionary packed his Mass kit and started back to his beloved Indian children, but not before the pioneer women had extorted from him a promise to visit them again in the near future.

To keep this promise, Father Pierz returned during the last part of January and again on February 6 to baptize another small pioneer.[1] This time the services were held in the log house of John Linneman. By now it was evident that the settlement needed a church. The small log house could not accommodate the faithful during the winter months. But no one could see how the project was to be carried out; they had not been on the land a year and there was as yet neither proper shelter for their families nor winter sheds for their cattle. Others argued the futility of building a church when there was no prospect of having regular services since Father Pierz was the only priest in that wide territory between St. Paul and Pembina. But, undaunted, he told them to build their church, that within a year he would have a priest for them. Encouraged by his words, the people organized their parish under patronage of St. Joseph. On July 12, 1855, blocks four and five were deeded by Peter Loso for church purpose.[2] The men of the parish were then allotted their share of work in procuring logs for the church building.

With the return of spring, the missionary's visits were resumed and the construction of the log church, twenty by thirty feet, was begun. In preparation for a resident pastor, the parishioners next year attached to the church a log house or shed fourteen feet by twenty feet and eight feet high. The attic room was so low that to place a bed there was impossible. The dwellers in these pioneer sheds simply laid a straw tick on the floor of the attic. When the shanty was completed and blessed, Father Pierz told his parishioners he would stop visiting them, for Benedictine priests would soon be with them.

Though the settlers at St. Joseph wanted the services of a resident priest at a time when only one or two parishes in the whole Territory of Minnesota enjoyed such a privilege, not all were willing to accept pastors belonging to a religious order. The following statement from the memoirs of an early pastor explains their state of mind.

A few turbulent spirits agitated against the expected monks and went so far as to send a petition to the Bishop of St. Paul begging him not to inflict the monks upon them and not permit them to come to St. Joseph. In consequence, the misguided hot heads had no services until August.[3]

For the same reason the neighboring settlements of St. James and Richmond also had no services that summer. When Father Francis Weninger, S.J., came to preach a mission in St. Cloud, the people at St. Joseph also wanted one. But Bishop Joseph Cretin of St. Paul would not listen to them until they had promised to accept the Benedictines. That mission, plus the grasshopper plague of 1856–57, would make the settlers more docile.

Father Weninger's mission of August, 1856, caused a flurry of excitement in the parish. A mission meant not only a revival of religious life; it also broke the monotony of dull days in a western prairie settlement. Those who had heard of the fame of Father Weninger could entertain their neighbors with stories of his power and eloquence. He was assisted by one of the Benedictine priests newly arrived in St. Cloud, Father Bruno Riess.[4] The St. Joseph church was so small that when both priests heard confessions one would go outdoors where an old log on the shady side of the building served as his confessional.

But there was to be more than the usual excitement. On August 15, while the congregation was listening to the eloquent missionary, darkness suddenly surrounded them and a clatter on the roof drowned the speaker's voice. The parishioners were startled, for no lightning or thunder accompanied this phenomenon. Fear clutched their hearts. But there was no consolation from Father Weninger. He seized the opportunity to speak vehemently on the obligation of obedience to proper authority. When the Mass ended, the people went out of doors to find that the air was full of grasshoppers in such numbers that they formed a cloud obscuring the sun. Already these winged creatures were at work destroying the crops. The loss was nearly a tragedy for St. Joseph. Not only was there nothing to show for a whole year's work, but there was a scarcity of food for the coming winter and no seed for the next spring's planting. Father Bruno himself describes the event in his reminiscences.

The 15th of August was . . . the beginning of a two-year aftermission sent by Divine Providence. . . . When we left the church our eyes beheld nothing but the greedy grasshoppers, which had darkened the sun. . . . This small voracious, yet invincible monster had in a short time devastated all that grows and blooms. . . . Within about two or three days the fields presented the appearance of having been newly plowed. Then indescribable misery entered the homes of the settlers. . . . The entire harvest was a dead loss for those settlers who had taken their abodes in this region during the previous year.[5]

But the mission and this tragedy of the grasshoppers worked the wanted change in the hearts of the people and they now welcomed Father Bruno Riess. One of his first acts was to open a school in the church. After teaching for two terms himself, he handed it over to a layman who conducted it as a district school.

The pastor and his people feared a return of the plague and the following summer in conjunction with two other neighboring parishes a vow was made to hold an annual procession on the feast of St. Ulric in July and again in the fall on the feast of St. Magnus that their crops be saved from these pests. The first procession was held on the feast of St. Ulric in July of 1857. On that occasion the parishioners of nearby St. James Church and of St. Joseph Church made their way toward the Sauk River where they were met by the pilgrims of the parishes of St. Cloud and St. Augusta. The rosary was recited along the entire route, interrupted occasionally by the singing of popular German hymns. An eyewitness has described their crossing of the river, which as yet was without a bridge. "At this point of meeting a line of wagons was placed in the shallow bed of the stream, and the procession filed across securely." [6] When the four processions arrived at the appointed spot, a field Mass was offered by Father Clement Staub, O.S.B. That day the new brood of grasshoppers lately hatched from the last year's eggs rose up in a cloud and left the country.

Freed from grasshoppers and blessed with good crops, the parish flourished, and in 1859 the people proudly hung their eight-hundred-pound church bell in its outside tower. With the help of the pastor they also erected a small log school house adjoining the log church. It was adequate until 1862 when the number of pupils reached eighty. Then the pastor hired two Benedictine sisters from St. Cloud to care for the school.

Mother Willibalda moved her diminished community to St. Joseph sometime in November of the year 1863. Here the Benedictine sisters were to make a new and successful attempt to establish themselves in Minnesota. Accompanying Mother to join the two sisters who were already teaching in St. Joseph were Sisters Boniface Bantle,

Bernarda Augé, and two novices. They were lodged in the old school house and parsonage for which they paid $1700. In December of that year , 1863, the bishop of St. Paul blessed the new convent and put it under the patronage of St. Joseph; for some years it was listed in the Catholic Directory as St. Joseph's Convent and Academy. Within a year or two the prior of St. John's, remembering the 3000 florins which Abbot Wimmer had retained to purchase government land for the monks, recompensed the sisters by erecting a new convent building as a wing to the string of older buildings.[7]

Now commenced a new struggle for existence, a doubtful conflict of fifteen years with just enough growth to encourage perseverance. The sisters had a piano and an organ, but the new settlers had no money for music lessons. The enclosure was again found to be a handicap in performing the many duties falling to the lot of sisters in a rough, new country. As in St. Cloud, there was trouble in school on account of the Eichstätt rule which permitted a sister to teach but one hour at a time. This change of teachers every hour created problems in discipline. The three young, untrained sisters who were forced by circumstances to help Mother Willibalda in the school often faced rough frontier boys as old as themselves and too big to discipline. This was the age when one of the very necessary requirements of a good teacher was physical prowess. Now the "irreconcilables" who had originally objected to the coming of the Benedictine priests and sisters to their settlement had something tangible on which to base their objections, and they made the most of their opportunity. It must be kept in mind that the school at St. Joseph was conducted as a district public school and as such was under the control of the district school board which at this time was made up of men who were opposed to employing the sisters and who were determined to keep their school free from parochial control. This group showed its power in the fall of 1864 when its members refused to rehire the sisters and in their stead gave the school to a Mr. Duerr with a contract for four years.

Deprived of their main source of support, the sisters were forced to break their enclosure to go on begging tours through the countryside. Michael Tilger, referred to by the early settlers as "Kloster Michel," would sometimes take the sisters from farm to farm in a wagon; but at other times the poor women were forced to walk. Their only income was that derived from choir work in the church and from their services as laundresses and seamstresses for the monks. Laundry work in those days was difficult. The water had to be drawn from the outside well and carried to the kitchen in heavy wooden pails. This was heavy work for young girls but when winter came it was not only heavy but dangerous work, for every splash of water from the pails helped to make the path from the well to the house more icy. After the water had been heated on the stove, it had to be lifted down again and put into wooden tubs. Often these had become warped during the interval between laundry days, and if this condition was not noticed the water ran out onto the floor. In winter the wash house with its earthen floor was miserably cold and damp. To prevent their feet from freezing, the sisters stood on bricks previously heated in the stove. Rubbing clothes on a wash board blistered the knuckles of the uninitiated and put kinks in the backs of even the best laundrywomen. Hands were burned by the undetachable iron handles which were as hot as the iron itself. Such heavy labor occupying several days of the week together with an insufficient amount of food soon affected the health of the young sisters and caused many early deaths. Finally in 1864 Mother Willibalda wrote to King Ludwig begging for aid and reminding him of his interest in her as a young school girl. This was the first time she had written to the king since Abbot Wimmer had denounced her to him.[8] The king replied to the letter with a gift of 1000 florins.

Because the religious spirit of the house was good, these hardships and disappointments were cheerfully borne — so grateful were the sisters that after six years of a restricted life in St. Cloud they could now carry out their conventual practices and recite the Divine Office with something of liturgical solemnity. Mother Willibalda pictured their new life when she wrote to King Ludwig:

While we were in St. Cloud we could perform our religious practices only piecemeal. Now for the past year we have been able to follow the Rule.[9]

The penances practiced in the old European convents for infraction of the Rule or mistakes at Office were scrupulously enforced. These included excommunication from the community exercises, prostration in chapel before the community, and loss of the veil. As in the Eichstätt mother house, the sisters were divided into two classes — choir nuns and lay sisters. The former carried the title, "Frau," and the latter were called "Schwester" or lay sister. The latter group recited the rosary in place of the Office, wore a veil, and followed the choir sisters in rank. Though all rose at midnight and again before six o'clock, no breakfast was served. Dinner at 11:30 consisted of a bowl of soup, potatoes, and pancakes or noodles. Meat was seldom eaten. At six o'clock in the evening some potatoes and a piece of bread were served. After the sisters took on the hard task of laundering for the monastery, Mother Willibalda mitigated the Rule and allowed the sisters a breakfast of a cup of coffee and one half ounce of bread. Strict in discipline, Mother Willibalda was careful of her subjects' spiritual and physical well-being. An old chronicler summed up her personality and her rule by declaring that Mother Willibalda had "a tenacious will and she was firmly imbued with monastic tradition. She was born to rule rather than to be subject to the rule of others. Her administration was marked by firm discipline, and good order prevailed. She had a kind heart, and there was love between her and her sisters." [10]

No doubt it was because the spirit of the house was good that new members asked for admittance despite the obvious hardships. In 1864 Mary Kump and Mary Muelken received the habit and took the names of Benedicta and Walburga. The four young women who entered the next year were known in religion as Sister Josepha Hassler, Sister Gertrude Petit, Sister Switberta Stacken, and Sister Mechtild Kohler. Sister Scholastica McNulty received the holy habit from the hands of the missionary Father Joseph Buh in 1867.[11] These were brave young women to join a religious community which as yet gave so little promise of permanence. But to these young women who believed they were called to religious life, this convent promised an opportunity to practice perfect trust in Divine Providence. This was the life these young women were looking for.

The sisters rejoiced at this increase of members but the problem of their support was a serious one. Other than laundering and sewing for the monks of St. John's Abbey, the sisters had no source of support for these additional members. When the sisters of Atchison, Kansas, called for help because of the defection of two of their members, Mother Willibalda willingly sent two sisters to their aid. She accompanied the two volunteers, Sister Gertrude Kapser and Sister Bernarda Augé, to Atchison.

A few days before they started on their journey the sad news of the assassination of President Lincoln seeped into the convent. Village gossips said the news was brought to this town by three strange men who had entered the general store across the street from the convent and in a political discussion announced the news. The strange thing about the story is that this news was related in St. Joseph, a town eighty miles from the nearest telegraph station, three hours prior to the assassination! It was suspected that the three strangers were privy to the plan formed in Mrs. Surrat's boarding house for the president's murder.[12] Though the merchant denied that such statement had been made in his store, the tale still lives. The village was in mourning before the sisters started for Kansas, and on their way they were destined to meet the funeral cortege.

An old manuscript chronicle at Mount St. Scholastica Convent in Kansas records that Mother Willibalda and her companions arrived at Hannibal, Missouri, at almost the same time as the funeral cortege of the martyred president. They left their baggage and trunks at the station while they went to attend the public burial services. During their absence their luggage was ransacked, and though their clothing and books were not very valuable, their loss meant a great hardship to the sisters.

Two old problems continued to plague the convent: that of uniting all Benedictine convents into a congregation under the headship of Abbot Wimmer and that of the pronouncing of solemn vows. Despite Rome's decree of 1859, which placed the Benedictine sisters under the jurisdiction of the bishops of the dioceses in which they found themselves, Abbot Wimmer again urged the various houses to form a congregation. His previous petition of 1858 had asked that the sisters' convents be incorporated into the monks' congregation with the abbot as its president, thus exempting the convents from diocesan rule. Now he suggested that they form a congregation of their own under the presidency of a mother general. Such a union would, he said, provide an opportunity for one convent to aid another by exchanges of sisters. Since the convents were situated in different dioceses and under the jurisdiction of various bishops, this exchange of sisters could not be authorized by bishops whose authority extended only as far as diocesan boundaries.

In 1865 Abbot Wimmer traveled to Rome to put this petition and one pertaining to solemn vows before the Sacred Congregation of the Propagation of the Faith. He also petitioned that the Benedictine convents already established be declared canonically erected, and repeated his request that the sisters be allowed to recite the Little Office of the Blessed Virgin instead of the Divine Office on ferial days. In the decree of June, 1866, the cardinals acquiesced to the last request. They also permitted the sisters to make simple vows instead of solemn. But to the other two petitions the answer was virtually a refusal. Propaganda commented that before answering them they wished to learn the attitude of the American bishops, who were to assemble in plenary council at Baltimore the following October. The abbot was informed he must defend his petitions before the bishops.[13] Responsible for the suggestion to consult the American hierarchy was Cardinal Reisach, one of the leading cardinals of Propaganda. As Archbishop of Munich at the time Mother Benedicta was in Europe in 1857–58, he knew something of the matters involving Abbot Wimmer, the bishops, and the Benedictine sisters. Abbot Wimmer, writing on June 24, 1866, comments:

The proposition was agreeable to the Most Eminent Cardinals but they refused the grant because Sister Benedicta through her complaints about my "oppression" had caused the cardinals [1859] to place the sisters under the bishops and they now did not wish to revoke their former decision without first learning the mind of the American bishops in the matter.[14]

In referring this matter to the bishops assembled at Baltimore, Propaganda was, however, virtually deciding the case against Abbot Wimmer, for the American bishops would not readily give up a jurisdiction expressly given them in the decree of 1859. Even if this had not been the mind of the bishops, Abbot Wimmer was doomed to lose his case for he returned from Europe too late to get his propositions placed on the agenda. The council leaders had already printed the program, and it was too filled to admit additional matter. Thus the decree of 1859 remained in force. The convents remained diocesan institutions and the bishops had the privilege of delegating their authority to the abbot if they wanted to do so.

It was in line with this decree that early in 1868 Bishop Grace of St. Paul delegated his jurisdiction over Benedictine sisters to the newly elected Minnesota abbot, Rupert Seidenbusch.[15] As soon as this responsibility was laid upon his shoulders, the abbot took an active interest in the material and spiritual welfare of the sisters. His first act was to restore to them the local district school in St. Joseph. This he did by commanding the entirely Catholic village either to hire the sisters as teachers in the district school or to send their children to a school which he would open. The village decided to hire Sister Evangelista McNulty and Sister Benedicta Kump to teach their district school.

Abbot Seidenbusch's second act was far more lasting and penetrating in its effect upon the life of the sisters and on the history of the community. No sooner was the jurisdiction over the convent delegated to him by Bishop Grace in 1868 than he deposed Mother Willibalda and appointed another sister in her place. The deposition was unexpected. Mother Willibalda and Abbot Seidenbusch had not seen eye to eye back in the Pennsylvania days when he had been prior under Abbot Wimmer. When he saw the poverty of the convent at St. Joseph he concluded she was not fit to be a superior and decided to depose her. Because the other members of the community were too young for the office, he was forced to look elsewhere for his appointee. His action was quick and peremptory. Without consulting the sisters, he traveled to Chicago. There in the Benedictine convent of St. Scholastica he chose a young religious, Sister Antonia Herman, professed six years and just recently relieved of the office of prioress. She accepted the appointment and with three other sisters left for St. Joseph, Minnesota, with the abbot. Sister Martina Amberg, one of the companions, relates in her memoirs that before starting on the journey when they packed the lunch for the trip, the abbot told them to bring no "stink cheese" with them.

The sisters at St. Joseph knew nothing of the impending change until the abbot and the four sisters arrived at the convent door and he presented Sister Antonia to Mother Willibalda and the community as the new prioress. He bluntly announced to Mother Willibalda that she was relieved of her office. Sister Evangelista McNulty often told the story of that day in July, 1868. Sister Evangelista was very busy in the classroom when she noticed a smart buggy with a clergyman and four women dressed in black dresses and Shaker bonnets pass through the convent gate. She was surprised to see such stylish equipage in the village and impatiently awaited the close of school so that she might satisfy her curiosity. Hastening to the community room, she looked about for the ladies with the Shaker bonnets but found none. Instead she was introduced to four sisters from Chicago. The clergyman was Abbot Seidenbusch. Part of the mystery was solved when she was told that because of the bigotry of the A.P.A., or

American Protective Association, the sisters had deemed it inadvisable to travel from Chicago in their religious garb. But then a new question presented itself. What were these sisters doing here? Consternation followed when she was told that one of the sisters was her new superior.[16]

Being called to rule a house under such circumstances was as embarrassing to Mother Antonia Herman as it was to the sisters. The difficulties of the situation were accentuated by the fact that her mandate to energize the community would entail changing old customs and this in turn would mean bruised feelings, and probably misunderstandings. For such work the utmost tact would be required. But Mother Antonia, though kindhearted and careful of the welfare of the sisters, was not always tactful. She was nervous of temperament and hasty in speech. One old chronicler records: "Mother Antonia Herman was austere with a mixture of mildness — hence she was feared rather than loved." She wished to follow some of the saints in exceptional works of penance and mortification and, therefore, introduced the discipline. Without guidance, she and the novice mistress read deeply on mysticism, and the young sisters were decidedly affected by their superiors.

Their strong faith and prayer is shown in the following incident. One day when there was nothing in the house to eat, Mother Antonia told the lay sister in charge of the kitchen to go to the chapel and pray to St. Joseph. Shortly after, the prayer was answered. A man came to the convent door with a sack of flour, saying that as he was driving past with a load of flour the horses stopped and refused to go on. Looking about and seeing the convent gate, he bethought himself of the sisters and decided to make them an offering.[17]

Strict about religious rules and customs, Mother Antonia was also careful of the physical welfare of her subjects. In the matter of food and rest she was lenient when it was necessary to conserve health. As the Rule and the statutes allowed the superior to use her discretion in regard to the number of meals a day, Mother Antonia continued Mother Willibalda's innovation of taking breakfast — a thing unheard of in the Eichstätt mother house. She changed the midnight recitation of the Divine Office to four o'clock in the morning and in accordance with Rome's decree of 1865 she substituted the Little Office of the Blessed Virgin for the Divine Office on ferial days. She also attempted to relieve the sisters of the task of laundering for the monks at the abbey. In this she was not successful.

Up to the time that Mother Antonia took office, no records and accounts either religious or financial were kept. But from Mother Antonia's induction in 1868, the convent kept its own financial records. These records carefully executed in Mother's handwriting are still in the archives of the convent. They reveal that it was by the hard labor of the sisters and not by donations and other outside aids that the foundations of the present-day flourishing establishment were laid.

In this record, such entries as the following help one to form a picture of the day-to-day life in a frontier convent which of necessity shared the activities of its neighbors. An entry of May 25, 1865, indicates that two pigs were purchased for $5. The plan no doubt was to fatten them during the summer months for the late fall butchering. Other preparations for this fall work are indicated by the entry of such items as the purchase of a brass kettle, an iron kettle, and a washboiler. Like their neighbors, the sisters churned the little butter they used and this same record shows the purchase of a churn for the price of $1.25. The following year, 1869, the greatest expenditures were for chapel equipment, an altar and an oil painting to be used as an altarpiece. Later a "Bethlehem Crib" is listed. Finally there is the inevitable entry: to a "carpenter for making a coffin, $10." The town carpenter was usually called into service when such need arose, and the neighbor women or sisters used their skill at lining the inside of the rough box. Coffins were not kept in stock in frontier towns; they were too bulky to transport from St. Paul, the nearest market.

There was now some financial security. Besides the salaries received for teaching in the local school, a new source of income was made available by "taking in" boarding pupils. Two factors made this new venture possible. The St. Paul, Minneapolis, and Manitoba railroad would soon reach the settlement. Not only would this make it easier to get supplies from outside markets, but pupils would no longer be kept away by the thought of the eight-mile carriage drive from St. Cloud, the nearest railroad point. The second factor was that the sisters now had room to accommodate boarding pupils, for to the old log church and parish house had lately been added the new convent building.[18]

Further support was given the sisters when in the spring of 1869

NEW STRUGGLE FOR EXISTENCE

the pastor of St. Mary's parish in St. Cloud asked that two sisters be sent to take charge of the district school conducted near the church. This parish had been without religious teachers since 1863 when the district refused to rehire the sisters. But their recall in 1869 did not indicate a change of heart, for it was under compulsion. Abbot Seidenbusch had given this parish the same ultimatum he had given the St. Joseph parish: they must hire sisters in their district school or turn their district school building, built on church property, into a parochially supported school which the pastor would superintend. The people of St. Cloud capitulated to the extent of hiring sisters. Sister Evangelista McNulty and Sister Benedicta Kump were withdrawn from the St. Joseph school and sent to teach in this district school at St. Cloud. The following year the St. Cloud district school became a parochial school, and the teaching staff was increased.

The next call for teachers came from Father Francis Pierz. He had lately retired from his Indian missions to the settlement of Rich Prairie or Pierz "to rest his eighty-year-old bones," as he put it. In 1869 he and his parishioners started to build a school which would serve as convent and school. It was not completed when the sisters arrived in 1871 and they were forced to live with some of the parishioners. The building was of logs, one story high with garret. The lower part with dirt floor was used for the school, and the garret or upper floor was divided into a kitchen, a bedroom, and a chapel. Because the logs had not been weather-cured and the cracks between the logs poorly chinked, it was impossible to warm the building in winter. The log church was as poorly built and was cold and drafty. During the Mass it was necessary to keep the Mass wine near the stove until the moment came to put it on the altar. Virtually blind after years in the smoke-filled tents of his Indians, the old missionary had his bishop's permission to say the Mass of Our Lady which he soon knew by heart. This deprived the sisters of the solemnity of the liturgy on many feast days. There were no high Masses. Instead, during the Sunday Mass the congregation sang their well-known German hymns accompanied by Mr. Rauch on his violin. Some one stood at Father's side throughout the Mass to see that he read all the prayers and had no accident with the sacred species. One of the sisters used to relate stories of the kindness and deference of the good Father Pierz. The unplastered church with its dirt floor could boast of only one pew, and much to their embarrassment, the pastor insisted it was to be occupied only by the sisters. In her memoirs describing their first Christmas spent at Pierz, Sister Placida Heinen relates how the old missionary's desire to gladden the day for the sisters found expression in the gift of a bowl of Indian maple sugar.[19]

What the sisters at Pierz lacked in decent living was due not to miserliness on the part of the pastor, but rather to the long-established habits of a man who had lived for years in Indian tents with none of the things the white man thinks necessary. To Father Pierz, Rich Prairie was everything the name connotes. He wrote to *Der Wanderer*:

> Rich Prairie is a parish ten miles from Little Falls in a beautiful place. Already a beautiful church has been built and blest and the building of a parish house has begun. A beautiful convent, as yet incomplete, is being built for the school sisters who are coming to educate our children. The place has good soil and beautiful pasture for light cattle raising. A railroad will soon be built near by.[20]

His ways were just not of this world, and age was making him more eccentric. He kept a pet goat loose in the yard between the convent and church much to the annoyance of the sisters and parishioners, for it was not only mischievous but dangerous to pedestrians. Only after it had butted and knocked down one of the sisters did the missionary tie up the animal.

With the organization of the church in northern Minnesota into a vicariate, there was promise of greater stability for religious communities, and from now on the growth of the Benedictine foundation was constant. On February 12, 1875, that part of the St. Paul diocese comprising all of the state from the southern boundary of Stearns County north to the Canadian border, and west to the Missouri River in Dakota Territory was created into the Vicariate Apostolic of Northern Minnesota with the bishop residing in St. Cloud. Abbot Rupert Seidenbusch, the friend of the convent, was appointed to head this new vicariate. Though the appointee was only forty-five years old, he had already spent nine years as abbot. It would take a young man to care for the settlements scattered over this vast territory stretching from Grand Portage to the Missouri River. Many of these settlements had never been visited by a bishop, for while they formed the outlying fringe of the St. Paul diocese, the bishop of St. Paul had found it physically impossible to visit all of the settlements or to supply priests for the territory. Now with a bishop especially assigned to these settlements Catholic life would grow. In 1876 there were only eight diocesan and twenty-one Benedictine priests serving the new vicariate, but within a dozen years the number of diocesan clergy would increase to thirty and the number of churches would double.

The growth of the convent at St. Joseph was equally striking. Within five years the community's membership also doubled. In fact, the log and plank convent buildings were so filled with sisters, boarding pupils, and some two hundred day students, that means were sought to relieve the congestion. Someone suggested moving the boarding pupils into St. Cloud to the old convent and log church where only four teachers were living. When the St. Joseph taxpayers and parishioners objected to giving space in their crowded school to pupils who were not of the village or parish, this suggestion appeared even more attractive. Bishop Seidenbusch, desirous of having a boarding school and academy in his see city, urged the sisters to make the move, and offered to sell them the old church and convent property on the corner of St. Germain and Hanover streets.

Soon the *St. Cloud Times* carried a notice of the new St. Agnes Academy:

The Sisters of St. Benedict have opened an Academy in this city for the instruction of young ladies where they intend to teach all the branches of English studies, also instructions in German, music instrumental and vocal, fancy needle and knitting work. They have also a private school for younger scholars which has been in operation for some time. The pupils in the primary branches pay 50 cents per month, those further advanced $1.00 per month.

More conspicuous and more detailed than the above was the advertisement in *Der Nordstern*. Large display type announced: "St. Agnes Academy. Under the Guidance of the Sisters of St. Benedict. Corner of St. Germain Street and Hanover Ave., St. Cloud, Minnesota." Below it was this description of aims and facilities:

The Academy is situated in one of the healthiest and most convenient parts of St. Cloud, and offers an extensive view upon the city, whilst the playgrounds about the building offer to the students opportunity for healthy exercises. The curriculum embraces all branches which are of use to young ladies. Time and attention will be given especially to those students whose relatives wish that they acquire a knowledge of languages, sewing, music, drawing, and painting, which subjects can also be registered for without following the regular school courses. Upon the health of the students care will be bestowed with motherly solicitude and their progress in virtue and science will be cultivated with the greatest zeal. . . .

No student will be admitted for a shorter period of time than one term. Spending money and stamps must be given over to the directress; likewise all incoming and outgoing correspondence is subject to inspection.

Instruction in English, German, and sewing, embroidering, as well as vocal lessons will be given. For tuition, board, and laundry a charge of $50.00 is asked.[21]

Church history and religious instruction were compulsory. General history and algebra were among the electives. That this academy was distinct from the grammar school and taught on the secondary school level is evident. At least it was so within the meaning of the term, "secondary school," in the 1870's. True, the academy did not offer the well-defined sequences of courses which are offered in present-day high schools, but in the 70's there were probably not six schools in the Midwest that did. Most of the public high schools of the period existed chiefly as the upper grades or as courses added beyond the grammar school level. A student was frequently enrolled in both upper and lower division work. Here at St. Agnes Academy was an institution not only offering such secondary school subjects as modern languages, higher mathematics, and art, but at the same time making a distinction between the primary school and the secondary school. Only after 1878 would the high schools of Minnesota be classified as separate units in the educational system of the state. The sisters of St. Benedict were, therefore, pioneers in the movement for distinct secondary schools.

This increase in members and in schools put in their care showed that the Benedictines had established themselves and extended their roots deep into Minnesota soil. The growth had been slow, it is true, but the sisters had never lost faith in their work which was personal sanctification and winning souls for God. From now on, despite two attempts to branch off into separate houses, growth was constant.

The first attempt at the formation of a separate house was made by the former prioress, Mother Willibalda, who had been deposed by Abbot Seidenbusch in 1868. Deeply hurt at her deposition from the office of prioress, she had obtained permission to change her obedience to some other Benedictine convent. Accordingly she spent some time in the convents in Shakopee, in Chicago, and in Pennsylvania.

NEW STRUGGLE FOR EXISTENCE

But finally, in 1871, she returned to St. Joseph. The next year in company with Sister Benedicta Kump and three other sisters she was sent to open a new parochial school in the small rural settlement at New Trier, Minnesota.[22] In the course of the next five years there arose a movement on the part of Mother Willibalda and Sister Benedicta Kump to make this place independent of the mother house at St. Joseph. In 1877 they were apparently independent and ready to accept members, but the bishop of the St. Paul diocese did not want two small Benedictine convents in his territory, and he determined the New Trier convent should unite with the St. Gertrude's Convent in Shakopee; and until such union was made they were forbidden to receive new members. In this predicament, Mother Willibalda informed Abbot Alexius Edelbrock of St. John's Abbey that the sisters strongly objected to the amalgamation. They would rather ask for readmittance to the convent at St. Joseph. She herself planned to return to Europe where she could forget the years of worry and suffering she had endured in this country. She concluded her desperate letter by begging the abbot to come and give them some advice; in the meantime they would all make a novena. What he did is not known, but the records at St. Benedict's show that the chapter on October 18, 1877, moved to grant the petitions of Mother Willibalda, Sister Benedicta Kump, Sister Hildegard Hasler, and Sister Ida Aschenbrenner for readmittance. That attempt to separate had failed.[23]

The second attempt at founding a new convent came toward the close of Mother Antonia's term of office. If not reappointed to the superiorship, Mother Antonia herself planned to migrate to Pierz, Minnesota, with a few followers. In May, 1875, Abbot Alexius Edelbrock had succeeded Abbot Rupert Seidenbusch, her sponsor, as superior of St. John's Abbey, when the latter became bishop of St. Cloud. In the course of the year relations between Mother and the new abbot had become strained to the extent that Mother was certain that he would not reappoint her at the end of her three-year term in 1875. With that in mind she prepared for the approaching event by making plans to start an independent house at Pierz where three of her sisters had charge of the parish school. She purchased ten acres of land there and erected a convent building large enough to accommodate a dozen or more sisters. But in 1875, to Mother Antonia's surprise, her friend Bishop Seidenbusch decided to call for an election of a superior and to preside over it. She was reelected by the sisters for another three-year term to terminate in 1878. Her movement for separation was dropped for the time being.[24]

In 1877 things finally came to a climax between Abbot Alexius and Mother Antonia. In her eagerness for the welfare of her sisters, Mother Antonia would not accept all the work and obligations that the energetic and enterprising abbot demanded. He was insisting that his priests open schools in their parishes and that Mother supply the teachers. In many cases he insisted on the opening of schools even when no houses were provided for the sisters. Sometimes they had to live in the school, now and then even in the same building with the pastor. To this Mother Antonia objected. In some locations no school building was provided. At times, when she had no teachers to give to these new schools, the abbot thought her uncooperative.

Surprisingly enough, however, the final break was not caused by demands for teachers but by Mother Antonia's attempt to get the convent released from the onerous task of doing the monastery laundry.[25] In the difficulties that followed, rather than have the convent suffer because of lack of understanding between the abbey and herself, Mother Antonia handed her resignation to Bishop Seidenbusch. The bishop promptly accepted it and appointed Sister Walburga Muelken in her place. But there was strong objection on the part of the sisters to this choice and to the loss of Mother Antonia, whom they all respected. The bishop then held a visitation at which each sister was interviewed as to her objections and her wishes. By February 15, 1877, Abbot Alexius was sharing information that must have come from the bishop: "I understand that Sister Aloysia will be appointed to fill the vacancy: a change for the better." [26] Only on February 21 was the appointment of Sister Aloysia made known.

Mother Aloysia Bath had come into the Benedictine family after having begun her religious life in the newly-founded community of the Sisters of St. Agnes in Barton, Wisconsin. This Agnesian community was small, poor, and as yet not well established, though its founder, Reverend Casper Rehrl, did his utmost for it. In her autobiography, Mother Aloysia described her reception of the habit of St. Agnes as follows:

I left home to enter the convent at Barton, Wisconsin, on November 7, 1864, exactly fifteen years of age. Received the dress of the Congregation and the name of Agatha on the twelfth of November in the poor little kitchen alongside of the kitchen stove and when the superior had finished the performance the founder of the Congregation, the old Rev. Father Rehrl said: "Now you are Agatha, that means good, but do not do as the other Agatha did." After six years spent in this Community which as yet could give no assurance of permanency of establishment, my confessor, Rev. Anthony Foeckler, advised me to seek entrance into the Benedictine convent at St. Joseph, Minnesota, and obtained for me the dispensation from Bishop Henni.[27]

On her reception into the Benedictine convent she was given the name of Aloysia.

Now in 1877, only two years after final profession as a Benedictine this young religious, 28 years of age, was placed over the Benedictine convent at St. Joseph to fill out Mother Antonia's term of office. She was an experienced teacher and had seen something of the country outside of Stearns County. She was also of a pious disposition and kindly nature. Guided by Providence, the bishop had made a good choice.

However, it is once more evident that Mother Benedicta Riepp's struggle in 1857 for free elections of prioresses, though won in theory, had come to naught in practice. For the second time a superior was appointed whose religious training was not that of the house over which she was to rule. The first, Mother Antonia, had at least been moulded by Benedictine tradition, but Mother Aloysia's formative years had been spent in a new and modern congregation inculcating a spirituality far different from the liturgical type produced by Benedictine training. This shift in piety and spirit was to leave its mark on the Benedictines at St. Joseph. It showed itself in the introduction of various novenas and practices, in the discontinuance of the grate in the parlor, and in lessening the strictness of enclosure. In regard to the latter, other factors were operative, too. With the bishop and abbot constantly seeking new sisters from the community to supply the schools of the diocese there was need for traveling from mission to mother house. The rule of enclosure needed to be mitigated. Since the sisters no longer made solemn vows and the enclosure was not so obligatory, mitigation was now permissible. This change was probably due as much to the needs of the sisters as to the new superior's attitude toward the enclosure and its restrictions in America.

Shortly after Mother Aloysia Bath's appointment the community was again confronted with the possibility of forming a Benedictine Congregation — the same question which had faced Mother Benedicta and Mother Willibalda. This time the movement arose in the Midwest and not in Pennsylvania. Abbot Innocent Wolf and Bishop Louis Fink, O.S.B., of Kansas felt something must be done not only for the Benedictine convent in Atchison but for all the Benedictine houses in the United States. They believed that the constitution of the various convents should be revised "in order to protect the sisters from the undue influence of the bishops and the abbots and from the unlimited power of the superioresses. Up to now the convents had to see the prior or the chaplain and later the abbot about everything." [28] They believed that the sisters' chapter should consist of all professed sisters in the convent, that this chapter should settle the affairs of the convent without outside influence, and that the prioress should be elected by this chapter and not appointed by the bishop or his delegate.

After writing constitutions embodying these ideas for the sisters at Atchison, Bishop Fink inquired of Cardinal Simeoni about getting Rome's approval of the document. He also inquired about the advisability of having all the Benedictine sisters adopt it and of their forming a congregation. On May 14, 1878, the cardinal replied that it was the wish of the Holy Father that the American Benedictine convents should form a congregation and that the bishops should be consulted in the process. With Rome's approval, the abbot felt that the bishops in whose dioceses the sisters were established could now hardly refuse their consent to the forming of a congregation.

With this document to support him, Bishop Fink called on a number of Benedictine convents and their respective ordinaries. He found that to be slow work and decided instead to call a meeting of Benedictine prioresses for August 4, 1879, at Covington, Kentucky. At the same time he sent a notice to the bishops in whose dioceses these convents were located to the effect that "the meeting will be attended besides the superiors by sisters — one from each community — previously elected for this purpose" and that after the constitution was agreed upon, it would be submitted for approval to the ordinaries of these sisters and then sent to Rome. At Bishop Fink's suggestion similar notices were sent out to the convents by Mother Theresa Vogel of St. Joseph's Convent at St. Marys, Pennsylvania. These notices declared that the purpose of the meeting was to carry out the will of the Holy See by the adoption of uniform constitutions and the establishment of a congregation, and added that Bishop Fink and Abbot Wimmer would help the sisters. [29] But all this work came to nothing. The meeting never took place: a smallpox epidemic broke out in Covington and the gathering was postponed indefinitely. No doubt the leaders discovered that the movement had not taken fire. Little interest was manifested and this last-minute obstacle was enough to make them drop the work for the time being.

Just what attitude the community at St. Joseph would have taken on the question of a congregation is not known because records and letters are lacking. That Bishop Seidenbusch of St. Cloud favored the formation of a congregation is evident from the fact that he appointed Abbot Alexius to guide the sisters in this matter.

The statutes and customs which governed the religious life of the sisters at St. Joseph were those carried over from the Eichstätt convent, with changes made at various times by the prioresses and the abbots in an attempt to adjust old practices to American conditions. During her novitiate each sister laboriously copied by hand the Eichstätt *Statuten* with the various amendments. No printed copies of the statutes or customs were made until the late 1880's and no formal ecclesiastical approbation seems to have been obtained for them until 1887. The collection in use in the 70's was a mixture of guidance in prayer and regulations of everyday etiquette. Many of the latter points were practices which would be taken for granted in any state of society then or today. The basic religious practices and customs practiced in the 1870's were those of the parent convents in Eichstätt and in Pennsylvania. Many remain unchanged today, as for example, the praying of five Paters and Aves with outstretched arms in the refectory on confession days, the silent recitation of the "De profundis" for the souls in purgatory when unfolding one's napkin at table, and the visit to the chapel after leaving the refectory at noon and evening. In the 70's the sisters recited the traditional Latin monastic "table prayers" turned away from the table, not facing it.[30] Likewise no longer observed is another Eichstätt table custom. Each sister cleaned her knife, fork, and spoon first on a piece of bread, then wiped them in her napkin, rolled them up in the napkin, and left them on the table for the next meal. A beautiful custom now no longer practiced is that of the prioress' blessing each sister on the forehead and breast with holy water as they left the refectory after the evening meal. Prostrating in the middle aisle in chapel as penance for making the wrong intonation or any other disturbance during the chanting of the Divine Office is no longer observed.

At this period the convent had no chaplain but was dependent upon the pastor of the St. Joseph parish. When he had an assistant, Mass could be offered in the convent chapel. Otherwise the sisters attended Mass in the parish church next door. The kindly interest which St. John's Abbey had in the sisters is shown in the assistance they rendered in time of affliction. When Sister Benedicta Hessler was buried in the late summer of 1877 the funeral took place in the parish church, for the tiny convent chapel could not accommodate the choir and clergy for a high Mass. The choir from St. John's sang the requiem Mass, and six Benedictine monks carried the remains to the grave in the parish cemetery where the sisters were buried until such time as the convent could have a cemetery of its own. Whether all of the sisters who died had such a funeral is not known. The convent buried thirty sisters during its first thirty-one years of existence, and like Sister Benedicta Hessler most of them died before reaching the age of thirty years.

Mother Aloysia soon discovered that St. Agnes Academy in St. Cloud was not having the results that had been hoped for. The mother house was still overcrowded and the attempt to establish a select academy in a group of old buildings was proving unsuccessful. Mother Aloysia and the community therefore decided that a new building was imperative, and planned to erect one that would accommodate both the convent and the boarding school. There was a difference of opinion, however, as to the location of the proposed building. Some held that St. Cloud had a future and would be the ideal place for an academy. Others, especially the older members of the community, clung to the quiet rural settlement of St. Joseph for they had only sad memories of St. Cloud. In August of 1879 the decision was made to build a large three and a half story brick building in St. Joseph. With only $900 credit this was a bold decision. But with Abbot Alexius's guidance and financial aid, work on the basement was begun and by November 4 the basement walls were nearly completed. Cold weather halted construction; then for two years lack of funds prevented more building.

But Mother Aloysia's greatest efforts were spent in supplying teachers to district and parochial schools, especially those which were springing up at the insistence of Abbot Alexius. During Mother Aloysia's administration of less than three years, the community staffed four new schools in Minnesota at Breckenridge, Moorhead, Minneapolis, and New Munich, one Indian mission school at White

Earth Reservation, and a parochial school at Bismarck in Dakota Territory. Staffing these schools cost Mother Aloysia less effort and worry than did the problems that arose in districts where the pastor and parishioners were at odds over the school question. In some instances, unable to persuade his people to employ the sisters in the district school, the pastor would take matters into his own hands by establishing a parochial school to which he required parents to send their children. This was done whether the people were willing or not. In either of these two situations the sisters themselves were subject to annoyance from Catholics who did not want sisters teaching in either public or private schools. In twenty-five years, the Benedictine priests and sisters in this predominantly Catholic territory had not been able to convert all the Catholics to the idea of religious teachers in their schools. So bitter at times was the opposition on the part of laymen that radical means were used to discourage and drive sisters away.

One such incident may be related here. The pastor of the church in New Munich, Minnesota, asked the local school board to hire sisters for their district school. The school board and some influential citizens refused. Nevertheless, hoping for submission, the pastor procured Benedictine sisters for the coming year, but before they arrived the board had quietly hired a lay teacher. The sisters arrived in the midst of the quarrel, and the pastor, not to be defeated, opened a parochial school in the basement of the church. Because of poor classrooms and bad feelings, the attendance was very small. Antagonism was so open that fear of insults made the sisters reluctant to leave the house. In fact, some of the irate men contaminated the well from which the sisters got their drinking water. The church trustees refused to supply the convent with fire wood and withheld the teachers' salaries. But within three months the two leaders of the opposition received great blows. One met with a violent death, but he had time to repent and retract; the son of the other was struck by lightning. The people saw the hand of God in this and the opposition was soon broken.[31] The parish agreed to hire the sisters and the next year, 1880, the school opened with over a hundred children enrolled. The whole miserable situation caused much talk and the newspapers of Stearns County and Minneapolis took up the controversy, thereby adding their bit to the general spirit of rebellion.

Yet these were the people who only six years before had built a handsome new church and invited the Catholics of the entire countryside to the blessing. It was a gala day for the parish. The pastor, Father Meinulph Stuckenkemper, O.S.B., chartered a train for the Sunday celebration. It left Sauk Rapids at 7 A.M. St. Cloud turned out en masse. A participant in the celebration wrote:

At St. Joseph, freight trains were fitted up with seats and St. Joseph individually and collectively added herself to the crowd. Along the route, red, white, and all colored flags waved as signals, the train stopped, and many added themselves to the throng. In due time we arrived, five hundred strong, not to any station, but to a point nearest our destination. There we found a temporary avenue of trees leading from the cars to the carriages, over a hundred in number. These latter were ornamented with fresh saplings so that the array of vehicles and farm wagons rather resembled a waving grove. After the ceremonies of blessing were over, the church was entered by the throngs. Seats not yet having been supplied, a vast number of people obtained entrance and only a few sat on the floor during the high mass and the two sermons.[32]

Despite initial opposition, the sisters by their prayers and works won these fundamentally good people of Minnesota to the mind of the Church and have remained in charge of these schools until today. They gave the people an opportunity to unite their prayer and work with that of the pastor and the sisters themselves. As a result, the Christian faith was firmly established in the hearts of the succeeding generations who in turn have given many sons and daughters to the service of the Church in the Order of St. Benedict.

8 AN EARLY DAKOTA EXPERIMENT

Bismarck and the surrounding territory is as rich in historical traditions as in the wild and varied beauty of its scenery. The large number of buffalo roaming the grassy plains had early attracted the Indians whom Father Severe Doumouslin and Father Joseph Provencher visited in 1820. The Indians in turn attracted the missionaries, and with the missionaries civilization as well as Christianity was brought to the Dakota plains. As early as 1830 the great missionary, Father Pierre-Jean DeSmet, S.J., visited the Mandan Indians. In 1848, on a buffalo hunt with his whole Indian parish, Father Tissiot reached a point not far from the site where the future city of Bismarck was to be located. This period of early missionary work among the Indians and half-breeds was of short duration, for gold was discovered in the Black Hills and with the great rush of white men to the mines, the Indian was pushed farther west. Towns sprang up along the route to the Black Hills, and Bismarck was one of these dusty plains towns. Father Jean-Baptiste Genin was appointed in 1866 to care for the straggling settlements from the Missouri River to Duluth.

Before the railroad reached Dakota Territory, Bismarck was a small town of about 170 inhabitants of white, Indian, and mixed blood and of all levels of culture and social standing. With the coming of the railroad to Bismarck in 1873 the character as well as the population of the town changed. Within four years the population jumped from 170 to 2,500, excluding the numerous soldiers from the forts near by. It became a mushroom town — a town of dusty streets crowded on Saturday night with soldiers, Indians, cowboys, and railroadmen; a town of restaurants, one-story shanties and makeshift hotels. Its best hotel has been described by one of the pioneers as

an immense log building with earth and thatched roof and a ground floor, the walls chinked but not daubed. There was no furniture but a long board table with wooden benches beside it. . . . The only other room, a back room, contained nothing but a cook stove and some blankets piled in one corner. . . . The overnight guest picked up a blanket from this corner and took his choice of sleeping place on the table or bench in the other room.[1]

The most western terminal of the railroad, Bismarck, was at that time the jumping-off place for all those venturesome souls who were going farther west to strike a fortune. It was the jumping-off place for those with a "past" who wished to be swallowed up in the unknown prairies as well as for lawless characters who wished to cut the ties that held them to law, order, and culture. Formerly, the inhabitants of Bismarck had been of a more uniform type, for only the strongest and boldest would attempt the long journey by mule or stage-coach. Now that railroads made travelling across the prairie hunting grounds of the Indians less hazardous, the town soon drew to itself physical and moral weaklings, the restless and ne'er-do-wells, running away from the officers of the law or the responsibilities of life. Other newcomers came from families of wealth and social position and thus another element was injected into the changing character of Bismarck. It was becoming a town whose dusty streets might be crowded with deserting soldiers, renegade Indians, railroad men, cowboys, a few millionaire ranchers and nobles. At one end of the social ladder were Three-fingered Dick, Muddy Jim, Liver-eating Johnson; at the other, a Marquise de Morres and a Teddy Roosevelt. Here were to be found people from virtually every state of the Union, from Bombay, Germany, England, and even from Russia.

It was a rough town and a life at times was not worth more than a good shot. Of the fifty bodies lying in the old cemetery ten were those of children and "all the others were adults who died with their boots on — men who were shot or were accidentally killed, and women who were beaten to death, shot or poisoned." It was a hard country. One officer's wife, Lynda Slaughter, has left an account of the mid-winter burial of her child. Because the ground was frozen so deeply that the grave could not be dug, the little coffin was put in the magazine house of the fort. This distressed the mother, and to quiet her the officers decided to bury the child. To do this they had to keep a fire burning over the ground until it was soft enough to dig. They soon found themselves in a predicament: they could not make a deep grave, and a shallow one would offer no protection against wild animals. They solved the problem by pouring several barrels of water over the coffin after it was lowered into the grave. Coated with ice, the small coffin was safe until spring.[2]

Into this crude, restless, and yet courageous settlement teeming with energy and hope the Benedictine sisters came in 1878 to teach religion and the three R's. Before the sisters came, Father Genin and Abbot Martin Marty, O.S.B., had labored with the Catholics of Bismarck in erecting a church on the western extremity of the main street.[3] Father Genin served a vast territory and he could visit Bismarck only occasionally. He was, therefore, forced to leave the raising of money for a church in the hands of the laity. His trust was not misplaced. The local newspaper carried accounts of numer-

AN EARLY DAKOTA EXPERIMENT

ous money-raising projects. A ball was given in Reardon Hall on St. Patrick's Day in 1874 which netted $200. Tickets sold for $3 each. With this money the lumber for the structure was shipped from Detroit Lakes, Minnesota. There are two stories about the origin of the timber. According to one version, Father Genin tore down the church of Detroit Lakes and shipped it to Bismarck on flat cars. According to the other version, the church at Detroit Lakes was blown down by a storm and rather than rebuild it there, Father Genin decided to do so in a more deserving settlement.

When the lumber arrived, priest and parishioners got to work and in a few weeks this 70 by 28 foot structure, as yet roofless, was used for devotions. On this occasion, Father Valentine Sommereisen from the Indian Reservation preached a lengthy sermon. Because of lack of funds, building stopped and another ball was held — this time in the unfinished church itself! The roof was on before the winter season set in, but the shingles had not been paid for. To pay for them, Mrs. J. B. Cleary went about collecting from friends and parishioners. The sum she collected plus that raised by another St. Patrick's Day ball, held in the roundhouse of the Northern Pacific Railroad, made it possible to complete the carpenter work. The church was blessed in June, 1875, by Father Genin, assisted by Father Labrine and Father Valentine Sommereisen. But all of this grand effort nearly ended in failure a few weeks later when a severe storm struck the building, moved it eighteen inches, and left it tipped at a dangerous angle.

Though the Catholics of Bismarck now had a church of their own, they still had no resident pastor. Father Genin continued to visit them about once a month, and occasionally priests from the Standing Rock Indian Agency served their needs. On those days weddings and baptisms were crowded in between Holy Mass and catechetical instructions, for the priest had to move on immediately to keep appointments at other Catholic settlements. These missionary priests used the stagecoach but often they resorted to railroad handcars. On one occasion when Father Genin missed the stagecoach leaving for Fargo, where he had promised to say Mass, he requisitioned a handcar. With the aid of a sail and a favoring wind he made the trip from Bismarck to Fargo in seventeen and one half hours. This bit of ingenuity was spectacular enough to be featured in the Bismarck newspaper.[4]

During the building period, the Bismarck parish was under the jurisdiction of Bishop Grace of St. Paul, but soon afterwards it came under the care of Bishop Rupert Seidenbusch, O.S.B., Vicar Apostolic of Northern Minnesota. After this churchman's first visit to Bismarck in the fall of 1875, he decided that the people should have not only a resident pastor but also teaching sisters. Father Chrysostom Foffa, O.S.B., was appointed resident pastor and for the next two years he slowly gathered funds for a school building. Finally in the fall of 1877 the foundation was laid for a two-story building 30 feet square attached to the west side of the church toward the river. It was planned to accommodate four sisters and twelve boarding pupils. According to the builders' plans, the first floor provided space for the kitchen, pastor's dining room, children's refectory, and a parlor. The upper floor was to be one large dormitory shared by the four sisters and the pupils. Classes were to be taught in the church and in a room attached to the church building.

As soon as the plaster was dry, the sisters were summoned. The *Bismarck Tribune* of March 21, 1878 carried a brief notice that Sisters of the Order of St. Benedict had arrived to open a new academy. The following issue of the paper carried an extended announcement that the boarding school and the day school would be opened on April 8 with "Boarding accommodations for twelve young ladies." Another issue stated:

No labor or expense will be saved to make it one of the best schools in the West. The three school rooms are admirably arranged and nothing is lacking for the progress of the pupils. All branches of study will be taught from the classics down to the alphabet. The text books used are to be the same as those in use in the public schools which close on April 2. The pupils can thus go from one school to the other without additional expense for books. . . . The charges for all grades for board and tuition are placed at an extremely low figure — just sufficient to make the school self-sustaining. Father Chrysostom wishes it known that the school is not a sectarian one.[5]

Perhaps the rather startling final statement — startling when one remembers that this was to be a parochial school — was simply an expression of the fact that the school would not be closed to non-Catholics. Besides, since funds had been collected from Protestant and Catholic alike, the whole project probably seemed as much civic as parochial.

AN EARLY DAKOTA EXPERIMENT

The boarding school or academy announcement must not be interpreted to mean that the sisters were opening a private school with its own classes taught separately from those of the parish school. The sisters had been brought in to teach the children of the parish in a school built by the parish. The "Academy" for the "twelve young ladies" mentioned in the newspaper was merely a venture on the part of the sisters to board some pupils whose homes were too far away to allow them to travel back and forth each day. These girls were to attend classes with the parish children.

Though the newspaper reported the arrival of five sisters, only four were assigned to the mission. These were Sister Magdalen Euste, who was in charge of the institution, Sister Ida Aschenbrenner, Sister Gregoria Thiekamp, and Sister Alphonsa O'Donnell. The fifth was Mother Aloysia Bath who accompanied them and saw them properly established. Sister Alphonsa was destined to remain but one year when she was called to open a new mission elsewhere. Sister Magdalen remained five years and then left to join the Benedictine community at Atchison. The three teachers were embarrassed but pleased on the opening day when, instead of 12 boarders, 21 applied and in place of the expected 50 day pupils, 80 pushed into the three small classrooms.

The first term closed in August, 1878, with exercises held in the church the following week. The part of the program which evidently most impressed the newspaper reporter was a Sioux hymn sung by Anna Goodro, a small Indian girl from Standing Rock Reservation. However from this statement it must not be inferred that the boarding school was attended only by Indian girls. The majority were daughters of military officers and government agents at the forts and Indian reservations of Dakota and Montana. Their parents were often Protestants who had no other means of schooling their daughters than to send them to this boarding school — probably the only one of its kind between the Rocky Mountains and Minnesota. Though they knew that the school was good, some found it hard to forget their early prejudices against nuns. The following anecdote was told by Sister Anatolia Langford, who was principal there in the early years. Two girls arrived from Jamestown. When helping to unpack their trunk, Sister found two clothes lines. Jokingly she asked, "Did you think we did not have clothes lines in Bismarck? Why did you bring these?" The girls blushed and bashfully said they would tell her sometime later. Weeks later when the pupils felt quite at home and had grown to love the sisters, one of them asked Sister Anatolia if she still wondered about the rope. "I blush to think of it," added the girl. "Our parents knew the sisters kept good schools but they were afraid that some of the old stories they had once heard about convents might have some truth to them, and so they supplied us with ropes that we might make an escape if it were necessary." [6]

The Catholics of the town were so pleased with the splendid work of the school that the next term found it impossibly crowded. The parish decided to erect a new two-story building, 20 by 48 feet, a few steps from the convent. The project was slowed up because of lack of church funds and the difficulty of getting lumber. Father Chrysostom told of his problems in a letter that throws light on one phase of the "opening of the West." He wrote:

I must build the schoolhouse now and collect for it during the winter in the forts and on the railroad. But we have trouble to get lumber, for all the cars going east on the Northern Pacific are loaded with wheat and those going west are loaded with material for the construction of the new railroad. For two weeks we could get no empty cars to fetch our lumber for our new buildings. [7]

However, not all of the citizens of Bismarck had been pleased at the establishment of a Catholic school. When the project was proposed, as early as 1876, two Protestant ministers denounced it as a threat to democracy and the free education of the public school system, and headed a campaign against Mrs. Lynda Slaughter, the county superintendent of schools, for her kindly attitude toward the sisters. Nor did the success of the school change their attitude. They campaigned vigorously against Mrs. Slaughter, who by this time had also aroused the opposition of Bismarck's numerous saloon keepers. On election day the citizens of Bismarck witnessed a strange contest: saloon keepers allied with ministers against the Protestant superintendent of the public schools who was supporting a Catholic school. Mrs. Slaughter herself has left an account of the incident in her memoirs.

I was interested in the building of St. Mary's Academy, having a high opinion of the sisters' schools. I contributed several articles to the *Bismarck Tribune,* earnestly commending the school and asking the people of Bismarck to give it patronage and financial support. This gave offense to Rev. Mr. Carey. He took a copy of the *Tribune* containing one of my articles into the pulpit and read it to the congregation, seriously censuring me as a Protestant for recommending a Catholic institution and as a public school officer for extending help to a sectarian school and one at variance with the public school system. He counselled all Protestants to remove their children from the sisters' school and advised them not to vote for me again for superintendent of schools. The sermon made a sensation in Bismarck. . . . At the county election when I was again a candidate for reelection as county superintendent of schools, the most bitter campaign ever waged in the county was carried on against me. . . . The result showed that I had not trusted in vain, . . . for I was elected by a larger majority than any other county candidate at the election, having received 413 votes. . . . At the county election in 1879 the same process was repeated, but on a larger scale there being many more people in the county. . . . On the Sunday before the election the new Presbyterian minister preached a sermon on the public schools counselling his hearers to vote against me at the polls and also attacking me as a teacher of the primary department of the city schools of Bismarck, on the grounds that I was a partisan of Catholic institutions and in favor of sectarian schools. . . . I gave up all hopes of election as the saloon keepers of Bismarck were opposing me because I had organized a ladies' temperance society. . . . The minister of the Presbyterian church worked against me and stood all day at the polls on election day, side by side with the saloon keepers, sparing no effort to defeat me. After all I received 962 votes and was elected. Thus again was my position toward Catholic schools sustained by the fair and impartial people of Burleigh County.[8]

Despite this opposition on the part of this block of residents of Bismarck the Catholic school's enrollment increased.

Stories of life on this frontier mission have been told again and again by those sisters who survived the test. True, it was a hard life — a life with bare necessities — but it never lacked color and change. It was a rough-and-tumble age, a life of "beginnings." With new problems and new situations, whether joyful or not, constantly arising, the monotony of a settled routine might have been welcomed. Many and exciting were the stories with which serene old sisters who had known Bismarck in the old days entertained their young successors. The tale of the mysterious prowler was one of these.

The convent and school were located at that end of town toward the river where the boatmen had to pass on their way downtown.

Their yells and coarse talk when returning from town in the wee hours of the morning used to frighten the sisters out of their deep sleep. Because this group of church and school buildings was the largest in this end of town, many of the boatmen took it to be a hotel. They would knock and demand admission at any hour of the night. One night when a rumor went about that a band of ruffians were planning on "shooting up the town" a kindly neighbor, an Episcopalian minister, warned the sisters to keep everything well locked. Then to relieve their fears he promised to sit up all night in his home next door so that no annoyance would come to the sisters or pupils. Too frightened to sleep, the sisters sat up in the dark all night fully dressed. If they were to die, they would die in their habits! They heard a noise in the kitchen, and their first thought was of prowlers. Frozen with terror, none was brave enough to investigate the source of the sound. Toward morning the neighbor came creeping over to the convent and quietly called out that he thought all danger had passed and they might get a little rest. They begged him to come in and examine the kitchen; they were sure that someone was there or in the cellar, for they had heard a thumping sound as of someone going down the steps to the cellar. The neighbor came in and with him at their head they fearfully entered the back room. The day's baking had been left out on the table to cool during the night and they now noticed that one loaf was missing. Crumbs led them to the cellar trapdoor, and then on down the steps to the bottom. There they found the loaf — and the culprit — a large rat. Apparently it had pushed the loaf off the table and from step to step to the bottom of the cellar steps, making that thumping noise which they had mistaken for a prowler. The sisters had many a good laugh over this scare.

On another night after a church collection four attempts at robbery were made on the convent and rectory. For several nights after that, volunteer vigilantes kept watch over the convent.

Another incident related by Sister Anatolia Langford gives further insight into the surroundings of St. Mary's, Bismarck. One evening while she and a companion were in church arranging the altar for the next morning's Mass, the pastor entered and asked that the candles be lighted. He was to take Holy Viaticum to a dying person. He left immediately, but he returned so soon that the sisters were startled. He was pale and showed signs of great excitement, and the sisters noticed he had no hat. But to their questions he answered only, "I did not have far to go. Leave the work and get into the convent at once." It will be recalled that the convent was attached to the church and could be entered from the sanctuary. The next day the pastor explained to the sisters that he had been called by an unknown person to visit a dying man; he was a bit suspicious about the affair and he was on the alert. As he turned the corner at the church, he was suddenly attacked by two men. At their first blow, he struck out and knocked one down. The other fled.[9]

As was more customary than not, the sisters boarded the pastor, and that meant his clerical guests as well. Though the sisters were glad to serve God's travelers, in Bismarck they did so at great inconvenience. Cooking by electricity or gas was unknown. Not even wood was to be had for cooking on this treeless prairie. Lignite coal was shipped in from Dickinson, and it was impossible to prepare a meal quickly with this fuel which gave more clinkers than heat. Adding to the trials of cooking was the scarcity of water — not only drinking water but water for any purpose. All water had to be carried from the muddy Missouri River and thoroughly boiled before it could be used.

Fresh vegetables were scarce and high-priced. Little gardening was done in a settlement of soldiers and transients, and vegetables had to be shipped in from eastern states. For other staple goods the inhabitants were likewise dependent on the railroad. This is illustrated well by an incident related by Sister Hilda Weisser who was in Bismarck as early as 1879 with Sister Bernarda Kurz and Sister Celestina Marschall. According to her account, the winter of 1879 was so severe that no attempt was made for a time to operate the railroad west of the Red River. During a particularly heavy storm Bismarck was cut off from all railroad communication for three weeks. At one time rations were so depleted that the commissary at the fort was anxious about the sisters and their charges. A detachment of soldiers was ordered to bring them hardtack and army crackers. The Indians were also hungry, and as the isolation continued the settlers feared an Indian uprising. It would have been a strategic time for an attack, for the settlement was helpless and the government would have been unable to send reinforcements to aid the soldiers at the fort. But the trains finally shoveled through and the tension was relieved. During this time of crisis the parish was without a shepherd: The pastor had left town a few days before the storm [10] and was snowbound between Fargo and Bismarck for 27 days. During this long period the sisters and children were deprived of Holy Mass and the sacraments.

Even the nights brought their hardships for the 21 pupils and four sisters crowded into a dormitory 20 by 40 feet. The sisters had one corner of the room curtained off to give them a little privacy. Even when Sister Euphrasia Hirtenberger contracted typhoid fever, there was no place other than this room in which to put her. The building was poorly constructed. The wind blew through window casements and chimney, and the rain dripped through the roof. The bell tower in the dormitory was a particularly leaky place in time of showers, the bell rope acting as a very effective conduit that brought the incoming rain down on the unfortunate who slept beneath it. Only a few rooms were heated by stoves. The stove pipe in the kitchen was supposed to give off enough heat to warm the children's refectory and play room as it passed through that room to join the general chimney in the church. If stoves were heated sufficiently to keep the children from freezing, smoke forced them out of doors.

The pastor, Father William Eversmann, O.S.B., was oblivious of the domestic problems of the boarding school. He could see no need of new buildings for he had no confidence in his parishioners. He complained to his abbot: "If a person goes to Holy Mass once a month or once every two months, and to Holy Communion three times during life, all will call him a good Christian." His judgment was somewhat unfair; another priest a few months later declared the place to be the liveliest city of its size in existence. "The church," he said, "was well filled last Sunday and the congregation showed as much religious feeling as any congregation that I have ever seen. I never saw a better behaved people." [11] Despite the primitive conditions at the institution the enrollment continued to increase.

With the opening of this parochial-boarding school in the West and the staffing of eight district and parochial day schools, Mother Aloysia could gratefully finish her three-year appointment as superior. The little convent at St. Joseph had passed through the uncertain period of planting and had at last taken firm root in the Midwest. The next decade was to be one of rapid growth and expansion as well as of increased range of apostolic and charitable endeavors.

PART TWO

FLICKERING LAMPS

9 A NEW SPIRIT AT ST. JOSEPH

The history of the Minnesota Benedictines through the period from 1857 to the close of Mother Aloysia Bath's term of office in 1880, shows it to have been a period of very slow growth. During that period the membership of the Community grew to the number of 57 professed sisters. The year 1880, however, was to mark the beginning of a rapid and constant development which was to continue down to the present day. Not only was there a rapid increase in members, in development, and in expansion of the physical plant at the mother house, but also a mushrooming of the apostolic work over the states of Minnesota, North and South Dakota, Iowa, Wisconsin, and Washington.

The beginning of this upsurge coincides with the coming of a new prioress. In the spring of 1880 Mother Aloysia, whose term of office was to end in July, handed in her resignation to Bishop Seidenbusch. On April 6, the Bishop delegated Abbot Alexius Edelbrock to appoint or to provide for the election of a temporary superior until such time as an election could be held after the bishop's return from a trip to Europe. Acting under these powers, the abbot came to the parish house next door and sent two documents to the convent. One accepted Mother Aloysia's resignation; the other appointed Sister Scholastica Kerst as temporary superior. The sisters objected to his action, considering it interference. They also felt that the abbot's choice was unwise, for it was less than three years since Sister Scholastica had transferred her obedience from St. Gertrude's Convent in

Shakopee, Minnesota, to theirs. The protest was ignored, and both
the bishop and the abbot soon left for Europe. Four months later,
Abbot Alexius returned, and on August 20, 1880, he presided over
the election of a prioress. Aware that a majority of the chapter members did not intend to vote for Mother Scholastica, he announced that
if she were not elected, she would be appointed. He wanted the community to grow. In his opinion she was capable of providing the
necessary leadership.

Mother Scholastica Kerst was born in Muringen, Prussia, on June
21, 1847, and came to St. Paul, Minnesota, with her parents in her
infancy. She entered St. Gertrude's Convent at Shakopee on October
11, 1862 — two days after its establishment. She received the habit
the following year and made temporary vows in 1864, but a period
of five years elapsed between the pronouncement of her temporary
and her perpetual vows. This may be accounted for by the fact that
the newly-founded convent of St. Gertrude's with only three sisters
and one candidate was unable to provide solid novitiate training,
and Bishop Grace required that before making solemn vows Sister
Scholastica should spend a year of strict novitiate in some well-
established Benedictine convent.[1] Sister Scholastica was sent to St.
Joseph's Convent, St. Mary, Pennsylvania, where she remained two
years. These years spent in that well-established and well-regulated
older convent with its German atmosphere and its system of prudent
economy made her sensitive to the contrast between it and the young,
struggling St. Gertrude's to which she returned. She had inherited
her father's good business sense, and the poor methods used in her
little convent irritated her. Her flair for leadership made it difficult
for her to accept these things as they were. Discontent is shown in
letters written to Abbot Alexius of St. John's Abbey during the years
1875 and 1876. Her letter of May 2, 1876, reveals that with four
others she planned to leave and establish a house in St. Paul. She
asked his help and that of the Benedictine priests.[2] The abbot took
no action and a year later Sister Scholastica through a priest emissary
petitioned Bishop Grace of St. Paul for permission to transfer to
another convent. The permission was granted, and in a letter to
Mother Gertrude Flynn of St. Gertrude's dated August 10, 1877,
Bishop Grace wrote:

> By this mail I send a letter to Sister Scholastica giving her permission
> to transfer her obedience to one of the convents of the Order in Pennsyl-

vania. She expressly asked this permission through Reverend Father Plut who was in St. Paul the same day you came here.[3]

Abbot Alexius, a friend of her parents, attributed Sister Scholastica's action to wrong direction and persuaded her to apply instead to the Benedictine convent at St. Joseph. The abbot presented her cause to the capitulars of that house a few days later, and on August 30, 1877, Sister Scholastica was admitted as a member. In May, 1880, two years and eight months later, the abbot appointed her to rule the convent.[4]

This young religious was gifted in many ways. She was practical, adventurous, self-confident, and gifted as a leader. The abbot had like qualities and his dominant concern was the growth and development of the Church and the Benedictine Order. He saw in Sister Scholastica the person who would cooperate with him in the expansion of Benedictine work in the field of education, of care of the sick, and of mission work among the Indians.

One of the first projects of the newly-appointed superior was to open negotiations for the suppression of her former convent at Shakopee and its amalgamation with the convent at St. Joseph. With her aptitude for finance, Mother Scholastica saw that the union of her former convent and that at St. Joseph would make one large well-established mother house; that the personnel of St. Gertrude's Convent with its English-speaking members was just what her convent needed for its academy; that the union would also double her teaching staff at St. Joseph. With Mother Scholastica, to think was to act; and in May, 1880, within a few days after her temporary appointment as prioress, she started to work through friends in St. Paul and Shakopee to persuade Bishop John Ireland, coadjutor to Bishop Grace, to suppress the convent at Shakopee.[5]

The story of this Shakopee Benedictine convent can be briefly told. St. Gertrude's Convent was founded from St. Joseph's Convent at St. Mary, Pennsylvania, October 9, 1862, when two choir sisters and one lay sister took up residence in Shakopee in a shed formerly used as a cow barn. Within ten years the convent had made considerable progress and was held in high esteem by Bishop Grace. It is true that the authorities at St. John's Abbey had from time to time suggested that the Shakopee convent close and merge with the St. Joseph convent, for Shakopee was too great a distance from the abbey for the abbot's care and guidance. However, Bishop Grace

A NEW SPIRIT AT ST. JOSEPH

expressed his unwillingness to lose the services of the sisters and obstructed the move. On one of these occasions he wrote to Prior Othmar Wirtz that "the sisters are doing great good in Shakopee and it would be a sad loss to religion were they to be removed." Again in 1865 he wrote to the prior:

It is very desirable that Father Matthew be retained in or around Shakopee on account of the sisters as well as on account of the populous missions. With the assistance of Father Matthew the sisters will, I have no doubt, succeed in building up a flourishing establishment in Shakopee, by means of which religion and souls will be greatly benefited.[6]

But in the early 1870's trouble began for St. Gertrude's. Unable to meet the payments for their $11,400 stone convent and academy built on property belonging to St. John's Abbey, they were forced to borrow money. This was difficult because St. John's Abbey, not St. Gertrude's, held the deed to the property. St. John's then borrowed money for them, putting the property up as security. The third superior, Mother Gertrude Flynn, resorted to outright begging for donations, begging which was reinforced by faith and prayer. In her old age she delighted in telling how she and the community placed in a money box a Blessed Virgin medal and a slip of paper on which were written the words, "God increases," and then started a campaign of prayer. She claimed that money came in from the most unexpected places, and that in less than three years $15,000 was paid out to impatient creditors. By January 24, 1877, Bishop Grace of St. Paul was able to write to Mother Gertrude:

I have looked over your report of the financial condition of the convent in Shakopee with a great deal of interest and was surprised and glad to find how much you had done towards diminishing the original amount of indebtedness that was on the convent when you undertook the administration of affairs. You have reason to thank our good God and to hope He will continue His blessings upon your efforts. I feel a sense of relief and am encouraged to believe that the convent will not only be extricated from its embarrassments, but will prove a most valuable aid in the cause of religion and piety in Shakopee. . . . Pater Valentine spoke to me about getting some of your Sisters to take charge of the Orphan Asylum he is thinking of opening up here in St. Paul for the benefit of orphan children of German parentage. I told him he could have them as it will be an additional relief to your community.[7]

By the middle of 1878 the debt hanging over the sisters was practically paid off. But troubles now arose from another quarter. The pastor of the local church in Shakopee became strongly antagonistic to the sisters. He refused to rehire them as teachers in his parochial school for the coming year and gave as his excuse that the sisters were unable to teach the German language in school. For a time he even went so far as to refuse them a pew in the church. It is true that two-thirds of the thirty sisters composing this convent were unable to speak the German language but, as Abbot Alexius wrote, commiserating with Mother Gertrude on this occasion:

> Our public schools are taught by young girls of sixteen years of age with little English at their command and nobody is dissatisfied with them, and others with little German at their command teach in districts where the Germans prevail and are accepted. . . . We live in a queer world and have to bear the crosses willingly. . . . If we are treated as our Master let us be satisfied. No doubt God will make all things right in due time. He is slow at times, but always sure. Although the Sisters have not any school in Shakopee they will continue to exist, to live, to do good. Perhaps Reverend Plut will change his mind in course of time.[8]

The real issue was not so much the inability of the sisters to use German in teaching as it was the pastor's bias against the members of St. Gertrude's Convent, helped perhaps by one member of the house. However, there was still plenty of work for the thirty sisters in staffing the academy connected with the convent, the three large parish schools in Minneapolis, in Carver, in Belle Plaine, and the orphanage in St. Paul.

Though Bishop Grace praised Mother Gertrude for her business ability, he did not approve of her inclination to pattern the life in her convent on that of the more cloistered Benedictines on the Continent and in England. The bishop, overwhelmed by the need of missionary workers in Minnesota, wanted a convent of women devoted to works of exterior charity. Mother Gertrude Flynn made the best of the situation, but a trip to England in 1875 where she visited the Benedictine houses renewed in her the old desire of a Benedictine cloistered contemplative life. At Ramsgate she and the prioress discussed the matter of the Shakopee convent's joining with the Ramsgate house in a congregation which was just then being approved by Rome. The proposal of such a union appealed to Mother Gertrude, for she felt that the consequent exchange of sisters and the requirement of chanting the whole Divine Office would raise the tone of the Minnesota house and give it security. Bishop Christopher Reynolds of Adelaide, Australia, even offered Mother Gertrude a foundation in his diocese if her convent joined with the Ramsgate Congregation. To these plans Bishop Grace refused his approval. When Mother Gertrude told him of her own desire to enter the community at Ramsgate where the sisters were cloistered and recited the Divine Office each day, he answered:

As God has placed you in a position now in which you can accomplish a great deal of good for the community . . . you should take it as His will that you should remain where you now are. You can gain great merit by striving to bring the community to a stricter observance of Rules of your holy institute as far as the circumstance of the times and place will admit.[9]

He probably considered Mother Gertrude somewhat of a visionary. Despite the fact that during her term of office financial conditions were greatly improved and the sisters had reelected her, the bishop of St. Paul passed over their choice and appointed Sister Ignatia Huntington, an invalid, in her stead.

This was the state of affairs at St. Gertrude's in Shakopee in the spring of 1880 when Sister Scholastica Kerst, lately appointed prioress of the convent at St. Joseph opened negotiations for suppressing her former convent and amalgamating it with St. Benedict's.

When the proposition of joining the community at St. Joseph was first put before the Shakopee convent it was unanimously rejected. When it was proposed a second time, the chapter again voted it down. But on August 31, 1880, Bishop Ireland again sent word that the convent was suppressed and that the thirty sisters were to join the convent at St. Joseph or be dispensed from their vows and return to the world. They were not given the right to join another Benedictine house of their choice. This notice did not reach Shakopee before the sisters had dispersed to their various mission schools. Sister Anatolia Langford first learned of the suppression from a priest in a railroad station on her way to her mission at Belle Plaine. Uncertain whether to return to their convent at Shakopee or to continue on to the school to which they were sent by their superior and for which their contract had been signed for the coming school year, she and her companions decided to continue on to their assignment until notice was sent to them. This accounts for the fact that they and a number of other Shakopee nuns did not reach the convent at St. Joseph until the next year.[10]

What the bishop of St. Paul did was in keeping with the powers of his office although he was misinformed as to the unstable financial conditions at Shakopee and also was unaware of the motives of those who wanted the merger. Abbot Alexius considered the act an injustice and in a letter to Bishop Ireland wrote:

The Sisters' home in Shakopee stands vacant and to hold that the Sisters are solely or principally to blame for having been driven from their convent is or will be a matter for Rome to decide. They believe and feel that they were wronged and my own impression is they were wronged.[11]

In later years Bishop Ireland admitted that he had acted unwisely in this matter, and on her death bed in the presence of two former Shakopee sisters, Mother Scholastica declared she had done wrong and asked for forgiveness.[12]

Though it worked a hardship on those sisters of Shakopee who had to give up their home to join another group, the amalgamation did have good results. The merger brought in a leaven of other nationalities and tended to make the community at St. Joseph more American. It gave Mother Scholastica a group of experienced teachers and, what is still more important, a group of zealous religious. It enabled her to open and staff hospitals in Bismarck, St. Cloud, and Duluth and to accept a number of new parochial schools. With all Mother Scholastica's genius for organization and business and her zeal for good works she would have been unable to forge ahead without this additional group of sisters to staff the institutions.

With additional capable teachers for the higher classes in Latin, English, music, and art, Mother Scholastica felt she could open an academy or finishing school of high school level. St. Agnes Academy housed as it was in the old log church and school in St. Cloud, had not been successful as a select boarding school. The faculty members were not particularly distinguished and the school was poorly equipped. Mother Scholastica in one of her many quick moves closed the school in St. Cloud, rented the Haarman building across the street from the church and convent in St. Joseph, and announced the opening of a select boarding academy at St. Joseph.

At the close of the year's work the abbot was so pleased with the results that he urged Mother Scholastica to complete the unfinished building begun in 1879 by her predecessor, Mother Aloysia. A week later the sisters assembled and voted to build a combination convent and academy despite the fact that no one knew how to raise the money except by begging. The chapter decided that the business men of the village and friends of the sisters should be appealed to for donations, and in case that failed, a lottery would be tried. On such expectations the masons were set to work in the early summer of 1881 with the hope that the structure would be under roof before the winter snow fall. But the work was slow and the donations did not meet expectations. Only on September 11 was the cornerstone laid. *Der Nordstern* carried this account of the ceremony.

The Right Reverend Bishop had promised to be present but was called away to attend the funeral of Bishop Henni [of Milwaukee]. In his stead Abbot Alexius laid the cornerstone. The exercises began at 3 P.M. People came from near and far. The band from St. John's College led the procession from the church to the building site where the ceremony took place. After the cornerstone was laid, the procession wended its way back to the church where Father Francis explained the ceremonies. The religious function was ended with the singing of the *Te Deum*. In the evening the sisters served a grand feast for the friends and benefactors of the convent.[13]

When spring came, the building was ready for occupancy despite all delays. Among pupils and sisters there was much excitement as well as hard work in moving books, maps, desks, and house furnishings across lots to the new convent and academy in preparation for the house blessing and graduation exercises of 1881. All took their share in the joyous work and by May 7 Holy Mass was offered in the large room which was to serve as both chapel and study hall. On June 29, 1882, the whole building was blessed and the title changed from St. Joseph's Convent and Academy to St. Benedict's Convent and Academy.[14] Mother Scholastica appointed Sister Alexia Kerst, her sister, to be directress of the academy. A printed catalogue was issued that fall, and St. Benedict's Academy could now take its place with the best schools of the day.[15]

The building was plain, within and without. Because funds were limited, there was none of the ornateness that made hideous so many buildings, both private and public, in the 1870's and 1880's. The very plainness of the structure gave it character. The Bavarian cultural background of its builders, together with a sense of conventual simplicity and practicality, served to produce a building that was at once monastic and mid-American.

During the 1880's there were a number of Catholic boarding schools for girls in the vast territory which stretched from St. Paul to the Rocky Mountains. Outside of St. Paul, however, only one could be described as a "finishing school" — St. Benedict's Academy at St. Joseph, Minnesota. With this exception, the girls' boarding schools of the period were of grammar school level or were bound up with mission work among Indian and mixed-blood girls.

St. Benedict's position as the westernmost Catholic finishing school of the 1880's drew many students from western Minnesota, Dakota Territory, Montana, Utah, and even Idaho. Others came from Illinois, Wisconsin, Indiana, and Iowa. The majority of the western students appear to have been daughters of state and federal officials, men living beyond the line of the frontier who had regular salaries and who appreciated all the more the benefits of a thorough education. The Minnesota students came from business and professional groups in the towns and cities of the state. Only a few farmers' daughters were enrolled at St. Benedict's. The Minnesota farmer seemed little minded to send his daughter to school beyond the eighth grade, possibly because he was reluctant to part with her labor, or with the money required for her tuition, or both.

Among the western girls was Melda McLaughlin, whose father, James McLaughlin, was federal Indian agent at the Standing Rock Indian Agency at Fort Yates, Dakota Territory. She was sent to the academy in 1887 partly for the schooling she would receive there and partly for her personal safety. The Indians of Fort Yates were restless because Sitting Bull, the powerful Sioux chief, was in custody there. Carrie Smith's father had a similar position at Coeur d'Alene, Idaho. The McKenzie girls were enrolled in the St. Benedict's grade school while their mother, who remained with them, studied music, art, needle work, and rhetoric. Their father, Alexander McKenzie, was one of the most prominent men in Dakota Territory. He was the political boss of the Dakota Territory. When North Dakota became a state he is said to have made and unmade governors; it was as a result of his efforts that the capital was moved from Yankton to Bismarck. The Gerard girls were daughters of Frederick Gerard, whose grandparents had emigrated from Bordeaux, France, in the late eighteenth century. Gerard himself, after having finished his courses at St. Xavier College in St. Louis, was sent by the American Fur Company to Fort St. Pierre and later to Fort Berthold in Dakota. On his visits to the academy he regaled the sisters and the pupils with stories of his adventures at Fort Berthold. He told how, in the absence of the friendly Arikara and Mandan Indians, seventeen men bravely fought off an attack on the post by six hundred Yankton

Sioux. But more often he told about the part he played in the Custer expedition to the Little Big Horn and its aftermath.[16]

The students from St. Paul and Minneapolis had an entirely different background. Theirs had been a city life, and they brought with them an element of sophistication. Elizabeth Will, Lena and Margaret Kerst were members of prominent German families in St. Paul; Josie Freund and Lena Schlick's fathers were businessmen in the same city.

The young ladies did not make the long journeys from Idaho and other remote places alone and unchaperoned. Neither parents nor teachers would have tolerated such action. Each year at the opening of the fall term two sisters traveled to distant points on western railroads in order to meet prospective students who previously had been instructed what train to board at what time. Even students traveling the short distance from St. Paul were chaperoned on the trip. The *Northwestern Chronicle*, a Catholic newspaper published in St. Paul, carried a notice in its issue of August 23, 1883, announcing that "The female Academy of the Benedictine Sisters at St. Joseph, Minnesota, opens on September 5." "Pupils will find a sister," the notice continues, "to accompany them to the school." On September 6 the same paper announced that twelve young ladies, accompanied by Sister Alexia, had left St. Paul for St. Benedict's.

The purpose and aim of the school, which was stated in each issue of its *Annual Catalogue*, was to offer a well-balanced education based on thoroughly Christian principles. The 1883 *Catalogue* announced: "Here facilities are afforded to young ladies for acquiring proficiency in branches that constitute an education, at the same time solid and refined. . . . The course of instruction embraces every useful and ornamental branch of education suitable for young ladies." [17] There was no thought of training girls for a career. Nevertheless, the curriculum was comprehensive in character. While covering the intellectual, the aesthetic, and the moral, it did not exclude the practical. A three-year high school course, which offered subjects differing not greatly from those of a classical secondary school of today, was outlined. The subjects for the first year were listed in the *Annual Catalogue* in the following manner: "Elocution, Algebra one-third through, Church History half through, Religion, Physical Geography, Ancient History half through, Hygiene, Rhetoric, Drawing." During the second and third years these subjects were continued, and logic, natural philosophy, bookkeeping, geometry, and botany were added.

In the science classes, the students used Dr. Joseph Martindale's *First Lessons in Natural Philosophy*, published in 1879. Written in the question and answer form, it deals with such topics as light, heat, air, water, sound, and motion. That the teacher or student should conduct experiments or demonstrations is never suggested. The text used to teach bookkeeping was written by J. C. Smith, a professor in the Iron City Commercial College at Pittsburgh.[18] It was intended "for use of schools, Academies, Colleges, and private learners." The author claimed that his work was based upon a "new and original plan altogether more simple, comprehensive and practical than any of the methods now in common use." A. S. Barnes' *General History*, published in 1883, was used as a supplementary text by the history classes. In his preface the author indicates that he was moving along with the historians who were interested in the social phases of the subject, for he asserts that "the political history which occupies most, if not all, of the ordinary school-texts, is condensed [in his text] to the salient and essential facts, in order to leave room for some accounts of the literature, religion, architecture, character, and habits of the different nations." As for the style of the book, he declares that "though intentionally written in a semi-romantic style," many of the situations and events described "are accurate pictures of what *might* have occurred." [19]

For the regular "classical" courses and for board and room, a fee of eighty dollars a term was charged. Since a secondary aim of the school was to teach womanly arts and accomplishments, all students took some courses in music, speech, or art. Lessons in these subjects cost from five to twenty dollars a term. Work materials, music books, and musical instruments loom large in the expenses of some pupils, as recorded in the academy's early account books, causing one to suspect that their academic loads must have been rather light. The variety of arts and crafts in which instruction was offered is reflected in the early catalogues of the academy. Students of music were offered lessons in playing the piano, the organ, the harp, the guitar, and the zither. Instruction in drawing and painting in water colors was available at eight dollars a term, painting in oils at twenty-four dollars, and on china for five dollars. The costs covered instruction only; students purchased their own materials. The school catalogues

A NEW SPIRIT AT ST. JOSEPH

of the 1880's list instruction in various handicrafts then in vogue. In addition to "ornamental needlework" and needle-point lace, pupils could learn to make wax fruit, muslin and wax flowers, and hair wreaths. Although the school catalogues indicate that accounts were to be paid in cash and in advance, the financial records of the late 1880's show that some accounts were paid in produce. One student's father offered two cows valued at twenty-five dollars each, some meat valued at eleven dollars, and a small amount of cash in paying a bill of some eighty-six dollars. Another account was settled by payments made partly in cash and partly in grain.[20]

The Benedictine sisters who served on the teaching staff of St. Benedict's Academy were as capable a group as could be found in many Atlantic seaboard academies of the day. The institution was proud of its faculty, and it did not hesitate to draw the attention of the public to the individual talents of its teachers when advertising or printing news in the local and in the St. Paul newspapers. The music teachers, Sister Willibalda Scherbauer and Sister Bede Linneman, had been trained in Bavaria and in Milwaukee. Several others, as Sister Gertrude Flynn and Mother Scholastica Kerst, had attended schools in England, Germany, and the eastern United States. Though the school catalogues indicate that the institution undertook to teach "every useful and ornamental branch suitable for young ladies," the sisters felt that education concerned the whole of man and that the heart and soul as well as the mind and hand must be developed. Character building was the *raison d'etre* of the school.

Except for instruction in religion and in etiquette, training in morals was not given in formal classroom procedure. Rather was it hoped that the student would absorb much from the tone and atmosphere of the school as set by the teachers, prefects, and older students. In those years — in fact, until the 1920's — academy life resembled conventual life in many ways. Formed as they were by the Holy Rule in a disciplined Christian family spirit, the sisters demonstrated in their own lives what was desirable for students who themselves came from Christian homes. There is no evidence that the sisters were acquainted with Newman's educational ideals, but they would certainly have understood his thinking about the character of teachers and about the atmosphere of a school better than many who can discuss "intellectual excellence" but see it in a vacuum never intended by Newman himself.

But all was not dependent on time and atmosphere. The sisters knew the adolescents with whom they were dealing. To assist new students and to refresh the memory of the older ones, a set of sixteen rules was printed and placed in the dormitory and recreation rooms. Proper regard for the natural right to property was embodied in the rules that "no student is allowed to go to the desks, stands, or shelves of other pupils," and that "No student is allowed to borrow or lend clothing." Respect for parents was stressed in a rule declaring that "Pupils will write to their parents once a week." The list concluded with the warning: "Pupils must cultivate, or create, if they do not possess them, amiable dispositions, polite deportment and gentle manners." [21] If a student failed to respond to the ideals of the institution, she was corrected in private and her monthly grade or mark in conduct was lowered.

The sisters frowned on vanity and extravagant display in the matter of dress. Wardrobe rules, which were strictly enforced, specified that school dresses could be of any color or style, but that black sateen aprons must be worn over them during school hours. On Sundays a plain black uniform with a "brooch for closing the collar, and earrings" was to be worn. For commencement in the late 1880's the graduate was allowed to wear a "white Swiss, French Lawn, or Nun's Veiling dress, neatly and plainly made, with high neck and long sleeves; no trimmings of silk, satin, or lace; black or white boots and white kid gloves," but all jewelry except a brooch and earrings was prohibited.[22]

An important aspect of the story of St. Benedict's that might easily be overlooked is reflected in the student's daily life, her reaction to institutional living, and the many adjustments she had to make to her new surroundings. It must be remembered that in this frontier academy conveniences were of a primitive type, wood stoves at times did nothing more than smoke, and water for use in the third-floor dormitories had to be carried up three flights of stairs bucket by bucket. Everyday life in this western academy, where luxuries were suppressed and where youthful spirits often broke into mischievous pranks, is vividly reconstructed in a series of letters based on the memoirs of a student of the 1880's.[23] An extract from one of these letters, supposedly written by a newly-arrived student on September 13, 1882, follows:

Two weeks ago today you and I were busy packing my little home-made trunk. . . . Everytime I open my trunk I have a siege of homesickness.

Last Sunday I wore my new black dress . . . and felt as well dressed as the best. Of course the bigger girls dresses are longer than mine and sweep along the stairs and floor in grand style. Maybe Mother will lengthen my dresses at Christmas and at the same time put in a bustle. All the big girls have bustles in their Sunday dresses. I should say *had* them, for last Monday Sister Bonaventura confiscated all of them. The loss of style was bad enough, but what is worse, the skirts sag in the back. But for next Sunday the girls have planned to take their black sateen aprons . . . and roll them up to replace the confiscated bustles. Won't the Sister prefect open her eyes thinking that bustles like cats have nine lives? . . .

Ann, I will not know what to do with my big room when I return home. Here fifteen of us sleep in a large room which is called a dormitory. Each girl has for her use a narrow cot, a small washstand, and the only floor space allotted to each is that between one's bed and that of her neighbor. . . . This space which we call our 'cell' is inspected every day by the prefect for neatness as well as for censorship of vanity. Stella Lacomb's talc powder which she kept hid in her Sunday shoes was found and confiscated yesterday. A new girl who did not know about inspection lost a bottle of perfume a few days after her arrival. Lena Kerst nearly met a similar loss in the matter of highly scented soap, but Sister's practical sense would not allow the soap to be destroyed so Lena kept it on condition that her next supply of soap would be plain castile.

In another letter, which is dated the "1st Sunday in Dec., 1882," a student told her mother about some of the inconveniences that existed at St. Benedict's Academy in the days before modern improvements in lighting and heating reached the small towns of central Minnesota. She wrote:

Julia O'Rourke of Montana was in tears the other day. She has charge of the lamps in the study hall and chapel. Think of keeping all those lamp chimneys clean. Someone opened a door or window causing a draft through the study hall and in less time than it takes to tell, the flame in each lamp was lapping at the globe and had smoked up to such an extent that Julia had to start cleaning them all over again. Another charge I would dislike to have here is to keep the fires going — say nothing of starting them in the morning. There is a large band stove in the study hall and chapel, one in each of two dormitories and one in each of the three class rooms and infirmary.

Visits at home or with guests, which tended to distract the students from their studies, were discouraged. When they received gentlemen callers at the academy, the students were carefully chaperoned in the parlor during the visit, unless the caller was a brother or a first cousin. At times the sister directress would smilingly say that it seemed as if nothing but cousins were enrolled in St. John's University at nearby Collegeville. Despite close supervision, the young people managed to carry their messages to one another. One alumna delighted to relate how her future husband slipped an engagement ring into her hand — if not onto her finger — all unknown to the sister directress, who was present during the interview.

The crowning point of the student's career at St. Benedict's was reached at the close of three years, when the young lady was "finished" and parents and friends went to St. Joseph to see her carry off her honors. Commencement day at St. Benedict's has ever been something of an event. Guests traveled by wagon, carriage, and railroad from many parts of the West. The assembly hall was decorated with ferns and flowers, and a bunting-draped stage was made more impressive by the illustrious personages seated on it. There were white dresses, flowers, and wreaths in profusion; lengthy orations by the candidates; distribution of gold medals for "proficiency" in studies and for "lady-like conduct." The prizes, often medals, were distributed with all possible pomp. The bishop announced the title of the medal and the name of the winner. The recipient, arising from the front row of white-gowned girls, went up to and across the stage to receive the honor in all finery, with sweet girlishness, and yet with the dignified step the sisters had taught her to use. Abbot Alexius of St. John's and Bishop Seidenbusch of St. Cloud were present whenever possible. They were sometimes accompanied by as many as twenty clergymen. Occasionally, as in 1884, a prominent layman gave the commencement address. In that year the Honorable John W. Arctander of Willmar, District Attorney and author, delivered the oration. Of an old Swedish family, he was related to the Nobel family, the petroleum kings of Russia and Sweden, and founders of the Nobel Prize Foundation. After finishing his university career, Mr. Arctander associated himself with Björnstyerne Bjornson in journalistic work but soon, becoming too radical for his country, was forced like Bjornson to travel. When Arctander came to the Scandinavian state of Minnesota, he opened a law practice and entered politics. His local reputation drew an unusually large crowd.[24] On an earlier occasion the guest speaker was Herman Zschokke, chaplain to the Austrian imperial court and ex-rector of the University of Vienna. His visit to Minnesota is described in a book entitled, *Nach Nordamerika und Canada*, which he wrote after he returned to Austria.

The early commencement exercises were of interminable length, and they often tried the patience of all except perhaps the proud parents. In an old chronicle under the date of June 22, 1881, is to be found the following note: "Commencement at the Academy in St. Joseph last night. The program was so lengthy that Bishop Rupert Seidenbusch, who was present, expressed his displeasure."[25] Although the exercises of the years 1882 and 1883 were doubtless abridged as a result of this criticism, the brittle and faded old programs indicate that the closing exercises still would be found too lengthy by modern audiences.

In the 1890's other finishing academies were to arise in northern Minnesota and in the Dakotas. Though St. Benedict's Academy lost its unique position, it continued to grow, and in time evolved into the College of St. Benedict and St. Benedict's High School.

10 PAROCHIAL AND INDIAN SCHOOLS

The rapid spread of the various types of work undertaken by the Benedictine sisters of Minnesota during the nine-year period of Mother Scholastica Kerst's administration, 1880–1889, is astonishing. In this short time the community accepted and staffed seventeen new parochial schools in Minnesota and Dakota and eight rural district schools situated within a radius of six miles from the convent. In addition to these, three hospitals, two Indian missions, and an orphanage were established in territory stretching from Minnesota to the Pacific coast.

One of these seventeen schools was in Stillwater, Minnesota — an old settlement as settlements go in Minnesota. As early as 1846 the people here had been attended by Reverend Florimond Bonduel of Wisconsin. On that visit he baptized six children and offered Holy Mass in the home of a Mr. Bruce. On this first visit he had entered the settlement riding on a Red River ox cart. At sight of him the inhabitants of the place laughed aloud, but he also laughed. Amicable relations were immediately established. Taking a bell in his hand, he went about the town inviting all to come to service within the hour. Though there were few Catholics in the town, fifty persons crowded into the small Bruce house. Twenty-two years later, because of the influx of immigrants, there were enough Germans there to form a small national parish of their own under the title of St. Mary. Though the old English-speaking parish had a parochial school conducted by the Sisters of St. Joseph from St. Paul the new German parish had to be content for some years with lay teachers. However when Father Willebrord Mahowald, O.S.B., was made pastor, he applied for religious teachers, and in 1882 St. Benedict's Convent sent to his aid Sister Irmina Kritzer, Sister Luitgard Billig, and Sister Winnibald Sauber. Though the Faribault-Stillwater School Plan, inaugurated in 1891, was to rock state and nation with its religious and national implications, the little Benedictine school in Stillwater was too small to play any part in it.

In October of the same year, 1882, Mother Scholastica sent Sister Benedict Kump, Sister Seraphica Kennedy, and Sister Genevieve Byrne to the school of St. Boniface Parish at Melrose. This place had been visited by priests as early as 1868 when a log church was built. For some years thereafter the parish was cared for by the pastor of New Munich, but in the 1880's Father Meinrad Stuckenkamper, O.S.B., built a school there and asked for Benedictine teachers. Two other missions were opened in 1882, Millerville and Morris. The Seven Dolors parish school at Millerville and the school at Melrose are still thriving missions.

Brainerd, a town on the Northern Pacific Railroad, applied for teachers in the parochial school in 1885 and the sisters staffed this school for two years. In 1885 a mission was also opened at White Lake, South Dakota. It was short-lived because of lack of proper support. In 1887 the community consented to supply two sisters for the district school at Buckman and sent Sister Clara Billig to teach the thirty pupils in the rough plank schoolhouse seventeen by twenty-one feet. Sister Appolonia Jensen was her assistant and sacristan.

PAROCHIAL AND INDIAN SCHOOLS

In the fall of 1888 Abbot Alexius accepted the care of the Catholic Indians at the Red Lake Reservation and asked assistance of the Benedictine sisters for the school. Sister Amalia Eich and Sister Evangelista McNulty were sent. They and their successors were to do valiant work in converting pagans and in strengthening the faith of those whose forefathers had been baptized by the 18th century French missionaries.

With the increase of schools came a multiplication of troubles to try Mother Scholastica's patience and to test her ability. The last two years of her administration were greatly disturbed by school problems. The people of the 1880's were the children of the pioneers of the 50's who had showed opposition to the coming of the Benedictine monks and sisters to St. Cloud and St. Joseph. It will be recalled that in some villages of central Minnesota where the population was predominantly German and Catholic some of the early settlers of the 1850's had tried to transfer the German idea of state schools to America. Instead of parochial schools they established district schools near the church and hired Catholic laymen as teachers. They had preferred this plan for it gave them, rather than the pastors, control of the schools, and it avoided the necessity of supporting two school systems. But now in the 1880's, Bishop Seidenbusch, Abbot Alexius, and their priests were convinced that the children were not receiving the proper religious instruction. Backed by the promulgations of the Third Plenary Council of Baltimore which declared in 1884 the obligation of building parochial schools, these two churchmen started a campaign for Catholic schools. The priests urged their people to establish parish schools or at least to hire sisters for their public schools, these sisters to hold county teachers' certificates and to be under the direction of the county superintendent of schools. As a further inducement the people were told that they could hire two religious teachers for the salary paid to one layman. But even the economic appeal sometimes failed to win favor. A few school boards simply refused to hire sisters. The ensuing struggle was invariably bitter and protracted. The situation in the small Stearns County village of Albany may be considered typical.

The district school of this predominantly Catholic village was controlled by men who opposed religious authority in the matter of schools. For some time previous the lay teachers had neglected their work. The pastor, Father Gregory Steil, O.S.B., tried to offset the neglect of the religion classes at least by giving instruction in the church after school hours. When it was finally evident that order could be restored to the school only by sisters, it was equally evident that there would be some argument with the school board. Two of the three members of the board were opposed to Father Gregory's proposition; they claimed that they were afraid to hire sisters, and they called a meeting of the school district at which the people could elect a new member for the school board. In an article written for the *St. Cloud Times* of August 13, 1884, the pastor described his actions preceding the school meeting as follows:

On the Sunday preceding the district meeting I told the parishioners of the obligations of giving their children a Catholic education. I showed them how their teachers in the past had not bothered giving religious instructions after regular school hours. I also stated that the number of children in the parish, being over 150, was too great for one teacher and advised the engaging of the Sisters as a safe remedy showing also that financially there would be no loss, since two Sisters agreed to teach for the same pay as the one [lay] teacher had formerly received.[1]

After urging the parishioners to elect a school board that would accept his plan, the pastor threatened that if his people did not comply they would be left without his services and without Sunday Mass.

The election was held, but out of the hundred family heads in the district only forty-six went to the polls that day. All but four voted against the pastor's candidate. That meant that the school board was back to where it was before — two to one against hiring the sisters. On the following Sunday, Father Gregory announced that he was leaving and that no priest would be sent to replace him.

From July to November, 1884, the quarrel was featured in the St. Cloud, St. Paul, and Minneapolis newspapers. Father Gregory explained his position. One member of the school board published in *Der Nordstern* a denial of Father Gregory's statements and claimed that the people were opposed to the sisters only because the parish would have to build a residence for them. He concluded by denouncing Abbot Alexius and Bishop Seidenbusch for supporting Father Gregory and declared that he for one "would not go to Canossa."[2] Bishop Seidenbusch then sent a letter to *Der Wanderer* in which he attempted to shame the people of Albany into obedience. At last, in late November representatives of the more respectable element of the village took it upon themselves to go to St. John's Abbey to petition for a pastor. A sort of compromise was effected. A pastor was sent to them on condition that they would accept sisters. Albany would once again have a pastor; it would also have sisters — but in District School No. 3 at Two Rivers, about a mile from the village, not in the school district that had provoked the conflict. Two years later, in 1886, a parochial school was opened in the sacristy of the church under the care of Sister Aurelia Bissen; and the sisters withdrew from District School No. 3.

Similar opposition showed itself in Melrose, St. Augusta, St. Wendel, Lake Henry, and St. Martin. Even in the districts which acceded to the pastors' wishes and hired sisters for their schools, the opposing minority made life miserable for the sisters. At St. Wendel, District School No. 34, where the people had accepted the proposition of employing two sisters for the same salary as one lay teacher the opposition party created trouble. They charged that one sister was not a certified teacher. Technically the school board had contracted for one teacher — the one with the certificate. It was implicitly understood, of course, that she would have an assistant. But strictly speaking, the assistant was not hired by the board as a teacher and the requirement of a certificate could not hold. The St. Cloud newspapers aired the affair and made it appear that sisters were not qualified teachers.

Such turbulent circumstances nullified much of the sisters' effort and made classroom discipline difficult. Nor could the attitude of parents fail to leave its mark on the children. If pastors, supported by their bishop and their abbot, insisted on having sisters in such parishes, it was the sisters themselves who had to carry the daily burden. Mother Scholastica had to select from her 80 teachers the ones best fitted to meet such school conditions. But as the years passed, the attitude of the people changed and more opened parochial schools, while others kept the district school system with sisters as teachers.

In Duluth, where the sisters were called to open a school at the Sacred Heart parish in 1881 and a hospital in 1887, opposition was of a different sort. It came not from those within the Church, but from the anti-Catholic American Protective Association, and it was aimed at the Catholic Church in general. At times feeling was so high that the sisters dared not venture on the streets. Men frequently pushed them off the sidewalk and made rough remarks about them; one man even boasted that he never walked on the same side of the street with the sisters. At the sight of them he would cross to the other side. With the opening of the hospital this prejudice slowly died out. Many of these people, brought into contact with the sisters in a time of sorrow or trouble, soon recognized their charity and their good lives. This is illustrated by an anecdote related by one of these sisters. One morning three men entered the hospital and told the sister in charge that they wished to see all the sisters. "We understand," they said, "that the nurses and the sisters are here under compulsion and are treated as prisoners. Now if we can see them and talk to them and find any who are anxious to go, we will give them the means." The sister in charge saw that they were honest in their purpose and after explaining that it was washday and all were very busy and could not be called away from work, she told them they were free to go to the laundry, the kitchen, and sick wards and talk to any or all of the sisters there. They looked surprised at this but made the tour of the hospital. They came back astounded at the joy and contentment they found among the sisters and apologized for their intrusion. The next day the hospital received a large gift from an unnamed donor — no doubt from these men.[3]

Among the numerous schools placed under the care of the Benedictine sisters at this time none had a more romantic and weird history than that of the mission at Rush Lake, Minnesota. This parish school to which the sisters were sent in 1886 had been founded twenty years previous by a group of schismatics from Ohio. Father Joseph Albrecht, their leader and spirit, had been mayor of a town in Germany. Feeling a call to a higher life, he and his wife had agreed to separate and enter some religious house. His choice was the Society of the Precious Blood. Eventually he came to the United States where he completed his studies for the priesthood in a seminary at Thompson, Ohio. There he was ordained by Bishop Amadeus Rappe of Cleveland in 1849. Ten years later he was the superior of the parish and monastery at Himelsgarten in Mercer County, Ohio.[4] He was a well-built man, tall and erect, with a bright countenance. High-spirited and bold, he had a determination which could bear no resistance. This determination of will together with a fanatic hatred of anything savoring of vanity, worldliness, or self-indulgence brought him into conflict with church authorities. It must be said in his favor that while denouncing vanities in others he was likewise hard on himself. He always spurned a horse and carriage and made his trips on foot or on horseback when necessity required it. To the poor he always showed mercy and kindness. Two subjects formed the matter of most of his sermons, dancing and feminine vanity in dress. He urged the women of his parish in Ohio to wear plain dresses and bonnets without ribbons or flowers. He specifically forbade the use of crinoline or hoop skirts at church services. One afternoon when, despite his strong admonition of the morning, some women returned to services in all their finery, he calmly walked to the pulpit, took the gospel book, and read an appropriate chapter. Then he took a long hickory rod, strode down to the body of the church, and drove the bedecked women out of the church. For this act he was reprimanded by his superiors. Refusing to accept the reprimand, he was suspended by Archbishop J. B. Purcell. With many of his sympathizers, among whom were included religious brothers and sisters of the Society of the Precious Blood as well as laymen, he now planned to withdraw from Himelsgarten and settle in some western spot where the group could live a simple and unworldly life.[5]

Scouts were sent out to locate land, and finally in 1866 some seven hundred acres of land were procured at Rush Lake in the name of this group. Here the religious worked one large farm but each family was allotted its own land. Father Joseph ruled them with a strict hand. The farmers and their families went to the church every morning at five o'clock for meditation and Holy Mass and again in the evening for spiritual reading and night prayers. At services each woman wore a black kerchief over her head and a uniform black apron over her dress. The sisters were kept in strict enclosure, Father Joseph himself taking care of all the outside business for them. They were refused the administration of any other priest even on their death beds. Parents whose daughters joined the sisterhood were forbidden communication with them. Tradition has it that in the middle of one of the fields was a large wooden cross before which he might send a sister to do penance, sometimes for the whole night.

Though still under suspension when he came to Minnesota, Father Joseph offered Mass each day and administered such sacraments as were necessary. This did not include penance; his people did not need it. Bishop Grace of St. Paul tried to get him to be reconciled with the Church; both Father Weninger and Father Pierz tried in vain to recall him to obedience. After four appeals to him to refrain from saying Mass, Bishop Grace excommunicated Father Joseph on November 23, 1871, and published the following notice in *Der Wanderer*:

As I, Thomas Grace, have for the first, second, and the third and fourth time commanded in the name of the Father, Son, and Holy Ghost the priest, Joseph Albrecht, to refrain from offering Holy Mass and he has remained obstinate and has failed to obey I now declare him excommunicated until he reforms. Given in St. Paul on November 23, 1871.

When even this failed to silence Father Joseph, Father Weninger opened a mission in a small church near by. One by one the schismatics made their submission to him and went to confession. Some fifteen families thus defied Father Joseph. But the remainder of the settlement, including the brothers, the sisters, and their leader, refused reconciliation.

When this eccentric man died in April, 1884, he was venerated as a saint by his loyal followers. In a ceremony from which all outsiders were excluded, his remains, in a metal casket, were placed beneath the altar of his church. His will disclosed that he had left all of his property, which was in reality community property, to the brothers and sisters of the Society of the Precious Blood and to the lay members to be held in common by them. Three members of the organization were to act as trustees. But without a leader they soon broke into factions over various matters. Bishop Seidenbusch of St. Cloud now offered them a priest and an opportunity to be reconciled, but the faction that held the property opposed this suggestion knowing that the property belonging to the parish would pass to another jurisdiction. The other group wanted to accept the bishop's offer but was defeated. These members soon joined near-by parishes. The stubborn schismatics, brothers, sisters, and laymen, then sold what private property they owned, mortgaged the real estate, and moved to Jordan, Oregon. Not satisfied with carrying off the money they had been able to get from the property, they determined to take with them the most valuable possession of the place, the body of Father Albrecht. Secretly and at night they dug through the wall of the church basement, removed the corpse, and concealed it in a box of vegetables which they smuggled into the immigrant train bound for Jordan. There they made another attempt to establish themselves as an independent schismatic church, but the magnetic influence of their founder was not there; and in time the community dissolved. After becoming reconciled to the Church, many of the sisters remained together in their religious institute and were reestablished by the archbishop of that diocese as a new congregation.[6]

In time the Rush Lake parish was placed in the hands of the Benedictine priests. The mortgaged church building and land were purchased by St. John's Abbey. It was in 1886, only two years after Father Joseph's death, that the Benedictine sisters were called in to take charge of the school. The sisters found it necessary not only to teach the children the fundamentals of their religion but, what was more difficult, to clear up many misconceptions prevalent among the adults. The parishioners had no understanding of the nature of sin for Father Joseph Albrecht had never instructed them in that matter. The adults were eager to be instructed, and when the sisters held religion classes for the children there were at times as many as twenty adults present. The young girls, of course, were delighted when Sisters Catherine Siefner and Ehrentrude Wessel told them that they need not wear shawls or kerchiefs over their heads but could dress as did the people of other parishes. Even so, the sisters never felt at home or at ease in this place and were at all times conscious of a strange atmosphere. No sister would let herself be left alone in the house or even in the fields.[7] Their uneasiness plus unusually poor living conditions caused Mother Scholastica to recall the sisters from that mission in 1889.

Life in these parochial schools was always hard. The poverty of the parishes and consequent poor buildings, the poor equipment, and the lack of appreciation for educational methods, all contributed to this situation. Only great zeal for souls could have sustained the sisters in most of the work. The pastor and parishioners must not be blamed for all the hardship which the teachers endured, for the country was new and had few of the conveniences found in cities of the older states. In the 80's most schools, both public and private, had little equipment outside of desks, a piece of blackboard, and a teacher. During the summer months the classroom accommodated the number of pupils registered, but during the winter months, after the harvest was in and the older boys joined the classes, there might be as many as 80 in one small classroom.

The school at Wahpeton, North Dakota, was no different from

BISHOP MARTIN MARTY, FIRST BISHOP OF THE VICARIATE OF DAKOTA.

ABBOT ALEXIUS EDLEBROCK, ST. JOHN'S SECOND ABBOT.

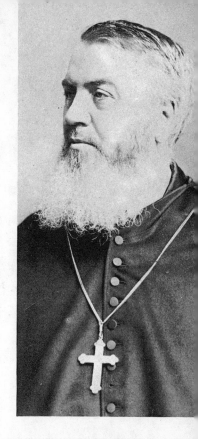

BISHOP OTTO ZARDETTI, FIRST BISHOP OF THE DIOCESE OF ST. CLOUD.

THE MOST REVEREND JOHN AND, ST. PAUL'S ARCHBISHOP.

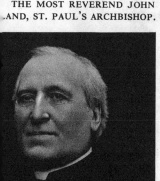

MOTHER SCHOLASTICA KERST.
SUPERIOR, 1880-1889.
MOTHER CECILIA KAPSNER.
SUPERIOR, 1901-1919.

TEACHERS STAFFING ST. MARY'S AND
HOLY ANGELS' PAROCHIAL SCHOOLS,
1889.

SISTER ANATOLIA LANGFORD,
SISTER IGNATIA HUNTINGTON —
SOME MEMBERS OF ST.
GERTRUDE'S CONVENT AT SHAKOPEE.

FIRST SUPERIOR OF ST. ALEXIUS HOSPITAL,
SISTER ALEXIA KERST.

SISTER BONIFACE TUMMINS, SECOND
SUPERIOR OF ST. ALEXIUS HOSPITAL.

EARLY BENEDICTINE SISTERS IN
GRANDE RONDE, OREGON.

CONVENT AND ACADEMY: FIRST BUILDING 1882, AND FIRST ADDITION OF 1884.

CONVENT AND ACADEMY: 1892 ADDITION.

A GRADUATE OF THE CLASS OF 1887.

A GRADUATE OF 1895.

A DELSARTE TABLEAUX PROGRAM BY
ACADEMY STUDENTS.

ACADEMICIANS OF
1887.

ORIGINAL ST. ALEXIUS HOSPITAL,
BISMARCK, DECORATED FOR A
CIVIC CELEBRATION.

FIRST ST. MARY'S HOSPITAL AND
ST. CLEMENT'S CHURCH, DULUTH.

ST. ALEXIUS HOSPITAL FLOAT IN A PARADE.

CHAPEL AT ST. BENEDICT'S, 1890.

REAR VIEW OF ST. BEN-
EDICT'S, 1910.

INDIAN INDUSTRIAL SCHOOL
AT ST. JOSEPH.

TEACHERS, PASTOR, AND PUPILS AT MOORHEAD, 1888.

FATHER HENRY BORGERDING, O.S.B.,
ST. BENEDICT'S FIRST CHAPLAIN.

FATHER HENRY AFTER THIRTY
YEARS OF SERVICE TO THE
CONVENT.

many others in the 80's. The town was new, and only ten years earlier its population was made up mainly of frontiersmen, trappers, soldiers, Indians, and adventurers. Sister Anatolia Langford, the superior of the first group of teachers, in her memoirs tells of the first days in Wahpeton.

When Sister Ursula Hoffman, Sister Baptista Lorsung, and I arrived, in 1886, we found no house had been provided for us. The pastor went out to look for one and got us two rooms, bedroom and kitchen, the best he could find, in the home of a woman who was not a practicing Catholic and who had some very rowdy friends. One night the landlady told us she was having some friends in for a dance and fun and we could come. We retreated to our rooms and locked the doors. As the jovial shouts of the dancers pierced the thin walls of our rooms, we prayed and prepared for the worst.[8]

The next day a relative of the landlady came and apologized for the insult given to the sisters. From September to November the sisters taught in the church — Sister Ursula in the front and Sister Anatolia in the rear near the holy water font and under the choir loft. Sister Ursula had a blackboard about a yard square; Sister Anatolia had none. The primary chart hung near the holy water font. In November of the following year, 1887, the parish rented a building which had been used as a store and a home. Sister Priscilla Schmittbauer, who taught there that year, has left us this picture:

The store was divided into two classrooms by means of a thin board partition. There was only one outside door and pupils from the back room had to pass through the front room on leaving the building. During the winter months when the boys and country children came to school there was not enough room and the woodshed was fitted up to care for the overflow. Two years later the pastor started to build a school building of two rooms. I told him we already had three crowded classrooms and he had better build larger. But he answered, "Pack them together." When school opened we "packed them in." I had 80 registered in my room. The pastor partitioned my room into two class rooms and sent to St. Benedict's for another teacher.[9]

But all was not hard work. The parishioners showed their gratitude to the sisters in many ways, and there were pleasant breaks in the routine. One teacher told how one day the pastor opened the door to the classroom in the front of the old store building and called out in German something she did not understand; but suddenly all the pupils were on their feet and racing outdoors, and those from the middle room moved by the noise in the front, were also on the run. Going outside to seek the cause of the trouble, she learned that the pastor had called the pupils out to see some Indians who had just arrived. They were going to do a war dance down on the island. Away the children ran. The sisters followed their charges at a more sedate pace and witnessed the performance.

Because of lack of room a great number of children had to be refused admittance. This aided the sisters in establishing standards to be met by the applicants. One of these was that no child who cursed or used vulgar language would be admitted. It is related that one eager lad came to school only to find that the lists were closed and no more pupils could be admitted. Looking eagerly at Sister he said, "Oh gee, I have kept from swearing for a whole month so that I could get in here and now —!" Sister relented and found a temporary place for him on a stool in the corner.[10]

Another mission, one opened by Mother Aloysia in February, 1880, at Long Prairie, was short-lived. When three sisters reached this former Indian Reservation Agency, they found a new school building and a home. But Mother Scholastica withdrew the sisters at the close of the next school year, and not until 1895 did the sisters reopen this school.

At Bismarck another problem faced the sisters. The combined parish and boarding school established in 1878 was so overcrowded that there was great danger to health and safety. But the parish did not seem to sense this and did nothing to remedy living conditions in the school or in the convent. In an attempt to lessen the work of the sisters and to give them more room, Mother Scholastica forbade them to accept boarding pupils for the school year 1883–1884. This brought about a storm of protest from the pastor but it did result in action. Though for that year the day school was continued in the same building as before, the pastor rented an old public school building for the school year 1884–1885. This gave room for the overflow from the grades and made it possible to open some commercial classes on the secondary school level.

That the sisters were interested in souls and were teaching more than bookkeeping and science is evidenced by an article which appeared in the June 24, 1885, issue of the Bismarck *Saturday Evening Journal*. The reporter stated that "the pupil here, first and above all, is taught that God's work is the most important and should be the foundation upon which to build his education." Despite this successful work with the young people of the parish, no attempt was made to build a new parochial school and convent. At the close of the school year just referred to, Mother Scholastica withdrew the sisters from the parochial school and opened a private school in the hospital which she had just established in Bismarck. Though the school had no connection with the parish, it retained the name of St. Mary's Academy.

This school and hospital combination could not last long. It satisfied neither the teachers, nor the hospital staff, nor the pastor. The hospital was growing and needed all the available space; besides, the combination was anything but ideal for either hospital patients or pupils. The pastor was dissatisfied because too few of his parishioners could have the benefit of a Catholic education. He, therefore, decided that the parochial school must be reopened. To this end he negotiated with St. Benedict's for teachers for the January term, 1891. His petition had to be rejected; there were no teachers available at that time of the school year. Another reason for the refusal, though not mentioned to the pastor, was that the sisters suspected that he planned to use the old buildings again without making any renovations. He was promised teachers for the fall term on the condition that the buildings be made habitable. In the end nothing was done and the sisters returned to the outskirts of the town to the old weather-beaten, leaky, dirty buildings which had been unused since 1885.

Teaching in the isolated rural district schools nearer home was work of an entirely different kind. It was lonely and burdensome, especially in winter when it meant daily journeys in an open cutter over snowbound roads. Two sisters would hitch up the horse in the morning, pack some hay in the back, put their lunch boxes between them so as not to have the food frozen, and then drive to School No. 1 on the Cold Spring road where one sister would alight. The other continued on to the District School No. 120 near the abbey — on the west side of Watab Lake. The same routine was carried out by the teachers for School No. 2 west of the Sauk River bridge on the St. Cloud road and School No. 47 southwest of St. Cloud. Arriving at the school, the sister would "put up her horse" and then go into the cold school room, light the fire, and try to thaw out. One of these rural public school teachers has told how watchful Mother

Scholastica was to see that these sisters were warmly dressed and that it was she who made sure that they had men's buffalo coats. Mother often went to the kitchen and examined the food packed for their lunch to assure herself that it was nourishing and palatable.

There was, of course, much more for her to attend to at the mother-house. Under her care were three separate schools — one, the academy; the second, an industrial school for Indian girls; the third, a small orphanage for boys.

It may surprise the reader to learn of an Indian school in the village of St. Joseph as late as 1886. But many such schools had been encouraged and established by the United States Government as a result of President Grant's peace policy of handing over the education of Indians on reservations to religious groups. Out of this grew the "contract system" whereby the government in 1876 began the annual appropriation for industrial schools on the reservation and contracted with religious groups to care for the education and keep of Indian children in such schools. Within a few years the Indian Bureau in Washington was convinced that better work could be accomplished in educating the Indian if the young people were removed from the reservation and the sordid surroundings of their homes. The government then contracted with private institutions in various states for "clothing, care, and teaching of ordinary English subjects, cooking, sewing, and all branches of domestic work" at $167 per capita. In the fall of 1883 Mother Scholastica, through Abbot Alexius, started negotiations with the United States Government to educate twenty-five to fifty Chippewa Indian girls. The government granted the right, and on March 19, 1884 the contract was signed to take thirty girls from the reservation and to educate them at St. Joseph.[11] By 1886 the number of girls in this industrial school had increased to one hundred, but only twenty-five were paid for by the government.

The pupils were gathered by the sisters, who made a tour of the various bands at White Earth, Cloquet, and Fon du Lac, interviewing and persuading parents to let their children leave the reservation. Indian parents were reluctant to let their daughters leave home, and the girls themselves did not take kindly to being put away in a boarding school. As a result most of the pupils were of mixed white and Indian blood.

Many an amusing story was told by the sisters when they returned home after gathering their charges. One thing lightened the task of travel with these thirty or more girls; they were allowed to take no luggage and no extra clothing. On arrival at St. Joseph, they were given a thorough bath and a complete new set of clothes. Those in which they had traveled were burned. Though the half-breed girls came more or less willingly and were quite adaptable, the Indians found the process of formal education too restraining and often took to the wide open spaces. They could not sit occupied over books. They fidgeted and squirmed when they should be quiet and they rebelled against the use of soap and the fine comb. What Agnes Repplier wrote of the Indian girl of the previous century was true also of these: "They were subject to spells of passionate nostalgia and sickened for the life of the woods. Nothing could hold them back when the desire was upon them. They would slip away by day or night." [12] In fact, the teachers used to notice that these girls in some unknown way seemed to sense or feel the approach of Indian relatives from afar and would go out stealthily to meet them. When relatives came to visit the school, they did not believe in making a hurried call but came with tent, kettle, and papooses and set up housekeeping on the edge of the campus.

Among the names enrolled in the school register were such picturesque ones as Lizzie Spry, Rose Rabbit, Rose Fedahbawnohewe, and Rose, the daughter of Chief Hole-in-the-Day. In this register were also the names of daughters of well-known fur traders such as the Morrisons, Beaulieus, Fairbankses, Warrens, and the Bellangers whose forefathers' marriages with Indian girls had been blessed by the early missionaries. Some proudly traced their lineage from the courts of France; others just as proudly from the tents of Indian chiefs. Rose and Maggie Hole-in-the-Day were full-blood Chippewa, as were Rose Rabbit and Mary Ognacagijiogok. [13]

Since the government's aim in schools was to train the pupils to a higher standard of living and to make them industrious housewives, more stress was laid on manual arts than on purely academic pursuits. Gardening, cooking, sewing, needle work, and other household arts as well as reading and writing were taught these Indian maids ranging in age from seven to twenty-two years. The sisters' aim in teaching the Indian children went further than the government's. They wanted to instruct them in the truths of religion as well as in housewifely arts. A day like the Sunday in late June, 1890, on which seven Indian girls were baptized, was always a happy one for the sisters.

But there also came a day in early April, 1886, when Mother Scholastica returned to the convent grounds to find ashes and tangled ruins, all that remained of the old log church and the row of wooden buildings that had housed the Indian girls and the orphan boys. In the convent itself the normal quiet was more than somewhat disturbed: the shelterless Indian girls had been moved into the sisters' own dormitory and refectory. Everyone was grateful that the fire had been timed as it was — at noon — so that though the buildings burned like tinder and threw sparks across the street to Linneman's and Loso's stores, there were no lives lost.[14] The orphans were being housed in another building.

Obviously something had to be done, and done quickly. The convent and academy buildings were not so spacious that they could accommodate a hundred additional girls. There were also problems other than space. Mother Scholastica decided to erect a new building. By April 13 she was writing to Abbot Alexius:

> We do not just know what to do for room. Some of the Indian girls were going home, but are satisfied since we told them we would very soon make things comfortable. Then, if we keep the Indians in the same house with the Academy it will injure the Academy, because people always want to know whether we have the Indians there. Heretofore we could say no; but now we are in a bad fix.[15]

The new red brick building was completed for the fall term, and a contract was made with the United States government through the Catholic Indian Bureau for one hundred and fifty pupils. The inspector sent in 1890 gave such a splendid report of the work done in this school that the Indian Commissioner sent a new contract permitting the school to take any number of pupils and to draw them from any reservation. But six years later the government dropped this contract system of Indian education and the school was forced to close.

The twenty-three orphan boys who were also made homeless by the fire of '86 were temporarily housed in an old building on the premises. The work of caring for orphans had been started in an informal manner as early as 1875. The orphanage was incorporated under the laws of the State in 1884, and the orphan boys and girls were moved from St. Joseph to St. Cloud. In 1885 because of overcrowding, the boys were moved back to St. Joseph and placed in the vacated old log church and convent. The orphan girls were moved to Pierz. The care was a noble work but seemed to have brought only trouble. Remuneration for the care of these orphans was made in part by the parent, in part by the diocese, and in part by funds gathered by the sisters on begging tours. But parents and the diocese were slow in making payments, and the whole venture brought heartaches as the following incident related in the St. Cloud newspaper illustrates:

Yesterday Mrs. Augusta H. Stevenson of Livingston, Montana, by A. C. Robertson of this city, her attorney, applied to Judge Collins through a writ of *habeas corpus* for the custody of her three little daughters aged eight, ten, and fourteen years, then supposed to be in the convent of St. Joseph. Two years ago, Mrs. Stevenson alleges she placed her daughters with the Benedictine Sisters . . . under an agreement to pay $24.00 a month for their care and education until she would demand them; she paid $100.00 on this contract and then sickness and reverses set in and prevented further payments. . . . Mrs. Stevenson came here last fall and demanded their custody which was refused until she paid what was due for their care under the contract, some $400.00; she tried but was unable to raise the sum, and again went to St. Joseph and demanded her children; and again was refused and then began these proceedings. Sister Pius on whom the writ was served, appeared yesterday . . . Messers Morse and Searle appeared for the defense.[16]

At the time Mother Scholastica became superior of St. Benedict's Convent the work of the sisters was already known in Oregon. Late in 1880 Archbishop Francis Norbert Blanchet and Very Reverend J. Brouillet asked them to take charge of an Indian mission school on a reservation at Grande Ronde. To send sisters to staff an Indian school in Oregon in the early 1880's was comparable to sending missionaries to the Orient today. Oregon seemed to be at the end of the earth to Sister Stanislaus Sauer, Sister Evangelista McNulty, Sister Agatha Nachbar, Sister Maura Schmidt, and Miss Monica Will, who were chosen to make the journey.

Leaving St. Benedict's on March 17, 1881, in the company of Mother Scholastica, they were forced by heavy snowfall to take a cir-

124

cuitous route by way of Chicago, Omaha, Ogden, San Francisco, and then by steamer to Astoria. The story of the trip is told in the following letter written by Mother Scholastica to Abbot Alexius.

After a journey of 17 days we have reached, or nearly reached our destination. No doubt, my Lord, you have heard of our proceedings as far as Chicago, also of our delay there. On the 23rd ult. we left for Omaha on the North-Western R.R. and arrived there 24th. at 5 P.M. but not having our half-fare permits we were obliged to remain until the 25th, but were once more obliged the same evening to return on account of a washout. On the next morning we started by a roundabout way not reaching the direct route until the 26th at 2 o'clock A.M. We passed over the desert-prairies of Nebraska and Montana where we saw the hundred, yes I dare say, thousands of cattle, horses and sheep which had died of starvation, not a sign of a human dwelling for many miles, with the exception of a miserable hovel now and then, apparently more fit for wolf's dens than for human habitation. I thought it a fearful country. Monday evening we were pleasantly surprised at Ogden when Reverend F. Becker of Salt Lake City walked up to us. . . .

On the 30th we reached San Francisco and remained there waiting till the steamer Columbia left on Friday about noon. We had a very pleasant voyage, but were all seasick with the exception of Sister Agatha. Sunday evening we were surprised on our landing for a few hours at Astoria when the Reverend Father from the place, Reverend Father Dillmann, and the superior and another Sister came to welcome us to Oregon and the Father accompanied us to Portland, where although 1 o'clock at night there were two hacks at the order of the Archbishop Seghers to take us to the hospital of the Sisters of Providence . . . His Grace is going with us to Grande Ronde as is also Reverend J. B. Brouillet.[17]

The sisters were anxious to see their new mission, to learn of its rich history, and to meet Archbishop Blanchet and Father Brouillet, the men who helped to plant the Church in that part of the country. The retired Archbishop Blanchet had come as a missionary to Oregon from Montreal in the 1830's and was early made bishop of the newly formed diocese. He had worked strenuously for the Church and the good of souls and had undergone many hardships and persecutions. With Father Brouillet he had stood the brunt of the anti-Catholic movement which reached a climax after the Indian massacre of a Protestant missionary, Dr. Marcus Whitman, and his family. The murder of these people was the result not so much of any religious antipathy as it was of an old practice of killing the medicine man who failed to stop an epidemic. Dr. Whitman was a physician and shared the danger. Father Brouillet discovered the deed and at great risk to himself warned Mr. H. H. Spaulding and other Protestant missionaries of their danger and enabled them to escape. These men returned the kindness by spreading abroad a rumor that the Catholic missionaries, Blanchet and Brouillet, had instigated the murders in order to exterminate all Protestant mission leaders. This story and the antipathy which it aroused handicapped the growth of the Catholic missions for years. But the Bishop weathered the storm. In 1874 with the aid of the Commissioner of Indian Affairs he had opened an Indian school at Grande Ronde and put it in charge of the Sisters of the Holy Names. Those sisters had withdrawn from this work in 1880 and Archbishop Blanchet then turned to the Benedictine sisters of Minnesota for help.[18]

It was a venture which seemed promising but which turned out to be short-lived. The Grande Ronde mission school at its peak had an average enrollment of thirty-five pupils ranging from five to twenty years of age. The teachers found the buildings large, commodious, and adequately equipped, but the ground on which they were located was so low that they were practically in a swamp. The mission had two heavy work horses, eleven cows, and plenty of farm implements; but, as the Commissioner of Indian Affairs stated in his official report, the land was in such a foul condition that it was a hindrance to farming. The sisters supervised the boys in performing such tasks as milking cows, but to get to the barns they had to don rubber boots. These unhealthful surroundings together with the fact that they had to teach male pupils twenty years of age caused the sisters much misgiving. When Abbot Alexius of St. John's visited the place in December of that year he remarked to the authorities that he would not have a dog there, much less his priests and sisters. Not only were the living conditions bad, but he found that even though the government paid $8.00 a month for clothing, food, and education of each child, there was not enough left over for the sisters' own living expenses. Under ordinary circumstances this sum would have sufficed to support the child while at school, but the Indian parents were intent on getting all they could out of the United States Government. According to the abbot's letter of December 9, 1881, there were no pupils for the first three months and consequently the sisters received no money.

For the children now in school they receive $8.00 a month for each child. Out of this $8.00 they board, instruct, clothe a child. After they have clothed a child, this child goes home, and generally returns after one or two weeks but without any clothes on. Well, the sisters must again give him clothes, boots, and shoes — and all this out of $8.00. The sisters must buy everything and at high price. It is therefore doubtful whether the sisters will be here after January 1882.[19]

On his visit the abbot broke the contract with the Catholic Indian Bureau, and he withdrew the sisters on January 15, 1882.[20] Thus the first attempt to plant the order in the far West failed. Mother Scholastica was sorely disappointed for she loved the West and had promised Archbishop Charles Seghers of Portland to accept the care of the Indian school at the Umatilla Agency. She had also promised Bishop A. Junger of Vancouver to staff a city parish school in Vancouver, Washington. But failure in this far western venture did not dishearten Mother Scholastica. Her parish schools were flourishing, and a new field of work, one not as yet undertaken by the American Benedictines, was being offered to her.

11 MEDICINE, A NEW FIELD OF WORK

As early as 1878 Abbot Alexius was busy prospecting for a site on which to establish a college for men in the vicinity of Mandan and Bismarck in Dakota Territory. On one of his visits to this new and booming country he became acquainted with some of the frontier speculators and real estate men who told him of the need for a hospital in that wild country and offered him inducements to establish one. The pastors at Mandan and Bismarck, convinced of the good that a Catholic sisters' hospital could accomplish in that country, added their voices to the cause.

For some reason the word "hospital" usually conjures up a picture of an institution in a city of some proportions, and at first thought one is surprised to find a hospital in frontier Bismarck. But Bismarck and the surrounding territory did have need of a hospital. It was a cowboy's country and therefore a place of few homes. It was also a town of soldiers and of prospectors who if married had left their families in the East. When sickness or accident struck any one in such a masculine settlement there was neither kith nor kin to nurse him back to health. When the sick were brought to town for medical aid, a lonely hotel room over a saloon with occasional visits from the doctor and the hotel keeper was all that money could buy in the way of care.

There was yet another class of men in this country who, though wealthy, had need of someone to care for them during times of illness. These were the millionaire "dude ranchers." As early as 1883 wealthy Easterners such as the Eatons and the Huiderkoopers of Pennsylvania had established ranches north and west of Bismarck. Their neighbors were men belonging to the nobility of France and England. There were the two sons of Lord North, Sir John Pender, the Duke of Sutherland, and Lord Nugent. Perhaps the most colorful of all of them were Teddy Roosevelt and the Marquis de Mores.[1] The marquis was a romantic man who planned great things for the West. Formerly a lieutenant in the army of France and now married to an American millionaire's daughter, he interested his father-in-law in establishing a business of raising and butchering cattle on the plains and shipping the dressed beef to the East. The project, of course, was premature and bound to fail, which it did. But long before the packing house was erected, the marquis had incurred the bad will of the Dakota cowboy, for as soon as de Mores and others started fencing in the ranches, the cowboys knew it meant the end of their cow business and the loss of their freedom to ride across country straight as the crow flies. The cowboy started to harass the millionaires out of the country; in one affray the marquis shot and killed Luffcey, one of the cattlemen.[2] Such were the men at the top of the social ladder in Dakota.

These millionaire ranchers as well as the cowboys needed proper care in the ever-recurring cases of typhoid or "plains fever" as it was called. Nature and geography treated all men alike, and at times no money could buy fresh drinking water. Springs and rivers were few, and at certain seasons many of these sources dried up into stagnant

128

pools. Nevertheless this water, barreled and brought to the ranch, was the only water to be had. Anyone other than a tenderfoot knew that it should be boiled before being used. But careless bachelor house-keepers often dispensed with this precaution, and typhoid was the result.[3]

The need for a hospital was apparent. Nursing was a type of work not yet undertaken by the Benedictine sisters in America but there was nothing in the Rule of St. Benedict forbidding such service. No group of Benedictines receives more explicit help from the Holy Rule itself than do the sister nurses. Chapter 36, "Of the Sick Brethren," gives supernatural motivation and encouragement. There St. Benedict states: "Before and above everything let care be had of the sick, serving them in very deed as Christ Himself, since He hath said: 'I was sick and ye visited Me.' And elsewhere: 'Whatever ye did to one of these My little ones, ye did to Me.'" The day may come when the Benedictine nurse will have an encouragement not available to the pioneers of Bismarck or to their successors: a history of the contribution of monasteries and convents to the care of the sick before 1885.

But perhaps for Abbot Alexius the more compelling consideration was the fact that it had been the practice of Benedictines throughout the ages to undertake whatever work the needs of the time or place dictated. He could see no reason why the care of the sick should not be undertaken by the sisters. He succeeded in interesting Mother Scholastica and her sisters in the proposition to the extent that she went to Bismarck and Mandan.

Mandan at this time showed better signs of growth than did Bismarck and was chosen as the site for the hospital. Plans were drawn up for a building three stories high to cost about $25,000. Money was collected in house to house calls and by parish socials. *The Bad Lands Cowboy* of Medora carried the notice of a church bazaar. "A church fair will be given for the hospital at Mandan on the 27, 28, 29, and 30th of October. If the new skating rink on Wright Avenue is finished in time it is the intention of Father Martin to hold the fair in the rink." [4] But that is the last heard of the proposed Mandan hospital, for the removal of the capital to Bismarck in 1833 destroyed Mandan's chance to outstrip Bismarck in size and importance.

Another determining factor in placing the hospital at Bismarck was the opportunity to acquire a hospital building already erected, or rather, a building which could easily be adapted to hospital use. This building, the Lamborn Hotel, located on the corner of Main and Sixth Streets, was built by two speculators of the type so common on the frontier — men who attempted big things on a gamble. Richard Mellon and Alexander McKenzie were the two most conspicuous characters in Dakota Territorial days. Mr. Mellon was from a family of bankers in Pittsburgh, a brother of Andrew Mellon who later became Secretary of the Treasury. Mr. McKenzie was the man on whom Rex Beach in *The Spoilers* based his character, Alec McNamara. McKenzie was the political boss of Dakota Territory and the brains of the deal that moved the capital from Yankton to Bismarck.[5] These two men and all Bismarck gambled in futures. They were busy buying lots and selling them. They foresaw that a large modern hotel would be needed by the legislators and politicians who would move to the town with the governor. They themselves had no intention of going into the hotel business for that was too slow a way of making money. They built to resell at a good price. As the building neared completion these exploiters met the abbot and used their high-pressure salesmanship to induce him to purchase the place. As an asset to the city a hospital was as valuable as a hotel, and they had made a good bargain when on April 14, 1885, the sale was made. The act is best described by the abbot in the following report written on the same day to his abbey:

Today after consulting with Father Bede and Father Martin, also with Reverend Mother, I bought from Messrs. McKenzie and Mellon the Lamborn Hotel and three lots of this city for $24,000 which is due two years after date but which amount may be paid off at any time during the two years. I bought the Lamborn Hotel for St. John's Abbey and I pledge myself and successors to turn the Lamborn Hotel over to the Sisters at once who will immediately open there-in a hospital. I reserve to myself the full control until St. John's has received full payment of capital and reasonable interest from the Benedictine Sisters. They will conduct the Hospital at their own expense and risk. All the money coming in from the patients or from gifts shall belong to the Sisters. If the venture prove a success it shall be handed over to them in due time. If it turn out to be a failure as a hospital, it shall be turned over again to St. John's.[6]

To staff this hospital Mother Scholastica placed Sister Gabriel McCoy in charge of general housework; Sister Thomas Ryan, in

MEDICINE, A NEW FIELD OF WORK

charge of the men's floor; Sister Juliana Venne, of the women's floor; Sister Opportuna Plemmel, of the kitchen; with Sister Alexia Kerst as superior. All was ready on May 3 when the abbot came to bless the building and to open the building to the public.[7] On May 6 the first patients were admitted.

Abbot Alexius aided the sisters in every way possible. He sent two brothers and some workmen from the abbey to make the necessary changes in the building and to help the sisters in moving equipment. He bought furniture and equipment to the amount of $2,000 and for two years he paid for all medicines and groceries and other supplies to the amount of $4,000. Added to the original cost of the property, this brought the sisters' indebtedness to $30,000. When at the end of two years the sisters had reduced this debt to $9,340, the abbot very generously cancelled the final indebtedness and gave the sisters a clear title to the property. Up to that year, 1887, the hospital's official title had been *The Lamborn Hospital* as that was one of the conditions on which the transfer of the Lamborn Hotel had been made to the abbot. Now when the property no longer belonged to the abbey, the condition was not binding and the sisters took this opportunity to give the hospital the name of St. Alexius, the saint under whose protection it had been placed when it opened its doors to the public.[8]

The records of the sixty-five patients received the first year — May, 1885, to May, 1886, fully illustrate the character of the territory which this hospital was to serve. The records show that these patients came from all parts of the earth. Some claimed Bombay and Russia as their place of birth. Others claimed Ireland, Sweden, England, Prussia, and Bavaria. The type of cases most frequently treated in the hospital is also a reflection of the frontier character of Bismarck. Accidents, fever, consumption, rheumatism, and delirium tremens outnumbered all other cases. Melancholia appears often in the records.

Shortly before the hospital opened for service, the sisters contracted with the county through Mr. McKenzie to care for the sick poor at the rate of $1 a day. They made another contract with the United States Marine Service to care for the river boatmen at the flat rate of 90 cents per day. These contracts were made at the suggestion of Bismarck's "boosters" and politicians who were eager to see any new business venture flourish and so enhance the name of their town. The first seven patients in the hospital were county poor cases, and the eighth patient was a boatman. The sisters soon learned that in the opinion of the boatmen the hospital was a convenient boarding-house when the Missouri froze over and left them jobless in Bismarck. All that was needed for entrance was a minor ailment. In December of that year the chaplain complained that "the two sailor patients will probably stay for the winter since the river is frozen over." [9]

Not only did the county and the marines patronize the hospital but the penitentiary sent its charges as well. Such features helped to strengthen the long-standing prejudices against hospitals as institutions for wayward and shiftless. One of the first patients from that institution was a notorious horsethief and jailbird, the well-known Osborn, captured at Jamestown with over twenty stolen horses. Wounded in the attempt to break jail he was brought to the hospital. He was heavily guarded; the sisters attended him with fear and always with the guard standing by. [10]

From the account just given it must not be inferred that only the underprivileged groups were served by the sisters. General G. Whistler and the American wife of Marquis de Mores were cared for, and tradition has it that Teddy Roosevelt as cowboy was nursed through a siege of fever. [11]

As the number of patients increased, the nursing staff was enlarged by the addition of Sisters Josephine McLean, Margaret Delmo, Mildred McGuire, and Crescentia Eich. But an increase in patients did not mean an increase in income, as the hospital cared for many a patient from whom nothing could be expected in return, and it cared for many patients who failed to pay for the care given them. At last the sisters resorted to begging. Two sister nurses were released at intervals to go on begging tours to the nearby Fort Lincoln Railroad construction camps as well as to Dakota towns. When these excursions took them to that area west of Bismarck where the railroad was in process of being built, the sisters had to resort to queer modes of travel. The construction crews used handcars when traveling from section to section or from their work to their camp. This was the only mode of travel available, and this the sisters took. The sight of a couple of sisters aboard a handcar propelled by sturdy railroad laborers was said to have won them many a friend. When a section point was reached, the sisters alighted and timidly went to the barnlike shed which served as a boarding house for the construction gang. There they begged for an offering. If the construction boss or the cook had his wife with him at the camp, the sisters would stay over night. If not, they then had to beg for room on another handcar to take them back to the hospital.

Begging was a hard task and at times dangerous. Sister Juliana Venne recounted that once when she and a companion were on a begging tour they were put off the train at the wrong station, Antelope, while traveling on the east side of the river. To their dismay they found not only that it was the wrong town but that it was a Lutheran settlement where the spirit was so hostile to all things Catholic that they had to leave immediately. They walked the ties to the next station. On another occasion when the sisters asked to be directed to a Catholic home in the town, they were maliciously sent to a house of prostitution. On reaching the house, they were met at the door by a woman who threw up her hands at the sight of them and told them to leave immediately, that they had been purposely misdirected. As they looked about, they could see that a group of people had gathered to watch the encounter. Covered with shame, the sisters left the town as soon as they could. Another story is told of Sister Thomas Ryan. One day in late summer she was released from nursing duty to solicit funds at Fort Lincoln across the river. She collected the meager sum of $22. This is not to be considered a reflection on the soldiers' generosity. The fact was that they had received their pay on Tuesday and it had vanished by Friday.[12]

During the first five years of its history the hospital was really nothing more than a nursing home. There was no equipment other than could be procured at the local market. The sisters had no special training in the care of the sick and the doctors had to direct their every step. Sometimes they were thrown into a piece of work without a bit of warning or preparation. This is illustrated by Sister Juliana's first experience in the operating room. When sent to assist at an operation her task was to hold a basin at the side of the surgical table. At the first sight of blood she fainted. The assistant surgeon put her on the floor, splashed water on her face, and ordered her back to finish her job. This she did and never again fainted at the sight of blood. But the doctors of that day did not consider untrained nurses as dangerous or undesirable. In fact, there were no trained nurses to speak of at the time St. Alexius Hospital opened its doors. Doctors ranked obedience and cheerfulness above formal training.

One physician complained, "What are we coming to! Lady nurses writing articles for medical journals! Training only makes lady nurses puffed up and quite useless as practical nurses." The same attitude is reflected in an item published by a medical journal in 1888. It reported that "lady nurses write queries to medical journals and express doubts as to the proper treatment of cases." The writer expressed the opinion that "trained nurses know just enough to make them dangerous when they attempt to practice in our absence." [13] Thus, as might be expected, the early St. Alexius nurses were without formal training. It was up to the doctors to train the nurses as they went about their work from day to day. To Sister Alexia Kerst, the superior, was assigned the dangerous and delicate work of administering the anesthetics.

Medical and surgical methods were simple and little concerned about bacteria. Ordinarily a doctor's outfit consisted of a knife or two, a pair of scissors, a few needles, and some drugs. These might or might not be thoroughly cleansed after use before being packed in a small carrying case or thrown loose in the doctor's coat pocket. With medicine as simple as this, it can easily be seen that a doctor would not object to taking on a staff of untrained nurses. The teaching of Lister on the absolute need of asepsis had hardly touched western United States. In far-off Dakota aseptic and antiseptic methods were not generally practiced. In fact, even Dr. Will Mayo did not become an advocate of the theory until 1887, two years after St. Alexius opened its doors.[14] So it is not surprising that the medical profession in the frontier town of Bismarck went blithely on, unconscious of the movement, or at least not practicing what the new theories advocated, until the coming of Dr. Quaine to its staff in 1899.

With Dr. E. P. Quaine the hospital soon followed the latest methods in antisepsis but never went to the extreme as did some hospitals of Europe and New York whose methods are described by an eyewitness in the following words:

The walls of the rooms were lined with large jars of many different kinds of antiseptic solutions, each a different color . . . The operating tables, designed for use in the extremely wet operations then in vogue, were covered with rubber and flanked all around with drain pans to catch the pailsful of plain boiled water, sometimes warm, sometimes cold, that was sloshed generously over everything in sight. The surgical staff all wore rubber boots. Much emphasis was being placed on the careful scrubbing of the surgeons' hands and . . . a few men were already using gloves, white cotton ones that were boiled after each wearing.[15]

In a modified form Dr. Quaine put into practice the techniques he saw in Michigan. In place of the wooden surgical table, he installed a new one covered with rubber and supplied with a drain. This appliance was not procured from an eastern or European supply house but was made by the local carpenter according to plans drawn by the doctor. The rubber covering and the drains were necessary to carry off the copious amounts of boiled water and chemical solution which was squirted from the syringes onto the wound, as well as the large amounts of bichloride water which was sloshed over the hands and instruments of the surgeon.

All of this required a large amount of water, and water was scarce in Bismarck. It was measured by barrels and distributed from house to house at 25 cents a barrel. So scarce was water that the sisters as well as the other residents often made a pail of water do two or three duties. Water used by the surgeons in "scrubbing up" preparatory to surgical work was saved to scrub the floor at close of day. Water in which the week's washing was done was saved for the same purpose.[16]

Surgeons such as the Mayos of Minnesota and the leaders in the medical centers of the East, tiring of this "unpleasant rite of wet antisepsis," after a few years turned to asepsis as a means of attaining the same end — the absence of bacteria. The doctors in waterless Bismarck were only too eager to follow this new method where all instruments, bandages, and appliances were to be made sterile either by dry heat or by boiling. St. Alexius' early attempts at this method were crude. At first they went no further than applying hot water to the instruments and bandages, water that was not always very hot after it had been carried to second floor from the kitchen stove in the basement. The next improvement was to place the instruments and bandages in a pan to boil. As soon as Dr. Boeckman's portable sterilizer was put on the market, St. Alexius Hospital proudly installed one and thought this was the last word in asepsis. This sterilizer, though an improvement over the pan, was nothing but a double boiler with steam going around the sides and then passing out through an opening into the room making the walls wet and dampening the coifs and veils worn by the sister nurses.[17]

At the close of the 80's the medical profession in the Midwestern states was slowly coming around to the teachings of Dr. Reginald Fitz of New York that the symptoms usually referred to as inflammation of the bowels or cholera morbus were really an inflammation of the appendix. This new theory was not as hard to accept as was the treatment Dr. Fitz recommended. His treatment, the removal of the appendix, was considered a drastic treatment by those conservative doctors who had been accustomed to prescribe ice packings, enemas, or oil in such cases. All through the 90's the pros and cons of this solution were argued. Even the Doctors Mayo of Minnesota were conservative in adopting surgery for such cases, and in the year 1895 performed only twelve appendectomies.[18] If surgery as a remedy for appendicitis was accepted slowly by those surgeons of eastern cities who were in close touch with the men who were preaching and practicing the method with success, it is not surprising that the first appendectomy to be performed in Bismarck hospital did not occur until July, 1899, the year Dr. Quaine took up work at St. Alexius.

What Dr. Quaine did for the hospital in the department of surgery, Sister Boniface Tummins did for the hospital in administration. She had great business ability and knew how to win the cooperation of the business men, the politicians, and the patients. The business men of Bismarck consistently backed her projects. During the forty-two years she held the position as superior, she was to see St. Alexius Hospital grow from a primitive frontier institution to one of the best in the land. The first thing she did on her arrival at St. Alexius was to throw out the old sheet iron stoves with which the rooms were heated and install a steam heating system.[19] Bismarck had no telephone system when Sister Boniface arrived, and the only way the doctors could be summoned at night was to send the hospital's handy man, Old Peter, to call them. The day came when the telephone system reached Bismarck. The doctors were slow in taking up this new aid, and Sister Boniface in desperation bought several telephone instruments and presented them to the doctors after she had used all her business arguments to induce them to put telephones in their homes or offices and have them connected with the main line. One doctor consented but only on condition that the hospital would not call him after he had retired for the night. At the same time, electric call bells were installed for the convenience of the patients who up

to this time used hand bells to call the nurses. Electric lights took
the place of the old kerosene lamps and lanterns. The coming of
electricity to Bismarck made it possible for Sister Boniface to intro-
duce still another improvement. Without an elevator or even the type
of dumb waiter which could be manipulated by man power, patients
as well as everything they needed had to be carried up and down two
and three flights of stairs. Sister Boniface and Dr. Quaine solved this
problem by installing the latest in electric elevator service.

Early in their work to modernize St. Alexius and to bring it into
line with the hospitals of the East, the hospital administrators had
turned their attention to the patients' rooms. The beds in use were
those procured in 1885 from local dealers, low beds of the type
used in homes. These beds not only put kinks in the nurses' backs but
at times they were a danger to the patient. The springs and mattresses
rested on loose board slats placed across the bed from side to side.
Often when a heavy patient tossed about, the slats would fall out of
place with great noise. Mattress and patient both fell to the floor.[20]

Early records at the hospital were not very thorough in regard to
the patients. The records covering the years 1885 to 1897 while quite
illuminating are at times most exasperating to the hospital historian.
The record book was a simple blank book ruled off into several
columns in which were recorded the name of the patient, his birth-
place, age, residence, ailment, name of physician in charge, and dismissal. No information was given as to the treatment administered
to the patient. Sometimes a case was laconically described as "fever,"
again simply as "a wound," or "an operation." At other times the
recorder's modesty caused her to state the case as "a private dis-
ease." On the other hand, the records occasionally give unnecessary
detail, as in the following entries: "Shot by turnkey of penitentiary,"
"Wounded by a runaway," "Hands frozen on Christmas day while
drunk," "Shot in the knee while trying to hold up a train at Dawson."
But in time the keeping of patients' records improved along with
medical procedure, and before the turn of the century the hospital
adopted up-to-date methods.

Long before Bismarck ceased to be a frontier town St. Alexius
had shed its pioneer character and took its place among the stand-
ardized hospitals of the country. It was the first hospital in the state
equipped with X-ray and pathological laboratories that met the requirements of the American College of Surgeons. As the city popula-

tion increased, the hospital expanded with new buildings and a larger staff of physicians and nurses.

That the work of the sisters was appreciated by the citizens of Bismarck is attested by the following eulogy which appeared in the local newspaper many years later on the occasion of the opening of the new hospital building:

Honor is due to the local and hard-working Sisters, not only for the magnificent edifice which stands as the physical result of their efforts, but more so because of the spirit that has been imprisoned within the masonry walls to become as much a part of the institution as the bricks themselves.

We recognize the Sisters as true pioneers who came conquering into the great northwest. The men who, around open fires, built cities and empires on our prairies were pioneers, as were the women who came with them as their wives. So also were the Sisters of St. Benedict, who came west to found the first hospital on the plains.[21]

The institution's importance to the Dakotas lies in its work of building better and healthier bodies, adding years of usefulness to some, and bringing peace of soul to many of its citizens. From Holy Mass and daily prayer within the framework of their Benedictine life, the sisters received the strength to raise hospital work from the plane of praiseworthy humanitarian activity to one that can sanctify both patient and nurse.

12 WORK AND PRAYER IN THE 1880's

The combined effort of St. John's Abbey and St. Benedict's Convent spread the order's work in the care of the sick and of the orphans and of the Indians from the Mississippi River to the Pacific coast. But these works, holy as they might be, were not the sole purpose of monastic life. The first purpose of the order is the service of God in prayer and the sanctification of the individual by leading a life in community in accordance with the Gospel counsels. St. Benedict in his Rule, Chapter 43, declares that "nothing is to be set before the work of God"—the public recital of the Divine Office. Nevertheless, his Rule gives freedom to undertake whatever apostolic work the needs of a country or time dictate provided it is compatible with monastic life. These works are secondary and no one of them is a part of the essential vocation of a Benedictine. They are a means to an end. From the beginning the Benedictines have endeavored to spread God's kingdom through charitable and missionary works, but those works rest on prayer and deep religious spirit. Down through the centuries the problem has always been to keep the two phases of Benedictine life in balance.[1]

During the period of the 1880's under the direction of the two strong leaders, Abbot Alexius and Mother Scholastica, there were many who thought that excessive stress was placed on external growth with a consequent weakening in the development of the liturgy and the spiritual life. There was danger of imagining that the greatest good was the meeting of present needs of Mother Church and of the convent. This danger was apparent when at Mother Scholastica's suggestion the recitation of the Divine Office was abandoned entirely and the Little Office of the Blessed Virgin Mary recited in its stead.[2] Many regretted this and for years they kept up a constant prayer for the revival of the full monastic office. To Sister Gertrude Flynn the change was particularly crushing. She made no secret of the fact that she thought St. Benedict's Convent no longer Benedictine and that it would not be so until there was a return to the recitation of the whole psalmody. The fact that the sisters recited the Tenebrae with the Church in Holy Week kept alive in the hearts of many the beauties and blessings of the Divine Office. The lay sisters continued as of old to pray in common the fifteen decades of the Rosary daily, together with the Litany of the Saints in the morning, of the Holy Name at noon, and of the Blessed Virgin in the evening. As the community had gradually moved from formal liturgical prayer, it took up public novenas and other popular devotional practices. There were the devotions of the Thursdays of Advent, of the Fridays of Lent, and the daily recitation of five psalms in honor of the Blessed Virgin. All prayers, with the exception of the Little Office of the

Blessed Virgin, were said in German, a custom continued until after World War I.

Despite the abolition of the Divine Office, most of the age-old monastic practices and penances were adhered to, for example, the Lenten penance of taking a meal kneeling on the floor and of confessing a public fault kneeling before the crucifix in the refectory. Still practiced was the custom of the prioress' washing the feet of twelve sisters on Holy Thursday in commemoration of our Lord's act at the Last Supper. The Lenten fast was strictly kept.

A half-hour meditation was made each morning before breakfast, the points being read aloud by the reader first in German and then in English. In the afternoon, after school was dismissed, the sisters gathered to listen for half an hour to the reading of some spiritual book.

But the daily schedule of prayer and work included not only hours of prayer and work, but also periods of recreation. The time between the evening meal and night prayers was spent in relaxation and innocent fun. Sedate walks, music, song, card games and fancy work were the favorite forms of amusement. Every mission house had its garden and many enjoyable recreation periods were spent weeding or picking the fruit and vegetables.

The real object of Benedictine life and the proper balance between prayer and work was fortunately recalled to the attention of the community when the Holy See suggested that all Benedictine convents in the United States unite to form a congregation. A union of houses would help a convent to tide over a dangerous situation and to check any deviation from the fundamental spirit of Benedictinism. The study of the way of life in other Benedictine houses which this proposed union brought about helped St. Benedict's to judge itself.

It will be recalled that Bishop Louis Fink, O.S.B., of Leavenworth, Kansas, in 1877 had formulated constitutions for the Benedictine sisters of his diocese and had sent them to Rome for approval. Shortly after this he was informed by Cardinal Simeoni that it was the will of the Holy See that the sisters of the Order of St. Benedict in the United States be governed by the same constitutions and form a congregation among themselves. In compliance with this information, Bishop Fink, on June 4, 1879, sent a circular letter to each convent inviting them to a general meeting to be held at Covington, Kentucky, on

140

August 4. The purpose of the meeting, he stated, was to carry out the recently expressed will of the Holy See. Unfortunately, the meeting had to be cancelled at the last moment because of an epidemic in Covington, and interest in the movement lagged until 1880. That year Mother Scholastica Kerst became prioress of the convent at St. Joseph. With her instinct for business and organization she felt that the Benedictine sisters should either go ahead with the matter or drop the idea entirely. She believed in the movement for a union and decided to take the initiative.

In May of 1881, Mother Scholastica, while on her trip to Oregon, took the initiative and asked the prioress of the convent in Chicago to meet her at St. Scholastica's, Atchison, on June 3. There, the three prioresses and Bishop Fink could plan how to put new life into the movement for a union. The result of this conference was that Mother Evangelista Kremeter of Atchison was induced to send out a call to Benedictine convents for a general chapter meeting in Chicago to examine the proposed statutes, to form a congregation, and to elect a mother general for the new union. A month later, three days before the Chicago meeting, Mother Scholastica told her sisters of the proposal of forming the union.

At the Chicago chapter meeting begun on July 19, 1881, the convents of Covington, Chicago, Atchison, Birmingham, Nauvoo, and St. Joseph were represented. The first day of the meeting was given over to the question of the advisability of forming a congregation. When that was approved, the remainder of the session was spent in a study of common customs and observances, and uniformity of headdress. In the end the constitutions as previously written by Bishop Fink were revised and adopted as the rule for all members of the congregation. On the third day the officials were chosen. Mother Evangelista Kremeter of Atchison was chosen to fill the office of mother general, Mother Alexia Lechner of Covington was elected first assistant, the prioress of the Chicago convent the second assistant, the prioress of Birmingham as scrutinizer and the prioress of Nauvoo as secretary.[3] The Congregation of St. Scholastica was thus inaugurated, but years were to pass before the congregation was approved by Rome.[4]

The constitutions of this congregation called for changes in headdress, chapter membership, and organization of the novitiate. These changes were placed before her sisters by Mother Scholastica the day after her return from Chicago. The new headdress was accepted without much opposition. The old Bavarian Benedictine headdress worn up to this year, 1881, was a pleated coif of coarse linen and a black veil lined with white and worn low over the forehead. For a simpler and less conspicuous headdress as well as for saving time and money in laundering, this white lining was removed and a small, stiff band of white linen across the forehead was used to raise the black veil from the face. At the same time the old custom of wearing the face-veil over the face until after breakfast on the three Communion days of the week was given up. The custom of wearing the face-veil over the face in all places outside of the enclosure was likewise given up. Henceforth, this custom was binding only when walking on the "public streets." This change was made in July of 1881 when most of the sisters were returning to their various mission schools after retreat. They were very self-conscious in their new array, and they felt lost without the veil covering the face. The habit and choir cloak worn then were practically the same as those of the present except that the cincture was of leather.[5] From this cincture hung a large fifteen-decade rosary.

The sisters were not as ready to accept the congregation's position on the status of the lay sisters. This topic caused much discussion. In St. Benedict's Convent there were two divisions, choir sisters and lay sisters. The lay sisterhood was an institution introduced from Europe where conventual conditions were different, and it can be traced back to the middle ages. Where the Divine Office was solemnly chanted and the enclosure in Benedictine convents was strictly observed, there was need for "outdoor" or lay sisters. Sisters capable of reading Latin and reciting the Office were placed in the group whose chief duty was to chant the divine praises from the Psalter. They were referred to as choir sisters.

Those whose education was deficient or who lacked ability for such duty were placed in the class of lay sisters. Instead of chanting the Divine Office, these sisters recited the rosary, litanies, and other prayers in the vernacular in common and were engaged chiefly in domestic work rather than in teaching. Their dress differed from that of the choir sisters as did their rank. Though a sister's rank was generally determined by the date of her entrance to the convent, the lay sister always took a place below the youngest choir sister in chapel and in the refectory. In another and more vital matter they differed from

142

the choir sisters. They were not members of the conventual chapter and had no voice in determining the policy of the convent. The constitutions of the proposed new union or congregation did not declare the system of lay sisterhood abolished — it did not even mention the group, but a clause at the beginning of that document would tend in time to do away with that institution. It declared: "The chapter consists of all sisters who have made vows." There was also the statement that "dress is to be the same for all sisters in any particular convent."

The third matter of debate was the establishment of a common novitiate for the whole union or congregation. This the sisters at St. Benedict's rejected as being impractical. The reasons were summarized by Mother Scholastica in a letter to Mother Theresa Moser, Atchison, November 12, 1882, when she declared:

1. The difference in climate is too great.
2. There would be an excessive amount of travel.
3. One novitiate would encumber us with such expenses that we could not meet them.
4. No one house has or will have for years to come suitable buildings for the purpose.[6]

The next general chapter had been scheduled to meet in 1884, but when Mother Evangelista of Atchison, elected mother-general of the congregation in 1881, had resigned her office of prioress of her convent, the question arose as to who should convene the general chapter. All the prioresses were reluctant and the year for the meeting passed. Finally, after fifteen months, Mother Scholastica sent out feelers to the various prioresses about who should take the initiative in calling a meeting. Her letters and the answers to them show the nebulous state of the movement at this time. In a letter to Mother Theresa she wrote:

What is there about the "Congregation of St. Scholastica" or is that union of the several houses effected in 1881 all gone up? It is really too bad that we should have made ourselves the laughing stock of the houses of the East.

If we had expected that these matters were going to be let go this way, I know we would not have joined.

I wrote to Mother Alexia last week. She is the first Assistant and should act: If she will not, would it not be well for all . . . to be in dead earnest? I do not blame you for not acting, you feel just as I do. Neither of us . . . had obligations to do anything, but since it pleases Almighty God to place us at the head of our houses, I feel bound in duty to do what lies in me to effect and confirm a union with as many houses as choose to join and adopt the same constitutions, being fully convinced that united we stand, divided we fall, as has so well proven itself in so many eastern convents. . . . Let us have your opinion on the subject and inform us as to your mode of action for the future. . . . Let all petty selfishness be banished, that little differences of opinion, etc., will not prevent us from taking a step which will certainly serve to promote a closer union of the houses of our order. I do not care who takes the lead, but do want a union promoted. It is now 14 months overtime since a general chapter should have been convened.

I should have written long ago, but was somewhat slow taking the initiative. Now our Superior wants to know just what we are at, and I wish to know *plainly*. Please answer at an early date and oblige.[7]

This letter was answered by Mother Theresa on September 24 in a friendly manner and with much news of local interest. But the letter was a little evasive on the matter of the general chapter. She did, however, state that she, too, was eager for a union and added, "If Mother Alexia (being first assistant) does not or will not act, which I hope is not the case, I think you who have the largest community are the proper person to take matters in hand. The way things are now, the matter must be well considered and talked over and I find it necessary to see you." A day previous, Mother Alexia of Covington answered Mother Scholastica's prodding by stating that no further steps in the matter could be taken until the statutes were approved by Rome. She denounced "this traveling about and holding chapters on our own hook . . . that to repeat it every three years without any special authority or sanction — and that from Rome — would in the end appear ridiculous. . . . Holy poverty and the enclosure would be infringed upon." She also disclaimed any responsibility as first assistant because the election and other acts of the chapter had not been recognized by Rome. Another prioress, Mother Luitgard of Chicago, wrote:

I see in the affair merely a form, would rather hear no more about it. Nothing will be done, for . . . as it is now planned we do not wish it to be, if, as I now know this union should leave us as the new associations, and leave nothing to us as distinctively Benedictine . . . then I will have nothing more to do with the whole affair, because such a union would dissolve us as Abbot Alexius always told me. . . . We will soon see.[8]

144

So no general chapter was convoked and the movement lay dormant for some years to come.

When there seemed to be no hope of working in a congregation, Mother Scholastica set about revising the statutes and customs of her house to enable it to stand alone. She also felt it was time to revise these statutes. Up to this date they consisted of handwritten copies brought from Eichstätt together with such changes and additions as had been made since the sisters had settled in Minnesota. Each sister, as was the custom, had made her own copy of this document from a copy of the document and in the course of time many discrepancies had crept in. It was to rectify this and also to bring the constitutions and customs of her house more in line with the document prepared by Bishop Fink that Mother Scholastica drew up a new body of rules. It differed from that of the congregation only in respect to the period of candidature, term of office for the prioress, and membership in chapter. To this document Bishop Seidenbusch gave his approval on April 21, 1887, although it had not yet been presented to the chapter for acceptance. Only on April 24 was the proposal to rewrite the constitutions put before the chapter. When certain features of the new constitutions were made known the lay sisters were disappointed. They had long desired a voice in the deliberations of the chapter and had asked that the differences between them and the choir sisters be abolished. But the new constitutions for St. Benedict's Convent made no changes in their status and the convent lost some of that family spirit and unity which should characterize a Benedictine house.

An undercurrent of discontent was evident not only within the mother house. In a number of the parish schools there were misunderstandings. Abbot Alexius of St. John's Abbey and Mother Scholastica were alike in personality, in aims, and in work. They both believed that opportunity must be grasped and risks undertaken. As has been mentioned before, they both put pressure on the pastors and the people to open parochial schools or at least to employ sisters in the local district school. In some places the parishioners opposed both plans and gave as their excuse the expense of building a convent to house such teachers. To nullify that excuse, the abbot and the bishop at times had sent sisters against the will of the people. They asked the priest to give up the rectory to the sisters and move to the sacristy. He then took his meals at the convent or food was sent to him. In other places the sisters were forced to live for some months in a house with seculars until a convent was provided. This was but a temporary arrangement until the parishioners could be won over to build a convent and a school, but while it lasted it was very unsatisfactory to both sisters and pastors. Finally, the abbot in a letter dated November 19, 1887, forbade such arrangements.[9] As restlessness grew, the situations described above were bound to be used as something tangible for complaint.

The nine years of rapid growth of schools and expansion of Benedictine work in hospitals and orphanages had culminated in a feeling on the part of the monks and sisters of being pushed and driven. Many longed for a change from the feverish expansion and external activity to a more peaceful, retiring, and spiritual life. They felt that the spirit of Benedictine life was being missed and held that "the greatest service to God and man is what they are, rather than what they do." This picture does not necessarily mean that religious discipline was low at St. Benedict's but it does mean that the balance of *Ora* and *Labora* was obscured.[10]

Then the inevitable happened. An ambitious and disgruntled monk abetted by some of his brethren went to Rome to present his cause. He charged the superiors of the abbey and of the convent with mismanagement and toleration of evils. Out of the conditions found in some parish schools described above, he presented an unsavory story to the Holy See. That resulted in Rome's commanding an apostolic visitation of St. John's Abbey and of St. Benedict's Convent. Archbishop John Ireland of St. Paul was appointed apostolic visitator and in 1889 during the months of March, April, and May he visited those institutions "to investigate the charges and to correct such undesirable conditions as might have crept in" the various parochial missions and the mother house. It was found that the wholesale charges had never applied to more than a few parishes; that where the irregular conditions had existed the abbot and the prioress had never approved but only tolerated them; and that at the time of the visitation those irregularities had already been corrected.[11]

When Archbishop Ireland had finished his visitation and had interviewed each sister, he found in the outward life or discipline nothing of any great moment to correct, but he was fully conscious of a general desire for a new prioress, for the right of a free election of the same and for less external activity. He also recognized that the activistic tendencies of the house tended to retard the spiritual development of its members. Up to this time, the convent had never had a free election despite the provisions of its statutes. Abbots or bishops had appointed the superior. When the motions of an election were made, it was to place in office a sister selected by the bishop.

Mother Scholastica's term of superiorship was to terminate in August, and to the majority of sisters the way now seemed clear for a free election. Neither Bishop Seidenbusch nor the abbot was in a position to interfere. Bishop Seidenbusch had resigned as bishop in the Vicariate of Northern Minnesota on October 18, 1888, and Archbishop Ireland had then become administrator of the vicariate. Neither could Abbot Alexius interfere in favor of Mother Scholastica, for he himself, having gone through the ordeal of a papal investigation, was on the point of resigning. The new constitutions and statutes adopted shortly before had also guaranteed the sisters' right of free choice of a superior. The reelection of a superior without the express approval of the bishop was prohibited.

The admirers of Mother Scholastica who believed in her policy of spreading Benedictine works and who wanted that policy continued, started their work for her reelection early. This group, led by Sister Bede Linneman, called a meeting of the chapter for June 24 to present their plan of obtaining permission from Archbishop Ireland to put Mother Scholastica's name on the list of candidates. The records reveal that a majority agreed to the motion, and that the sub-prioress, Sister Cecilia Kapsner, and the former Mother Aloysia Bath were charged with presenting the petition to the archbishop. In the meantime, notices were sent to the sisters on the missions that a particular sister, usually the superior, would attend the election and cast the votes for the rest of the sisters on that mission. This aroused consternation because the new constitutions gave each member of the chapter the right to be present for the election and to choose her own candidate. When the two delegates, Sister Cecilia and Mother Aloysia, approached the archbishop for permission to put Mother Scholastica's name on the list of candidates, he did not commit himself but told them they would hear from him in time. He never answered them, but instead wrote to Mother Scholastica advising her not to accept the reelection or to be a candidate for it. He also demanded that all sisters, even those from Red Lake, Duluth, and Bismarck, be present at the election. When the list of those eligible for the office was made up, Mother Scholastica placed on it the name of Sister Cecilia Kapsner, even though she was not of the required age. On the day of the election, August 28, Sister Cecilia told the archbishop that her name should not appear and asked to have it canceled. He agreed and declared he would have a free election.[12] Mother Aloysia, who, it will be remembered, had been appointed to fill out the last two years of Mother Antonia's term, was not considered as ineligible for election and her name was placed on the list of candidates. One amusing thing happened during this tense meeting. When Mother Aloysia saw the votes going her way she got up and declared she could not allow that, for her health was too poor to carry the burden of being prioress. The archbishop told her: "Sit down; you are not yet elected." But by eleven o'clock that morning Mother Aloysia had been chosen prioress for the next six years.[13]

Thus ended the administration of Mother Scholastica as prioress of St. Benedict's Convent. One of the early chaplains described her as "gifted with more than ordinary talents, having an excellent education and unlimited ambition for progress. She had, in addition, an indomitable will to carry out her plans for extending the work and the influence of the Benedictine sisters in Minnesota. She was a born leader who courted opposition for the sake of overcoming it, a firm believer in the aid of Divine Providence, nevertheless believing in doing her share in furthering the plans of Providence. Because of her dominating disposition she had more foes than friends, and while her friends admired her wonderful abilities others felt crushed." [14] During her administration of nine years, membership in the community had increased from 57 to 164, and the number of parochial schools had grown from 10 to 28. The orphanages, schools, and hospitals she built stand today as monuments to her enterprise and executive ability. What was said of Abbot Alexius Edelbrock could be said of Mother Scholastica: her bent was toward external achievements and the spirit of the American frontier was in her blood.

13 PRAYER AND WORK IN THE 1890's

For an institution devoted to the worship of God and the personal sanctification of its members a perennial problem is the manner of adaptation to the times which apparently demand an increase in external works. The danger of over-emphasis on external good works at the expense of the monastic spirit which had threatened St. Benedict's Convent in the period of the 1880's was lessened. It retreated with the passing of the western frontier spirit of feverish growth and with the withdrawal of Abbot Alexius and Mother Scholastica from the leadership of their respective houses. Two events in the summer of 1889 were decisive in bringing back a better balance between *Ora* and *Labora* — the election of Mother Aloysia Bath as prioress and the erection of the Diocese of St. Cloud.[1]

The community was to welcome the comparative quiet of Mother Aloysia's term as prioress. A woman of poor health and weak constitution, Mother Aloysia did not have the vitality to do the things her predecessor did, even if she had had the desire and the same outlook. Her contemplative quiet stood in strong contrast to Mother Scholastica's burning energy. In character and disposition she was the opposite of Mother Scholastica and was probably chosen for the office for that very reason.

Saying that this period of the 1890's was one of peace and quiet does not mean that there were no problems and worries. But with the intensification of the spirit of prayer and under the rule of a gentle superior who had sympathy for the weak, peace came to the house. There were to be trials, but the new spirit animating the community enabled the sisters to meet them serenely.

Convinced that a convent should be, first of all, a place where the Christian life is lived fully and intensely and that material advancement is secondary, Mother Aloysia soon applied to the abbot of St. John's for a full-time chaplain. Up to this time the sisters and the pupils of the academy, orphanage, and Indian industrial school had been under the spiritual care of the priests of the nearby parish church. The parish funerals, sick calls, and weddings had always and properly held first place with the pastor; the convent and school had to accommodate their chapel services to the parish program. St. Benedict's needed a full-time chaplain—one whose first interest was the welfare of the sisters and their charges. The sisters offered many prayers that a wise and pious priest would be appointed. It so happened at this time they were visited by a false priest claiming to beg for his South American missions. He simulated saying Mass and deceived the sisters by his appearance of great piety. They were so impressed that they even prayed that their new chaplain would be a man like him. They were greatly chagrined when Archbishop Ireland exposed the man as a fraud.

Reverend Henry Borgerding, O.S.B., was assigned to the chaplaincy and took up his work in September, 1890. A good and pious clergyman with unusual common sense, he served the convent for twenty-nine years. He often teased the sisters about his bogus predecessor. Holy Mass was now offered in the convent chapel every day, and religious instructions were given by the chaplain to novices and students. These instructions were limited to the elements of the catechism and his sermons never varied from year to year.

A few months after Mother Aloysia's installation, the Diocese of St. Cloud was erected and on November 24, 1889, the Most Reverend Otto Zardetti was installed as its first bishop.[2] These new superiors would work to raise the tone of religious life in convent and diocese, gradually introducing the order and discipline that had been impossible to achieve during the days of the vicariate. This new diocese comprised 12,251 square miles which included sixteen counties. At the date of the erection of the diocese in 1889 the eastern part of this territory was well settled and boasted of railroads, good wagon roads, and telegraph service. Most of the 58 churches and 40 stations in the diocese were in this eastern or St. Cloud area. Catholics farther west were, as a rule, too scattered to establish parishes. Even if they had been able to, there were not enough priests to care for them.

Perhaps the reception given to Bishop Zardetti on his arrival in St. Cloud, the one city of any size in the diocese, may have hidden from him the actual rural tone of the remainder of his territory. St. Cloud itself was a city boasting of a teachers college, a hospital, and several hotels. The day before his arrival a delegation of clergymen went to St. Paul to meet their bishop. There Archbishop Ireland joined them and Mr. J. J. Hill, "President of the Manitoba Railroad," as the newspaper referred to him, gave the party his special car for the trip to St. Cloud. An hour before the arrival of the party in St. Cloud, church societies of the various nearby parishes formed in processional line. The official paper of the diocese described the reception as follows:

There were over 2000 people in the procession and perhaps as many more who did not take part. They were stretched in line from the depot to the corner of St. Germain Street, on Sixth Avenue, a distance of six blocks. At the regular time the train pulled into the depot and the reception committee at once boarded the special car in which the Bishop, ten priests, and the lay delegation rode from St. Paul. At the platform the mayor and the city council awaited the Bishop. . . . The Bishop was then escorted to a carriage in front of which the priests to the number of 50, marched in advance. At the Church of the Immaculate Conception he alighted and entered . . . and proceeded through the nicely decorated church to the altar, where after the usual ceremonies he delivered a short address in German. From this church he proceeded on his way to the Cathedral amid the crowds of people, the strains of music, the displays of welcome, and the gorgeous decorations everywhere meeting with an ovation never witnessed before.[3]

In the evening a reception was held "at the parlors" of the Grand Central Hotel where Catholic and non-Catholic had an opportunity to meet the new churchman. On Sunday, November 24, Archbishop Ireland and Bishop Martin Marty of Sioux Falls, South Dakota, installed the first bishop of the new diocese of St. Cloud with all the pomp of the Church's ceremonial.

The half dozen years he had already spent in America had not given Bishop Zardetti an understanding of America and its democratic ways. He remained an aristocrat. A priest of the diocese once said of him that he "had the highest idea of the episcopal dignity and authority, with no understanding of the common people and their needs. He could not bring himself to their level; neither did he understand the ways of missionary priests. His purpose was of the highest but he employed measures which seemed drastic to priests and people alike."[4] His zeal for uniformity made him command the clergy to have their copies of his official monthly magazine bound and preserved in their rectories. The order read, "If they [the clergy] have difficulty in getting volumes bound we invite them to send their volumes well marked with their name to us and we will get them bound for them for a trifle. But bound they must be." In his meticulous way he asked Rome to change the title of the diocese from Claudii as used in the brief of his appointment to that of Clodoaldi. Having looked into the history of the origin of the name of the city of St. Cloud, he discovered it was "not named after S. Claude or Claudius, bishop of Besancon, France, but after the city of St. Cloud near Paris which claims as its founder and patron, Saint Clodoald or Cloud, son of Clovis." [5]

In line with his purpose of molding the pioneer diocese into a replica of what he had known in Europe, he soon turned his attention to St. Benedict's. It will be recalled that in 1887 the sisters had attempted to bridge the chasm between choir sisters and lay sisters by allowing the latter to wear the same apparel as that of the choir sisters. Now Bishop Zardetti ruled that the old distinction between the two groups be revived and that the lay sisters should not be permitted to wear the religious ring nor the choir cloak, nor should they be granted a voice in the chapter. He was finally persuaded not to insist upon this rule and the matter rested there until the interim between the reigns of Bishop Zardetti and Bishop Marty when the diocese came under the ecclesiastical jurisdiction of Archbishop Ireland. That American prelate, who had a great repugnance to the division of religious into classes, urged the sisters to abolish the system. This they did at a meeting of the general chapter on December 11, 1894, when the lay sisters were transferred into the ranks of choir sisters and took their places in rank according to the date of their final vows. [6]

Bishop Zardetti's second directive to St. Benedict's lengthened the term of novitiate to two years and the period of temporary vows to eight years. The custom of making final vows at the end of three years of simple vows was therefore abolished in favor of triennial vows followed by another period lasting five years before being admitted to perpetual vows. This long probation was the general rule in the Benedictine convents of Europe because the European Benedictines made solemn vows. The American Benedictines did not and therefore had a shorter period of trial. Bishop Zardetti, it may be observed, was trying to govern things in America by the pattern he was acquainted with in Europe. And both of these directives created in the mind of the community a fear that he was planning eventually to force the enclosure on them.

Two days before Bishop Zardetti left for his *ad limina* visit to Rome in 1892 he gave his third directive to the convent. He visited St. Benedict's, called a meeting of the members of the chapter, and announced that he wanted the academy transferred to St. Cloud, this despite the fact that the sisters were in the midst of building a north wing to the convent and academy which was designed to relieve congestion in the academy and to provide a chapel large enough to accommodate both sisters and pupils. The chapel in use was so small that the pupils were forced to attend Mass in the parish church. For the same reason the convent ceremonies of the reception of new members, the profession of vows, and funeral services had to be held in the parish church. The bishop's directive was a blow. The new building could not be left half finished and yet, without pupils, it would be useless. But the following spring, before the bishop returned, the building was completed and occupied. Either he had changed his mind about transferring the academy to St. Cloud or the larger and more pressing problems which had arisen during his seven months' absence in Europe caused him to postpone to a later date the moving of the academy. The project was not mentioned again.

Such interference with the character and aims common to all American Benedictine houses combined with regulations of minor details caused uneasiness in the convent. The three regulations pertaining to the lay sisters, the novitiate, and the academy seemed to portend that the bishop was aiming to transform the sisters into cloistered nuns. It was believed by some that the bishop meant to restrict the activities of the order.[7] Preparing for such an eventuality, Mother Aloysia at the suggestion of the abbot began to look about for a place of refuge if their fears materialized. This explains why, during Bishop Zardetti's absence but with consent of the Very Reverend Administrator Joseph Bauer, she accepted the invitation to staff two schools in the widely separated dioceses of Seattle and LaCrosse. In case of necessity the sisters teaching in these places could form the nuclei of independent priories.

Once more Benedictine sisters set out for the far West. But the journey made by Sisters Alphonsa O'Donnell, Perpetua Pick, and Rosina Loecken was short and simple when one compares it with the seventeen-day trip to Oregon made by Mother Scholastica in 1881. Now three days by rail brought them to Tacoma. The trip, though short, was full of excitement; scenery, the fellow travelers, and the train itself were sources of wonder to these sisters who had never before been out of their native state. It was all a pleasant dream, but at the end of the road they came up with a jolt against the work-a-day world with its admixture of the ridiculous. Because of a mistake in the telegram announcing the time of their expected arrival, no one was at the station to meet them when they reached Tacoma on the midnight train. Some friendly soul directed a cab driver to take the sisters to the parish house. The cabby aroused the pastor from his slumbers and together they brought the sisters to a small shed or cabin in the yard back of the church, and here the sisters stayed for the remainder of the night. This leaky, unplastered, one-room cabin built on stilts on sloping ground, the pastor intended should serve as the sisters' refectory, kitchen, and community room. It had been equipped with a stove, a table, and one chair. A classroom in the school building some distance away was to serve as dormitory.

In justice to the pastor it must be said that this lack of proper housing for the sisters was not entirely his fault. He had made arrangements with a local convent to supply him with teachers who would return to their convent home in the city after class each day. Then at a late date the abbot of St. John's ordered him to make an opening for the Minnesota Benedictines instead. Caught on short notice, he had had no time to procure a proper residence for them before the opening of the school year. Though St. John's Abbey went ahead and eventually established a priory in the West, the sisters' plan of an independent convent did not need to materialize, for the danger threatening the life of the mother house in Minnesota had passed before this convent ever promised any growth.

The two parishes of Tacoma, Washington, and Eau Claire, Wisconsin, differed as much in character as they did in their geographic locations. Eau Claire was a lumber town with a large anti-Catholic population and an Irish Catholic minority. These Catholics were a warm-hearted people, respectful to the sisters. Sisters Anatolia Langford, Theodora Dunne, Patricia Egan, Modesta Wieland, Ildephonse Carlin, and two candidates received a warm welcome from the parishioners when they arrived on August 28, 1892, and were directed to the convent and school buildings in which the Franciscan sisters from Joliet, Illinois, had served the parish for several years. But the children were unpredictable. School opened with 309 pupils. On the sisters' first trip to the postoffice the postmistress wished them success with the school but warned them that the children were mischievous and daring and that the school was a difficult one.

Mother Aloysia had opened this mission not only to have a house in another diocese but also to have a school and mission in which she could use the English -speaking sisters who had come to St. Benedict's when St. Gertrude's Convent, Shakopee, had been closed. Within a few years there was a movement to establish an independent priory in Eau Claire. However, though Bishop Joseph Schwebach of La Crosse approved this movement, the dissensions which had accompanied the establishment of an independent house in Duluth made Mother Aloysia fearful. So, like the Tacoma mission, Eau Claire was to wait more than sixty years to become an independent priory.

In the meantime, the evidence of concern for Catholic education in his diocese makes one wonder whether the danger of their claustration by Bishop Zardetti was ever as great as Mother Aloysia and her advisors considered it. Education was something that held his interest constantly. Bishop Zardetti had taught in the seminary near St. Gall in Switzerland and after coming to the United States he was on the staff of St. Francis Seminary in Milwaukee. Now as the first bishop of a growing diocese he was in a position to point the way for others in the field of teacher preparation.

When Bishop Zardetti came to St. Cloud in 1889, Catholic education needed direction and organization. There were many schools in the area but only twelve parochial schools. For the most part these were small schools and employed only two to four teachers. Eight of these parochial schools were staffed by Benedictine sisters, three by Franciscan sisters and one by Sisters of Mercy. The Catholic children in the other eighty-six parishes and station churches were attending public schools. The attorney general held that the Minnesota constitutional amendment of 1877 forbade any distinctive doctrines, creeds, or tenets of any particular Christian or other religious sect to be taught in tax-supported schools.[8] This plus the attorney general's later opinion that the reading in school of the King James version of the Bible did not come under this ban showed Catholics what they could expect. In many of the predominantly Catholic localities of the diocese the Catholics found a way of avoiding this danger. In eleven such places the district school board had become accustomed to engaging Catholic laymen or Benedictine sisters as teachers who conducted catechism classes after school hours. By doing so the people avoided supporting two school systems. But this system had no assurance of permanency, and in fact it was soon to be outlawed.

The position of the Catholic schools in the St. Cloud Diocese was not unique and the Catholic bishops of the United States were fully awake to the situation. The Sacred Congregation of the Propagation of the Faith as early as 1875 had forbidden Catholic children to attend public schools; and in 1884 the Third Plenary Council of Baltimore expressed the ideal of Catholic school education and legislated explicitly for the attainment of that ideal, at the same time binding the clergy and the laity to build schools. To this end the council legislated that parochial schools be erected as soon as possible in every parish, preferably within two years after the promulgation of the decrees.[9] Though results were not attained as soon as was expected, the legislation did establish a norm toward which Catholics should work, namely that parochial schools be available for all. In the St. Cloud area these decrees had been taken seriously by Bishop Seidenbusch and Abbot Alexius but not by some of the parishes. Bishop Seidenbusch's efforts to establish parochial schools among reluctant parishioners have been described in earlier chapters of the book.

One of Bishop Zardetti's first important acts in the diocese was to promulgate the decrees of 1884, at the same time ordering every parish to have a parochial school within two years unless the parish was expressly exempt.

The support of parish schools by citizens who were also supporting public schools by their taxes became a burden. By the 1890's double taxation began to weigh heavily on the Catholic population. A solution of the troublesome question of how to have public education and at the same time have Catholic training despite the attorney general's opinion on the Amendment of 1877 was attempted by Archbishop Ireland in 1891. With the cognizance of the archbishop, the pastor in Faribault rented the parochial school building to the local school board for one dollar a year with the proviso that the sisters be retained in the school and their salaries be paid out of public money. The superintendent of schools was to have supervision of the school and religion was to be taught after school hours. Non-Catholics were free to send their children to this school or to another in the town. When, soon after, a similar arrangement was completed in Stillwater, Protestant ministers made a state-wide protest. At a conference of Protestant ministers of Minneapolis the school plan of Faribault was denounced as a scheme, a subtle attack of the Roman hierarchy. They asked the state attorney general for his opinion as to the constitutionality of the Faribault and Stillwater plans, but when he failed to give a definite answer and suggested that they petition the court, the ministers hesitated.

In the state, and out of it, too, the Faribault and Stillwater Plan was opposed also by a Catholic group who defended the parochial school system. They were also motivated by national antagonism against the archbishop, by "Cahenslyism," and by religious politics. This opposition was hardly becoming to a group which had been using the very same school procedure in fifteen Catholic settlements in the St. Cloud diocese, in eight places in the Milwaukee diocese as well as in Poughkeepsie, New York.[10] As a result of this agitation the Faribault and Stillwater experiment came to nothing. The whole episode, however, helped Catholics to see that they must build and support schools of their own.

Increase of school population, compulsory school attendance laws, absence of suitable religious training in the public schools, and the statutes of the dioceses of the country caused so rapid an increase of schools that it was impossible to supply qualified teachers. Religious teaching communities throughout the United States found themselves hard pressed to supply this need and in these circumstances were forced at times to assign members to teach who were insufficiently prepared. One writer declared that a consequence of the rapid increase of public and private schools throughout the land was that "young girls would be sent out to teach when they were little older than some of the pupils and when they had little more education." A survey in Minnesota in 1885 showed that 40% of all Minnesota teachers had less than a common school education.[11] If this was true of the public schools of the state, it is not surprising that teacher preparation at St. Benedict's was also spotty.

Taking seriously the directives of the Council of Baltimore, Bishop Zardetti determined not only to raise the Catholic schools to the level of the public schools but to surpass them. To this end he created a diocesan school board of priests. The first purpose of the board was to supervise the certification and preparation of diocesan teachers. A second purpose was to inspect the schools annually. The bishop also appointed a committee of two clergymen to formulate a program of studies for the sisters preparing to teach. At the same time he declared that before being allowed to make vows, each Benedictine novice destined to teach was to pass a teachers' examination administered by his examining board.[12] The school board met for the first time on January 25, 1892, and decided that all parochial schools should in the future use the same textbooks. They stopped short of drawing up an outline of the course of studies for all of the schools of the diocese as was at first proposed. Instead, they required that each school have an outline for the classes taught in that particular school which all of its teachers must follow.

Mother Aloysia was wholly in accord with these provisions for she too was an educator and saw only too clearly that the great demand for teachers during the preceding decade had lowered teaching standards.

The work of the school board had some good results but it was not given a fair trial. It functioned but a year or two because the bishop was transferred to another diocese and another year was to pass before his successor took charge of the diocese. An added reason for the failure of Bishop Zardetti's educational plans was that busy pastors who were appointed as examiners and inspectors of the parochial schools found little time for this extra work during the year 1892–93. The members of the board also found it embarrassing at times to inspect and criticize a neighboring priest's educational plant, and they were inclined to make superficial inspections. When the bishop's plan broke down, Mother Aloysia put into operation a community teacher training plan for her sisters. Furthering the bishop's aim, she appointed a sister as supervisor of teacher preparation and inspector of schools conducted by Benedictines. She also ordered attendance at summer schools and encouraged the holding of exhibits of school work. In order to improve teacher preparation, Mother Aloysia recommended that St. Benedict's be asked to staff no new parochial schools for the next three years. This three-year period was to be spent in giving the young members a better education and in reserving sisters to relieve the teaching load of some who were overburdened. All of this was a step in the right direction and showed an awareness of the educational needs of the day. In all these forward-looking plans the community and the bishop worked in harmony toward the same end.

158

The spirit of the community was good. Great fervor and zeal were shown in the recitation of the Little Office of the Blessed Virgin Mary and in attendance at the numerous prayers and devotions which had been taken up in the course of the decade since the Divine Office had been dropped. Public novenas were increased and the number of days on which Benediction of the Blessed Sacrament could be given was increased by the addition of all days in May and October, all days during the octave of Corpus Christi, all Wednesdays and Fridays of Lent, all days of retreat, and the first Sunday of each month. Daily reception of Holy Communion was not then the practice in the Church, but professed sisters were given the privilege of communicating on four days each week and on major feast days. The simple professed communicated on three days, novices on two, and candidates on one. After attending Holy Mass and making a half-hour meditation, the sisters were served a simple breakfast. Then all went to their assigned work. At 11:45 the bell rang for examination of conscience in the chapel. After that the sisters went to dinner. Silence was observed at all meals. During dinner and supper all listened to holy reading in German.[13] At one o'clock Vespers and Compline were prayed. Then the sisters returned to their assigned tasks in silence. In the afternoon a cup of coffee was allowed to those who needed it. At five o'clock the bell was rung for the recitation of Matins and Lauds. This was followed by a half-hour of spiritual reading in the community room where the sisters would sit in a group crocheting or darning while one read aloud to them such classics of the spiritual life as Alphonse Ligouri's *Die Herrlichkeiten Marias* or *Die Regel das Leben und die Wunder unseres heiligen Vaters Benediktus,* based on St. Gregory's account.

After supper there was recreation until seven-thirty. This evening recreation period was spent in the community room in winter and outdoors in summer. It was at this time that the sedate lady-like game of croquet was introduced, an innovation indeed, for hitherto exercise was taken by weeding the garden or picking the fruit or vegetables. But a great part of the recreation period was given up to pleating coifs. At this time the coifs or wimples were made by hand by putting the dampened piece of linen on a board and painstakingly fingering in the tiny pleats. In 1896 this work became less burdensome, for two men working about the school and convent in Moorhead, Minnesota, invented a machine which pleated the linen more evenly and in seventy-five percent less time. From then on, coif making no longer had a place in the recreation period. In winter the evening recreation was enlivened by simple games such as checkers, by song and conversation. The older sisters delighted in relating jokes and affectionate stories and anecdotes concerning convent events.

After recreation came night prayers and a preparation of the points for the morning's meditation, read aloud in German by the one appointed. Examination of conscience followed, and after that it was nearly bedtime. As the clock in the parish church tower struck nine, all lights were put out except a lantern placed in the corridor between the dormitories.

In the midst of this piety, unity and peace reigned. But the spirit of the house was put to the test when a movement was made to withdraw a large group of sisters from St. Benedict's for the purpose of creating an independent priory at Duluth.

The Benedictine sisters had been sent to work in Duluth schools and in the hospital at a time when that city was included in the Vicariate of Northern Minnesota under the care of Bishop Seidenbusch. In 1889 Duluth became the see city of the newly-created Diocese of Duluth with Bishop James McGolrick as its head.

This movement to detach the sisters in the new diocese from the convent at St. Joseph and to form an independent priory originated in Duluth. A few sisters there felt so strongly the deposition of Mother Scholastica Kerst as prioress in 1889 that they conceived the plan of withdrawing from the jurisdiction of St. Benedict's and erecting an independent priory at Duluth with Mother Scholastica as superior.[14] As superior of a new diocese, anxious to build up religious institutions rooted in his diocese and under his ecclesiastical jurisdiction, Bishop McGolrick was ready to cooperate in a plan that would make the Benedictine sisters in the hospital and in the schools independent of the mother house at St. Joseph. He requested Bishop Zardetti to allow the sisters to make this foundation. On April 13, 1892, Bishop Zardetti consented to Bishop McGolrick's petition but on the condition that the division be a complete separation and take place within two months. Despite the fact that the leaders of the movement used influence to get the forty-three sisters working in the Duluth diocese to agree to stay as the nucleus of the new priory, only twenty sisters chose to remain.[15] Twenty-three exercised their right to return to the house in which they had made their vows.

Because twenty sisters would not suffice to staff the hospital and schools, Mother Aloysia of St. Benedict's promised assistance. She offered to take over and staff three of the parochial schools until such time as the Duluth foundation could supply its own teachers. Mother Aloysia preferred to staff a complete school rather than to lend individual sisters to fill vacancies in the various schools or the hospital conducted by the Duluth mother house. To this plan both Bishop McGolrick and Mother Scholastica, whom he had appointed superior, objected. As a result lay teachers were employed.

Through all of this, relations between the two convents became strained. Then matters of finance nearly brought about a complete rupture between the mother house at St. Joseph and this new foundation.[16] Yet in time the rift between the two convents was healed, for as daughters of St. Benedict both worked toward the same goal. This new mother house, Villa Sancta Scholastica, grew rapidly and in a few years was itself able to establish other foundations.

While St. Benedict's was carrying the financial burden of a new foundation it was also involved in an important court case. This was the "Will Case," famous for its bearing on the right of religious to inherit property. The mother of Sister Julia Will died August 2, 1892, leaving an estate valued at $30,000. A will made March 19, 1891, stipulated that this estate be divided between her son and her daughter after the husband's death. On October 5, 1893, Sister Julia, like all other members of St. Benedict's Convent, had made a will bequeathing to the convent all she had inherited or would ever inherit. Sister Julia died August 21, 1894. When the community presented her testament to the probate court after the death of her father in 1896, the brother objected to the admission of his sister's will and claimed he was the sole surviving heir; that Sister Julia had not been a free agent, being bound by vows; that Sister Julia had never come into possession of the estate and therefore could not bequeath it. The probate judge before whom the case was heard decided to admit the testament to court, and the brother then appealed the case to the district court in Ramsey County where Sister Julia's will was again declared valid. Mr. Will then brought the action to the state supreme court where he again lost, for the court declared that members of religious orders are free moral agents notwithstanding their vows of poverty and obedience. Thwarted in his attempt to invalidate his sister's will and testament, Mr. Will now attacked the validity of his father's will and started a new series of proceedings in the Ramsey County probate court. The judge of this court gave a verdict favorable to Mr. Will. It was at this point that the sisters, backed by the clergy of the diocese and guided by a capable attorney, decided to fight the decision and appealed to the district court in St. Paul where they obtained a reversal of the lower court's decision. Mr. Will in turn then appealed from this decision to the state supreme court which in May of 1898 handed down a decision in favor of the sisters when it declared the validity of the father's will.[17] The case was given wide publicity in the St. Cloud and the Twin City newspapers, and it gave many a heartache to the sisters.

Another period of uncertainty came to the community when Bishop Zardetti was named by the Holy See to be Archbishop of Bucharest, Roumania. Whatever anxiety the sisters might have entertained about Bishop Zardetti's successor was allayed when they learned that the man chosen was Bishop Martin Marty, O.S.B. Bishop Marty had left his European monastery of Maria-Einsiedeln in 1859 to join the new Benedictine foundation at St. Meinrad's in Indiana and in time he became its abbot. Later, because of an insufficient number of priests for the Indian missions in Dakota, he had offered his services and established missions at Fort Totten, Standing Rock, Pine Ridge, Rosebud, and Cheyenne River. Before he was appointed to the bishopric of St. Cloud he had served as vicar apostolic of the Dakota Territory and later as bishop of the Diocese of Sioux Falls.[18]

Under the guidance of this experienced bishop who was also a Benedictine, the community in 1896 revised its constitutions and statutes. There were no drastic changes. However, Bishop Zardetti's lengthening of the time of preparation for profession was abrogated. Once more the term of the novitiate was one year, to be followed by three more years of probation, at the end of which the sister would be permitted to pronounce simple perpetual vows. There was also an addition made to the number of non-liturgical prayers already being said in common.

Ill and worn out by his missionary work with the Sioux, Bishop Marty was not to be the sisters' protector for long. He worked with them for only eighteen months when he was called to his eternal reward. Now the sisters entered another period of suspense and for one year they prayed daily for a good bishop. Their prayers were heard; Bishop Trobec, a priest of the Archdiocese of St. Paul, was appointed by Rome to succeed Bishop Marty. In him the sisters found another wise protector.

By the close of Mother Aloysia's term in 1901 the community had grown in religious spirit as well as in members. In territory including Minnesota, North Dakota, Wisconsin, and the state of Washington, the community was administering two hospitals, one in Bismarck and the other in St. Cloud, one home for the aged, one orphanage in St. Paul, two Indian missions, and thirty-one schools. Mother Aloysia ruled her sisters with prudence and skill, but her health, never very strong, was weakening under the cares of office. When her term was finished in 1901 both she and the community thought it advisable to have a new prioress. On July 27, 1901, Sister Cecilia Kapsner was elected to lead the community for the next six years.

Attracted by a pamphlet in which Father Pierz extolled the wonders of the climate and the soil of Minnesota, the Kapsner family had come from Prussia to Pierz when their daughter Mary was fifteen. Two years later Mary entered St. Benedict's, where upon receiving the holy habit she was given the name Cecilia. Now in 1901 Sister Cecilia, at the age of forty-five had already served the community eighteen years as sub-prioress, several years as mistress of novices, and some time as convent procurator. With this broad experience in administration, Mother Cecilia brought to her new office qualities of heart and mind that were to endear her to her sisters.

PART THREE

FULL FLAME IN A NEW CENTURY

14 BUILDING PROJECTS 1900 TO 1957

During the period from 1857 to 1900 when the Convent of St. Benedict was very slowly gaining members, there were four attempts to make new foundations. The first division had occurred in 1863 when such a large group left to found the convent in Atchison, Kansas, that St. Benedict's was crippled. This was followed in the next decade by the two unsuccessful attempts to make independent foundations at Pierz and at New Trier. The fourth attempt was made in 1892 when the Benedictine sisters working on the missions in the Duluth diocese formed an independent priory in that see city. It is somewhat ironical that these threats to the growth of St. Benedict's should have come when it was ill-prepared to withstand them and that in the period from 1900 to 1940 when it was numerically strong, no new foundations were made.

In fact, instead of threats to the growth in numbers, there arose on two occasions danger of such an increase as to make St. Benedict's lose all resemblance to a religious family. The first occasion occurred in 1913 when the bishop of Lead, South Dakota, asked that the Benedictine convent in Sturgis be amalgamated with St. Benedict's. This would have added sixty or more new members at one time. Because the Sturgis community based its practices and interpretation of the Holy Rule on those of the Swiss Congregation, and not the Cassinese, such a large number of religious would have been difficult to assimilate. Nothing came of the proposal, and both convents escaped the great problems of such an amalgamation.

The second incident of this kind occurred in 1931 when Bishop

165

Vincent Wehrle of Bismarck decided to improve conditions for the Sacred Heart Convent, a small community of Benedictine sisters at Garrison, North Dakota. This community's chief work was with the Indians of North Dakota. It had been leading a struggling existence and to all appearances would have difficulty developing into a permanent institution. Since the Indian schools were not a source of religious vocations, the community did not grow. Because their economic prospects were not better, the bishop feared that neither he nor they could finance the building of a much-needed mother house. In 1931 he resolved to suppress this community and to have its members merge with St. Benedict's whose sisters had been working in his diocese since 1878. Once this change had been accomplished, he planned to found a new mother house the members of which would be all those sisters of St. Benedict's Convent who were working in his diocese. The hospital property would pass into the hands of the new community.[1] The first step Bishop Wehrle took to realize his plan was to request that St. Benedict's Convent accept the sisters from Garrison as members of the Minnesota community. St. Benedict's agreed and sent its invitation to them.

The whole plan was unfeasible, of course, based as it was on a failure to investigate the provisions of canon law. Bishop Wehrle was at that time an old man, in poor health. Previous to his elevation to the bishopric, he had been a missionary to the Indians of the territory of the two Dakotas. There details of canon law were sometimes put aside, for quick judgments under pressure were often a necessity.

With this background he was surprised to find his apparently simple plan of the fusion of two convents frowned upon by Abbot Alcuin Deutsch of St. John's Abbey and by the abbot primate. He was reminded that shortly before his petition for the suppression of St. Gertrude's and its amalgamation with St. Benedict's was sent to Rome, he had given a letter of recommendation and approval to the sisters at Garrison to join the proposed Congregation of St. Gertrude —an organization of Benedictine convents under pontifical jurisdiction.[2] Though warned that he could not push for the amalgamation of Garrison with St. Benedict's until Rome had answered his petition of suppression he nevertheless placed the Garrison convent under a superior from St. Benedict's. New members were ordered to make their vows of stability to St. Benedict's Convent rather than to the Sacred Heart Convent which they had entered.

Mother Louisa of St. Benedict's tried to postpone this step until Rome answered the bishop's petition.[3] But even word that the Congregation of St. Gertrude had been approved by the Sacred Congregation of Religious and that, consequently, the Garrison convent now had pontifical status did not discourage Bishop Wehrle in his plans of amalgamation. As yet, Rome had not answered his petition of suppression, and until it had, he would proceed with his plan. Finally in the summer of 1937 papers from Rome stated that the bishop's reasons for disbanding the Garrison convent were not grave enough for the drastic action of suppression.[4] The bishop then dropped the matter, and the Sacred Heart Convent at Garrison as well as St. Benedict's, never very eager for the proposed fusion, were both happy at the outcome.

The annual reception of thirty or more new members taxed the physical capacity of St. Benedict's. That together with the growth in attendance at the academy had made necessary additional building. Though 90 per cent of the sisters did not reside at the mother house during the school year, the ever-increasing number of candidates did. At the opening of the new century the novices had been moved to the building formerly occupied by the pupils of the Indian Industrial School. The candidates still occupied rooms in the academy where they attended classes with the boarding pupils. This crowded condition of convent and academy called for expansion. At the same time there were plans for the establishment of a college which would also need space.

Building plans were made as early as 1910, and in September of the following year contracts were let for the erection of a college hall and a chapel. The location of the proposed college building was easily decided, but the location of the chapel, the center of Benedictine life, was not so easily settled. It had to be in a place easily reached by the aged and ailing sisters and at the same time be accessible to the students and the public. The general preference was to extend the chapel out from the east front of the main building toward Wisconsin Street. But because the distance was only ninety feet, such a plan would necessitate moving the street one half block east. The sisters sent a petition to the village council on March 28, 1911, requesting that Wisconsin Street follow the quarter section line from the parish cemetery due north and enter Minnesota Street through the block east of the old line. The village did not grant the request and the sisters were forced to place the chapel in the rear of the main building.

The architect chosen for the new college building and the chapel was Mr. George Stauduhar of Rock Island, Illinois, and plans were drawn up for a $50,000 chapel and a $50,000 college hall. Before the buildings were completed, however, the total cost was $335,467. On October 5, 1911, ground was broken for the chapel. The day was well remembered for some years by those who took part in the ceremonies. A large group of sisters had crowded on a wooden porch to get a better view of the rite when all of a sudden the porch collapsed. Fortunately no one was injured. In October of the following year, 1912, the cornerstone was laid and blessed by Bishop James Trobec. The building was completed in 1914.

The Sacred Heart Chapel is connected with the college on the south and with the novitiate on the north by means of cloister walks. The main entrance of the chapel opens into the convent. This building appears to be a church rather than a chapel because of its size and beauty. A Roman renaissance style building in which sixteen columns of polished Rockville granite with Minnesota marble bases support six main arches and a dome that rises above the transept to a height of 135 feet, it provides space for 550 worshippers in two areas. In the transept there is an antiphonal choir of 145 light red southern gumwood stalls, while the nave has pews of the same wood. Most impressive is the Carrara marble high altar in a sanctuary elevated four feet above the floor of the body of the chapel. Executed from a design found among the papers of the early eighteenth century Roman Jesuit architect, Reverend Andrea Puteo, this altar is surrounded by light golden Sienna marble columns on a base of pale gray Georgia marble. A carved entablature resting on these columns supports six great angels in Levitical garments who hold aloft the great crown which is the baldachin.

The ceremony of the opening of this new place of worship was held with great solemnity on March 25, 1914. On the night preceding, many of the sisters kept an all-night vigil in reparation for all the faults committed in the presence of the Blessed Sacrament in the old chapel, and the next morning the Te Deum was chanted in thanksgiving for all the graces and blessings received there during the past years. A diary in the convent archives gives the following account of the event:

On the morning of the 25th the chaplain, Father Henry Borgerding, celebrated Holy Mass for the last time in the old chapel; they carried the Blessed Sacrament in solemn procession; each sister and novice carried a lighted candle, and the students were dressed in white. There was also a long line of acolytes and clergy accompanying the Blessed Sacrament to its new resting place. During the procession all joined in singing appropriate hymns. Pontifical High Mass was then celebrated. In the afternoon the statues were blessed and the Stations of the Cross were installed by the Right Reverend Bishop, after which Benediction with the Blessed Sacrament was given.[5]

The new college hall, St. Teresa's, was a four-story brick structure with a full basement and a flat roof, the first of its kind on the premises. The basement contained the gymnasium; the first floor, the library, the museum, and art and sewing rooms; and the second, the assembly hall and two classrooms. The two upper floors, the residence section, were planned as a unit in which all the rooms opened into a spacious "rotunda," an oblong social center, with a balcony, and a full skylight as a ceiling. Like the chapel, the college soon became a show place of central Minnesota.

After the college and the chapel buildings were opened for use the older buildings underwent a complete renovation from roof to basement. A new tiled roof replaced the wooden shingled one, a cloister porch was erected on the west side of the community room, and an unsightly covered walk connecting the convent with the novitiate was torn down. The old chapel occupying the third and fourth floors of the north wing of the convent was then remodeled and turned into private rooms and dormitories for the sisters. The basement of the same wing, formerly used as the sisters' refectory, was redecorated and given to the candidates. The fourth floor of the old academy building was remodeled and converted into student rooms and infirmary.[6]

The addition of these two buildings to the convent and school required a complete change in the heating system and this in turn called for a new boiler house. Fortunately, the electric light plant installed in 1906, the 60,000 gallon water tank built in 1908, and the well dug in 1909 were considered sufficient to carry the new load. At this time when the small towns of Minnesota were not as yet supplied with electricity, large institutions located in such towns had to provide their own power. Therefore, in 1906 St. Benedict's installed its first power plant. Electric lights were considered such a luxury in the convent that for years the electric light plant operated only from five o'clock in the morning until nine in the evening. When the nine o'clock retiring bell was rung, a central switch turned off all lights in the school as well as in the convent. However, kerosene lanterns were hung at various points in the corridors and burned all night. Heat was likewise turned off during the night for there was no night shift of engineers. As late as 1920, Sundays were days of shivering, for the engineer was a member of the parish choir and sang at the late Mass and at Vespers in the afternoon. Between Mass time and Vespers some heat might be turned on.

The addition of the chapel, college, and power house necessitated the removal from the west campus of such service buildings as the root cellar, storage buildings, and stables. The two acres of orchard on the south campus had ceased to be profitable as an orchard when the new college building was built, for it was so close to the building that it was subject to constant raiding. Those acres were turned into campus and the orchard placed farther south. The sisters' cemetery was enlarged and improved.

Another building improvement undertaken under the direction of Mother Cecilia was the erection of an isolation infirmary for students.[7] This was a timely act, for shortly after its completion in 1906, over a hundred students and candidates were stricken in a diphtheria epidemic.

Mother Cecilia's next project was the construction of a new St. Alexius Hospital in Bismarck. For some time the administration and staff of this hospital had been asking for a new building. Though only twenty-nine years old, the building had become overcrowded and outmoded in several respects. St. Benedict's understood the need and despite the fact that it had just erected the $335,467 buildings at the mother house it bound itself in 1914 to the erection of this new hospital. Mother Cecilia also realized that the St. Raphael's Hospital in St. Cloud would in time need enlargement. In anticipation, she and her counselors purchased land on the bank of the Mississippi River.

While the home plant and the hospitals were being enlarged, the same growth was going on in the field of education. During Mother Cecilia's superiorship twenty-four new parochial schools and a boarding school were opened. To these new missions Mother sent a total of 103 sisters.[8]

171

Although she was busy with this expansion program it must not be thought that Mother Cecilia neglected the spiritual life of the community. She had a very capable procurator, Sister Priscilla Schmittbauer, who took the details of building construction from her shoulders and left her time to see that attendance at prayer and other religious exercises was regular and that the sisters were living the life they had vowed. In 1919, after eighteen years spent in caring for the spiritual life of her sisters and erecting a chapel, a college, an infirmary, and service buildings at the mother house and a new hospital building at Bismarck, Mother Cecilia retired from her office. One chaplain wrote of her: "Gifted with a keen perception and a ready judgment she could grasp almost intuitively every phase of a question presented to her for immediate decision and it was next to impossible to take her by surprise in any transaction. With broad charity she loved peace — often nearly to a fault." [9] Near the end of her administration minor differences arose between Mother and Bishop Busch. At the close of her term she withdrew to the small mission convent at Millerville.

Mother Cecilia was succeeded in office by Sister Louisa Walz who had been acting as her subprioress for the past seventeen years. Mother Louisa was born in Baden, Germany, on December 19, 1864. She had come to America with her parents when she was eight years old and entered St. Benedict's Convent in 1886. Her years of experience gained as novice mistress and as subprioress gave her a good preparation for the office of prioress to which she was elected in 1919. Mother Louisa continued her predecessor's policy of brick and mortar expansion, and like those of Mother Cecilia, her projects were not ventures into new fields of work but were rather the enlargement or replacement of institutions already established. To make space for classrooms in the college it was decided to erect a new building for the needle art department. Fancy needle work and the making of church vestments had been a work of the sisters from the day of their arrival in Minnesota, and by 1910 St. Benedict's had become the center for liturgical apparel in central Minnesota. Under the direction of Sister Justina Knapp this work had been carried on in rooms in the academy and then in the college building.[10] Finally in 1922 St. Walburg's, a four-story brick building, was erected as a workshop and a dormitory. Shortly afterwards the Scholasticate, another four-story building, was erected to accommodate the

98 candidates who had up to this time occupied a section of the college. The erection of these two structures released much needed space in the college and in the convent.

The flu epidemic which struck the country during World War I had proved the inadequacy of hospital service in St. Cloud. Bishop Busch in this emergency opened up the Institute or Community Center for the care of the sick, and he called for priests and sisters to aid the nurses in caring for the victims of the epidemic. The demand for a new hospital large enough to meet the needs of the vicinity became louder. Some even threatened to build a second, competing hospital. World War I with its resultant good wages and easy money filled the college, the academy, and the hospitals. These conditions made it possible for St. Benedict's to meet the payments on the new buildings which had been erected between 1900 and 1922. The relative ease with which these payments were made had given the sisters a false sense of security, and when in 1925 St. Raphael's Hospital in St. Cloud called for a new two and a half million dollar building, Mother Louisa and her counselors were not as fearful of the undertaking as they might have been. The sisters did not know, of course, that the great depression of 1929 was about to throw the whole country into chaos.

This new hospital, which would be named the St. Cloud Hospital, was built on the previously purchased twenty-acre site of wooded land on the banks of the Mississippi River far enough removed from the business district of the city to ensure quiet. The architect's plans called for a ten-story building with 475 rooms. It would accommodate 250 patients and a few staff members. Work began in July, 1926. Two years later, on February 9, 1928, it was completed and blessed. The patients were moved from the old St. Raphael's Hospital to the new St. Cloud Hospital.

No building of any sort was contemplated for the next seventeen years. By that time, under the guidance of the new superior, Mother Rosamond Pratschner, the indebtedness of the convent had been reduced and its total assets sufficiently increased so that when a call came from Ogden in the predominantly Mormon state of Utah to do apostolic work in the medical field, St. Benedict's gave the matter some consideration. In the summer of 1941 the federal Bureau of Public Health had made a survey of the hospital facilities in Ogden which showed only 1.9 beds per 1000 people. This low ratio was due to the sudden influx of military and governmental personnel which had raised the population from 43,000 to 75,000. The four military depots and the air base established in and near Ogden employed over 26,000. When the military forces planned to establish a 512-bed hospital in a temporary structure for the soldiers and the civil personnel working at those posts, the Ogden business men and the doctors objected. Wanting a permanent hospital under local control, the Ogden Chamber of Commerce had already applied for federal aid under the Lanham Act. When notified that funds would be available if suitable sponsors could be found to operate the hospital, they asked Monsignor W. J. Giroux of Ogden to find a sisterhood which would be willing to undertake the building and staffing of such a hospital. He contacted the Sisters of St. Francis of Denver, Colorado, who agreed to take over the management and building of the proposed Ogden hospital. They applied for a federal grant and submitted plans for a large two-story building. But because the army was planning on building its own large hospital, the Federal Works Agency saw no need of a large city hospital and limited the proposed sisters' hospital to a one-story building. The sisters withdrew their application for a federal grant in July, 1942, and gave up the project entirely.

Undiscouraged, the Ogden citizens turned to new tactics. They opened negotiations with the army to the end that it give up its plans for an army hospital and accede to Ogden's desire to build a large private 150-bed hospital to service both the military and the civil populace. Certain of winning their point, they sent Monsignor Giroux to scout for sisters to sponsor the undertaking. Early in 1943 this emissary called on Mother Rosamond at St. Benedict's and laid before her the following proposal: The sisters would erect a 150-bed hospital plant together with a nurses' residence and a heating plant at the cost of $1,250,000. Their request for federal aid would be backed by the city, and the city itself would aid in various other ways.

Bishop Duane Hunt of Salt Lake City then wrote declaring that a "Catholic hospital is the finest missionary agency which the Church can have. At present there is only one Catholic hospital in the state of Utah." [11] Mother Rosamond and her advisors gave the matter much thought. Unlike the other building projects of the past forty years, this was not the expansion or rebuilding of an institution already in successful operation and in a territory well-known. This was an adventure into a state not yet penetrated by Benedictine sisters nor to any great extent by Catholics. In this Mormon state of Utah the Catholics were a scattered minority. In the diocese of Salt Lake City which comprised the whole state of Utah there were but forty-five priests, twenty-nine parishes, four parochial schools and one Catholic hospital. But it was just this aspect that appealed to the missionary zeal of the majority of the sisters at St. Benedict's. Weighing all these considerations, Mother Rosamond declared the convent was willing to undertake the work if the army hospital plan was dropped for there was no need of two new hospitals. On receipt of this answer the Ogden Chamber of Commerce and the army held a meeting on October 16, 1943, in the office of Brigadier-General Talbot with the representatives of the armed forces, the state and county medical associations, and the representatives of the Sisters of St. Benedict. The purpose was to determine whether a private hospital could be constructed in lieu of the proposed army hospital. A few days later Colonel Lanza recommended to General Willis, the medical officer in charge of the Utah area, that the army hospital be dropped and that priorities available for the construction of the proposed army hospital be transferred to the Ogden community project.[12]

On the strength of Colonel Lanza's report, the sisters at St. Benedict's with the approval of Bishop Busch formally accepted the Ogden proposition and on February 18, 1944, applied for federal assistance. President Roosevelt signed the grant authorizing the expenditure of $900,000 toward the construction of this $1,250,000 hospital. Work was begun in October, 1944, and in the summer of 1945 the cornerstone was laid by Archbishop John Mitty of San Francisco. The first unit, the nurses' residence, was completed May 22 of the following year, and the first high Mass was sung in that building on July 11, the feast of the Solemnity of St. Benedict. Though a hospital signifies charity and love of brother, there crept into the hospital on that day a faint note of war. The organ used for the services was borrowed from the Italian soldiers' prison camp nearby. Not until September 18, 1946, was the hospital formally opened and put under the protection of St. Benedict. The *Standard Examiner* of Ogden in its issue of September 19, 1946, gave a glowing account of the blessing and the opening of the hospital. Bishop Hunt in his address on this occasion stated, "This building is now set aside for a two-fold purpose, that of giving glory to Almighty God and service to man."[13]

The crowd of 7,000 visitors who were shown through the building on that day was indicative of interest in an enterprise of commercial and social benefit to the locality. It was also indicative of a curiosity about Catholic sisters and their institutes — a trait common among all people but especially among those in localities where few convents are to be found. This new undertaking has done much to break down misunderstanding of the Church and her work and has given solace to many Catholics in the Ogden area. During the first four and one half years of work the hospital cared for 21,125 adult patients, and 18,644 out-patients; 4,113 children were hospitalized and 5,193 were born there.[14]

This hospital was no sooner put into operation than Mother Rosamond and her sisters were asked to build another. This call came from the town of New Prague, Minnesota. Since 1924 a group of citizens of New Prague had operated a non-profit hospital, which by 1946 had become outmoded and too small. At this point the hospital corporation offered to turn over all its assets to the town to be used in building a new hospital. The doctors pushed the matter of a new hospital building and in 1947 the city fathers agreed to build. On October 24, 1947, a municipal bond election was held and the people of New Prague bonded the city for $175,000 to finance it.[15] Federal funds were soon made available for financing 45 percent of the cost. The rest would be made up by city taxes and by gifts of private citizens. It was to be a community project and the Catholic parish joined the good work by donating the site for the building. The pastor told his people that a Catholic hospital was what that locality needed and induced them to put a Catholic sisterhood in charge. The doctors agreed. From 1946 to 1951 efforts were made to interest a sisterhood to take over the management and control of the local hospital. The first request, one sent out as a feeler, was directed to St. Benedict's during August, 1947. Mother Rosamond, after consulting with her community, replied that financial circumstances and the shortage of nurses compelled her to refuse the offer. Finally in August, 1951, St. Benedict's was again petitioned and Father Cyril Popelka was sent as the town's emissary with the proposal that if the sisters would take charge of the forty-two bed hospital, the city of New Prague would deed it over to them, provided the sisters would assume the $143,000 debt still due on the building. After consulting with Bishop Peter Bartholome of St. Cloud and

Archbishop John Murray of St. Paul in whose diocese the hospital was located, Mother Richarda Peters (prioress since 1949) accepted the offer on September 3, 1951. Papers were signed that "the sisters shall assume full and complete control of the said hospital and operate same at their own expense and for their own profit and at their own risk . . . as soon as the same is substantially completed and as soon as they arrive to assume control." [16]

This forty-two bed hospital was equipped for every type of surgery, basal metabolism, X-ray, and other work usually found only in larger hospitals. It is a red brick two-story structure of contemporary design with large areas of glass as one of its main architectural features. A floor in one wing is set aside for the sisters' residence and for the chapel.

The sisters moved into the new Community Memorial Hospital in January, 1952 but it was not open for service until the following month.[17] This hospital is truly a community project and demonstrates the spirit of cooperation and good will of the town and the surrounding country. Wives of Protestant ministers and members of the Protestant groups worked side by side with the Catholic women and the sisters in cleaning, scrubbing, and performing other tasks to prepare the hospital for the opening day. The men of the locality, regardless of religious affiliation, volunteered for the heavy work.

On the opening day a baby was born — a good omen for the patronage to be given to the hospital in all of its departments in the future. During the first year of service this small hospital cared for 1,408 patients and 584 newborn infants. The next year the number of patients increased to 1,555.

The erection of the four hospitals at Bismarck, St. Cloud, Ogden, and New Prague had so absorbed the attention and the financial assets of the community that nothing had been done to enlarge and improve the college buildings at St. Joseph. A residence hall had long been needed. Since in its early years the college was located too far from St. Cloud to draw a large number of day students, most of the students enrolled would have to live on the campus. Insufficient residence accommodations compelled the college administration to refuse entrance to a large number of students each year and hampered the growth of the institution. Finally in 1954, the situation became so acute that building was imperative. A committee chosen from the college faculty was appointed by Mother Richarda to study the needs of the college and to make plans for its future growth. After putting the project under the patronage of St. Joseph, they called in the assistance of the architects, Mr. Richard Hammel and Mr. Curtis Green of St. Paul. The committee and the architects after weeks of investigation decided that three units of construction were necessary — a dormitory to house 200 students, a recreational center, and an auditorium. The vacated dormitory space in the old building would provide room for the expansion of instructional facilities. It was soon evident that an auditorium would not be built until a later date.

The plans drawn up by the architects provided for a three-story dormitory to accommodate 200 students and for a commons building or recreational center to include guest rooms, recreation rooms, snack bar and a lounge for day students. Though both buildings were to have a brick exterior to harmonize with the older buildings on the campus, the plans revealed a decidedly contemporary handling of materials and spaces. To prevent bigness from destroying the family spirit which has been such a marked feature of school life at St. Benedict's during its century of existence, the dormitory was divided into six units, each having its own living room, kitchenette, and laundry. Early in 1955 the building contract was given to the Wahl Construction Company of St. Cloud. The estimate for construction, furnishing, and architects' fee was $981,117.68. The expansion of the power plant necessary to provide heat, light, and other utilities for the new buildings brought the total cost to over one and one half million dollars.

To meet this cost the sisters broke their century-old tradition of building up the plant at the mother house by their own efforts and savings and those of a few interested friends. They now decided to call on outside help. Because a professional fund-raising campaign was not feasible in a small village, the sisters decided to raise the money by personally soliciting funds from foundations, from business firms, and from parishes, as well as by appealing to relatives, alumnae, and friends. This work has been carried on by a committee of sisters appointed by Mother Richarda. This committee also coordinated the activities of the community in planning sales of articles such as bread, fancy work, and rosaries made by the sisters at the missions as well as at the mother house.

On April 6, 1955, ground was broken. The work of excavation

and construction of concrete foundations was pushed in order to have the ceremony of the laying of the cornerstone on home-coming day, April 30. On that day Bishop Bartholome in presence of the clergy, sisters, students, and alumnae blessed the cornerstone with all the ceremony of the Church's ritual, placing Mary Hall under the special protection of Mary the Mother of God. In September, 1956, the first group of students moved into their residence hall to find there under the broad sweep of the low-hanging roof of the new commons building the same spirit of dedication to God that had prompted the establishment of the college over forty years earlier and had inspired all the growth of the community.

15 EDUCATIONAL MOVEMENTS 1900 TO 1957

Building expansion was only one of the community's achievements during the fifty-year period since 1900. Teacher preparation and the staffing of the ever-increasing number of parochial and district public schools was another accomplishment. Increase of population, compulsory school laws, the action of the prejudiced American Protective Association, and the decrees of provincial and plenary councils had caused extraordinary growth in the parochial elementary school system from 1880 to 1900. Like the members of other religious orders for women whose work included education during these years previous to 1900, the Benedictine sisters were engaged primarily in elementary education. Though this has continued to be true, the fifty years following 1900 were spent in expanding to the secondary and college level, and at the same time in perfecting the elementary school.

Of the sixty-eight new missions undertaken during the period 1900 to 1949 fifty-two were schools. Among them were thirteen incomplete high schools and one complete one, all opened in connection with elementary schools already established. During this same period some schools were relinquished by the Benedictines to the care of other and newer religious communities. Such for example were the schools in Wahpeton, North Dakota, and Moorhead, Little Falls, and Waite Park, Minnesota. St. Benedict's Convent now had a number of sisters of Polish descent and it was able to undertake the care of several Polish parochial schools in such places as Gilman, Sobieski, and Little Falls in Minnesota. In the St. Cloud diocese most of the elementary parochial and public schools staffed by the Benedictine sisters were located in small towns or rural centers. The territory comprising the diocese is rural, and this determines the size of parish and school. As late as 1920 about half of the Benedictine elementary schools required fewer than eight teachers. Nevertheless, in that year the total number of pupils under the sisters' care numbered 12,241. This was due to the large city parochial schools located in other dioceses. Among these were schools in Minneapolis and St. Paul, in Tacoma, Washington, in Eau Claire, Wisconsin, and in Bismarck, North Dakota.

A change was made in the community's system of educational supervision in 1914. Until then the supervision of these parochial schools from the Mississippi River to the Pacific coast rested mainly in the hands of the mother superior or the directress of St. Benedict's Academy. But with the beginning of the century because of the increase of schools and the multiplication of laws relating to teacher qualifications this task became so complex as to demand the appointment of a community supervisor of schools. The first appointee to this office was Sister Digna Wieland. Though her academic preparation was adequate, Sister Digna was without experience in the parochial elementary schools; consequently her position remained to a large extent nominal. In 1928 she was succeeded by Sister Patricia Egan, who had taught for many years in the parochial schools of Minnesota and Wisconsin. After her Sister Pacifica Beste successfully continued the work until 1937.[1]

While the parochial schools were multiplying, many predominantly Catholic and Lutheran settlements in the state continued the old custom of employing Catholic sisters or Lutheran teachers as instructors for their district public schools. In the St. Cloud diocese alone there were at one time as many as fifteen district schools employing Benedictine sisters. This system received its first setback in 1904 when the Minnesota attorney general declared that the wearing of the religious garb was prohibited because the teaching of any distinctive doctrine, creed, or tenets of any particular Christian religion in the public schools is forbidden by the state constitution.[2] To this declaration Catholics answered that the dress did not teach a distinctive doctrine, that religion was taught only after school hours, and that the constitution did not forbid the employment of sisters or ministers. Despite the dictum of the attorney general most of these Catholic and Lutheran school districts continued their old system, but special pains were taken to allow no formal religious instruction or prayers during regular school hours. In this way the schools kept within the letter of the law.

But nine years later, in 1913, opposition to this custom again appeared and the attorney general was asked if it was lawful to employ sisters in public schools and whether such schools could receive state aid from public taxes. He gave the following opinion on March 31, 1915:

I may inform you . . . that the wearing of such garb by teachers while teaching in the public schools was unlawful . . . The statutes of this state make the opinions of the Attorney General rendered to the Superintendent of Public Instruction decisive until the question involved shall be decided otherwise by a court of competent jurisdiction.[3]

The basis of this opinion was that, because a religious garb is a religious symbol, wearing it is in itself teaching the religion of a particular sect, a practice forbidden by the state constitution. But even after this ruling many schools employing sisters continued to request and receive state aid. Among these places were Richmond, New Munich, Luxemburg, Freeport, and St. Augusta. Other schools such as the ones at St. Joseph and Melrose were converted into parochial schools.

Opponents of religious education now felt that the only way to get the sisters out of the public schools was to settle definitely the constitutionality of teaching in the religious garb and of teaching religion after school hours. But these two matters could be settled only by litigation in the courts — a procedure for which somebody would have to pay and which would be uncertain as to results. No one seemed willing to risk a case at the time. But by 1915, the rapid increase of parochial schools in the state caught the attention of the anti-religious group. This group was more alarmed by the rapid increase of parochial schools than by the relatively few district schools staffed by Catholic sisters. A plan was then made to bring all private schools under state control and to limit their growth and expansion

BISHOP JAMES TROBEC, THIRD BISHOP OF ST. CLOUD.

BISHOP JOSEPH BUSCH, FOURTH BISHOP OF THE DIOCESE OF ST. CLOUD.

SISTER PRICILLA SCHMITTBAUER, THE BUILDER.

MOTHER LOUISA WALZ, 1919-1937.

SISTER JUSTINA KNAPP, FOUNDER OF THE VESTMENT MAKING DEPARTMENT.

THE CHAPEL IN 1914.

BISHOP BARTHOLOME AND
CLERGY IN CEREMONY OF
CONSECRATION OF THE CHAPEL.

THE 1914 COLLEGE ADDITION.

THE CHAPEL.

THE FARM AND BARNS.

SAINT WALBURG'S HALL, THE CENTER OF
CHURCH VESTMENT DESIGNING.

THE SCHOLASTICATE.

SOME OF THE FIRST FACULTY. SISTER ADELGUNDIS, SISTER DOMINICA, SISTER GRACE, SISTER IRMA, SISTER JEANETTE, SISTER MAGNA, SISTER URBAN, SISTER VIVIA.

THE FIRST BOARD OF DIRECTORS, MR. FRANCIS GROSS, MR. JOSEPH MATT, AND MR. FRANCIS MULCAHY.

EARLY DAYS IN HOME ECONOMICS. ST. BENEDICTS, 1913.

NE OF THE FIRST "BENNIE" BUSSES.

IRST MEETING OF THE ST. PAUL CHAPTER OF ST. BENEDICT'S ALUMNAE.

RECREATION IN THE 1920's.

THE ANNUAL PAGEANT.

RED CROSS WORK IN WORLD WAR I.

MAKING BANDAGES DURING WORLD WAR II.

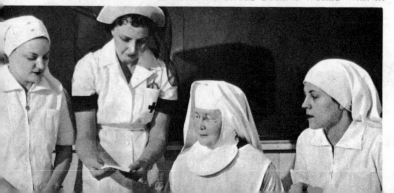

INTERRACIAL CHARACTER OF ST. BENEDICT'S STUDENT BODY.

STUDENTS' RESIDENCE AND COMMONS: INTERIOR, FRONT AND COURT.

LAYING OF CORNER STONE OF MARY HALL
BY BISHOP PETER BARTHOLOME.

THE GROTTO WALK.

EARLY SECTION OF THE CONVENT CEMETERY.

SOME MONASTIC CRAFTS: CANDLEMAKING,
VESTMENT DESIGNING, BOOKBINDING.

and force them to close. If an expensive court case could not be risked in order to remove sisters from the district schools, neither could that means of suppression be used for curtailing the parochial school system and placing the system under state control.

Another means had to be sought. The opportunity came in 1919. It had been known that a number of district and parochial schools in Minnesota and in other states were still using German or Norwegian instead of English as the chief language medium of instruction. This came to public notice during the period of World War I when national feeling ran high. A bill was introduced in the Minnesota state legislature in 1919 declaring that the compulsory education law could be satisfied only by attendance at a school in which all the common branches were taught in the English language and taught by teachers qualified to teach in the English language. On the surface this law of 1919 seemed harmless enough in its demands, but it was an opening wedge in the program of state control of all Catholic schools. To compel parents desirous of obeying the compulsory school attendance law to send their children only to those schools in which teachers held certain qualifications is equivalent to prescribing who may teach in private schools and is therefore state control. The group in Minnesota opposed to Catholic parochial schools quickly joined forces with the earnest public-minded educators who were working to raise the standards of the schools. But their motive in this collaboration was the hope that high state standards would drive religious teachers out of the district schools and prevent the increase of parochial schools. *Der Wanderer* of St. Paul warned its readers that under the mantle of patriotism this bill was a step toward state control of Catholic education and a violation of the rights of parents in educating their children.[4]

Up to this time, the qualification demanded of the teacher in the public school was a certificate issued by the town or county superintendent to the applicant after a successful examination.[5] The sisters teaching in the district schools had long complied with this rule. The parochial teachers had done the same, not because the state controlled parochial schools, but because they wanted to assure themselves and the parishioners that they were qualified teachers and that their schools compared favorably with the public schools. The records in the office of the Stearns County superintendent of schools show that the sisters continued to apply for these examinations and certificates down to the year 1921 when the qualifications for teaching were changed.

The educators of the country had long been convinced that the old system of certification of teachers was defective. It was known that frequently those in charge of issuing certificates were lax and that in many instances the examinations were a mere formality. As late as 1900 many states issued certificates to teachers with little more than a primary school education. Even as late as 1925 one fifth of the country's elementary school teachers had not advanced beyond high school. In the Catholic schools of the country the percentage of teachers with only high school training was somewhat higher. On the other hand, there were 10.4 per cent more Catholic teachers than public school teachers who had four years of advanced training in a normal school or a college. Gradually it became evident that in teacher certification more emphasis should be placed on academic and professional training and less on written examinations. In 1921 Minnesota succeeded in requiring all candidates for teacher's certificates to have a diploma from a Minnesota state teachers college or from the College of Education of the University of Minnesota.[6]

St. Benedict's was in full sympathy with raising the standards in public and private education and with the standards set by diocesan school officials for improvement in teacher preparation. Like the other teaching orders of the state, it responded by sending large numbers of sisters to the state teacher training schools at St. Cloud and Moorhead and to the University of Minnesota. In 1915 St. Benedict's opened a normal school of its own. However, because a diploma from a private school fulfilled certification requirements only for the rural or semi-graded schools whose numbers were decreasing, it was closed in 1924. During the following ten years an average of 120 sisters from St. Benedict's attended the summer sessions of the University of Minnesota and of the state normal schools. A number enrolled in the teacher training institutions in other states, especially North Dakota, to enable them to be certified in those states. Mother Louisa Walz sponsored this program of teacher training in state institutions fully aware of the hazards to the religious life that her sisters would meet away from the convent environment. Therefore, if there was no Benedictine convent in the college town, she would arrange to rent a house near the campus so that the sisters could live their conventual life in all details.

When the anti-religious school elements saw that a state normal school diploma requirement did not banish the sisters from the district school or disqualify them from teaching in schools which must satisfy the compulsory school attendance law, they formed a new plan. This scheme would make it impossible for the sisters to obtain such a diploma. In the Minnesota teachers colleges and normal schools practice teaching was mandatory. In the summer of 1923 a group at Moorhead, Minnesota, discovered that since the practice teaching at this and other normal schools was done in the model school connected with the college, it constituted teaching in a state-supported school and was therefore closed to those wearing the religious garb. When asked to give a ruling on the matter, the state attorney general based his decision on the opinion given by his predecessor in 1915. He declared that practice teaching in teachers colleges or other state-supported schools by those wearing a religious garb is forbidden by the constitution which declares that no particular religious tenets shall be taught in state-supported schools. He, too, reasoned that the wearing of the religious garb was in itself teaching a particular religious doctrine.[7] This opinion given in the midst of the summer session, brought to an immediate end the sisters' practice teaching. The other state teacher training schools followed the example of Moorhead. Their action made it impossible for the sisters to earn the diploma which was the prerequisite for a state teacher's certificate. Consequently, no sister would be able to teach in the public schools. Closing the Catholic schools would now be easy; all that was needed was a declaration that to fulfill the compulsory school attendance law the child must attend a school staffed by teachers holding state certificates.

As a result of the action of the Moorhead school, the religious orders of sisters in Minnesota withdrew their members from the Minnesota teachers colleges and sent them to schools in North Dakota, where practice teaching was not required for a diploma. But transportation to these distant schools and lack of proper accommodations limited the number of sisters thus trained. The greater number of prospective teachers was enrolled in the department of education opened in the fall of 1926 in the College of St. Benedict. Others were sent to the St. Paul Diocesan Teachers College which opened its doors in 1927. Though these sisters were all getting a training equivalent to that provided by any state institution, state law did not permit the issuing of an elementary teacher's certificate on a diploma from these private colleges. However, the state was soon to issue permits for teaching in secondary schools to holders of degrees from private colleges.

This was the *status quo* until July 23, 1938, when the State Teachers College Board relented somewhat and made it possible for a woman wearing the religious habit to obtain a diploma or a degree from a state college. To the board it was evident that the Catholic schools were here to stay and that thousands of citizens were being trained in those schools. For the good of the state and public welfare the State Teachers College Board decided to make it possible for the religious teachers of parochial schools to obtain a state diploma. At the meeting on July 23, 1938, the board adopted the following resolution:

Resolved that the State Teachers Colleges permit students of religious orders to register and to complete the practice teaching requirement in either of the following ways: (1) The practice teaching to be done in the parochial schools but supervised by the State Teachers College in which the degree is being asked, upon the recommendation and approval of the college faculty. (2) Where an accredited college is available and able to offer practice teaching, such shall, upon the opinion of the college, be accepted in lieu of the practice teaching requirement of the State Teachers College.

The state attorney general sanctioned these resolutions with the proviso that "this practice teaching is not to be done in a tax-supported college" but in "privately endowed colleges as distinguished from those owned by the state." [8] This ruling made it possible for a woman wearing a religious habit to receive a diploma from a Minnesota state teachers college or from the College of Education of the University of Minnesota.

Not many sisters took advantage of this ruling permitting them to graduate from a state college, for by this time the four Catholic women's colleges in the state were accredited to the University of Minnesota and other standardizing agencies and had training schools of their own.

In 1941 some anxiety was aroused when the compulsory school attendance law was changed to require attendance at a school taught by teachers "whose qualifications were essentially equivalent to the minimum standards for public school teaching." [9] But nothing harmful to the Catholic schools came from any interpretation of this law. In 1949 the law requiring a state college diploma or degree was repealed, and degrees from private, accredited colleges were recognized. Henceforth, the qualifications were not set by law but determined by the State Board of Education. Since the work done by the College of St. Benedict was recognized by the University of Minnesota and this college was a member of the North Central Association, the State Board of Education readily granted teaching certificates to its graduates on application. Thus was settled the question of professional qualifications for those staffing the primary and secondary schools of both the public and the private school systems.

During this fifty-year struggle to raise the standards of teaching and to gain control of private schools another problem, already referred to, ran its course. That was the right of teachers to wear the religious garb when teaching in public schools. The difference of opinion in this matter rested on the interpretation of the meaning of the state constitution and could be definitely settled only by the highest court in the state. Minnesota had long acted on the dicta or opinions of the State Attorney but North Dakota definitely settled its problem with a court decision in 1936. In this court case the Benedictine sisters were involved. In 1935 Sister Etheline Heid and three others sisters from St. Benedict's Convent were employed by the school board of Gladstone, North Dakota, in the hope that the sisters could remedy conditions there and bring order into Gladstone public school. One man whose daughter lost her position as teacher when the sisters took charge of the school was greatly incensed. Soon after the opening of school in the fall of 1935 this man had worked up enough sympathy among his townsmen to start opposition to the school board and to the sisters. Claiming to represent a majority of the patrons of the school district of Gladstone, he attempted to put the sisters out of the school and to replace them with lay teachers. He and his followers sent a notice to each sister teacher in the school and to the school board stating "we do hereby warn and inform the board that it is illegal and unlawful to employ as teachers in the public schools of North Dakota any individual wearing or exhibiting any religious garb or uniform, identifying such individual with any religious sect; and that if said school board disregards this warning and notice, proceedings will be forthwith commenced in court enjoining said school board from permitting such individuals to wear any uniform or garb in school identifying such teacher with any religious sect." [10]

No charge was made that sisters were not qualified, for they all had state permits. The pastor, sisters, and the school board ignored the warning, for the sisters — though wearing their religious habit — exhibited no other religious insignia, and there were no laws forbidding Catholics to teach. Under the contention that hiring sisters as teachers was against the North Dakota constitution which declares that no public school shall be under sectarian control and that no money raised for the support of the schools of the state shall be appropriated to or used for the support of any sectarian school, a Mr. Gerhardt then brought action against the school board and against the sisters in the district court of Stark County. The district court rendered a decision in favor of the sisters and the school board, but Mr. Gerhardt appealed to the Supreme Court of North Dakota in the case of Gerhardt et al vs. Heid et al.

The object of the action was to enjoin the school officers from paying the sisters' salaries from the treasury of the school district and to restrain the teachers from wearing the religious habit while teaching. Before this court the plaintiff claimed that the presence of Catholic sisters as teachers changes a public school with a right to public funds into a sectarian school with no such right. To this the Supreme Court countered that the word *sectarian* means *denominational* and when used in the state constitution describes institutions affiliated with a religious sect or under the control or governing influence of a religious denomination whose aims are promotive of interests of that sect. The court also explained that the constitutional phrase "No money shall be appropriated or used for the support of any sectarian school" means that no public money shall be used for schools governed by or under the control of some religious sect.[11] In the court's opinion Gladstone was not *sectarian* within this meaning of the word because the school was neither affiliated with nor governed by a sect or denomination. On the contrary, it was a public school operated under the supervision, direction, and control of the public officers of the state and county, offering courses prescribed by those officers, employing teachers who had received certificates and who taught in compliance with the laws of the state and who were as much subject to the control of the superintendents of the district, county, and state as are other teachers.

The court next disposed of the charge that the school, though not operated by the Catholic Church, was under sectarian control because the sisters were members of a religious order of the Church.

The precise question here was whether a teacher in a public school who is a member of a religious order and wears a distinctive garb of such an order puts the school under sectarian control. To this the court answered in the negative and gave its reasons: first, that the school was subject at all times to the control of the state and county superintendents and not to the order or to the Catholic sect, and second, that the wearing of the religious garb in this case described "does not convert the school into a sectarian school or create sectarian control. . . . Such habit, it is true, proclaimed the wearers were members of a certain denominational organization, but so would the wearing of the emblem of the Christian Endeavor Society or the Epworth League. The laws of the state do not prescribe the fashion of dress of the teachers in our schools." [12]

To the contention that the constitution was violated in cases where the teachers contributed all their earnings beyond their support to the treasury of their order to be used for religious purposes, the court answered that the constitution was not violated, that on the contrary "to prevent anyone from contributing money for the support of some religious body of which she is a member would in itself constitute a denial of the right of religious liberty." To bring weight to this opinion, the court referred to a Pennsylvania case where it was declared that "It is none of our business to inquire into this matter; American men and women of sound mind and 21 years of age, can make such disposition of their surplus earnings as suits their own notions. . . . It would be impertinence in us to inquire." [13] Thus the contention that the school at Gladstone was not a public school because it was taught by Catholic sisters was thoroughly quashed.

This case was anxiously followed not only by St. Benedict's but by many Catholics in Minnesota and the Dakotas and by the various religious congregations which supplied teachers for schools similar to that at Gladstone. The vital point in the dispute was the question of the right of Catholic women to teach in public schools and of the right of Catholic parents to educate their children as they think proper.

After the Supreme Court of North Dakota had handed down its decision, the Benedictine sisters continued to teach in the Gladstone school for some time. Then because of the attitude of some local malcontents, the sisters withdrew in 1948. [14]

In the summer of 1951 Mother Richarda Peters decided to withdraw her sisters from all district schools. Notice was given to the school clerks at Elrosa, Greenwald, Luxemburg, Richmond, and St. Augusta that sisters would be available only for parochial schools. Within a year or so all of these schools became parochial.

Parallel with this struggle about teacher qualifications, the religious garb, and the very existence of the Catholic school system ran another phase of the educational problem. This was a movement to make a greater distinction between the elementary and secondary schools, between secondary schools and colleges, and to give the secondary schools a more practical character. Hitherto academies had been interested in the ornaments of education to the slighting of the more solid subjects. They were "finishing schools for young ladies" in which lady-like accomplishments were stressed. But by 1910 girls' academies had universally established a standard program of sciences and languages. After the opening of the century, St. Benedict's Academy showed evidence in its curriculum of the contemporary educational trends. The "lady-like accomplishments of tapestry, painting, and music" still continued to receive attention; but now more courses of an academic and a scientific nature were injected into the curriculum. The high schools staffed by Benedictines at St. Cloud, Bismarck, and Altoona, Wisconsin, adjusted to the new movement more readily than did St. Benedict's Academy for these were co-educational institutions.[15]

Caught up in the nation's increased interest in secondary education, Catholics began to add high schools to their parish school in 1904. Catholic interest in high schools is evidenced in the pastoral letter which the American hierarchy issued in 1911 and in the amount of time given to that subject in the discussions at the 1918 National Catholic Educational Association meeting. The prosperity immediately following World War I also stimulated and encouraged the movement throughout the United States. But the Diocese of St. Cloud is rural, and the parishes, though numerous, are in villages or small, rural towns, unable to enter the field of secondary education. However, desirous of retaining pupils in the parish school for a year or two after finishing the eighth grade, some pastors added secondary school subjects to the grade school curriculum. This informal lengthening of the elementary course to include one year of secondary school subjects may have been well-motivated but its efficiency was often questioned. Of ten such incomplete high schools staffed by the

Benedictines in 1919 only one, that at Pierz, eventually grew into a well-established institution. Finally through the efforts of Mother Rosamond and of Bishop Busch these incomplete schools were closed during the 1940's.[16]

The heavy mortality of these incomplete high schools and of many small high schools throughout the state was due in part to their inability to graduate students able to meet college entrance requirements and their own difficulties in meeting the standards of accrediting agencies. Colleges had complained about the poor preparation of their freshman students and asked the state to set up an agency to inspect and rate high schools. If the state inspectors approved the work of a school, it was put on the accredited list. Students from these approved schools could then enter normal schools or colleges without entrance examinations. The incomplete and the small high school could not hope to meet the standards and many had to close. As early as 1912 St. Benedict's Academy underwent state inspection by Mr. Albert W. Rankin of the University of Minnesota and was placed on the list of accredited high schools. The other high schools staffed by the Benedictine sisters, St. Mary's in Bismarck, St. Patrick's in Eau Claire, St. Mary's in Altoona, and Cathedral in St. Cloud, were in time also accredited by their respective state agencies.

To meet the rising standards of state accrediting agencies, secondary school teachers had to hold professional certificates issued by the state. At first these were issued on the basis of a written "professional examination" given once a year at the state capitol. Each year a group of sisters had journeyed to St. Paul to fulfill this requirement. To aid them St. Benedict's Convent had been accustomed to hold summer school classes in the subjects in which the sisters were to be examined. Others were assigned several subjects for private study during the year in preparation for the examination. In 1921 these examinations were abolished by the state and in their stead a degree earned by four years of study at a state college or university was required. Fortunately, many of the sisters holding professional certificates had been working toward college degrees at the College of St. Benedict and were prepared for this development. More than two hundred sisters were attending the annual summer sessions at St. Benedict's while some were always able to pursue college studies during the regular sessions.

The College of St. Benedict had been established to answer the needs of the convent in preparing elementary and secondary teachers. As early as 1905 some far-seeing sisters, led by Sister Dominica Borgerding and Sister Adelgundis Bergmann, had proposed the establishment of a college at the mother house. They realized that teaching in parochial schools was to be the chief external work of the sisters. A college on convent grounds would enable the sisters to stay within the Benedictine family while earning their degrees. Mother Cecilia was hesitant about the matter even when the economic and spiritual benefits were shown to her. But Sister Adelgundis was not one to give up easily, and finally Mother Cecilia and her council were won over. With the convent committed to the new project, they began their long-range planning.[17]

Since no Catholic university as yet admitted women students, the sisters chosen to staff the future college were sent to the University of Minnesota for their advanced training. During the summer these sisters together with high school teachers working in some specialized field rented a house on the campus so they could live the conventual life while studying. In 1911 the Catholic University at Washington, D.C., and later some eastern Jesuit universities, opened their doors to sister students; and sisters of St. Benedict's hastened to avail themselves of this privilege. In 1912 Sister Jeanette Roesch and Sister Digna Wieland were sent to do graduate work at the Catholic University. They were soon followed by Sister Adelgundis Bergmann, Sister Magna Wirth, Sister Irma Schumacher, and Sister Grace McDonald. When it became known that the summer of 1914 would bring an extension division of the Sisters College of the Catholic University to Dubuque, Iowa, arrangements were made to enroll a group of sisters there.

While the faculty was being prepared, the new college building, St. Teresa's Hall, was completed and opened for classes in the fall of 1913. The first students registered were sisters, candidates for the order, and a few lay students. Helen McDonald of Eau Claire, Wisconsin, was the first lay student to sign. She was followed by Esther Mueller of St. Joseph, Margaret Grant of Minneapolis, Margaret McKeon of Montgomery, and Josephine Skluzacek of Lonsdale, Minnesota. The old records show that Helen McDonald's program of studies included logic, psychology, geometry, Greek, and history. Margaret Grant registered for history, English, philosophy, Latin, and chemistry. During the first ten years, very crucial years, the classes remained small, but the staff under the guidance of Sister Dominica Borgerding and Sister Adelgundis Bergmann pursued its way through all sorts of trying circumstances. After all, the idea of a Catholic women's college was still novel in the Midwest.

The teaching staff of the college during the first year, 1913–1914, consisted of Reverend Henry Borgerding, O.S.B., Sister Dominica Borgerding, Sister Adelgundis Bergmann, Sister Jeanette Roesch, Sister Irma Schumacher, and Sister Grace McDonald. The following year the staff was the same except that a lay teacher replaced Sister Adelgundis, who left to pursue further graduate work at the Catholic University of America. In 1915 Sister Magna Wirth joined the staff.

Despite the very small student body the administration within two years opened third and fourth year classes. The decision was made because the faculty believed that a two-year offering was an obstacle to growth, for many students refused to enroll in a college in which they could not finish. Accreditment came early for this embryo college; in 1918, within five years after its founding, the University of Minnesota inspected the institution and placed the junior college on its list of accredited junior colleges.[18]

Discipline in a Catholic women's college during the early part of this century was strict. At St. Benedict's, where the college evolved as it did under the same roof as the academy, retaining the same officers and at times the same teachers, it was but natural that the life and the discipline of the college students would differ little from that of academy students. It was some time before such things as "late pers," uncensored mail, and the privilege of receiving calls from young men of St. John's University were taken for granted. School parties, picnics, dramatics, debates, and musicals helped to break the routine. Entertainment of a higher order was provided by the administration, and in its first years the college established the policy of arranging programs by noted speakers and musicians and of bringing the best of artistic talent to its students. During these years such well-known Shakespearian interpreters as Francis O'Donnell and C. E. Griffith made annual appearances, as did Henry Southwick, president of Emerson School of Expression at Boston. Among the musicians were Madame von Unschuld and Rose D'Arina. Professors of the University of Minnesota frequently spoke at student convocations.

The first college degree was issued in June of 1917, but the first group or class to receive the degree of Bachelor of Arts was that of 1918. The affair was memorable not only because it was the first time that a class had finished, but also because of the political excitement which unexpectedly entered into the exercises. That summer Charles A. Lindbergh was running for the office of governor of the state of Minnesota on the Non-Partisan ticket and the campaign was a bitter one because of Mr. Lindbergh's attitude toward the Catholic Church. Two years earlier, on July 5, 1916, presenting a resolution to Congress asking for an investigation of alleged political activity of the Catholic Church in the affairs of the nation, he had declared that the Church of which the Pope is the head was opposed to and sought to destroy the free institutions of the United States and to bring the country under the complete dominance of the Pope. Now in 1918 the Catholic bishops of Minnesota had decided to take concerted action in opposing such a candidate for the office of governor. What occurred at St. Benedict's first college commencement exercises is best told by a local reporter. *The St. Cloud Times* carried the following story of the event.

When Rt. Rev. Bishop Busch arrived at St. Benedict's . . . Thursday evening to attend the Commencement exercises he discovered among the many automobiles lining the front, one having a Non-Partisan streamer: *Lindbergh for Governor*. It filled him with indignation that, on such an occasion, anyone should have the assurance and cheek to park an auto before the Academy [College] with such a placard. He tore it off and bore it into the institution. When the Bishop rose to give the Commencement address he looked perturbed and said: "The Socialists are in Minneapolis and I blush to say that right here in Stearns County there are 2000 members of that party." After an impressive pause, the Bishop produced a great placard, inscribed, *Lindbergh for Governor*, which many recognized as one they had seen earlier in the evening, on an automobile parked before the Academy. With righteous indignation, the Bishop proceeded to lash, figuratively speaking, the man who had placarded his automobile with *Lindbergh for Governor*. . . . He begged the good Sisters of the Academy and all women to throw their whole souls into the prayer: "Lindbergh shall not be Governor." [19]

There was a moment of consternation, but quiet was soon resumed and the degrees were conferred with due solemnity.

The College of St. Benedict located as it is in the quiet of a Minnesota village might have been out of touch with the general current of national and international affairs. However, the student body soon

included young women of various races and from many countries.
A glance at the guest book for one year will show that among the
many guests were such personages as the Lord Abbot Wilfred Up-
son, O.S.B., of Prinknash, England; Reverend Nicholas Maestrini,
the founder of the Catholic Truth Society in Hongkong; and Masie
Ward of England. Others were Arnold Lunn, the English debator
and speaker; Reverend Xavier Thaninayagam of India, who was
on a good relations tour for the government of India; as well as
visitors from Belgium, Bavaria, and all parts of the United States.

When the disturbances of two world wars broke in upon the normal
life of the college, students and faculty cooperated with the government's war efforts. During World War I sisters and students did all
they possibly could in sewing and knitting for soldiers. In World War
II the college was permitted to establish its own Red Cross unit — one
of the first college units to be set up in Minnesota. The output of this
surgical dressing unit doubled that of any other unit of the county.
Faculty and students signed up as blood donors each time the mobile
blood donor unit came to St. Cloud. On one occasion seventy sisters
from the college and the convent responded. Several of the sisters
were so generous that they were enrolled in the gallon club. Some
sisters and students joined in first aid classes; others conducted the
sale of war bonds and stamps.[20]

World War II brought to the college some of the same problems
that it brought to other colleges. On two of these the administration
and the faculty took a conservative stand, unswayed by war hysteria.
Should St. Benedict's follow the lead of the colleges which were
planning to shorten the four-year term by means of long summer
sessions? Should the college stress subjects and courses of a more
practical nature? To the first question Mother Rosamond and the
faculty answered that a great number of students were dependent
on summer employment to help defray the expenses of their college
education. Part-time work the year round would enable students in
large cities to dispense with summer salaries, but such opportunities
were not available in the small village of St. Joseph. To the second
question, should St. Benedict's follow the new trend or keep to the
traditional Benedictine cultural program of the sciences, literature,
and arts and prepare its students not only for earning a salary but for
the richness and beauty of living, there could be but one answer.

From its very beginnings the college (like the academy) had not considered the education of the mind the sole nor the adequate object of education. In the years between the wars, the deepening liturgical formation of the sisters was making itself felt on the campus. So, too, were the pronouncements of Pope Pius XI on education. As a result, even the war years and subsequent pressures have not changed the Christian cultural orientation of the college. In accordance with the teachings of Christ it seeks to elevate and perfect the whole of human life, intellectual, physical, and moral. Each day's work begins with participation in the Sacrifice of the Mass in the Sacred Heart Chapel and ends with the recitation or singing of Compline in English in the respective residence sections. Sunday is solemnized by high Mass and sung Vespers. St. Benedict's has been fortunate that the monks from St. John's serve as chaplains and members of the teaching staff and are available to the students who desire guidance.[21] Each year in the past two decades a group of students have availed themselves of the opportunity to join the League of the Divine Office and so to share more intimately in the formal worship of the Church. Frequently these, and others as well, have become Oblates of St. Benedict. The institute of the oblates is an old association made up of laymen wishing to affiliate themselves spiritually with a monastery in order to share in the spiritual life and work of the monks. Though living in the world they endeavor to mold their lives according to the ideals of St. Benedict. Under the direction and inspiration of Sister Alfreda Zierden, a group of students were prepared to become oblates and on June 3, 1935, the abbot of St. John's Abbey admitted them into the Institute of Benedictine Oblates and two years later received their profession. The Sodality of the Blessed Virgin Mary is also active on the campus. The liturgical spirit of the student body is such that the editor of *Worship* wrote in January, 1957, "There is to our knowledge no other college in the country in which the daily living of the liturgy forms a more formative part in the students' education."

Inspired by the liturgical and Christian social movement directed from St. John's, St. Benedict's during the 1930's advanced in the work of applying Christian social principles to modern problems. The two institutions invited leaders in the various Catholic social fields to speak to faculty and students. Among those who came were Monsignor Luigi Ligutti of the National Catholic Rural Life Conference along with Ralph Borsodi, advocate of family living; Peter

Maurin and Dorothy Day, founder of the Catholic Worker movement; Joan Overboss of the Grail movement; and the artists,
Graham Carey and Ade Bethune. Others who came were Barbara
Ward, secretary of the Sword of the Spirit group, and Baroness de
Hueck, of Friendship House for Negroes in New York. On one visit
the Baroness declared to a news reporter: "When I come to St. Benedict's, I come to a place I love. St. Benedict's has sent me two of my
finest helpers in the persons of Betty Schneider and Josephine
Zehnle." This attempt to unite the liturgy with the Church's social
doctrine took fire. It not only affected the lives of the individual
student but brought the college into harmony with the liturgical
apostolate fostered at St. John's in the 1930's.

One very apparent result of this liturgical-social thought was the
change in character of student personnel. During the first fifteen
years of the college's existence the student body was made up mainly
of young women from Minnesota and the Dakotas with an occasional
student from Canada, Montana, and Nebraska. But during the
1930's the college took on a more cosmopolitan character. In 1930
Lucy Chung and Florence Chi of Peking were enrolled, and since
that date students from the Far East have continued to be registered
at St. Benedict's. During the same decade students from Mexico,
Puerto Rico, and Russia applied. Small though the student body is,
it has the international and interracial character of the Church itself.
The feeling of camaraderie is such that at the traditional St. Patrick's
day basketball game, for instance, it is not uncommon to see a Negro
student lined up with the Irish green and a student from Puerto Rico
with the German blue. To date, students from thirteen states of the
Union, from Canada, Russia, Germany, France, Haiti, China, Japan,
Korea, Formosa, the Bahama Islands, Puerto Rico, Mexico, Colom-
bia, and Guatemala have enrolled at the college.

These developments were taking place despite the pressures
inherent in the effort to conform to the pattern of state education.
Looking for full accreditment and recognition it had been natural
to turn to the University of Minnesota and to the State Department
of Education rather than to regional or national agencies. As a
result, the college had in some things patterned itself on the University. Like the University, St. Benedict's divided the school year into
quarter terms instead of semesters. The sequences of studies often
followed that of the University. To be assured of state approval,

most of the faculty continued to attend the University of Minnesota and received advanced degrees from it. Full accreditment of the senior college to the University of Minnesota came more slowly than had recognition of the junior college. The reason was that after 1918 it became the policy of the University to accredit but a few departments at a time instead of accrediting a college as a whole. This policy prolonged the suspense and uncertainty of the standing of the college in the educational system of the state. Besides, the sisters began to see the possibility of developing the more distinctly Christian character of the college by looking beyond the state university for educational advisement and leadership. With the appointment of Sister Claire Lynch as dean in 1932 the college entered on a new program — that of throwing off its dependence on one local accrediting agency and of seeking membership in the North Central Association of Colleges. Some of the faculty feared that such a powerful organization might exert undue influence in Catholic institutions. But neither the president of the college, Mother Rosamond Pratschner, nor the dean, Sister Claire, was of that mind. Under their guidance the college applied for membership in the North Central Association in 1932 and was admitted within a year. With this step taken, administration and faculty worked to bring the program of studies back to a more traditional Catholic liberal arts pattern with philosophy as a central discipline. The departments of studies were reorganized and grouped into eight divisions. Because of pressure from the University of Minnesota inspectors, philosophy as a distinct department had been dropped and only a few courses had been offered. In 1937 the department was not only reinstated but ten quarter hours of philosophy were required of all students. Today the requirement is sixteen semester credits for both the Bachelor of Arts and the Bachelor of Science degrees.

Another indication of the general change in policy was evident in the choice of graduate school to which future college teachers were sent for training. Hitherto many of these had been sent to the University of Minnesota but during the 1930's and the following decade they were more likely to be sent to Catholic universities or to other universities in which a desired department was outstanding.[22] This policy has been maintained by Mother Richarda Peters and by the college deans who have succeeded Sister Claire Lynch — Sister Incarnata Girgen and Sister Enid Smith.

The college at present is affiliated with the Catholic University of America and is a member of the National Catholic Educational Association, the National Commission on Accrediting, the Association of Minnesota Colleges, and the State Council of Minnesota Colleges. At the time application for membership in the North Central Association was made the College Advisory Board was formed at St. Benedict's. The laymen who generously consented to give time and counsel to the college were: Mr. Frank Gross, president of the German National Bank of Minneapolis; Mr. Edward Callahan, an attorney in Minneapolis; Mr. Frank Mulcahy of the Northwestern Mortgage Company in Minneapolis; and Mr. Joseph Matt, publisher of *The Wanderer* in St. Paul. St. Benedict's is also a member of the Minnesota College Fund Association which, together with thirty-eight similar organizations of the country, is presenting the needs of the small liberal arts college to businessmen of the nation. So, as a college president, Mother Richarda found herself in the autumn of 1956 in offices of Minnesota businessmen reminding them of what industry owes to the kind of college she represented.

Many of the student organizations date back to the early days of the college. The Ardeleons, a dramatic club, carries on the work begun by Sister Dominica Borgerding and Sister Marcine Schirber. Since 1952, Ardeleons of St. Benedict's and the Johnny Players of St. John's have collaborated in such plays as Christopher Fry's *The Lady's not for Burning*, Moliere's *The Miser*, Claudel's *The Tidings Brought to Mary*, as well as in several by Shakespeare. Each school has its own schedule and is responsible for plays on its own stage. The Choral Club is another organization dating from the foundation of the college. *Our Lady's Juggler* presented in 1953 on the stage at St. John's was the first of the annual operas in which musicians of St. Benedict's and St. John's collaborated. The International Relations Club introduced in the early 1930's at the invitation of the Carnegie Peace Foundation continues to draw the more politically minded students. The Sigma Kappa Phi gives members of the home economics department opportunities for experiences not possible in the classroom. On March 29, 1940, St. Benedict's established the Omega Chapter of Delta Epsilon Sigma, a national scholastic honor society for students of Catholic colleges and universities, founded in 1939 in Washington, D.C. The National Federation of Catholic College Students and the National Student Association are strong organizations tying the student body at St. Benedict's in with the students of other colleges in the nation.

Campus publications include *The Benet,* the *Facula,* and *St. Benedict's Quarterly*, the literary magazine which has evolved from *College Days,* its 1914 predecessor. Faculty members have found time to publish books and to write articles for scholarly publications in the fields of English, history, sociology, and Latin. Others have won research grants or scholarships.[23] The pageant, *So Let Your Light Shine,* is presented at the close of freshman orientation week. Each year since 1935 every one at St. Benedict's — students and faculty, sisters old and young, men employed in the various maintenance departments — have worked together during the first week of school so that on the evening of her second Sunday in residence, the freshman may be inducted into her college and the Benedictine heritage of culture. This induction, symbolized by the presentation of the academic cap and gown and a flaming torch, is the climax of an outdoor spectacle which by means of choral reading, interpretive dancing, and dramatization depicts the continuity of Benedictine influence through fourteen centuries and shows the freshman her own role. By receiving the torch, she accepts the responsibility of handing it to those who come after her.

In 1938 St. Benedict's opened its doors to the first Negro students who applied for admission. During that summer, Betty Schneider and Josephine Zehnle had decided to see for themselves what Friendship House was like. Thus they met two young Negro women, Kathleen Yanes and Gertrude Danavall, ready and eager to attend college. Remembering all they had learned of Christian sociology, Betty and Josephine knew there was only one place for their new friends, St. Benedict's.

Two recent developments at the College of St. Benedict have extended its influence. One was the establishment of a Department of Elementary Education. The regular curriculum leading to the bachelor's degree was conceded to be adequate training for teaching at the high school level. But it did not satisfy the needs or requirements for teachers of elementary schools. When the Minnesota Department of Education announced that in 1960 it would require all elementary teachers to have a bachelor's degree in order to obtain a teacher's certificate, St. Benedict's decided to offer its students the opportunity of earning a degree with a major sequence in elementary education.

By setting up a program that leads to a Bachelor of Arts degree and stressing the principles of teaching as well as the techniques of teaching, the college is able to give the students a liberal education while providing professional training.

The other and most recent expansion of college instructional activities occurred in 1955. In cooperation with St. John's University at Collegeville the college initiated an adult education program to comply with requests received for evening classes and to fulfill a long-standing wish of the local ordinary, Bishop Peter Bartholome. Through a registration form published in the *St. Cloud Register* a pre-registration was taken on twelve courses with the understanding that the courses receiving the highest number of registrations would be offered. Theology for laymen, American Church history, music appreciation, social ethics, children's literature, art expression, and speech fundamentals were the courses selected. The first classes met on January 10, 1955, at the Cathedral High School in St. Cloud. Courses were open on a credit basis to any registrant who had graduated from a high school and who wished to register for college credit.

The loyalty of former students is reflected in their desire to form an alumnae association. In 1919 the St. Benedict's Student Association was formed and held its first meeting under the leadership of Irene Beresford O'Neill, Claire Frances Prinz, and Rose Broker. The nucleus of the new organization was not large but it was a loyal one. Plans were made to have annual meetings and to have nongraduates as well as graduates for members. In 1936 the constitution was rewritten and the name of the organization changed to St. Benedict's Alumnae Association. In 1955 the title was again changed — this time to the more specific one of Alumnae Association of the College of St. Benedict. Chapters of the association were formed as early as 1921. Today such groups are found scattered from Washington, D.C. and New York to California. Nowhere is there a more loyal body of alumnae than those who recognize St. Benedict's as their Alma Mater. The annual homecoming week end always finds a large number of "old girls" in brief residence, happy to be with their former teachers once more.[24] Since 1936 the Alumnae Association has had its own publication, *The Handshake*. In 1941 the name was changed to *The Benet*. The paper serves not only as a bond among the alumnae themselves, but between them and the college so that the school's ideals will continue to inspire them. The annual home-coming serves the same purpose.

Among the women who received their education at the College of St. Benedict some have gained national renown or local recognition because of wholehearted dedication to professional careers, but most alumnae are serving God and neighbor in relative anonymity. Many religious communities, contemplative as well as active, have among their members sisters who were trained at St. Benedict's. In hundreds of civic communities, solidly Christian families stand as a bulwark for the Church and the state because splendid women have estab-lished homes inspired by Benedictine ideals.

During the first fifty years of St. Benedict's educational work in Minnesota the major objective was the staffing of elementary schools. It was a period in which the foundations for the Catholic school system were laid. The next fifty years was a period of advancement to the collegiate level and a further spread and perfection of the elementary and secondary Catholic schools. In 1947, the ninetieth anniversary of the Benedictines' arrival in Minnesota, the sisters were staffing seventy-four parish elementary schools and six sec-ondary schools. Sixty-one of these were in Minnesota, six in North Dakota, three in Washington, three in Wisconsin, and one in Mon-tana. The great army of Benedictine sisters conducting these schools had developed from the original band of four teachers who came to the West in 1857. The members who followed in their footsteps have never wavered from the purpose which called the Benedictine sisters into this diocese.

His Excellency, Bishop Peter Bartholome of St. Cloud, on Pro-fession Day, July 11, 1953, expressed his appreciation of the educational work of Catholic sisters. He told the parents and friends present at the ceremony:

The Bishop is charged with the great duty of "feeding the flock" of Christ. This duty is laid on him on the day of his consecration and it is, of course, very evident that he cannot carry that out through his own effort; thus Christ through the Church established centuries ago an institution to aid the bishop in carrying on the great ministry of teaching all nations. These young women here today have decided to give their services to Christ, most of them for the sole purpose of aiding their bishop to plant the truths of Christ in the minds of youth and children, to aid the parents in carrying on the great traditions of the Faith. These sisters play a devoted part in implanting the truths of Christ in generations of youth. These women are contributing a service that you and I can never begin to evaluate. We can admire them; we can express our gratitude. But all this is only a weak expression of the greatness of the sacrifice made by the sister who manifests her love for God and fellow man.[25]

16 THE LITURGICAL MOVEMENT

Building, expansion, and the work of staffing parochial and public schools through the years 1900 to 1957 absorbed much of the time and energies of the sisters. But the seeking of God to which the sisters were dedicated retained first place in the community. Fortunately, the office of prioress was given in 1919 to Sister Louisa Walz, a woman with a motherly heart and prayerful disposition. Under her guidance from 1919 to 1937 the sisters experienced a spiritual quickening and strengthening of the bond of unity among themselves in the perfecting of liturgical worship and in the enforcement of canonical rules.

No better way could be found to bring about this unity of Benedictine family spirit than in wiping out language differences, and Mother Louisa soon declared that the German language was no longer to be used when reciting prayers in common. Neither were books in that language to be read aloud in the refectory. She further declared that the retreat preceding the reception of the habit and the taking of perpetual vows would be an "English retreat." At this time all the sisters in the convent understood English, but there were many who were unacquainted with German.[1] Likewise, Mother Louisa dropped the quaint old German custom of inserting the title of the mystery between the two halves of the Ave Maria when reciting the Rosary.

The second step in her endeavor to strengthen the spirit of the house was the enforcement of canon law as it applied to the novitiate. Until 1917 novices went to all parts of the buildings in performance of duties. It was not unusual for some classes in the high school department or elementary department to be assigned to novices who had come to the community with teaching experience. Strict enclosure of the novices was now enforced.

Mother Louisa was also successful in bringing her community into the liturgical movement which was making itself felt in the United States in the 1920's — the movement which had as its purpose to make the public official prayer of the Church the center of the lives of the people and to unite all in the same act of worship at Mass or in the recitation of the Divine Office. Undoubtedly the most outstanding achievement, liturgically speaking, of Mother Louisa's administration was the return to the recitation of the Divine Office in place of the Little Office of the Blessed Virgin.

The particular Benedictine work of the *Opus Dei* had been dutifully performed until the year 1866 when, on the petition of Abbot Wimmer, the Holy See had dispensed the American Benedictine convents from reciting the Divine Office on ferial days. In 1881 at Mother Scholastica's suggestion, and with Bishop Seidenbusch's permission, the Divine Office had been dropped entirely. The inevitable result was that in the course of time innumerable devotions and prayers, non-liturgical in nature, were adopted and added to the Little Office. In time they became more of a burden to the overworked teachers and nurses than the Divine Office had ever been. The love of the *Opus Dei* had never died out in the community for down through the years many of the older members lamented and regretted that they could not join the Church in its official prayer. One of them, Sister Gertrude Flynn, treasured her set of breviaries to the time of her death in the hope that the Divine Office would again be resumed. She often declared, "We are not Benedictines for we do not say the *Breviarium Monasticum.*"

The liturgical spirit infused in the Church in the United States in the 1920's helped to turn the sisters' attention again to this Benedictine form of community worship. But the immediate incentive for the readoption was that the Divine Office seemed to be one of the requirements for the convent's becoming a pontifical institute or for joining a congregation. In 1918 when St. Benedict's took steps to join the proposed Congregation of St. Scholastica, it was realized that the monastic office was the Benedictine ideal and as such was to be restored by Benedictine houses wherever possible. Four years later when the constitutions of the Congregation of St. Scholastica were approved by Rome, Mother Louisa Walz and her advisors decided that whether St. Benedict's joined that congregation or formed a new union, the *Opus Dei* would have to be restored. Immediately they set about making inquiries at various Benedictine convents and monasteries about customs, books, instructors, and ritual. By November of the year 1925 they were deep in negotiations with a Belgian firm about bindings and the cost of printing breviaries for one thousand sisters.

The project caused much discussion. There were some sisters, busy teachers and nurses, who felt that the Office would be a burden beyond their strength. There were others who felt the task to be beyond their intellectual abilities. Finally Abbot Alcuin Deutsch of St. John's Abbey was asked to address the sisters on the subject. He convinced them that the Divine Office need not become an added burden. He suggested that all of the non-liturgical prayers and devotions be dropped; that the time for formal meditation and for spiritual reading in common be greatly shortened; that the night prayers in common be discontinued because Compline was the Church's night prayer. These changes would not only give more time for the *Opus Dei* but would be more in conformity with the mind of the Church and with Benedictine tradition. He assured the sisters that the official prayer of the Church would be for them a bond of union and strength. With their fears thus dissipated the sisters in chapter on March 31, 1926, readily agreed to adopt the Divine Office. In a few weeks the order for one thousand sets of the *Breviarium Monasticum* was sent to Belgium.[2]

No doubt few of the sisters had any idea of the work and study the adoption of the Divine Office would entail if it were to be recited properly in a manner befitting an act of praise to God. Few realized that a year or more would be spent in training and study before the three nocturns of Matins could be prayed. Abbot Alcuin graciously gave instructions of a general nature to the sisters. The chaplain, Father Henry Borgerding, O.S.B., held evening class on the rubrics. Several times a week, Sister Albertine Kacher and Sister Urban Gertken, the choir mistress, drilled pronunciation and pitch with all of the sisters, young and old. Because the sisters were accustomed to

praying the Office of the Dead with the Church on November 2, All
Souls' Day, and in private at the death of a sister, it was decided that
the community could use the new breviaries in choir for the first time
on the afternoon of November 1, 1926, for the recitation of Vespers
for the following day. At last on Christmas morning in 1926 the
regular Office was said for the first time when the hours of Prime,
Terce, Sext, and None were prayed. It was a happy day and the
sisters felt they had recaptured something of the old Benedictine
spirit of divine praise. Vespers and Compline were prayed for the
first time on the feast of St. Scholastica, February 10, 1927, and after
a period of strenuous practice Lauds were chanted on Easter. The
time between Easter and Christmas was spent in the study of the
psalms and lessons and in the rubrics of Matins. Two more years
passed before the community was able to pray the Office for all
days of the year—ferial and feast—in a worthy manner.[3]

Today, after thirty years of devotion to the public recitation of
the Divine Office, the community at St. Benedict's realizes with
gratitude what a privilege it is to join Christ in the praying Church
throughout the world in His praise of the Father. During these years
the sisters have given much time to perfecting themselves in the
rubrics and in the chanting. Through study and meditative reading
they have deepened their understanding of the meaning and of the
spirit of the Divine Office. In recent years there has been a marked
trend toward greater solemnity in this public worship. Since 1950
the final anthem of the Blessed Virgin Mary is sung daily, and since
the Marian Year of 1954 the Magnificat is daily chanted on appropriate psalm tones instead of on one note. On feast days the greater
portion of the Office is sung. After various experiments to bring the
canonical hours as close as possible to the time for which they were
designed as well as to make it possible for the sisters to perform their
apostolic works efficiently, this is the schedule that is now being
followed at the mother house: the sisters rise in time to chant Lauds
and Prime before the holy Mass which is followed by Terce. Sext and
None precede dinner; Vespers and Compline precede supper. Matins
are prayed at 7:15 in the evening.

In line with the liturgical movement, opportunity for corporate
worship was provided for all at St. Benedict's by the introduction
of the *Missa Recitata* and the restoration of Gregorian chant. In 1925
Dom Ermin Vitry of Maredsous Abbey gave a course of instruction
in ecclesiastical music. On other occasions Father Gregory Huegle,

O.S.B., of Conception, Missouri, and Dom Adrian Eudine, O.S.B., originally from Solesmes, France, worked with the sisters to perfect their rendition of the Mass chant and the Divine Office. Sister Urban Gertken was appointed director of the convent choir. She also trained sisters to take charge of parish choirs. The *Missa Recitata* was introduced on February 4, 1931.

The Sacred Heart Chapel has provided a dignified setting for liturgical worship which has been enhanced by the beautiful vestments that sisters trained by Sister Justina Knapp have designed and made. The influence of the liturgical movement itself has been strong in the vestment department at St. Benedict's and from it has spread to many parishes and Catholic institutions.

Immersed in this movement of common prayer by all for all, the sisters saw ever more clearly the meaning of the doctrine of the Mystical Body of Christ, binding all men of every race together in a brotherly covenant with Christ. When the sisters doing mission work in the Orient in 1947 presented two young Chinese women for entrance to St. Benedict's Convent, they were readily accepted. Two years later a Negro student attending the college applied for the habit; she too was accepted without hesitation. Since that time six Chinese, four Japanese, and three Puerto Ricans, together with two young women from Haiti, have become members. St. Benedict's, though a pioneer in this interracial movement, was doing nothing more than putting into practice the doctrine of the Mystical Body. And still it was not something entirely new at St. Benedict's, for as early as 1894, an Indian girl of the Chippewa tribe had been admitted and given the name of Sister Marciana.

Though the spiritual life of the sisters was Mother Louisa's chief care, the souls of others were likewise to benefit by her zeal. Her influence reached out to Catholic lay women. On August 28, 1920, she opened the college and chapel to 138 women who wanted to spend a few days in contemplation and prayer under the guidance of a priest. This marked the beginning of the laywomen's retreat movement in Minnesota. The Reverend Clement Theunte, O.P., the master of the retreat, had for fifteen years conducted missions from Philadelphia to Honolulu and from British Columbia to San Diego. As he himself wrote years later, "I went about for thirty years as a preaching friar never stopping more than four weeks in any place." [5] Such work never gave him opportunity to learn the good he was accomplishing but his work in another field did leave a tangible record. This was his work in aiding Rose Hawthorne Lathrop in the formation of the Dominican Congregation of Servants of Relief for Incurable Cancer. This man of great experience in directing souls and of great discernment was the priest chosen to start the laywomen's retreat movement in Minnesota. The following twenty-four years saw ever-increasing numbers attending these retreats until in the summer of 1944 the number was so large that St. Benedict's could not accommodate all applicants. Plans were then made to conduct two retreats during the summer of 1945, but war transportation regulations put a stop to many meetings with the result that for the first time in twenty-five years no laywomen's retreat was held at St. Benedict's. After the war, the work was again resumed. As the retreat movement grew, other convents and schools opened their doors to the lay retreatants but St. Benedict's still has to turn away fifty or more applicants each summer.

Another field of apostolic work entered by Mother Louisa and her community in the decades of the 1920's and 30's was that of religious vacation schools and release-time classes for children not attending Catholic schools. Long before the opening of the century the Benedictine sisters in parochial work were accustomed on Saturdays and Sundays to prepare for first Holy Communion and confirmation those children of the parish unable to attend the parochial school. Not content with instructing these children of their own parishes, the sisters began as early as 1905 to travel each Saturday to an outlying parish which had no parochial school. There they held classes for half a day to prepare the children for first Holy Communion and confirmation. Such, for example, was the religious instruction given by the sisters in Mandan, North Dakota, in the year 1910. These sisters traveled from Bismarck to Mandan by train, or wagon and ferry, and sacrificed their much-needed free day for this good work. This week end type of religious school was antecedent to the vacation religion schools and release-time classes.

Many parishes were too far from a convent to call in the aid of sisters each Saturday. Moreover, many of the pastors who were fortunate enough to have Saturday classes realized that a brief Saturday instruction was not sufficient for an intelligent faith and for strong Catholic living. A few priests began to seek means whereby the children could have longer periods of instruction and contact with the religion teacher and decided that a regular school with all-day sessions for a period of two weeks would better answer their needs. They found a pattern in the summer religion schools success-fully conducted by the Lutherans in Minnesota and Wisconsin.

As early as 1904 two priests in Kansas had organized summer religion schools taught by themselves or by seminarians. But these were isolated instances. In Minnesota in 1912 seminarians of the Duluth diocese spent their vacation days in conducting three-week vacation schools patterned on the Lutheran type common in Minnesota. In Oregon in 1921, Father Edwin V. O'Hara experimented with four such schools with great success. But in 1919 the Benedictine sisters were already teaching such classes in Minnesota. Such, for example, were the instructions given by Sister Miriam Stoick and Sister Consilia Nesges at Clear Lake in the summer of that year when 80 children were enrolled. Classes were held until 3:30 in the afternoon and the remainder of the day was spent in visiting the parishioners in their homes. For good will and better understanding among the townspeople the pastor asked the sisters to visit the non-Catholic homes as well. However, this system of vacation school did not come to general notice until the 1921 meeting of the National Catholic Educational Association at which Father O'Hara told of his catechetical work in Oregon and publicized the need of vacation schools by his report that 10,000 Catholic parishes and missions in the United States had no parochial schools and therefore thousands of children received little or no religious instruction. Two years later at the meeting of the National Catholic Rural Life Conference in St. Louis, as director of the conference he gave the vacation school plan greater publicity and captured the interest of a number of bishops. Since the object of the conference was to strengthen and develop Catholicity in the rural districts, this organization readily accepted the promotion of Father O'Hara's vacation school plan as part of its program. From this meeting the Archdiocese of St. Louis took fire, as did the Archdiocese of Milwaukee, and the movement spread throughout the nation while it took on the organized form it has today. In the Archdiocese of Milwaukee the superintendent of schools made vacation schools the rule for rural parishes and thus initiated the trend toward bringing these schools under the supervision of the diocesan superintendent of schools. When Father O'Hara was consecrated bishop of the Diocese of Great Falls, Montana, in 1930, he continued his crusade with greater fervor and brought the Confraternity of Christian Doctrine to take over the responsibility of the religious vacation school system.[6]

THE LITURGICAL MOVEMENT

The plan was to staff these vacation schools with sisters who would conduct classes for a couple of weeks in outlying parishes. But for some time most of the instruction had to be given by Catholic laity and seminarians, for the sisters of the country were slow to go into the work on a large scale. This was not because of lack of zeal but due to the fact that there were no convents in those parishes, and the sisters had to reside in private homes, schoolhouses, or rectories. Living outside of convent walls was foreign to the sisters, and in many cases was forbidden by their constitutions or rule.

It was not until the meeting of the National Catholic Rural Life Conference and Confraternity of Christian Doctrine in St. Paul in 1934 that the dioceses of Minnesota and North Dakota went into the work on a large scale and established vacation schools on a diocesan basis. As a result the Benedictines at St. Joseph took up the work on an enlarged and official scale, sending sisters into the Archdiocese of St. Paul, the dioceses of Superior and LaCrosse, and to the far West. While attending this 1934 conference in St. Paul, Bishop O'Hara became acquainted with the Benedictines' earlier work in vacation schools in Minnesota and Dakota and asked for fifty Benedictine teachers for his territory in Montana. The invitation was favorably received, because the sisters were convinced of the importance of this apostolic work, but the full number could not be spared. One after another in rapid succession, other dioceses organized vacation schools, and requests for sisters to staff these schools came in steadily increasing numbers. In the following summer, 1935, the sisters conducted forty-five vacation schools. Seven of these schools were in the Archdiocese of St. Paul, nine in the Diocese of Bismarck, two in Seattle, six in Great Falls, five in Superior, ten in La Crosse, three in Fargo, and three in the home Diocese of St. Cloud. Eleven years later under Mother Rosamond Pratschner's careful guidance the number of these catechetical schools conducted by her sisters increased to sixty-nine in which 3,551 public school children were instructed in the truths of their faith. From the beginning of the movement till the present day St. Benedict's Convent has given its full cooperation to this work.

Work of a slightly different nature because of language differences was undertaken in 1940 among the children of the Mexican migrant sugar beet workers in the Fargo and Crookston dioceses. The headquarters were at Moorhead, Minnesota, and Grafton, North Dakota. Each day during the months of July and August, 1942, the children from Oakwood, Minto, St. Thomas, and Drayton were brought to the Grafton center. The Mexican children near Moorhead were cared for at the parish school in Moorhead, and the sisters lived in the nearby convent.[7] The following year the children were gathered at Wild Rice under the care of Sister Jeanette Roesch and Sister Jean Smisek. These Mexican vacation schools were staffed by three shifts of sisters, so planned that no sister taught more than three weeks.

While these vacation religion schools were proving their usefulness, more attention was also turned to those children who for one reason or another did not or could not attend the parochial school in their town. In the decades of the 1930's and 40's the "release time" classes were inaugurated. For this work a priest or a sister would be especially assigned to teach religion to pupils who were released from classes at the public school. But in places where no convent was established a pastor at times asked for two or three sisters to come and establish themselves in his parish for the school year to teach religion to all Catholic children during their "release time." Such a school was opened at Litchfield in 1935 and at Farmington in 1938.

Most of this work was done without any plan of distributing the burden of the sisters' summer assignments, of relieving those whose health required rest, or of giving an opportunity to others to advance professionally. Some of this lack of planning was due to the fact that pastors could and did apply to local superiors or to the mother house for teachers at almost any time. Some pastors waited until the eleventh hour with a consequent confusion and change in assignment of teachers. Order was in time achieved when Bishop Busch asked the pastors to fill out an application form which would be sent to the mother house through the Chancery Office.

Among the benefits brought to the parishes conducting vacation schools have been the return to the faith of lapsed Catholics, the validation of marriages, the conversion of non-Catholics, an increase of the number receiving the sacraments, and the formation of a more enlightened generation of Catholics. In some instances the whole parish was transformed as the result of one or two weeks of religious teaching. Only recently have the sisters been required to send in reports of their vacation work to the mother house. Even if statistics had been kept one would not have the whole picture, for some of the important effects are of a nature which escape figures.

The same is true of the work done in the regular parochial schools.

THE LITURGICAL MOVEMENT

While Mother Louisa gave a great deal of attention to the liturgy and to religious vacation schools, she did not slight the parochial schools, and she repeated the success of her predecessors in staffing new schools. New missions were opened at Breckenridge, Effington, Greenwald, Little Falls, New Richmond, Onamia, Minneapolis, Robbinsdale, Sauk Rapids, and Waite Park in Minnesota; at Dickinson, North Dakota; at Tacoma, Washington; and at Mauston and Richland Center, Wisconsin. These schools brought 2,607 more pupils under the care of the Benedictines. This additional work the community was able to undertake only because its membership had increased to 1,069 sisters during this period of 1919 to 1939. The recitation of the Divine Office and the community's full participation in the liturgical movement had already brought their rewards to St. Benedict's.

Further deepening of the spiritual life of the sisters came as the result of an event that occurred in 1950 — an event which tended to bring back to the community something of the early Benedictine ideals of religious life. In that year Pope Pius XII issued an indult which made it possible for the sisters in North American Benedictine convents to be consecrated in the ancient rite of the Consecration of Virgins. This rite is one of the sacramentals of the Church. It is solemn re-consecration of a virgin and the acceptance of her by the Church as a bride of Christ. While "religious profession is the complete giving up of one's self to God through vows of poverty, chastity, and obedience, consecration consists in receiving through the Church a blessing or spiritual power that places the recipient in a higher rank with corresponding obligations to foster greater innocence of life." [8]

The ceremony is one of the most ancient rites of the Church. Though always kept in some Benedictine houses, the ceremony fell into disuse during the late Middle Ages and for centuries this privilege has been reserved to only a few orders of strictly enclosed nuns and those of solemn vows. During the twentieth century the custom was revived to some extent in Europe. The movement was slower in the United States because the American Benedictine sisters do not have strict enclosure nor do they pronounce solemn vows. But a number of American Benedictine convents had long desired a revival of the rite. During their Holy Year pilgrimage to Rome, the Benedictine prioresses discussed with the abbot primate, the Most Reverend Bernard Kaelin, the possibility of gaining the privilege of consecration for Benedictine sisters in the United States. Pope Pius XII on October 24, 1950, most graciously granted the indult for the use of this rite without the obligation of solemn vows and papal enclosure. Shortly after this, however, the promulgation of *Sponsa Christi*, a papal directive to contemplative nuns, caused some anxiety. Would this later document abrogate the indult so recently given? Monsignor Larraona, Secretary of the Sacred Congregation of Religious, relieved this anxiety on September 24, 1952, when he declared that because the indult was a privilege, it was not abrogated by *Sponsa Christi*.[9]

The Convent of Perpetual Adoration in Clyde, Missouri, was the first to make use of the privilege and admitted the first group of sisters to Consecration on November 16, 1952. On December 27, 1954, Bishop Bartholome consecrated the first group at St. Benedict's Convent. A year later the same rite was performed at St. Paul's Priory and at St. Bede's Priory. The efforts of Mother Louisa Walz and Mother Rosamond Pratschner in encouraging the sisters to make their praying of the Divine Office ever more worthy were climaxed by Mother Richarda Peters' introduction of the rite of Consecration, a vital means of deepening and intensifying the religious life at St. Benedict's.

17 THE CONGREGATION OF ST. BENEDICT

A Benedictine congregation of papal or pontifical jurisdiction is a union of autonomous Benedictine communities erected and approved by the authority of the Holy See. St. Benedict had fashioned a system which made each monastery a family group in which the superior was the authority around which the religious family centered. For centuries each monastery was a separate entity. A change came in this system at the beginning of the thirteenth century when the Fourth Lateran Council decreed that a provincial or national chap-

ter of monks should meet "every three years where regular observance and like questions should be discussed." In time, through a
gradual application of this Lateran system to the Benedictine monasteries, a congregation of independent houses was formed. Such
were the two congregations of Benedictine monks — the American
Cassinese and the Swiss-American. For it was only in monasteries
of men that this idea was operative.

During the nineteenth century the Holy See had allowed the
establishment of convents by bishops of the United States but always
preferred that convents apply to Rome for erection and recognition.
The Holy See held that a religious institute of diocesan jurisdiction
had not reached its final or complete state until approved by Rome
and thereby brought under papal jurisdiction. The plan to gain
Rome's approval for the American Benedictine convents and to
make them members of the American Cassinese Congregation had
been proposed unsuccessfully by Abbot Wimmer in 1858. Later he
(1867) and Bishop Fink (1880) had proposed the formation of a
congregation of convents under its own president. During the twentieth century the question of papal approval continued to occupy the
attention of St. Benedict's Convent and the other Benedictine institutes in the United States.

At the head of the congregation is a mother president who admin-
isters the affairs of the entire congregation, convokes the general
chapter, and visits individual priories. The chief work of the general
chapter, which is made up of the prioresses and a delegate from each
priory, consists in deciding on common undertakings, in promoting
religious spirit, and in determining what seems necessary to maintain
discipline.

In 1905 the Holy See urged all Benedictine religious houses in
the United States to seek papal approval. The necessity for such
approval became more apparent as time went on. The customs and
constitutions of the Benedictine convents of the country varied greatly from diocese to diocese, these variations having been brought
about at times from pressure of diocesan needs. With the changing
views of successive bishops there was a danger to the normal and
common development according to the spirit of the Holy Rule and
the traditions of the order. The rapid succession of superiors elected
for terms of office within the convent also brought with it the danger

THE MOST REVEREND PETER W.
BARTHOLOME, D.D., BISHOP OF ST. CLOUD.

MOTHER ROSAMOND PRATSCHNER,
FIRST PRESIDENT OF THE CON-
GREGATION.

MOTHER RICHARDA PETERS, PRES-
IDENT OF ST. BENEDICT'S CON-
GREGATION IN 1957.

JUBILARIANS OF 1922. STANDING: DIAMOND JUBILARIAN SISTER GER-
TRUDE FLYNN, GOLDEN JUBILARIANS SISTERS BONIFACE TUMMINS AND
PHILOMENE KETTEN. SEATED: SISTER IDA ASCHENBRENNER, MOTHER
ALOYSIA BATH, AND SISTER EBBA SCHIFFRER.

OUR 90-YEAR-OLD SISTERS ATTEND DIVINE OFFICE.

GRADUATE NURSES, 1911.

SISTER BENEDICT KLEIN, SUPERIOR OF ST. JOSEPH'S CHILDREN'S HOME IN THE 1880's.

SISTER JULIANA VENNE AND THE ORPHANS OF ST. JOSEPH HOME, 1879.

BENEDICTINE SUPERIORS MEET IN 1917 TO FORM THE CONGREGATION OF ST. SCHOLASTICA.

ST. RAPHAEL'S HOSPITAL, 1905. THE FIRST HOSPITAL IN
ST. CLOUD, 1886, IS SHOWN AT EXTREME
RIGHT OF THE PICTURE.

THE SECOND HOSPITAL BUILDING, TODAY
USED AS A HOME FOR THE AGED.

ST. CLOUD TORNADO OF
1886.

PATIENT'S ROOM, 1912.

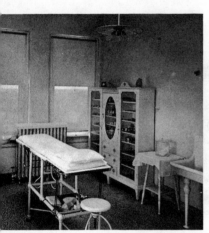

OPERATING ROOM, 1908.

ST. JOSEPH'S CHILDREN'S HOME IN ST. PAUL.

BISHOP JOHN TREACY IN CEREMONY
OF ERECTION OF ST. BEDE'S PRIORY.

ST. PAUL'S PRIORY, ST. PAUL,
MINNESOTA.

ST. MARY'S PRIORY, NAUVOO,
ILLINOIS.

ST. PLACID'S PRIORY, OLYMPIA,
WASHINGTON.

ST. BEDE'S PRIORY, EAU CLAIRE,
WISCONSIN.

MOTHER ROSAMOND READS DECREE OF ERECTION
OF ST. BEDE'S PRIORY.

FIRST MEETING OF THE GENERAL CHAPTER
OF THE CONGREGATION.

BBOT PRIMATE BERNARD
VISITS ST. BENEDICT'S,
1948.

BISHOP JAMES BYRNE IN CEREMONY
OF ERECTION OF ST. PAUL'S PRIORY.

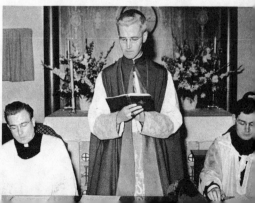

ABBESS AUGUSTINA OF
EICHSTATT AND MOTHER
RICHARDA.

SISTERS AT PRAYER.

THE 1955 CLASS OF NOVICES.

ST. BENEDICT'S SEEN FROM A DISTANCE.

of the introduction of personal attitudes and practices which might destroy its Benedictine character.[1] Bishop Ullathorne of England had seen this danger and many years earlier had warned the American Benedictines that the longer the delay in obtaining papal approval of their houses, "the more difficult it will be to accomplish it, as the houses multiply in the meanwhile and diversities get introduced in observance which become great obstacles against the agreement in, or the establishment of, any uniform observance."[2] In the opinion of the abbot primate and other superiors of Benedictine houses the only safeguards against the dangers inherent in the American convents lay in their becoming pontifical institutes with constitutions only Rome could change.

When Pope Pius X issued his *Motu Proprio, Dei Providentia* on July 16, 1906, declaring that bishops could not approve congregations without permission of the Holy See, Abbot Innocent Wolf of Atchison took action to get approval for the Convent of St. Scholastica. Other Benedictine houses then showed a desire to follow the mind of the Church and asked for papal approval. Full papal approval of a convent is gained in three stages: the decree of praise, temporary approval, and final and perpetual approval.[3] Abbot Innocent Wolf believed that Rome preferred to deal with a group or union of houses rather than with a series of single houses each of which would present its own constitutions and rules. He suggested therefore that it was more advisable for a number of convents to band together, adopt the same constitutions, and then ask to have that instrument and the union recognized by the Holy See. The constitutions would contain those things common to all Benedictine houses, on which they all could agree. Smaller differences such as type of work and dress could be cared for in each convent by a book of customs.

Under Abbot Innocent Wolf's direction a call was sent out to all prioresses to meet in Chicago in 1908 to write such constitutions and to send a petition for approval to the Sacred Congregation of Religious in Rome. Some members of this meeting withdrew from the movement when the proposed constitutions declared that teaching was to be the sole work of this union of Benedictine sisters. When those who remained had agreed to the new document and all of the other required papers had been assembled they placed them and their petition in the hands of the abbot primate, the Right Reverend

Fidelis von Stotzingen, to present to the Holy Father. Before action was taken on this petition, World War I cut off all attempts to carry the negotiations to completion.

Under the assumption that the petition sent to Rome in 1909 had through the course of the war been lost, the various convents decided that a new petition would have to be made. Mother Regina O'Donnell, prioress at Elizabeth, New Jersey, took the lead and asked all interested parties to meet in Chicago on August 5, 1917, and there again agree on common constitutions and a new petition. St. Benedict's, still eager to belong to a congregation and to have its constitutions approved by Rome, sent Sister Emiliana Von Drehle and Sister Othmar Thompson as delegates to this meeting. They were especially directed to see that the new constitutions would be so written that houses engaged in hospital and other charitable works would not be excluded from the union. This they accomplished, and upon their return home St. Benedict's enthusiastically voted to join the Congregation of St. Scholastica. The convent started immediately to revise its rules and customs to conform with the union's new constitutions.

A few months after the formal papers of the 1917 meeting had been forwarded to the Holy See, Mother Aloysia Northman of Atchison was surprised to receive a report from Rome showing that the Congregation of Religious in Rome had, despite the war, been working on a petition and had approved it. But it was the petition of 1908 and not the one they had signed in 1917. The Congregation of Religious was unaware of the existence of the second constitutions and petition. Therefore, when the constitutions were approved and returned to the sisters in 1918 the document approved was discovered to be the one which had been written ten years earlier. Rome's approval being thus given to the earlier constitutions which stated explicitly that teaching was the only field of work to be undertaken, St. Benedict's was automatically excluded from the Congregation of St. Scholastica.[4] Upon receipt of this news, Mother Cecilia Kapsner wrote to the president of the congregation asking that the constitutions be changed to include charitable institutions among the works of the congregation because she could not dispose of the hospitals and orphanages under her care. When Mother Cecilia was advised not to insist on asking Rome for this revision of the constitutions lest it spoil the project for all of the other members, she wrote on February 11, 1918:

We are most anxious to have the Declarations approved by Rome, and we are equally desirous of joining the Congregation. But when we once have the approval of Rome we want to live according to the Declarations so approved. We cannot dispose of our hospitals at present. If the Declarations remain as they now read and we should continue operating the institutions which we have and cannot dispose of, we would be exposed to apparently just criticism for engaging in work not authorized in the Declarations. . . . We are anxious to join the Congregation and should not like to have these few points debar us from becoming members.[5]

Abbot Ernest Helmstetter, President of the American Cassinese Congregation, Abbot Innocent Wolf of Atchison, and Mother Aloysia Northman, then suggested that St. Benedict's remain out of the union until present constitutions and declarations were approved and the Congregation of St. Scholastica put on a good footing. Then St. Benedict's could petition Rome for entrance into the union with special dispensation to conduct such charitable works as hospitals.[6] The door of entrance to the congregation was closed even more firmly when Bishop Joseph Busch of St. Cloud declared his opposition to the whole movement because from it he feared the end of many of the charitable works of his diocese.[7]

The bishop's attitude together with the coolness of the Congregation of St. Scholastica toward the needs of St. Benedict's blocked all immediate hopes of membership. But the leaders of the movement for union likewise met with disappointment. Despite the fact that St. Benedict's did not join the congregation, things did not work as smoothly as had been anticipated. The new secretary of the Sacred Congregation of Religious, Abbot Maurus Serafini, informed them that the constitutions and declarations were not in accord with canon law. He also stated that "if the Benedictine sisters were *Moniales* they could not form a congregation," for then each convent is independent and the members of each convent are enclosed. The secretary offered them the alternative of becoming *Sorores* with the vows of poverty, chastity, and obedience, but omitting the vow of stability and submitting themselves to a mother general. As *Sorores* they could form a congregation. But that would mean that the sisters were no longer Benedictines. At this juncture Aidan Cardinal Gasquet and the abbot primate, Fidelis von Stotzingen, took the question directly to His Holiness, Pope Benedict XV. Knowing that the Congregation of Religious would not even consider an organization whose constitutions were contrary to canon law, Cardinal Gasquet in 1919 induced Pope Benedict to appoint a small special commission of cardinals to examine the constitutions with the understanding that if the commission approved the union it would become a congregation *juris Pontificii*.[8] This was done and the Congregation of St. Scholastica was approved, but because of their work in hospitals the three Minnesota convents in Crookston, Duluth, and St. Joseph were excluded.

Between the years 1918 and 1920 Abbot Alcuin Deutsch of St. John's Abbey had become interested in these Minnesota convents. In 1920 when the constitutions were before the special commission of cardinals, he had asked the abbot primate to petition the cardinals to broaden the scope of the work of the congregation. Sensing that any suggested changes in the constitutions at this critical stage would turn the cardinals against the proposed congregation, the abbot primate did not present the petition.[9]

It was then that Abbot Alcuin began to promote the idea of a new congregation made up of western and Minnesota Benedictine convents — a congregation which would make special provision for hospitals and other charitable works. Made up of western houses it would be a group harmonious in character, environment, and outlook. Because this union would allow care of hospitals it would more readily receive the local bishop's recognition and approval. Abbot Alcuin pointed out that St. Benedict's Convent must sooner or later join a congregation, for the apostolic delegate to the United States was urging convents to seek papal approval.

In 1922 Abbot Alcuin took up the cause with greater enthusiasm. He urged St. Gertrude's Convent at Cottonwood, Idaho, to send out a circular to the western Benedictine houses inviting them to form a western union on the lines of the Swiss-American Congregation of monks. In November the movement was given an added impetus when it was learned that the Sacred Congregation of Religious had again made a statement encouraging all religious houses of women to look to the Holy See for documents of erection. The same ruling of the Sacred Congregation of Religious on November 30, 1922, also asked the bishops of the United States to see that all religious houses had papers of erection either diocesan or papal. If none could be found, the bishop was to issue a document of recognition.[10] When Bishop Busch could find no formal papers, St. Benedict's realized more than ever the precariousness of its position. He did find records of episcopal visitations and other facts which gave evidence that St. Benedict's had been approved by the bishops from the day of its foundation. Bishop Busch then graciously issued this formal decree of erection:

Although the formal decree of the canonical erection of this Congregation does not exist, nevertheless through examinations of candidates, through reception and profession of novices, through episcopal visitations it therefore always existed virtually approved from the time of its foundation.

Moreover, the Sisters of this Congregation through their excellent instruction in the spirit of St. Benedict, through the strict observance of the Rule of the common life, edified the people by their examples of virtue and always labored with great spiritual fruit not only in this diocese but also in others.

Therefore, with the consent of the bishops in whose dioceses this Congregation exists, according to the decree of the Sacred Congregation of Religious, we, on November 30, 1922 formally and authoritatively recognize and declare legitimately erected through the present letter this Congregation of Diocesan Jurisdiction in the Diocese of St. Cloud under the title of Sisters of the Order of St. Benedict.[11]

This incident not only renewed the interest in raising the canonical status of St. Benedict's Convent but showed how uncertain had been its position during the previous sixty-six years.

At the same time, Abbot Alcuin succeeded in getting St. Gertrude's Convent at Cottonwood to call a meeting to form a western congregation. Anxious as the community was to obtain papal approval, Mother Louisa and her councilors did not show much enthusiasm for the proposed new union of western convents. This was partly because most of the convents interested in the movement were of Swiss origin with government and customs based on those of the Swiss-American Congregation and with backgrounds somewhat different from the American-Cassinese group stemming from Bavaria. This lack of interest on the part of Mother Louisa Walz was also due in part to the invitation the Congregation of St. Scholastica had lately extended to St. Benedict's to join their group with the understanding, of course, that St. Benedict's would have to ask for exemption to retain its hospital work.[12] Besides, Mother Louisa was timid about taking the leadership which would naturally fall to her as the prioress of the largest priory among these western convents. To her mind it would be much easier to join a congregation already approved by Rome than to go through years of toil in forming a new union. Bishop Busch's attitude toward a union *juris pontifici* also made her hesitant to join the movement.

Despite the proddings of Abbot Alcuin, who had looked to St. Benedict's to take the initiative, the project lay dormant. His hopes were revived in the summer of 1928 when the abbot primate wrote to him approving of the union and again in August of the same summer when His Excellency, Peter Fumasoni-Biondi, the apostolic delegate, was directed by the Pope to visit all the dioceses of the United States. On his visit to the Diocese of St. Cloud and to St. Benedict's he inquired about the ecclesiastical status of the institution and on discovering that it was diocesan, he encouraged the sisters to join a congregation having papal approval or to form a western congregation of their own. With this backing and encouragement Abbot Alcuin declared he would take up the work anew. The sisters too renewed their interest, but Mother Louisa, who had been ill for some months, had not the physical strength to lead her community into a new venture.

After waiting three more years for Mother Louisa and her councilors to take part, the abbot announced to Mother Louisa and the prioress at Duluth that he would go forward and make his plans without them. Mother Louisa then definitely withdrew from the movement giving as her reason that her term of office would terminate in a few months and that she did not care to take any action that might embarrass her successor.[13] The abbot then put the leadership into the hands of the Sacred Heart Convent in Yankton, South Dakota, and issued an invitation to interested convents to meet at St. John's in August, 1932, to formulate plans for further procedures. An agenda was set up and a second meeting was held at St. Benedict's in the following year. At this second meeting the four convents at Duluth, Yankton, Sturgis, and Crookston were represented. Five other convents declared their interest in the movement but were unable to send delegates. It was at this meeting in St. Joseph that

St. Gertrude's Congregation was formed, but the convent of St. Benedict did not become a member.

For five years St. Benedict's let the matter rest. With the advent of a new and younger prioress, Mother Rosamond Pratschner, the work was taken up once more. A less strong personality than that of Mother Rosamond might not have been able to weather the storm ahead and bring to St. Benedict's the coveted papal approval.

Shortly after Mother Rosamond assumed her office, word came from the abbot primate that His Holiness, Pope Pius XI, wished all Benedictine houses to belong to a congregation and to be approved by the Holy See. Prompted to action by this notice, Mother Rosamond and her council on April 25, 1939, asked Bishop Busch for permission to join the Congregation of St. Scholastica and under its protection to obtain the approval of the Holy See.[14] The reasons given for joining a union of houses were that the convent would share in the good works of other Benedictines and would be strengthened by a union with other religious houses that followed the same rule. To this petition the bishop and his consultors gave a negative answer. St. Benedict's was then advised by Benedictine canonists to seek approval for its own constitutions and institute and after that to divide into three or more houses or priories and thus form a new congregation. It was also agreed that such a plan of dividing St. Benedict's into three priories situated in the nearby dioceses of St. Paul and La Crosse might more easily win the approval of their bishops than the plan of having those sisters join a congregation made up of convents in distant states. This proposal to divide St. Benedict's into three priories appealed to most sisters, for St. Benedict's with over a thousand members had become too large for one prioress to direct.

About this time it was learned that when the apostolic delegate, Archbishop Peter Fumasoni-Biondi, had made his official visit to the dioceses of the United States nine years previous he had informed some religious houses of diocesan jurisdiction that they might forward their petitions for papal approval directly to the Holy See even though it was usual to do it through the local bishop. But Mother Rosamond and her sisters preferred to take the regular procedure and to ask once more for their bishop's approval. Accordingly therefore on November 21, 1941, Mother Rosamond with three officials and the members of her council called on Bishop Busch to ask him to commend to the Holy See their appeal for the Decree of Praise. They left with him the following document:

Most Reverend and dear Bishop:

On several occasions during the past few years, we have presented petitions to obtain Your Excellency's blessing on our efforts to secure recognition from the Holy See. It is now our purpose to renew this petition.

We wish today to ask Your Excellency for a letter of commendation and your blessing on this undertaking. Your letter, together with one from the Archbishop and from the other Bishops of dioceses in which we have missions will assist us in securing the first step — the Decree of Praise (decretum laudis).

The large majority of Benedictine communities in America have already obtained pontifical approbation, and it is our earnest desire to share in the benefits derived from such a union.[15]

At this meeting Bishop Busch dissuaded the sisters from the undertaking and said he doubted that a decree would be given to them.[16]

Mother Rosamond and the sisters returned home convinced they would have to make their petition to Rome through other channels. After assuring themselves that the community favored a continuation of effort to obtain papal approval, they appealed to Rome through the abbot primate.

Abbot Primate Fidelis von Stotzingen succeeded in bringing the sisters' case before the Sacred Congregation of Religious in the spring of the following year, 1942. During the course of the next twelve months an agreement was reached with Bishop Ryan of Bismarck in which St. Benedict's agreed to establish a priory at Bismarck before it would become a papal institute. Then in November, 1943, Bishop Busch sent to the apostolic delegate a letter of approval of the convent's petition for the Decree of Praise. After that the sisters entered upon a period of prayer and sacrifice that God might make fruitful the work of the abbot primate on their behalf. Their prayers were answered on March 24, 1947, when Pope Pius XII gave his approval in the following decree:

The Congregation of St. Benedict, a congregation of Benedictine sisters, consists of independent priories, united in a federation under the vigilant and maternal direction of the mother president with her council. Its establishment is in conformity with the character of the Benedictine Order and it promotes the success of good works, as has been discovered by experience from similar institutes.

The mother president with the consent of the prioresses of the priories has sent a copy of the constitutions to our Holy Father, by Divine Providence Pope Pius XII, and has expressed her most humble petition . . . that he might deign to bestow some special favor upon that congregation and approve its constitutions and declarations by apostolic authority.

Accordingly, on March 24, 1947, in an audience granted to Cardinal Aloysius Lavitrano, prefect of the Sacred Congregation of Religious, His Holiness was regardful of the commendatory letters of the local ordinaries mentioned above, and of the favorable report made by the Most Eminent and Most Reverend Cardinals of the Holy Roman Church at the head of the same Sacred Congregation, who at a plenary meeting held in the Vatican had considered this matter maturely. In view of these recommendations His Holiness deigned graciously to bestow ample words of praise and commendation on the aforesaid institute as a congregation of simple vows under the government of the prioresses of the priories and under the direction of the mother president. His Holiness deigned, further, to approve and confirm for seven years, by way of testing them, these declarations and constitutions written in Latin as contained in this copy, the original manuscript of which is preserved in the archives of the Sacred Congregation. By this decree, therefore, the congregation is praised and commended, and its declarations and constitutions are approved and confirmed, the jurisdiction of the local ordinaries being safeguarded in accord with the sacred canons.

Given at Rome, from the secretariate of the Sacred Congregation of Religious on the day, month, and year as stated above.[17]

With this Decree of Praise St. Benedict's had reached the first stage in becoming a pontifical institute.

Since the whole juridical government of the institute formed by the Decree of Praise presupposed several autonomous priories, with their own superiors and capitulars, to be united and joined together into one congregation under the rule of a mother president, the next step was to divide the Convent of St. Benedict into several priories. In May, 1947, Mother Rosamond (whom Rome had appointed temporary president) informed the sisters that "these priories would naturally be founded in the dioceses where we have established branch houses. . . . We have secured the approval of the Archbishop of St. Paul and the Bishop of La Crosse who graciously invited us to establish a mother house in their dioceses." [18] After several months of prayer and deliberation it was announced that each sister might freely choose the priory of the congregation to which she wished to belong: St. Benedict's at St. Joseph, Minnesota; St. Bede's at Eau Claire, Wisconsin; and St. Paul's at St. Paul, Minnesota. When the lists were all in, on January 15, 1948, they showed that 178 sisters chose St. Paul's Priory, 83 St. Bede's, while 915 chose to remain at St. Benedict's.

The formal erection of St. Bede's Priory took place on June 21, 1948, and St. Paul's Priory was formally erected on the following day. At St. Bede's, Coadjutor Bishop John Treacy of La Crosse read Holy Mass in the chapel. After Mass the members of the priory assembled in the chapter room where Mother President Rosamond read the decree of erection. Bishop Treacy's authorization for the erection of the new priory in his diocese was then read. After that Sister Ethel Cushing was elected the first prioress of St. Bede's.

The afternoon of the following day, June 22, 1948, in St. Paul, Most Reverend James J. Byrne, auxiliary bishop of the archdiocese, blessed the new priory there. After Mother Rosamond read the decree of erection, similar in form to the one used at Eau Claire, Bishop Byrne presided at the election which made Sister Loraine Tracy the first prioress of St. Paul's.

With the erection of the new priories, the Congregation of St. Benedict was a congregation in fact and could now function as such. Mother Rosamond called the first general chapter to meet at St. Benedict's Convent the following month. The chapter, made up of the prioresses of the three priories together with a delegate from each priory, deliberated on matters dealing with the furthering of religious life of the sisters.[19] At the election meeting of the chapter, Mother Rosamond was chosen mother president, Mother Ethel Cushing first visitator, Mother Loraine Tracy second visitator, while Sister Myron McGinley became secretary general.

As is evident from the Decree of Praise, the Congregation of St. Benedict now entered upon a seven-year period of probation during which time special attention was given to the constitutions and declarations to make certain that they would serve the purposes for which they had been formulated. Toward the close of this seven-year period, Mother Richarda Peters, now president, and the other officials of the congregation with the guidance of the abbot primate, took steps to secure final and permanent approval. Again the bishops in whose dioceses the priories were located, St. Paul, St. Cloud, La Crosse, and Seattle were asked to send letters of commendation to the Holy See.

After Archbishop John Murray of St. Paul, Bishop Peter Bartholome of St. Cloud, Bishop John Treacy of La Crosse, and Bishop Thomas Connolly of Seattle graciously sent their testimonial letters to the Holy See the Congregation of St. Benedict sent the following petition to Pope Pius XII on December 4, 1954:

Most Holy Father:

Seven years have elapsed since Your Holiness graciously granted to the Congregation of St. Benedict the Decree of Praise. . . . At that time the Declarations and Constitutions of the Congregation of St. Benedict were approved for a period of seven years.

Prostrate at the feet of Your Holiness, the members of the Congregation of St. Benedict now earnestly petition for final approval as a Congregation of Pontifical Jurisdiction. . . . At the General Chapter held in July of this year, the Declarations and Constitutions were again reviewed, and copies of the revisions were submitted to the Holy See for approval.[20]

Every step in the final procedure had now been taken. Hopes were high that the final approval would be granted during the next year, 1955, but an unforeseen obstacle loomed up when death took Monsignor Robert Sposetti, the member of the Sacred Congregation of Religious who had the Benedictine cause most at heart. The sisters had to wait another year, but on May 12, 1956, the Sacred Congregation in plenary session gave its final approval to the declarations and constitutions of the Congregation of St. Benedict and on June 9 issued the decree which made St. Benedict's and the other priories of the congregation pontifical institutes.[21] In the interval of waiting for final approval, St. Benedict's had formed its western missions into an independent priory under the patronage of St. Placid and on June 28, 1952, it became a member of the congregation. Sister Placidia Hoehn was chosen to be the prioress of this new house. Three years later, the old, well-established convent of St. Mary in Nauvoo, Illinois, joined the congregation. St. Mary Convent had been established in 1875 by the Benedictines of Chicago. With the admission of this priory the congregation now numbered five members.

In the hundred years that have elapsed since Mother Willibalda and her companions disembarked in St. Cloud, the sisters have met the challenge of adapting Benedictine life to new world situations and of finding their place in the formal organization of the Church. The restoration of the Divine Office to its rightful place has deepened the religious spirit according to the ideals of St. Benedict and has enabled the sisters to preserve the balance between worship and work. Like the wise virgins of the Gospel they have kept their lamps burning.

THE CONGREGATION OF ST. BENEDICT

PART FOUR

CONVENT OF ST. BENEDICT'S INSTITUTES

18 CHIPPEWA INDIAN MISSIONS

The Chippewa nation of Algonquin stock was originally located on the St. Lawrence River as far east as the New England states. When the Chippewa Indians were driven from their homes by the Iroquois, they found the Sioux Indians in the way of their westward flight. But in the latter part of the seventeenth century possession of firearms gave the Chippewa an advantage over the more warlike Sioux and enabled them in turn to push their enemies south and westward. By the middle of the nineteenth century the Chippewa occupied the northern part of Michigan, Wisconsin, the southern shore of Lake Superior, and the upper part of the Mississippi Valley in Minnesota. Those Chippewa bands located in Minnesota in the Lake Superior region had given up their land to the United States government in the Treaty of 1854. These same treaties set aside some lands where the Chippewa Indians could live — in the area around Mille Lacs, Cass Lake, Sandy Lake, Pokegama and Winnibigoshish Lakes.

In 1867, a few years after the Sioux massacre and the consequent removal of the Sioux tribe from the state, the United States government decided to have the various bands of Chippewa give up their several settlements and lands and to gather them into one large reservation at White Earth.

It was at this time, too, that the government realized that frequently officers placed in charge of the Indians used their powers unscrupulously. President Grant decided to avoid future scandals, and to this end he inaugurated the peace policy of 1869. He felt that honest men could be had for the office of Indian agent if they were first nominated or recommended by some religious denomination. He also felt that he could not get the United States Senate to ratify his nomination of good agents unless there was some strong organization back of the nominee. Certain senators would fear to vote against such a nominee lest they incur the displeasure of the church which had made the nomination. He also believed that the only solution of the problem of christianizing and civilizing the Indian was through the united force of church and state operating together. His plan was to give the agencies over to such denominations which had for the longest time maintained missions among the Indians of each of the several reservations. At the same time President Grant asserted that the religious preferences of the Indians would be respected. To that church body was given the right of naming the agent, and he in turn would appoint the teachers of the government school, the farm director, and sometimes the interpreter; all of whom would belong to the religious persuasion of the agent. Thus, in a sense, the government school established on each reservation was in reality a denominational school subsidized by the government, and the church on the reservation was a state supported church. For the five years following 1874, the governmental authorities were adamant in seeing to it that one and only one religious group would be recognized or allowed to work on a reservation. For this reason a Catholic missionary might be expelled from a reservation after years of work if, under the new plan, that reservation had been assigned to a non-Catholic group. This rule violated the principle of liberty of conscience. In theory a reservation was allotted to the religious denomination which had conducted mission work at the place for the longest period of time. If the allotment had been carried out according to the intention of the act, the Catholic Church should have received 38 out of 72 agencies distributed. But only eight reservations were allotted to the Catholic missionaries. Despite President Grant's public assertion that he would respect the religious preference of the Indians and despite the fact that three-fourths of the Indians on White Earth Reservation were Catholics, and Catholic missionaries had preceded the Protestant missionaries in point of time, the Indians were by this new policy to be given over to the care of the Episcopalian Church. The agent who was beholden to the church of the reservation for his job would do all in his power to aid that church.

Having charge of the government warehouses, the distribution of supplies of food, clothing, and tools, he often was inclined to favor the Indians who were members of his church — thus exerting pressure on non-members to join.

It was this barrier which Father Ignatius Tomazin met when he was sent to work with the Chippewa Indians at White Earth in the spring of 1874. Father Ignatius Tomazin had worked for some years with the Chippewa at Crow Wing, Gull Lake, and Red Lake. When in 1874 most of these Indians had reluctantly moved to the reservations at White Earth and Red Lake he was told by his bishop to make his headquarters at White Earth. This priest, who had left his home in Krain, Yugoslavia, to work among the Indians of the United States, was a zealous and tireless worker — a man of determination, of fiery temper, intolerant of injustice. Upon his arrival at the agency he was notified that neither a Catholic church nor a Catholic priest was acceptable on the reservation and that not a cent of money would be allotted for his support. To this he answered that he was sent by his Church and would remain there until recalled by his bishop. Then he set about to obtain money from his friends. The Catholic Mission Society of Austria gave funds enough to build a small log church 20 by 30 feet a few miles from the agency buildings.

With the arrival of Agent Lewis Stowe, Father Tomazin's real troubles commenced. They started with the agent's method of distributing government annuities. When an Indian presented himself for his supplies, he was asked his religious affiliation. If he answered "Episcopalian," he was given a whole suit of clothes and maybe two suits. If he answered "Catholic" or "pagan," he received only a shirt. After three years of such discrimination, the missionary protested. In return he was threatened with expulsion, and on April 10, 1877, received a notice to leave the reservation within ten days.[1] When he read this notice to his parishioners the following Sunday, they excitedly declared that they would guard him with their lives. Mr. Stowe did not force the issue, but during the summer the Episcopalian Bishop Henry Whipple and his missionaries held a conference to plan a campaign. In September they called in United States Inspector Kemble who brought two charges against Father Tomazin.[2] Again the missionary was ordered to leave, and again he disobeyed. Troops were then summoned from Fort Snelling.

Friendly Indians warned the missionary of the approach of the troops. He barricaded himself in the church and rang the church bell to call the Indians from far and wide to his aid. A contemporary account of the trouble gives the following vivid picture of this dramatic phase of the struggle.

In the meantime, a large band of armed Indians had massed together summoned by the wild ringing of the church bell which was kept up incessantly throughout the day, and mounted parties from all sections of the reserve hurried to the scene, aroused by the alarm. Bonfires were lit in the church yard and the tolling was kept up through the entire night.[3]

The Indians to the number of three hundred came armed with guns, pitchforks, and knives and surrounded the church. The young and the old, and even women and pagans came to fight for the Blackrobe. The United States inspector ordered Colonel Bates to arrest the missionary but he refused, saying that he had no orders to that effect, that he had been sent to preserve order and to quell any riot and that it would be folly to provoke three hundred armed Indians and thus expose his twenty-five soldiers to massacre. The agent then attempted to break into the church but was confronted by the pagan chief, Shabascamsaid, who blocked the way saying, "What do you want? I am a medicine man, not a Christian, but what do you want? Is it justice the way you treat the Catholics and the pagans? Here is my knife; you will be the first to be killed if you try to take this man away."[4] The inspector then asked the colonel to starve out Father Tomazin but the colonel refused. Colonel Bates did bring about a compromise whereby Father Tomazin was not to be taken a prisoner but was to give his promise to leave the reservation of his own accord and immediately. The colonel promised that if this were done he would see to it that the priest would be returned to the place within six weeks. The missionary started out on foot but did not leave the reservation because two Indians kidnapped him and hid him on a lonely island. When things quieted down, he returned to his mission and Agent Stowe was removed.[5]

As may be seen from the events related here, the missionary had reason for his complaints against the agent. The evils were great, and no doubt the only way to get his cause heard was to fight, but he was quick tempered, stubborn, and very eccentric. Though zealous, he lacked the patience and the diplomacy which the situation at White Earth called for, and by his eccentric life he laid himself open to charges against his life of celibacy.

Father Tomazin had been assisted in his work by three men who called themselves Franciscan friars or brothers and wore the Franciscan habit. Two of them taught in the school that Father Tomazin had opened and the other went about the country begging for funds for the mission. One of these self-styled brothers, Francois Louis de Gonzague de Malissey, was a nobleman who, according to his own account, was descended from the famous Gonzaga family of which St. Aloysius was a member. Though French, he had spent his early years in the Province of the Rhine near the Holland border, and at the age of six he was going to school in Bonn. In his unpublished autobiography he describes his life as attendant and sacristan of a chapel in the port of Marseilles.[6] Because of his German accent he was one day accused of being a German spy and had to flee from Louis Napoleon's officers. He boarded the first boat possible, a sail boat, and landed in the United States. After two years in Baltimore and St. Louis he found his way to Minnesota and joined Father Tomazin at White Earth. Here with two other brothers he taught school. But Brother Malissey was also the beggar of the house and he loved his begging tours. With a flair for the dramatic, he would preach in the churches on Sundays, standing outside the communion rail dressed in the Franciscan habit. His group of Indian boys in wild attire danced outside the church door thus giving added interest to his cause. Though he was successful in raising funds for a mission which was sustained wholly by Catholic charity, the irascible Father Tomazin was never quite satisfied with the results. Brother Malissey left aggrieved and spent the rest of his life going from place to place, periodically returning to White Earth. He was a man who did much good and suffered much for souls. One who knew him said he was zealous even to fanaticism, an enthusiast with too much persistency. Today a plain cross in the cemetery ground at White Earth marks the grave of this descendant of the noble house of Gonzaga.

With two such eccentric characters as Father Tomazin and Brother Malissey peace could not be expected either between themselves or between them and the officials who were the agents of the Episcopal Church. It is true the two missionaries fought for the right of the Catholic Indian but their eccentricity made it possible for their enemies to bring charges against them and so to interfere with their success.

Fearing that Father Tomazin would embroil the Church in further disturbances, Bishop Seidenbush of St. Cloud decided to transfer him to the mission at Red Lake and in 1878 asked St. John's Abbey and St. Benedict's Convent to supply a priest and some teachers for White Earth. Mother Aloysia Bath consented to send two sisters. The Holy Spirit surely guided her choice of the two missionaries. Both sisters were very young. Sister Philomena Ketten was small and sprightly, with large sparkling black eyes and a vivacious manner. The other, somewhat older and of a more deliberate nature, was Sister Lioba Braun, who had been teaching school in St. Cloud. Sister Philomena had volunteered for the missionary work. Sister Lioba had not; she feared the Indians. These two souls were the complement of each other. Sister Philomena's impulsive, zealous nature was needed to carry them over the hard spots, to give initiative, while Sister Lioba's more conservative ways kept the impulsiveness of the other within bounds and gave the guarantee of perseverance. But when on November 4, 1878, they set out for White Earth in the company of Abbot Alexius Edelbrock, of Father Aloysius Hermanutz, O.S.B., and of the veteran missionary, Father Joseph Buh, they could not know they were destined to spend fifty years together among the Indians.

The journey to White Earth was made by wagon as far as St. Cloud and by railroad from St. Cloud to Detroit Lakes where the party remained over night. A twenty-two mile wagon trip faced them the following day. The road was little more than a trail, rough and tortuous, and the wagons were loaded down with the five passengers, two trunks, a barrel of flour, and a keg of lard.

At two o'clock on the afternoon of November 5, 1878, the party came in sight of the mission and started making the long climb up the road leading to the summit of the hill on which the mission buildings stood. Deeply afraid of Indians, Sister Lioba was sick with fright and white as a sheet; she thought she was going to her martyrdom. Her companions years later were to tease her about her first fears.

On the very summit of that hill was the graveyard; down from it on the sloping side was the log church. Near the church were the house, school, barn, and garden and down still farther in the valley was the spring. Even Father Buh, the veteran missionary accustomed to hard times, was aghast at the poverty of the place.[7] The church was a log structure thirty feet long and twenty feet wide with four windows on either side. It was unplastered and without a ceiling.

Bared and stripped of its coverings, the altar was nothing but a rough plank box with another smaller box as tabernacle. The house was a small log structure sixteen feet square. The logs forming the walls were covered with siding but the cracks and joints let in the cold winds of the north. Except for two rusty stoves, the interior was bare. Indians and half-breeds had long since appropriated the few things left behind by the former missionary. Having surveyed their home, the new missionaries designated one room, seven by twelve feet, as a general living room, a similar room as Father Aloysius's office and living room, and the third room, the size of a small clothes closet, as the place for the altar.[8] The garret under the eaves was reserved for the sisters' dormitory.

With the inspection of the premises finished, the sisters pinned up their habits and looked about for a broom, for the dismantled and dirty place must be put in order if Mass were to be offered the next day. A rough plank resting on two kegs was made to fit into the small two by eight foot closet. They found that with the door open the priest would be able to stand in the doorway before this altar and offer holy Mass. A stove was purchased at the agency store and placed in the living room together with a rough table and bench. Thus this room served as kitchen, refectory, community room, and chapel. Recollection at Mass was often disturbed by the gurgle of the coffee pot on the stove near them. The sisters had thoughtfully come supplied with a tick which when filled with straw, corn husks, or grass would serve as a mattress. But the priest, man-like, had come unsupplied with bed clothing. The sisters generously put one tick in his office. Their own they carried to the garret where for lack of bedstead it was placed on the floor.

The next day the abbot left them, and the sisters started to clean the church. This cleaning required quantities of water from a spring half a mile away. Father Buh, the experienced missionary, soon found a slough near by and in it sank a barrel which gathered water fit for scrubbing purposes. Four plain wooden candle sticks were polished, a statue taken from the sisters' treasures, the altar linens ironed, and all was finally ready for services in the church the following Sunday. On November 11, six days after their arrival, a day school was opened with an enrollment of twelve girls and three boys, which increased to a total of forty the following week.

The first winter was a hard one for these missionaries. They had expected to find the mission provided with such necessary articles as ax, spade, hammer, and some household furniture. The abbot had left with them but ten dollars to cover the expenses for the winter. After the purchase of a kitchen stove, a sack of flour, and a pound of tea at the agency store, there was little left of ten dollars. There was plenty of wood about the place but no ax with which to cut it. The sisters had mattresses or straw ticks but no beds. The roof leaked and on rainy nights they spent most of the hours trying to avoid these openings in the roof and to find a dry spot on which to place their straw ticks. On clear nights they could count the stars in the sky. But all movements in this upstairs vermin-infected apartment were made with gentleness and care so that the eaves and their coverings were not jarred. Before the winter had set in they had attempted to patch up openings and put in doors, but lumber was precious and had to be carried from the agency store two miles away. The openings between the logs and in the joints they filled with mud or cement of a sort, and they covered the inside walls with newspapers. Nevertheless the wind blew through the cracks, leaving little heaps of snow in patches on the floor and table. These little patches of snow did not melt, for when the Minnesota winds blew, the stove was incapable of heating even this small house.[9]

When Christmas came, the sisters did what they could to decorate the church and to dramatize the feast. A crude manger with straw was set up in one corner. A Chippewa girl, a boy, and a papoose were chosen to represent the Holy Family. But an unforeseen event made the poverty and cold of the first Christmas night even more realistic than had been planned. The missionary, Father Aloysius, described the event in a letter as follows:

Never in my life did I suffer so much from the cold as I did that winter and then more in the house and church than outside. I shall never forget my first Christmas on the mission. . . . I had sent the [church] bell away to be recast. To give the signal for the midnight Mass on Christmas I had procured three mortars, which some Indians were to fire off at the proper time. Wrapped in my buffalo coat I had been sitting in the confessional from 6 o'clock in the evening. It was 40 degrees below zero. When the mortars were discharged at the specified time, the violence of the explosion shattered every window pane on the north side of the church. We covered the openings with blankets. . . . During Mass the cold in the church became so intense that burning coals had to be brought to the altar to keep my hands and the contents of the chalice from freezing. The Indians did not complain and said they had a glorious Christmas.

Misfortunes never came singly. New Year's Day was just as cold. I had just completed my toilet on New Year's morning when a man rushed in saying the school was on fire. The evening before some half-breeds had asked to be permitted to use the school for their night's lodging as they wanted to attend Mass the next day. Through carelessness the woodwork near the overheated stove caught fire. I ran to the church to give the alarm. We succeeded in saving the books and furniture. The building burned down. In my excitement I had forgotten to put on my cap as I ran out. When I returned to my room I noticed that my ears were frozen and before long they began to assume unsightly proportions. As I had to celebrate High Mass I covered my head with a white cloth. After Mass I felt a dull pain in my head — I had also frozen my scalp. . . . Thus I came near losing my scalp without being scalped by an Indian. . . .[10]

This exposure to the cold exacted its toll of the sisters' health. Sister Philomena became ill with pleurisy and Sister Lioba was weakened by a siege of the grippe. Two weeks later they were still ill. This was enough to discourage any missionary. In his letters at this time, Father Aloysius continually mentioned his concern for the sisters. "Sisters cannot endure this weather much longer." "The sisters are still ill from the fire of New Year's." "They suffer much from cold, for we have only green wood to burn." One wonders if he himself was not ready to give up.[11]

To Sister Lioba this school fire seemed a God-send for with the school destroyed there was no reason for their remaining there. But young, vivacious Sister Philomena, though ill with pleurisy, proposed that the barn be used for a school. So the missionary and a carpenter fitted it up for $35.

The duties and services that fell to the sisters were varied and at times surprising. Being young, full of zeal, and blessed with good health, they went ahead and took charge of situations in a way that appeared audacious to them in their later years. At times when Father Aloysius went to visit other bands of Indians at Red Lake or Leech Lake or went on sick calls miles away, the sisters were left unprotected in the wilderness two miles away from any white person. But before leaving on such journeys the priest would see that enough wood was cut and that a barrel or tub of water was stored near the building. For company the sisters had with them two small Indian girls — orphans who had been given to their care. Food was scarce and so was room but the sisters were glad to have their company. At times they proved a burden as the following incident will show.

During one of Father Aloysius's long absences a messenger came, saying that a man two miles distant was dying and wanted a priest. Told that the Blackrobe was not at home, the messenger insisted that the sisters come instead. Little Sister Philomena in her quick and impulsive way was ready to comply but Sister Lioba weighed the matter. The children could not be left alone nor could they walk the two miles. Neither did the sisters care to go alone with the messenger. Sister Philomena solved the problem by offering to carry the four-year-old child on her back Indian-fashion if Sister Lioba would lead the other by the hand and lift her over the deep drifts. At the end of their walk they found the sick man at death's door. Prayers for the dying were said and the sick man was aided in making an act of contrition. He lived to receive the sacraments when Father Aloysius returned but died a few weeks later during another period of the priest's enforced absences. Now the Indians insisted that the sisters conduct the funeral services. They consented. The corpse was brought to the church where the sisters said aloud the prayers of the Church for the deceased and blessed the corpse with holy water. The procession led from the church to the graveyard on the top of the hill. So far the ceremony had gone well indeed, but on the top of this windy hill their perseverance was tried. The newly opened grave was found to be too short for the coffin and the funeral cortege had to wait in the bitter cold until the grave was enlarged.[12]

It is easily seen that these affairs interrupted the school work. But Indian mission schools as well as Indian government schools were never regularly attended. Of the forty registered pupils, as few as five were present on some days. Nothing but gifts of food and clothing could entice the lively Indian child to school every day. Then, too, during the hunting and maple sugar seasons the whole settlement packed up and left for other parts to be gone for four or five weeks. Of the original forty pupils, seventeen were boys ranging in age from six to seventeen years. Among the girls were children of the Parker, Howard, Jourdan, Morrison, and Fairbanks families as well as the daughters of Chief Hole-in-the-Day.[13] Most of these were of mixed Indian and white blood but there were a number with such names as Kedagigowiash and Nishegwoan. These children tried the patience of their teacher for it was not their nature to stay half an hour in one place. Sister Lioba noted their "ineptitude for intellectual culture" when she started to teach them reading, but she could quiet them by music which they loved. To things of religion they took more readily. And they did continue to come to the mission despite the fact they were derided for attending a school taught in a converted barn.

When more orphans were crowded into the convent garret with the sisters, the need of a home for waifs was seen to be imperative. Then, too, Indians and half-breeds living at too great a distance but eager to have their children instructed in their faith were importuning the missionary priest and sisters to take their children to live with them. The sisters longed for larger buildings but thought their case hopeless. But help was to come unexpectedly on a cold blizzardy day in January of 1881. Father Aloysius told the story of their good fortune in a paper written some years later:

A genuine Minnesota blizzard from the north was sweeping over the prairie. I had been cutting wood for the house and school; at 3 o'clock in the afternoon the thermometer showed 38 degrees below zero. I was sitting in my room and had just laid aside my Chippewa grammar to rest my brain from the exertion of trying to memorize the long forms of the fourth conjugation. I was puffing clouds of smoke into the air and watching the storm. Suddenly I heard quick steps, and a strong knock at the door and in stepped Abbot Alexius. I noticed that his face was frozen and began at once to rub the frozen parts with snow. When the Abbot had warmed himself he said: "We are going to build a church and a school." I looked doubtful. I had no money and no prospects of getting any, as I had no time to go on a collecting tour and my request to the Abbot for means to repair the old church had been refused. But when the Abbot laid before my eyes complete plans for a church and school, my doubts vanished. "Tomorrow," said the Abbot, "we will select the location for the buildings; we must have good land, timber, and water, these are necessary for such an institution." . . . Three days later we went to Detroit where we contracted for the necessary brick and lumber. Detroit was at the time the nearest railroad station, a distance of twenty-two miles from the mission. This was glad news for the Indians; they began to bestir themselves, and in February hauled the building materials on their sleighs from the station free of charge.[14]

The Indians of Buffalo River eight miles away thought they too should have a mission school and asked Father Aloysius to open a school for their settlement. The government school was conducted by two Protestant teachers and a Protestant minister. The Catholic Indians of the place wanted a Blackrobe's school. When the request was made to Father Aloysius in the fall of 1882, he rashly promised them teachers if they would build. But neither Abbot Alexius nor Mother Aloysia had at the time any extra teachers to send and Father Aloysius was placed in the difficult position of having to break his word with the Indian, a thing which the Indian found hard to forgive. Once more Sister Philomena saved the day. She offered to teach the Buffalo school if the missionary would lend her his pony. The offer was accepted and Sister Philomena made the daily sixteen-mile round-trip for many months. The lack of a woman's saddle did not deter this zealous woman. She rode astride the pony until the bishop made his visitation. Then she pleaded so valiantly for a saddle of her own that he promised to send her one. This plan worked out well until Father Aloysius had to visit his Indians at Red Lake or other points. Then she would have to borrow a pony from some native. One day she asked a half-breed for a horse. He had two, one lame, the other very spirited. Sister Philomena insisted on taking the latter even though she was told she might be thrown. She was thrown, of course. Getting up and shaking herself, she went back for the lame horse and proceeded bravely on her way to school. After one or two such experiences she made bold to beg the abbot for a pony of her own.[15]

When winter set in, the Buffalo River school was closed because of the danger in this solitary trip over the unmarked prairie snows. Such a respite was well deserved, for while teaching in the new school Sister Philomena had continued her duties as cook. To get through her daily charges before starting to Buffalo River, she had to rise at three o'clock. She fed the half dozen chickens and the horse, prepared the breakfast and part of the noon lunch, prayed the Office and attended Mass. Only then was she ready for her eight-mile jaunt to school. This was no eight-hour-day job.

The years from 1878 to 1883 may have brought hardships and suffering to the missionaries, but they brought joy also in the number of conversions made, marriages blessed, and children baptized. If one dips into the old church records he finds that in 1881 baptism was administered to 170 persons of whom 100 were converts from paganism. Likewise recorded is the conversion of 23 Indians of the Pembina band in January of the following year. The sisters did their part in instructing the children in their religious duties and in contacting the Indian women. Conversions were not made wholesale; soul after soul had to be gained by patience and prayer and years of hard work.

The dedication of the newly built church and convent school in June, 1882, seemed to climax their efforts. Church dedications are always great events in the history of a parish. On this occasion the sisters, Father Aloysius, and the Benedictine fathers outdid themselves in making it a memorable day for the Indians and themselves. One of the participants wrote the following account of the festivities for *Der Nordstern*:

As early as Friday, June 9, the Rt. Rev. Alexius Edelbrock, and Rev. Fathers Stimler and Severin Gross arrived at White Earth. With them came the Reverend Mother Scholastica Kerst, Sister Agnes, and Sister Aloysia. . . . The Indians had prepared a parade but since the twenty-two mile ride over prairies could not be timed to a nicety the paraders were not on hand to welcome the guests who arrived earlier than was expected. Disappointed in this the Welcome Committee succeeded in shooting off some fire works in greeting. Since they knew that the visitors must be hungry after their long journey and that it was now two o'clock they withdrew to let them eat their belated dinner alone. After this the two leaders welcomed the Abbot and clerical guests with a short address. They told their guests that the Pembina Indians would arrive in two or three hours with their famous leader, Chief Apotabega.

About half past six there was seen in the distance two flags the red of which harmonized with the green verdure of the forests. . . . Slowly moving toward us, some on horse, some in wagons, and some on foot, the Indian caravan wafted the flags on high and the golden waves of the setting sun threw over all an enchanting halo. They came from the banks of the far off Wild Rice River. Nothing could keep them from making this journey. . . . As true sons of the Church they made a visit to our Lord in the Blessed Sacrament before they took part in the celebration. After a short prayer they then went to the house to greet the clergy. Chief Gabone greeted the Abbot in the name of his people and they then dispersed to set up wigwams. In the meantime a group from Red Lake arrived. Soon the landscape took on a new appearance for where before there was but a broad expanse of land far off into the distance one saw now a large wigwam village. . . .

At nine o'clock the next morning the Indians sprang to their ponies and formed an escort for the Bishop on his arrival. . . . But hunger called and after the parade the Indians cooked or roasted a great ox and served it at tables under the green maple trees near the mission house.

After this they went to church to prepare for confession. Such great numbers approached the confessional that the priests were in the confessional until late at night. At ten o'clock the next morning the ceremonies of blessing commenced with the Abbot as celebrant. During the Mass two hundred and sixteen Indians and half-breeds were confirmed by the Bishop.[16]

The new convent building, called St. Benedict's Girls Orphan School, was built to accommodate twenty orphans. The classrooms were located in the basement of the church. These were, however, not dark underground rooms, for the church located on the brow of a hill was so constructed that one side of the basement was above ground. Having the classrooms here kept the day pupils away from the boarders except for the time spent in the classroom. No board or tuition was paid by these Indians or by the half-breed pupils. Their support came from St. John's Abbey, St. Benedict's Convent, and the Ludwig-Mission Society of Bavaria. Such an uncertain and irregular income could not be depended upon to support the ever-growing mission. Fortunately, in 1876 the government had changed its policy of aiding only one school on each reservation. There was now an annual appropriation for the support of industrial schools for Indians and any mission school which met requirements was eligible for aid. Under this system the churches constructed the buildings and operated the schools while the government contracted to pay the school a flat rate for tuition, board, and clothing of the children at a rate varying from $100 to $150 per pupil annually. The school at White Earth took advantage of this policy and in 1883 asked for aid. The Indian agent approved it, and only in 1885 did the school succeed in getting a contract for the care of ten orphans —the other fifteen to be cared for by charity. By pinching here and saving there the sisters made this sum go a long way. At least the $1,000 was an assured annual income and along with aid from the Catholic Indian Bureau it was something on which they could work and budget. At the close of 1885, the first year of the contract, the mission came out with a balance of $2.75. At the close of the second year the mission was in debt 31 cents. These same old account books show how pitifully small were the things these missionaries and children enjoyed over and above the mere necessities. Only one little luxury is listed: $2 for candy for the children at Christmas. Possibly the item of $2.50 for a pair of geese might by some be called superfluous, but no doubt it was a bit of thrifty housekeeping, goose grease being one of the pioneer remedies for sore throats and chest colds.[17]

Quarterly reports had to be sent to Washington with the names of pupils, their ages, their tribal bands, together with information as to the number who could read in the vernacular of the tribe, the number who could read and write English, and "those who can work the first four rules of arithmetic." In these reports the federal government also asked for an estimate of the amount of staple foodstuffs consumed per quarter by the boarding pupils. The report from the spring quarter of 1886 records that the boarders and the two sisters consumed 540 pounds of meat, 12 sacks of flour, 70 bushels of beans and 20 of potatoes, ¼ of a barrel of sugar, 50 pounds of rice, and 5 gallons of syrup. Only one half box of soap was used. This seems skimpy, but soft soap was made from waste fats in many a pioneer kitchen of that day.[18]

The school day here was similar to that of any other American school. The hours from nine in the morning to four in the afternoon were spent not too happily in learning the three R's. But music and singing were a pleasure, and the sisters soon had a choir able to sing a high Mass. Someone praising the White Earth school reported that the children were taught all sorts of things, useful as well as ornamental. Evidently the three R's were considered ornamental. The sisters and the government agreed that unless domestic arts were taught, the three R's alone would be ornamental and would not raise the Indian's standard of living. Accordingly in the hours "before and after school" the girls were taught to card wool and spin it into yarn. With this yarn they knitted their own stockings and hoods. They were taught plain and fancy sewing and took turns in assisting the sister in the kitchen, laundry, and dairy. Under the supervision of Sister Philomena, the boys cared for the large garden, and at times they went with her into the field to gather potatoes and to rake hay.

The work of this school was so satisfactory that it came to the notice of Miss Catherine Drexel, the renowned member of the Philadelphia family who was interested in the Indian and the Negro.[19] Miss Drexel visited White Earth and was so impressed with the work done there that she made arrangements for the erection of a new school building large enough to shelter 150 orphan and dependent children. The brick for the three-story building was made near the mission during the summer of 1890, and the lumber and other mate-

242

rials were gathered during the winter. Two years later, on February 10, the Feast of St. Scholastica, the school was opened for work with a government contract to educate and clothe one hundred Indians. The teaching and prefecting staff was increased to seven sisters, and Father Aloysius received an assistant in his work.

Heating such a large building was a problem where furnace or hot water system was not to be thought of for some years to come. For the thirty old-fashioned box stoves used in the building, the sisters and the girls carried wood from the outside shed up to the fourth floor of the school. Each morning and afternoon recess, every child able to carry a stick of wood was lined up and given a load proportionate to her strength. Imagine a train of girls with arms full of wood plodding up the stairs to the fourth floor. Sometimes accidentally, sometimes mischievously, one of the carriers would drop a stick and then enjoy the clatter and the disordered ranks. Supplying water was another task. During the winter months water had to be pumped by hand, for then the windmill did not function well. Water for morning "wash up" purposes was carried up the stairs to the dormitories where before morning it froze in the pitchers and basins.

The school grew in its reputation for good solid training, and the teaching force too continued to grow until it numbered eighteen teachers and helpers. Up to date over 5,000 pupils have been enrolled in the school.

An incident occurred in 1898 which showed Father Aloysius's bravery and sterling qualities as well as the respect and confidence in which the Indians, both Catholic and non-Catholic, held him. Some Indians, Chippewa of the Pillager Band under the leadership of Bugonaygeshig on Bear Island in Leech Lake, for a long time past had been in an angry mood because of the results of the Nelson Act of 1889. Though on the basis of this act the Indians were to be paid well for the sale of a great part of their old reservation, they had received almost nothing. The money had been eaten up by exorbitant charges for estimating the timber and for the expenses of the Chippewa Commission which had been foisted upon them. The Indians also complained that the pine estimates were fraudulent; that government agents connived with the loggers who removed great amounts of live timber instead of the dead timber which they were permitted to cut. In the end, the Indians received only 8 cents per thousand feet instead of the promised $3.

The immediate cause of the Pillager uprising at Leech Lake grew out of a local incident which though small was nevertheless the culmination of years of discontent. For the sake of fees the United States marshall had been in the habit of arresting Indians on the reservation and carrying them to the federal court at St. Paul or at Duluth. The Indians were often arrested for no cause, brought to St. Paul, and then told that the case had been settled out of court quietly through the kindness of friendly officials. After that such an Indian was released to find his way home as best he could. But the marshall was reimbursed by the government for the traveling and court expenses of the Indian and himself. Bugonaygeshig, or Bug, as he was called, had been brought to Duluth on one of these excursions and had been forced to walk back to his home, a distance of about one hundred miles. He swore he would never again answer a summons to court. When in June, 1898, he was subpoenaed as witness, he refused the summons and when arrested for contempt of court he was rescued by his tribesmen on September 15 and taken to Bear Island. The United States marshall at St. Paul procured warrants for the arrest of the rescuers and sent Fort Snelling soldiers to take them in charge. When the forces arrived at Sugar Point, a skirmish took place. The white men withdrew and went into consultation. At this point Father Aloysius stepped in. Fearing that the revolt would spread to the Indians at Red Lake if not quashed immediately, he suggested sending runners to the camp with an invitation to come to the agency for a meeting with himself, Flatmouth, and an officer of the agency to discuss the surrender of the braves and to settle complaints in regard to timber. On October 10 the United States Commissioner of Indian Affairs, W. A. Jones, arrived from Washington and appointed Father Aloysius his intermediary. The commissioner decided that if the Indians refused to come in for the meeting he would not go out to meet them. He was, in fact, afraid to meet them. When the Indians did refuse, Father Aloysius decided that he would go to them alone. At the risk of his life he left for the Indian hideout late one afternoon, refusing the company of the military guard and taking with him only Guss Beaulieu, Red Blanket, and another Indian.

They reached Bear Island about midnight. A council was called, and the commissioner's letter was read. Father Aloysius warned them of the inevitable results of their uprising and urged them to come to meet the commissioner. They refused to meet the commissioner anywhere except on Bear Island and insisted he come to them without military guard. Father Aloysius reported this and the next day he alone accompanied and guided Jones to the meeting place. They met the council; the Indians refused the demand for the surrender of the kidnappers unless immunity were guaranteed to all of the rebels. Then it was that Father Aloysius used all his influence and urged them to give in to authority, at the same time gently chiding them for disobeying the law. Twenty-five of the chiefs and braves finally capitulated, and eleven of the seventeen kidnappers surrendered themselves. A special train took these Indians and Father Aloysius to Duluth, but old Bug and his son were not among them. They received their sentences, but the government thought leniency the better way and let the sentences fall.[20]

During the days that Father Aloysius was absent on this mission of peace, the sisters prayed for his safety and their own. In some occult way the 150 pupils were aware of the uprising among their people and were restless and secretive. The tension was relieved only when Father Aloysius, worn out but happy, returned to them.

In Minnesota and throughout the country the mission schools were a great help to the Indians and to the federal government. In spite of this, in 1895 the government completely reversed its policy of giving aid to the education of Indians in sectarian schools and declared it to be the settled policy of Congress that after 1899 no public money would be given. This change of policy was due to the activities of American Protective Association, better known as the A. P. A., which looked with hatred on the growth of Catholic Indian schools. Its members declared that congressional aid to such schools was uniting Church and state — a thing forbidden by the constitution and tradition and utterly repugnant to American sensibilities. They forgot that the contract system of government aid had originated in Grant's Peace Policy and had owed its inception to the influence of Protestant leaders. Now after assiduously patronizing the contract system for about twenty years, the non-Catholic bodies suddenly claimed that Congress had no right to legislate public money for private institutions. In their anxiety to stop the growth of Catholic mission schools, the non-Catholic groups were willing to lose the funds they themselves were receiving for sectarian schools. That, however, did not mean that they were giving up their work. They could sell their

SISTER PHILOMENE.

FATHER ALOYSIUS HERMANUTZ.

SISTER PHILOMENE AND INDIANS
AT BUFFALO RIVER (CALLOWAY).

WHITE EARTH SCHOOL AND CHURCH.
EARLY LOG SCHOOL AT RIGHT.

RED LAKE LOG BUILDING,
SCHOOL AND CHURCH.

WHITE EARTH BOARDING SCHOOL
AND CONVENT.

RED LAKE CONVENT AND SCHOOL.

RED LAKE TEACHERS AND
INDIAN PUPILS, 1889.

WASH ROOM IN EARLY
WHITE EARTH SCHOOL.

LITTLE FLOWER INDIAN
MISSION AT MILLE LACS.

HOSPITALS AT OGDEN, UTAH;
NEW PRAGUE AND ST. CLOUD
IN MINNESOTA.

MEETING OF SISTERS WORKING IN THE DIOCESE OF ST. CLOUD.

CEREMONY OF DEDICATION OF
ST. CLOUD HOSPITAL NURSES' HOME.

REV. F. CLOUGHERTY AND
MOTHER LOUISA WITH
FIRST GROUP OF SISTERS TO
LEAVE FOR CHINA.

BENEDICTINE SISTERS IN THEIR PEKING HOME.

SISTER RACHEL LOULAN IS BURIED IN KAIFENG, CHINA.

THE SISTERS WORKED IN REFUGEE
CAMPS IN KAIFENG IN 1937.

BENEDICTINE SISTERS GIVE MEDICAL
CARE TO WOUNDED CHINESE
SOLDIERS IN 1938.

PAGAN CHILDREN OF TOKYO, ANXIOUS
FOR RELIGIOUS INSTRUCTION, EVEN
LISTEN THROUGH OPENING UNDER
THE GATE.

SISTERS FRANCETTA AND REGIA GIVE
A DEMONSTRATION IN COOKING TO
THEIR CLASS IN TOKYO.

STUDENT, TEACHERS AND
SCHOOL IN FORMOSA.

THE SCHOOL AT HUMACAO,
PUERTO RICO.

OUR FIRST MISSIONARIES
TO PUERTO RICO.

A POOR LABORER AND HIS FAMILY
IN PUERTO RICO.

YOUNG WOMEN FROM PUERTO RICO, CHINA, AND
JAPAN HAVE BECOME POSTULANTS
AT ST. BENEDICT'S.

mission schools to the government and still retain religious control of them by having their teachers employed as government teachers in those same schools.

This withdrawal of congressional support was a severe blow to St. Benedict's Mission with its crowd of one hundred and fifty destitute children. It was a threat to the existence of all Catholic schools established on reservations. There were two alternatives open to them. They could sell or give their establishments to the government, as did the Protestants, and have their teachers "covered into" the classified government service and rehired to continue teaching in the same schools. A few Catholic schools attempted to do this but were blocked by the attorney general's opinion prohibiting the wearing of the religious garb while teaching in tax supported schools. The second alternative for Catholic Indian schools was to throw themselves on the charity of their fellow Catholics. Though the Catholics were generous in their support, the missions soon found that this aid would never be sufficient. Even under the government contract system the sisters at White Earth had never been able to draw salaries and were wholly dependent on St. Benedict's for their living. Then before things became too desperate, a means was discovered whereby support could be solicited from the tribal fund held in trust by the government. Someone had discovered that there was a law on the statute books giving the Secretary of the Interior power to use certain moneys of the Indians held in trust in any way he might see fit. This could include aid in the education of their children. Ever since the days when the government had forced the Indians to sell their lands, the United States had been keeping in trust for the Indians a large sum of money—interest on which was spent for Indian needs when so petitioned. Since these funds belonged to the Indians and could not be said to be public moneys voted by Congress, there was no legal or constitutional objection to their use in mission schools. When Father Aloysius learned of this law, he urged his Chippewa band to sign a petition for use of their tribal funds sufficient to cover the expenses of his school for the year and, like many another Catholic mission, this school remained open. But the legality of the system was attacked despite the fact that the attorney general had declared it legal. Agitators contended that if these funds were tribal and held in common for the tribe, then using some of them for educating Catholic Indians in Catholic schools made the non-Catholic Indian pay for Catholic education, and that money taken out of this fund reduced the general fund without giving the non-Catholic any advantage from it. To this Father Ketcham of the Bureau of Catholic Indian Missions in a statement before a United States Senate committee countered that a number of government schools among the Osage and Menominee Indians had been supported by these Indian funds for years, and thus money for the Catholic Indians had been expended for maintenance of non-Catholic government schools. If this practice was acceptable, then there was nothing illegal or unjust in a similar use of these funds for Catholic children.[21]

The necessity of annually collecting the signatures for this petition had the bad effect of reversing the positions of missionary and Indians. The missionary was now the beggar and the Indian could refuse or agree to sign. The disagreeable position in which the system put the sisters and Father Aloysius each year and the uncertainty of the attitude of the tribe made the missionaries desirous of giving up the mission boarding school in favor of a day school which would serve the children of the immediate vicinity rather than those brought to them from other localities. As the Indians exchanged their nomadic way of life for a more settled one, the government advocated district day schools instead of the boarding schools which had been established to isolate the child from its savage surroundings. Such district day schools would also be patronized by the white settlers who were moving into the reservations. These general developments tended to change the boarding school, classed as a mission school, into a day school belonging to the parish church at White Earth. On May 19, 1945, the Indian Council met at Cass Lake and voted to use no more of the tribal funds for the mission school. Then it was that St. Benedict's mission school became a parochial day school.[22]

The record of this school will always stand as a tribute to the courage of the religious who have worked there since that November day in 1878. In 1928 the three founders celebrated fifty years of service with the Indians and then retired to make way for younger laborers. Though retired from active service, Father Aloysius remained at the mission, and he died the following year. Sister Lioba and Sister Philomena returned to their mother house.

When the Benedictine sisters entered the missionary field at Red Lake in 1888 they had been preceded in the work of evangelizing by the veteran missionaries, Father Francis Pierz and Father Lawrence Lautischar. These two men had founded the mission in the 1850's. After a few months of training, Father Lautischar was left alone to care for the place while Father Pierz worked among other bands of Chippewa Indians. This young missionary was not destined to work long in his field for he lost his life while on an errand of mercy to a pagan Indian across the lake. While he was returning from this ten-mile sickcall a snow storm arose, and he was later found frozen to death not far from his mission. His good Indians brought his body to Crow Wing where Father Pierz gave it proper burial. Father Lautischar was succeeded by Father Tomazin. As had happened at White Earth this priest was soon embroiled with the government officials in his championing of the rights of the Indians. This time the controversy was the Pine Swindle. His cause was just, but he was indiscreet in dealing with the officials. In March of 1883 the situation came to a head, and the United States Commissioner of Indian Affairs asked the Catholic Bureau to remove the missionary. The bureau agreed to this on condition that the Indian Commissioner would accept another priest in his place and allow sisters to work on the reservation. The bishop of St. Cloud also agreed to remove him but said he had no priest just then to replace Father Tomazin. But Father Tomazin refused to obey the Indian Agent's orders to leave, and, resorting to the same trick which he had found effective at White Earth, he barricaded himself in the church building as soon as the soldiers arrived. He tolled the bell to call the Indians to his aid, but this time the Indians, out gathering maple sap, were too far away to hear the summons. The soldiers took him by force and put him over the boundary.[23]

From this date to 1888, when Miss Drexel paid a visit to White Earth and Red Lake, the poor Red Lake Indians were without a resident pastor.[24] When she heard the Indians implore for a priest and sisters to teach their children, she was touched at their plight and begged the abbot of St. John's to take over the mission. In her generosity she offered to pay the traveling expenses and the rent for temporary buildings for the missionary and the sisters. Not to be outdone, the abbey sent two priests, and the convent sent two teachers.

On Sunday, November 11, 1889, Abbot Alexius of St. John's Abbey with the two newly appointed missionaries, Father Simon Lampe and Father Thomas Borgerding, started for Red Lake. With them traveled Mother Scholastica and the two missionaries, Sister

Amalia Eich and Sister Evangelista McNulty. The party traveled by railroad as far as Detroit Lakes and there they engaged a team to take them to White Earth, twenty-two miles north. They stayed there five days getting acquainted with Indian ways under the tutelage of the veteran missionaries stationed there. The time was well spent, for the White Earth sisters found that the neophytes lacked many things essential to mission life, and they proceeded to supply them from their own meager possessions. Then the group piled themselves and their luggage into two lumber wagons and with two Indian teamsters started out on the long, long drive to Red Lake. This wagon trip was not a holiday jaunt as is learned from an account written by one of the priests of the group. He wrote:

The air line distance is 80 miles, but zigzags and stygian windings of the road make the distance on a lumber wagon from White Earth to Red Lake over 100 miles. The road . . . pierces primitive forests, winds about lakes and ponds, passes over streams, meanders about swamps and hills. . . . To measure them on a lumber wagon is no poetry. During the first 18 miles of our journey we met but an occasional habitation of some son of the forest. . . . At 6 PM we arrived at Knute Thompson's place, where we drew up for the night. We had made 22 miles during the afternoon and had seen only two dwellings — the log habitations of Simon Roy and of Truman Warren. . . . We got on our lumber wagon early that [next] morning, and traveling all day without seeing a human habitation, we reached Red Lake at 5:30 of the same day, November 15. The 40 to 50 miles passed over between Thompson's place on the Clearwater river to Red Lake is the domain of the deer and moose, and of the bear and wolf.[25]

Government officials and natives received the missionaries kindly and did what was possible under the circumstances to make them comfortable. "The Indians rejoiced," wrote Father Thomas, "to have two blackgowns stay with them, and in two councils freely expressed their joy and happiness. Apropos, at the first of the two councils, Saturday, November 17, the council room was packed full of Indians all smoking vigorously. The air became thick with smoke. The effect was such that one of the missionaries became ill." The sisters took over the government teacher's house near the lake and lived there for six months. The church, a log structure 18 by 24 feet with a log lean-to for the priests' dwelling, was located a mile away. An old warehouse made of upright logs and formerly used by the

Hudson's Bay Company was put in order, and with a few rough log seats, school was opened with an enrollment of 25 Indian day pupils; but blackboards, books, and slates were lacking for some time. Since the church was a mile or more from the school the convent Mass was offered in this warehouse-school on week-days, and for the first few mornings the top of a barrel was made to serve as an altar. Not only school equipment was lacking, but also such essentials as flour, kerosene, and potatoes. The buildings were in a dilapidated condition. The house roof leaked and was open to snow and wind. When years later Sister Amalia was asked, "How did you keep warm in that drafty house?" she replied, "We didn't. We froze."

The missionaries had just got settled when Christmas was upon them. Something, they decided, must be done for the children. Evergreen trees were plentiful, but where were the presents to come from? There was no time to send out begging letters to friends. They decided that candied popcorn and home-made candy would have to do. Late in the afternoon of Christmas day, a tree was decorated with lights and candy and set up in the blacksmith's house. The "children were astonished at the lighted tree and the hanging presents" wrote Father Thomas, and he continued, "All of the white men and children, numbering seventeen, were gathered around the tree at the blacksmith's." For the church the missionaries prepared another tree and decorated the altar with evergreens. At midnight Mass the church was filled with Indians and half-breeds; many could not find standing room.[26]

The next spring boarding pupils to the number of 27 were accepted. These, together with the day pupils, raised attendance to 60, and Sister Augustine Terhaar, Sister Euphrasia Hirtenberger, and a candidate were sent to help. This candidate was a young Chippewa girl, Jane Horn, who had been educated by the sisters at White Earth. As one of their own she was soon taken to the hearts of the Chippewa of Red Lake. So the gulf between the inexperienced white missionaries and the Indians was more easily bridged. With her, the sisters went to the Indian homes, visited the sick, and even accompanied the Indians who left for the deep woods to gather maple sap each spring. But the sisters could not go on the hunts, and here the Indians showed their generosity by supplying meat to the convent whenever their own supply would permit.

In this atmosphere of friendliness the number of applicants to the boarding school increased, but no more could be admitted unless there were more buildings. Fortunately the charitable Miss Drexel came to their aid with a gift of $6,000 toward the erection of a new boarding school. This school proved so popular that within two years it had to be enlarged. Contracts were made with the government for boarding and educating these pupils, but when that assistance was withdrawn in 1899, other means such as tribal funds, the Bureau of Catholic Indian Missions, and private charity had to be depended upon. During the first 35 years the sisters received no salary but were supported by the mother house. This was true also of the White Earth missionaries.

On the spiritual side the work was fruitful, for within the first five years of Benedictine activity at Red Lake 300 baptisms were administered and many souls were brought back to their religious duties. During the first month of their apostleship fifteen marriages were blessed and three converts were made. The Red Lake missionaries endured the same trials of destructive fires, of hunger, of cold, as did their sisters at White Earth. They had likewise the same joy and happiness of bringing the knowledge of God to children of the forest. Through these two missions thousands of Indian children and adults were not only christianized but civilized and made into better citizens.

The two mission schools continue their splendid work down to the present day, but they operate under different conditions. For reasons already mentioned, boarding schools have been replaced by parochial day schools. These have the additional advantage of making the school a more integral part of the immediate community and of helping to develop in the people on the reservation — both white and Indian — a greater sense of responsibility for the support of their school. Today neither St. Benedict's of White Earth nor St. Mary's of Red Lake is considered a mission school, but they are still dependent on the charity of apostolic Catholics.

St. Benedict's most recent mission work among Indians was undertaken at the request of Bishop Peter Bartholome. In 1941 he asked that sisters stationed at Onamia work among the pagan Chippewa Indians who lived near them at Mille Lacs Lake. Sister Laura Hesch was put in charge of this mission work. Her zeal was challenged by obstacles unknown to the early missionaries in White Earth and Red Lake who worked with Indians who had at least known Catholic missionaries and did not resent them. The primitive band Sister Laura was called upon to help evangelize was under the domination of actively hostile medicine men. Despite this, and because of the continued encouragement of the bishop, the mission today has its own chapel and hall, and after sixteen years of effort twenty per cent of the Indians have been received into the Church.

19 THE ST. CLOUD HOSPITAL*

It is not surprising that St. Cloud had no regular hospital until thirty or more years after it was founded. Although the site of the future city attracted settlers as early as 1851, the place remained a frontier settlement until after the Civil War. Only in the late 1870's and early 1880's did it become a city. As long as the settlement remained a small village, where neighbor knew neighbor and the people were united by bonds of friendship and charity, the sick were cared for in their homes with the help of family and neighbors. There was probably little need for hospital care of the sick. Furthermore, there was a strong prejudice against hospitals as places of cold charity.

By 1880 a change came over the settlement — a change which brought about the need for a hospital. After the railroad reached St. Cloud, its population and that of the surrounding territory increased rapidly. St. Cloud itself grew to such an extent that the charitable neighborliness of early days became dimmed. The settlement changed not only in size but in character. The population was more transient. Unmarried men and women without established homes had no one to care for them in times of illness or accident. If travelers bound for points farther west or soldiers en route to frontier military forts became ill or met with accidents, they were sometimes left in St. Cloud, ultimately to become problems for the local officials.

* Reprint of an article in *Minnesota History* 33:291–297.

The change in the character of the population was only one reason why the need for a hospital became acute about 1880. A second, and probably a more positive one, was the fact that the medical world of the 1880's had become fully aware of the dangers of infection, and the best doctors were beginning to advocate the "ceremony" of anti-sepsis. This consisted of drenching the table and patient with boiled water and chemical solutions — a thing which could not be done effectively in private homes. Young doctors trained in the best medical schools of the East were beginning to find their way into St. Cloud. Unlike their predecessors, they were not content to operate on kitchen tables in the homes of their patients.

One young physician, Dr. A. C. Lamothe Ramsay, lately graduated from Rush Medical College in Chicago, began practice in St. Cloud in 1882. He was anxious to put the latest methods into use, and soon after his arrival he started agitating for a regular hospital. Whether it was he who interested the Sisters of St. Benedict in this project or whether the sisters themselves saw the need for a hospital is not known, but the records of the local Benedictine convent, now part of the archives at St. Joseph, and of the city council for 1882 show that the sisters decided to go into hospital work provided the city would help finance such a project.

To this end in 1882 the sisters and Dr. Ramsay petitioned the city council for funds to help them erect a three-story hospital building. At a meeting on August 26 the council appointed a committee of three to look into the matter and to report on it. The minutes of the next council meeting, held on September 30, show that the committee asked for an extension of time, and it did the same at the two meetings that followed. Then the matter was mentioned no more.

The city council records for August 25, 1883, however, state that "the City Council committee on health reported it had rented the Mitchel Building at $14 a month for use as a hospital for a pauper sick with diphtheria, and had hired a nurse at $3 per day." Further progress is revealed in the council records for June 30, 1884, which show that "Kropp and Delaney presented their bill to the City for $238.00 for building a city hospital and outhouse." [1] This so-called hospital, of course, was nothing more than a nursing home, and not what Dr. Ramsay was advocating. It was the type of institution that created in the public mind the idea that hospitals were largely for the homeless and the shiftless and the unfortunate.

In desperation Dr. Ramsay decided to open a hospital of his own. A contemporary newspaper reports that he purchased a newly erected house from Joseph Pendel and opened it to the public as a hospital late in September, 1885.[2] He soon found that he could not run the institution and at the same time care for his regular practice. He then persuaded the sisters to take over the hospital work so that he might be free to carry on his own practice. The matter was put before the diocesan authorities in December and with their approval the sisters accepted the work.

Mother Scholastica, always a woman of quick decisions and rapid action, went to St. Cloud the day after the community chapter meeting and contracted with Peter Smith to add another floor to the St. Agnes Academy building and to refit it for hospital use. But on December 22, the day the carpenters started the remodeling, Mother Scholastica arrived on the scene, called the laborers from the work and sent them to make adjustments on a building on Ninth Avenue —a newly erected building just purchased from Mr. Kropp for $2,000. They soon announced the opening of the hospital under the name of St. Benedict's Hospital. On February 25, the building was blessed by Abbot Alexius Edelbrock assisted by ten priests. At a reception given in the afternoon physicians from St. Paul, Little Falls, Sauk Centre, and St. Cloud were present together with the city officials. On that day $600.00 were subscribed by friends of the institution. This cream-colored brick building is still standing next to St. Raphael's Rest Home on Ninth Avenue.

The new hospital could boast of a modern heating system, an operating room, two private rooms, wards, a kitchen, and a morgue. One newspaper gave the following account of its facilities:

Proud as a castle this edifice stands. The main part of the building is 34' x 36' and is three stories high. . . . If the exterior of the building is such a delight to the eye, our wonder is heightened when we view the interior. At the left of the main entrance is the reception room; the next adjoining room which is especially lighted by a bay window serves as an operating room. Back of this is a patient's room. To the right of the main entrance is a large room used as a ward for those not dangerously ill. A door from this room leads into a dining room, and next to this is the kitchen. . . . The entire building is heated by hot air. . . . The front of the building has a porch and the back of the building is a morgue. The patients will be under the care of four Sisters.[3]

THE ST. CLOUD HOSPITAL

This glowing report did not, however, attract patients. Perhaps the mention of a morgue in connection with the hospital frightened some people. Perhaps the following frank account of the patients' ills, published with the intent of praising the hospital's work, turned others away. It reads:

St. Benedict Hospital has already received four patients. One is Mr. Joseph Schmidt, of Melrose, who recently underwent a severe surgical operation, in which six of his ribs were removed. Another is a gentleman from Perham, to be operated upon for cataract; another from Little Falls, from whom an eye is to be removed; and the fourth from Melrose, a medical case. . . . The medical and surgical staff, and the attendant Sisters, too are not likely to want for occupation, it seems.[4]

Despite such encouraging publicity, only two patients were received the first month and eight the second. The sisters feared their new project was to be a failure.

There is a story that the sisters, worried about the venture, decided to pray together for nine successive days asking for Divine help in deciding whether or not to close their hospital. On the fifth day the answer came! A cyclone swept over the city and neighboring towns on April 14, 1886, injuring hundreds and killing many. It made a path through the city, wrecking all in its wake save the hospital, which was left intact. It thus became the center of rescue work and gave the sisters a chance to show their worth. For forty-eight hours the sisters toiled, until finally relief came from near-by towns and from the Twin Cities. As a result the sisters gained unstinted praise from the public. This catastrophe did much to break down local prejudice against hospitals in general and against sisters as nurses.[5] Thereafter, the hospital did not lack patients, and at the close of the second year of service the number of patients received reached the 400 mark. The majority of these were of course surgical cases or hopeless cases, for hospitals in those days were patronized only in extreme necessity. The result was that most patients needed extra care and special night service. "Night nurses" were unheard of. The day nurses simply took turns at night duty and the next day went on regular duty without sleep.

Thus, as might be expected, the early St. Cloud nurses were without formal training. It was up to Dr. Ramsay and the other doctors to train the nurses as they went about their work from day to day. To

the superioress, Sister Anselma Billig, was assigned the then dangerous and ticklish work of administering anesthetics.

The equipment used in the sisters' first hospital, like that of most
hospitals of that date, was of the simplest. The surgical table was
made of wood by the local carpenter working under Dr. Ramsay's
direction. It differed little from the kitchen tables in the patients'
homes, but the doctor could be sure that the hospital table was clean
and sterile. Although other items of equipment were just as primitive,
it must not be inferred that members of the medical profession in St.
Cloud were old-fashioned and unaware of the latest developments
in the field of medicine. Such men as Dr. Ramsay, Dr. Beebe, Dr.
Albert O. Gilman, Dr. George S. Brigham, and Dr. William T.
Stone received their degrees from some of the country's best medical
schools, and several went East from time to time for graduate courses.
Some local doctors had such wide and substantial professional repu-
tations that they became officers of the Minnesota State Medical
Society. Dr. Beebe, for example, was its president in 1890–91.[6]
Others were invited to read papers before meetings of Twin City
and Rochester doctors.

One innovation introduced in this pioneer St. Cloud hospital anticipated such modern hospitalization plans as the Blue Cross. In 1888
the sisters initiated a system of selling, at $10 each, tickets which
would entitle the purchaser to hospital treatment and care at any
time for a year. According to the *St. Cloud Times* of May 30, 1888:

There are three hospitals now in operation under the direction and
care of the Sisters of the Order of St. Benedict, one in St. Cloud, one at
Duluth and the third at Bismarck, D.T. The Sisters have adopted a system
of admission to these hospitals (in addition to the usual one by payment
of stated weekly accounts), which is received with much favor. They have
issued and are selling "Hospital Admission" tickets at $10 each. A pur-
chaser is entitled, without further pay, to admission and treatment, sub-
sistence and nursing at the three hospitals named, at any time during one
year from the date of the ticket, in consequence of wounds, injury, or
illness received or contracted, disabling him from manual labor. Insanity,
contagious, infectious, venereal diseases, or injury received before the
date of the ticket, or arising from the use of intoxicating drink or fighting,
are excluded from the benefits of the ticket.

By the end of the third year, in 1889, the number of patients using
St. Benedict's Hospital had increased to such an extent that the

256

sisters were faced with the need for larger quarters and a larger staff. Many considered the present location too limited for continued expansion. Others believed the site to be too close to the railroad track and shops for the quiet usually looked for in the choice of a hospital location. As soon as this became known, local real estate dealers began offering sites for a new building. A suitable one was considered, but was rejected because the price was prohibitive. Then John Coates and Daniel H. Freeman offered the sisters as a gift five acres of land on the east side of the Mississippi near the state reformatory, where their firm owned a large tract.

Partly because they wished to see St. Cloud expand in the direction of their holdings, and partly because they also owned a local transfer and livery business, Coates and Freeman were eager to encourage the development of an area two and a half miles from the heart of the city. No public transportation system connected the site with St. Cloud proper, and there was not even a foot bridge across the Mississippi at this point. The sisters were assured by some prominent citizens that if they selected the site, a bridge and road to connect it with the main community west of the river would soon be built. They were also promised that the streetcar line would be extended to the hospital. City officials and local businessmen alike encouraged the sisters to make the move, giving them every assurance that they would be wise to build their hospital in this new district. Unfortunately, however, transportation facilities did not materialize. After accepting the land, the sisters met one disappointment after another, and from the first the location proved unsatisfactory.

Work on the new building, which was named St. Raphael's Hospital, was completed in May, 1890.[7] Contemporary papers praised the up-to-date establishment, which had a large basement and was equipped with dumb-waiters, bathrooms and toilets. The new operating room was the pride and joy of the sisters and the medical staff. The surgical table, designed by Dr. Ramsay and constructed of iron and steel, cost $31.

The room itself, however, was designed for the use of the wet antiseptic, or Listerian, method, which was first used in Minnesota in 1886. Because boiled water or a carbolic acid solution was poured over wounds, instruments, and practically everything in the room, it had a concrete floor with a drain in the center. Steam atomizers kept the air humid, and the nursing sisters were hard put to it to keep their coifs or wimples from wilting. Although the St. Cloud Doctors Brigham, Stone, and Gilman used it regularly, the Listerian method was soon to be outmoded by a new method of asepsis, achieved simply by sterilizing everything which was to come in contact with a wound. This method reached St. Cloud in 1893, when Dr. John B. Dunn arrived in the city. He had studied surgery both in Germany and in the eastern United States, and it was not long before he introduced to St. Cloud radical new medical methods learned elsewhere. They made useless much of the surgical equipment of the new hospital.

Despite modern equipment and up-to-date doctors, the first St. Raphael's Hospital never had more than seven patients at a time, and it accommodated only 94 patients during its entire first year.[8] The lack of patronage can be accounted for largely by the inconvenient location of the institution. Visitors, patients, and staff who did not have conveyances of their own were forced to hire them or trudge two and a half miles on a muddy road. Doctors found it difficult to get through the snowbound roads in winter. After seven years of vainly waiting for the promised transportation facilities and more patients, the nurses and doctors decided that the hospital must be moved back to the city proper. The sisters and their friends were on the alert to dispose of the property, and the prospects were good when early in 1897 the state entered the market for a location for a women's reformatory. The hospital site was close enough to the men's reformatory that if purchased for a women's house of correction both institutions could be directed by the same administrative board. But nothing came of this dream, because the representative of this district failed to push the matter in the state legislature.

For the third time the sisters took up the burden of financing a hospital building without help from the territory they served. Restricted finances caused them to use once more the old site of the first hospital on Ninth Avenue. There in 1900 they erected a plain brick structure large enough to accommodate fifty patients. In late July the building was solemnly blessed by Bishop James Trobec. Present on this occasion was Archabbot Boniface Krug, O.S.B., of Monte Cassino, and his secretary, Father Angelo, O.S.B. The newspaper reported that a choir of six sisters "furnished the vocal music in a very creditable manner."[9] The building had two operating rooms, one of which was equipped with the latest type of surgical table and all the newest gadgets. The old steam sterilizers were replaced by a new copper Rochester sterilizer. As pictured on old photographs, this hospital shows little resemblance to the present building, now St. Raphael's Rest Home.

Originally the structure was two and a half stories high with a mansard roof. Certain changes, however, were made after the two upper floors were destroyed by fire in the fall of 1905. The fire started in the garret where a small motor, used to operate a food elevator, must have become overheated. Splendid work was done in carrying the fifty-three patients to safety. Four had been operated on only the day previous, and a dozen or more typhoid cases were in the isolation ward. All recovered from the shock, and no lives were lost. The people of St. Cloud opened their homes to the patients, and it was said that every available hack and carriage in the city was hurried to the scene. The work of rebuilding began at once, despite the fact that the insurance did not cover half the loss. A flat roof replaced the old dormer type roof, and fire escapes and iron porches were placed across the front, sides, and back with safety rather than beauty in mind.

Although schools for nurses had been established in Duluth and in St. Paul, St. Cloud was slow in following their example. The Minnesota State Nurses Association in 1905 declared that it favored professional standards and licensing. Aware that the day was not far distant when a staff of formally trained and registered nurses would be necessary to maintain the standing of a hospital, Mother Cecilia Kapsner and Sister Secunda Hansen decided that it was time to institute a school for nurses. In 1908 the hospital engaged a superintendent of nurses from Chicago to train the sisters and any other young women who wished to become nurses.[10] Sisters Cunnigund Kuefler, Salome Amschler, Julitta Hoppe, Leobina Gliszhenski, and Natalia Schmittbauer, with four lay nurses, formed the first group.

About the same time the hospital improved its method of keeping case records. Heretofore, as in Bismarck, patients' records were gathered by the head nurse, who copied them in a large notebook. The pages were ruled off into columns, with spaces for the patient's name, date of entry and dismissal, the nature of the case, and comments on methods of treatment. Unfortunately the data gathered was vague, too brief, and at times unreliable. When Dr. C. B. Lewis arrived in 1905, he took the matter into his own hands, making the rounds each Sunday morning, interviewing patients and doctors, and recording data. He did this for some years until the modern system of case recording came into use.

Twenty-six years after the third hospital opened, it had become inadequate to serve St. Cloud and the surrounding territory despite the fact that twenty beds had been added. To provide space for them, nurses, laborers, and laundry had been moved out of the main structure and housed in a service building. The public had become hospital minded and people no longer used hospitals only as a last resort. Automobiles and good roads enabled residents of near-by towns and rural areas to take their sick to St. Cloud for care. So a hospital which in 1900 was sufficient for the city, was in 1926 wholly inadequate for the broadened area. To meet the new and expanded needs the sisters set about erecting their fourth local hospital building. With fear and anxiety they shouldered a prospective debt of $2,000,000 to finance the handsome structure erected in 1928 and known as the St. Cloud Hospital. The businessmen of the city promised aid and showed great enthusiasm for the project. They agreed that a city-wide drive should be made to raise $300,000 to help finance the sisters' undertaking. Twenty captains with their aides were named to solicit funds. A large barometer some fifteen feet high was erected on St. Germain Street to register the gifts as they were made. Meanwhile, a fire whistle called the attention of the city to the fact that the indicator was going up. Sad to tell, the red liquid in the barometer never moved very high, and the whistle was blown only a few times, for it had become generally known that the sisters had already signed the building contract and the structure would go up whether the citizens contributed or not. Only $10,000 was collected. Thus for the third time the city as a civic body failed to aid this enterprise which was not only humanitarian but also an economic asset to St. Cloud. There were in the city, nevertheless, many individuals who contributed generously to the cause.

Shortly after the building was opened the great depression struck the country, and the sisters of St. Benedict's Convent saved and economized in all ways possible to be able to meet the payments due on the hospital. Though the hospital beds were consistently filled with patients during the depression many could not meet their hospitalization payments. This made it difficult for the hospital to pay its running expenses, to say nothing of paying the interest on the building loans. Fortunately the depression ended without too much suffering and worry, and the hospital was then free to staff and equip the institution so as to meet state requirements. Previous to 1944 the lay nurses lived on one floor of the south wing of the hospital building. But by this date the number of patients asking for admission required that these rooms be given up to their needs and that a residence for nurses be erected near by. Plans were accordingly made to provide a building giving residence to thirty student nurses and to provide recreational, library, and classroom facilities for about one hundred and fifty student nurses. It was finished at a cost of $141,000 with the assistance of a grant of $66,500 from the federal government and $15,330 from friends.[11] On August 29, 1945, Bishop Busch dedicated the building under the title of St. Benedict's Hall. Eight years later four more floors were added to this two-story structure to enable the entire body of student nurses to live on the hospital grounds.

In 1956, St. Cloud marked the completion of seventy-three years of hospital work, during sixty-six of which the Benedictine sisters were leaders. Their record of accomplishment is well reflected in the hospital itself. Though the sisters began with a building that cost only $2,880, their present hospital represents an initial investment of $2,000,000. It is currently appraised at nearly twice that figure. During the same sixty-six year period the accommodations increased from 20 to 315 beds. The hospital lay employees grew in number from 1 to 395, the medical staff from 1 to 60 and the nursing sisters from 4 to 75. During the year 1956 the number of bed patients cared for was 13,854; the number of out-patients, 11,229. The St. Cloud Hospital has kept pace with the community in which it is located, as well as with medical progress in the state and nation. It has received national and state rating; it is a member of the Catholic Hospital Association, the American Hospital Association, and it is approved by the Joint Commission of Accreditation. Besides conducting a school of nursing, it has established schools of X-ray technology, medical technology, and anesthesia.

Buildings and equipment alone do not make a Catholic hospital; it cares for souls as well as for bodies. The patients in the St. Cloud Hospital are particularly blessed in the fact that Bishop Bartholome has assigned to their care two young resident chaplains. Of the spirit in the hospital one may permit a monk to speak. In an article which appeared in the *Catholic Digest* for November, 1952, Father Emeric Lawrence of St. John's Abbey wrote:

Though living intimately with suffering, these women never become used to it, never hardened. They know that suffering and death have no value in themselves; but they also know that suffering and death motivated by love can become the most powerful and sanctifying of prayers. They give others motivation. This suffering and grief the sisters bring with them to daily Mass where they offer it together with themselves and their love on the altar.[12]

20 HOMES FOR THE AGED AND ORPHANS

The Diocese of St. Cloud can take pride in the fact that its old people are well cared for. Two of the three homes for the aged conducted by Benedictine sisters are in the area of St. Cloud. One is outside the city limits; the other is close to the center of the city. The former, St. Joseph's Home, is located on an estate of seventy-eight acres about one and a half miles east of the city. The building was originally erected as St. Raphael's Hospital, but in the pre-auto age distance and poor roads made the site inconvenient for doctors, patients, and visitors. This forced the sisters to build a new St. Raphael's Hospital nearer to the center of the city. The problem remained of putting the vacated building to some profitable use. The State of Minnesota was at this time looking for a site for a women's reformatory. Friends of the sisters saw an opportunity to sell the hospital property to the state. Since the site was but a mile or so from the state reformatory for men, it was argued that to put the two reformatories under one management would be good state economy. When this plan failed, Bishop James Trobec and Mother Aloysia Bath decided to use the building as a home for the aged. While the location had been inconvenient for patients and doctors making daily visits to the hospital, it was ideal for a home for older people who loved the quiet and the beauty of the countryside and who had no need or desire to travel back and forth to the city.

During the 1880's and 1890's most Catholic hospitals harbored a number of aged people whose only affliction was the pain of old age. The hospital in St. Cloud had them too, and in May, 1900, when the patients were transferred to the new St. Raphael's Hospital eight elected to stay to form the nucleus of the new St. Joseph's Home. Sister Placida Heine was appointed superior. Their first guests ranged in age from sixty to eighty-four years. Two more guests entered each succeeding month until by the end of the year they numbered twenty. All of these first twenty guests had been born abroad in some one of the German states, and nearly all were Catholic. However, among the people registered in 1902 there was one Lutheran, one Universalist and one Spiritualist.[1]

Some of the house rules in vogue in the early 1900's indicate the kind of discipline that was required for peace, order, and cleanliness. The following list was printed and posted in each room:

1. Papers and valuable articles should be given to the Sister Superior for safe-keeping.

2. If anyone desires to leave the Home for the City, that person must inform Sister Superior.

3. Everyone is at liberty to take walks around the premises and if the weather is favorable, to be outdoors as much as possible.

4. No one is allowed to cross fields or climb through fences when going to the City or visiting neighbors, but must keep to the public road.

5. Unbecoming manners, quarreling, or fighting is not allowed.

6. No spitting is allowed in the building, nor outside the building, but use cuspidors (spitoons), or handkerchiefs.

7. It is forbidden to strike matches on the walls, or to put hard articles in the toilet, such as orange peelings, matches, rags, etc.

8. It is not permitted to lean against the radiators in rooms or halls, or soil them with dirty hands, or by spitting on them.

9. At 9 o'clock all must retire in a quiet manner.

10. No one is allowed to stay in the boiler room, except the ones in charge.[2]

In 1904 when eighty residents filled St. Joseph's Home to capacity, another wing was added. From that date to the present the number of aged in annual residence approximates ninety-five.

The religious life of guests at St. Joseph's Home is amply cared for. Resident chaplains are there to attend to the spiritual needs of those who wish aid, and a chapel is open at all times for those who wish to pray and to meditate.

Much of the food is raised and processed on the premises. Sixty-eight acres are used for farming, gardening, fruit growing, and pasturing. The dairy herds produce enough milk and butter for the institution. Enough hogs and chickens are raised to supply the pork and eggs used. The garden and orchard products are ample for summer consumption and for canning.

Recreation is provided by occasional parties and bazaars held in the general recreation room, but most of it is of an informal nature. In summer many take an interest in flower gardening.

The second home for retired men and women is located on the corner of Ninth Avenue and Fifth Street in St. Cloud. This building, like that of St. Joseph's Home, was originally used for a hospital and consequently is well-equipped with sun porches and elevator service. St. Raphael's Rest Home opened the doors to its first guests in May, 1928, a few weeks after the hospital staff and patients had moved to their new St. Cloud Hospital.[3] The superior, Sister Rufina Hansen, received five guests the first day, and ten more entered in a short time. Today about eighty-two are accommodated and there are as many more on the waiting list.

The Mary Rondorf Home in Staples, Minnesota, is of a later date and of a different type. This institution is parochial and the title to the property does not rest with St. Benedict's Convent. In 1953, Sacred Heart parish, under the leadership of its pastor, decided to undertake a much-needed charitable work, a home for retired people of the parish and the town. It was to be a parochial cooperative work. Two apartment houses and a residence were purchased and the local women were asked to contribute their services to the care of their aged friends and neighbors. To coordinate the work and to comply with state law, a superintendent had to be appointed. The pastor asked Mother Richarda Peters to send a sister to fill that position. His request was granted, and on May 23, 1953, Sister Sophonia Lang was put in charge. It was soon evident that an institution caring for some twenty-five guests needed more than the donated services of parishioners. To give stability and regularity to the daily routine, St. Benedict's Convent sent two sisters to assist in the work, one to act as a nurse and the other to take charge of the kitchen. At present three sisters assisted by six full-time workers carry on the work of bringing joy and security to fifty elderly men and women.

The great influx of immigrants into Minnesota in the period preceding the Civil War brought with it many social and religious problems. One of these problems was the care of orphans. The ravages of plague and epidemic often left the immigrant children with neither parents nor friends. With this in mind a group of German Catholics in the St. Paul area took steps in 1869 to organize the St. Joseph Orphan Society to care for German orphans. Among the leaders of this movement were Frank Schlick, Henry Timme, F. J. Metzger, A. Springer, and M. Throze. In time zeal died down, and at the end of eight years nothing much had been accomplished in the way of providing a building for an orphanage. The project took on new life in 1877. With the election of Mr. George Mitsch to the presidency of the society, a committee was formed to get a building for an orphanage and to apply to St. Gertrude's Convent, Shakopee, for two sisters to care for the children.

Temporary quarters were rented on the corner of Ninth and Robert Streets, St. Paul. The household articles were furnished or begged by Balthasar Schweizer, Jacob Simmer, Charles Friend, George Mitsch, and Henry Timme. The regular members of the society were assessed ten cents a month. The honorary members contributed one dollar a month to the cause. The Assumption parish assumed responsibility for the education of the orphans by permitting them to attend the parochial school free of charge.

The orphanage opened its doors on the Feast of St. Joseph, 1877. Its first charges were six children taken from a Catholic orphanage established at Grove and Olive Streets by Bishop Thomas Grace of St. Paul. Five other children were admitted the next day. Sister Benedict Klein and Sister Agatha Nachbar of St. Gertrude's Convent, Shakopee, were in charge. They received a salary of ten dollars a month.[4] Because of the distance from the Assumption church and school, this home could be only a temporary one. In June, 1879, an eight-room house on Ninth Street, on property across the street from the Assumption rectory, was purchased and a building constructed for a new orphanage. During the summer of the following year, the seventeen children moved to their new home, and on December 9 Bishop Grace blessed it. Preparatory to purchasing this new property, the society changed its name to St. Joseph's German Catholic Orphan Society of St. Paul. According to a previous agreement the children continued to attend the Assumption parochial school, but when an epidemic broke out among the children of the parish the orphans were blamed as the carriers. The incident was used for propaganda by certain parishioners who were opposed to supplying school space and teachers for children not of the parish. Because of the strong feeling against the orphans, the children were withdrawn, and classes were taught in the orphanage. Within five years the school was so overcrowded that building was the only alternative to turning away many homeless children. The society's board of directors with the aid of various German parishes throughout the state generously undertook the expense, and the new wing was blessed on October 23, 1887.[5] The home then gave shelter to forty-seven boys and forty-three girls. This increase in the number of children in turn caused other problems, and the lack of proper playground space, together with the down-town location of the home, forced the directors to look for property in a less congested district.

A suitable place was found at the outskirts of the city on Randolph Street where a forty-seven acre tract of land was purchased. Here a spacious structure was built during the course of the summer of 1900. In addition to the main building, the plant included a number of farm buildings and a shop for the boys.

Some time previous to this building venture the society had taken steps to become incorporated under the laws of the state. To bring the orphanage under the care of the diocese it had named Bishop Ireland as president of its board of directors. By so doing, the institution received a share of the annual diocesan orphan collection, though it was not a diocesan institution but one whose title was vested in St. Joseph's German Catholic Orphan Society of St. Paul. Previous to moving to the Randolph Street location, the home had been supported only by the society and by funds collected by the sisters on regular begging tours from parish to parish and from door to door. Down through the years the sisters drew the salary of $10.00 a month, and at times they had to go out and collect the money that was to be paid for their salary.[6] Even after they began to receive diocesan aid, the sisters went begging throughout the state during harvest time. Some went about with a wagon soliciting food from hotels and bakeries. Reports from the sisters who did the begging for the orphans attest to the generosity of the people of the St. Paul area in responding to their appeals. In her memoirs, Sister Juliana Venne relates how she begged from time to time for money for such improvements as the building of a porch, a laundry, and the installation of a new heating system, for sidewalks, and for a flag pole. The Orphans' Picnic and Fair became an annual event and was patronized by many different parishes. Hundreds attended despite the fact that the street car lines ended at Grand and Snelling Avenues. On that day, friends of the orphans supplied carriages to bring guests to the picnic grounds at the orphanage.[7]

The orphanage farm gave the boys training in manual work and at the same time taught them responsibility. They were allotted such tasks as helping to milk the cows, tend the chickens, and work in the garden. The girls shared in the housework. *The Northwestern Chronicle* of April 30, 1904, in describing the work done at the institution revealed that the boys as well as the girls were taught to darn their own stockings and to sew on buttons and that the superior was "as proud of the boys' sewing as she was of the girls'."

Administrative changes have been made to meet the demands of legal requirements. Previous to 1907 the children were placed in the orphanage by its board of directors and this same board placed them in homes for adoption. In 1907 the State Board of Control made its first inspection of the institution, and thereafter all placement of children in private homes had to have its approval. The sisters, however, were the persons who had to inspect the private homes previous to the placement and to do the follow-up work. In 1921 when the number of orphans registered at the home was 214, the State Department of Social Welfare licensed the newly incorporated Bureau of Catholic Charities of the Twin Cities to take over the work of admission and placement of orphans. With the opening of World War II, the consequent dislocation of family life, and the need of close relations of Catholic charitable agencies with the public agencies, Archbishop John Murray of St. Paul established the Diocesan Bureau of Charities for the whole archdiocese. This bureau was incorporated as a child-placing and family agency under Minnesota statutes on May 29, 1943. The first purpose of the bureau is to integrate the work of Catholic agencies within the archdiocese, to plan, supervise, and finance social work under Catholic auspices. Another purpose is to enable Catholic charities to work in intelligent harmony with civic organizations. Under this arrangement, St. Joseph's Home for Children, as it is now called, is one of the St. Paul institutions to be supported partially by the Community Chest Fund.

Under the old system of placement the child of a broken home would be admitted without question to a home such as St. Joseph's. The practice today is to study the whole background and if possible prevent the child's home from being broken, or, if that is impossible, to place the child in a foster home rather than in an institution. Though the whole trend is away from institutional care of the child, there is still need for an institution like St. Joseph's Home for Children. From its opening until 1955, the sisters have cared for 5000 boys and girls, counteracting the handicaps which might easily have led to warped personalities, and so prepared them to fill the vocations for which God destined them.[8]

21 FOREIGN MISSIONS

Though St. Benedict established his monastery as a school of the Lord's service, it was soon found that as the monks grew in the love of God their love expressed itself in love for souls who knew not the God Who had created them. St. Benedict himself had sent his monks to teach the people of the surrounding countryside, and the Benedictines down the ages have followed his example. In the sixth century Benedictines were sent by St. Gregory the Great to christianize England. Two centuries later the Anglo-Saxon monks and nuns were able to furnish missionaries to convert the Teutonic tribes of Europe. It was from one of these convents established in Germany that monks and nuns were recruited to work in the United States in the nineteenth century. Missionary work to peoples in strange lands has always been a part of Benedictine tradition. It is for this reason that the Minnesota Benedictines when called upon in their turn to carry the light of Christianity across the Pacific to the Far East did not view the call as something new and foreign to the Benedictine spirit.

But the call of China when it came in 1929 was as unexpected and as sudden as was the call of America to the Eichstätt convent in 1852. Reverend Francis Clougherty, O.S.B., of the Catholic University of Peking in China appeared at the doors of St. Benedict's Convent on Saturday, August 24, 1929, asking Mother Louisa Walz for sisters to open classes for women in conjunction with the Catholic University at Peking. This school for higher Chinese studies was a young institution located in Peking and sponsored by the Benedictine abbeys of the American Cassinese Congregation. Its origin dated to 1912 when a Catholic scholar, Mr. Vincent Ying, petitioned Pope Pius X to found a Catholic university in Peking. As a preparatory measure Mr. Ying opened Fu Jen Shê, a school for Chinese studies. After waiting six years for the Church authorities to take action in the field of higher studies, the school was forced to close. But Mr. Ying did not give up. He knew that the ancient literature and culture of the Chinese people was in danger of being lost in their eagerness to become westernized. He also believed that a university was the best means of bringing the truths of Catholicism to the intellectuals and of training Chinese Catholic leaders. When in 1920 the Reverend Dr. G. B. O'Toole, an American priest closely connected with St. Vincent's Archabbey at Latrobe, Pennsylvania, visited Mr. Ying, he was so impressed by the latter's views that he traveled to Rome to lay the matter before the Chair of Peter. On his return to the United States Dr. O'Toole did his best to interest Archabbot Aurelius Stehle and other Benedictine abbots in the project of establishing a Catholic university in Peking. His reward came two years later when the Sacred Congregation for the Propagation of the Faith asked the abbeys of the American Cassinese Congregation to undertake the work. In 1924, Rome issued the official documents necessary for the projected university, and in the fall of 1925 the newly constituted university organization revived Mr. Ying's school and opened a few classes in the Fu Jen or Catholic University of Peking.

In 1927, two years before Father Clougherty's visit to St. Benedict's, the university had received recognition and accreditment from the Chinese Nationalist government. Father Clougherty, then chancellor, and the university officials immediately began to plan a women's college as an affiliate of the university. It was in pursuance

of that plan that the chancellor visited St. Benedict's on Augu¹
1929. Told that the convent was diocesan and that Bishop B
consent must be obtained before such a venture could be consiᵤᵤᵤ
Father Clougherty hastened to place his cause before the bishop. He
returned that same day to report that Bishop Busch looked with favor
on the proposal and had even offered to address the sisters. He convinced Reverend Mother Louisa and her council that they could no
longer hesitate to accept this Chinese mission since their bishop
approved and the Holy Father had asked Benedictine sisters to
undertake it.

Monday morning, August 26, Father Clougherty and the bishop
addressed the sisters. Father Clougherty spoke eloquently on the
cause of China and stressed the fact that the Pope had particularly
picked out the Benedictines for this university work. When Bishop
Busch addressed the sisters he gave his consent for the undertaking,
but only on the condition the necessary funds be raised by the diocesan Propagation of the Faith, and that the mother house be in no
way held responsible. This was done as a matter of precaution, for
he knew St. Benedict's had lately incurred a two-million dollar debt
in erecting a hospital in St. Cloud and hard times were already threatening this country. At the end of the meeting, all were enthusiastic
over the venture.

At the chapter meeting of the convent held on September 1, the
sisters gave their formal approval of the undertaking. They did this
without full realization of what was in the mind of the Church officials
in China. Apparently the details of the agreement with Father
Clougherty were not as clear as they should have been and there was
room for misunderstanding. The sisters and Bishop Busch understood that the Catholic University of Peking, of which Father Clougherty was the chancellor, was simply asking for sisters to teach in the
women's department of the university — not to found or to build
that school. Their salary plus funds gathered in America would be
sufficient to support them. Later events proved that Father Clougherty and the apostolic delegate to China had been asking not only for
teachers but for a Benedictine convent which would found, build, and
maintain a women's college at the university. In the fall of that year
a novena to the Holy Spirit was made by all the sisters at the mother
house and at the missions, and at its close 109 sisters felt moved to
offer themselves for work in China. Mother Louisa pondered and

prayed long over that list of names and in April of 1930 chose Sisters Francetta Vetter, Donalda Terhaar, Regia Zens, Rachel Loulan, Ronayne Gergen and Wibora Muehlenbein. While enthusiasm for the foreign mission was increasing among the sisters, the bishop in the meantime had discovered some of the problems of this undertaking and had lost interest. He had even become antagonistic to the venture. But then zealous Father Clougherty reappeared on the St. Cloud scene and the bishop again warmed to the enterprise, not only giving his formal approval but making a substantial donation toward it.

These six sisters left St. Benedict's Convent on August 30, 1930. On their arrival at Peking in late September, they were domiciled in a house belonging to the university but located some distance from it. The house and its location were suitable enough while the sisters were studying the Chinese language and people and becoming acclimated. It was, however, too small to accommodate the students that the university soon sent there in increasing numbers. When the sisters complained of lack of room they were told to purchase a larger building. It was now apparent that neither the apostolic delegate at Peking nor the university officials ever planned to build a women's college but had intended that the sisters accept complete responsibility for this project. To force the sisters to purchase school property, the university continued to send young women to them. In 1932 the apostolic delegate notified the sisters that at a certain date the Sisters of Disciples of the Lord, a congregation of sisters which he had founded, were to occupy their house and it must be vacated. With the help of Father Clougherty and others a new home was rented and classes were re-opened. But classes were no sooner opened than the prince who owned the property put it on the market for sale. The missionary sisters were worried, for any day this new home could be sold over their heads. The university again insisted that it was understood from the first that the mother house in Minnesota would found and build a women's college. The apostolic delegate himself urged Mother Louisa to act, but she and Bishop Busch withheld their consent. This was the time of the great depression; and burdened as St. Benedict's already was by a debt the weight of which grew ever heavier, Mother Louisa had to refuse. Bishop Busch protested that he had never committed St. Benedict's to found or build such a

college; he had only agreed to the purchase of a convent f[...]
sisters, and that to be made only after a period of five years' res[...]
in China. Acting on the advice of the bishop, Mother Louisa [...]
August 31, 1930, sent a cablegram to the sisters in Peking ordering
them to return to the United States should the university insist that
the sisters finance the women's college.

It was fortunate, indeed, that the sisters were not permitted to buy
the property, for control of the Catholic University was soon to pass
from the hands of the Benedictine priests to the Fathers of the Divine
Word. Lack of funds, together with lack of teaching personnel, had
forced the American Benedictine abbeys to ask Rome to transfer
control of the university to another religious body of the Holy See
and Rome had replied early in 1933 by commissioning the Society
of the Divine Word to take charge of the institution. The Benedictine
sisters were then worried. Would the new administration build a
women's college and if they did would they retain the Benedictine
sisters or call in other sisters of an order allied with theirs. Only in
December of that year did the Fathers of the Divine Word declare
their stand: the Benedictine sisters could continue their work in the
women's college, but that college would not be supported by the
Catholic University. On receipt of this news, St. Benedict's informed
the sisters that they must plan to return to Minnesota at the end of the
next school year, August, 1935.[2] That year would mark the end of
the five-year contract that St. Benedict's had made with the Catholic
University. The missionaries were reluctant to leave China, because
they saw the great work that could be done there. Although their
five years of work had not produced many converts, they had broken
down prejudice against the Catholic Church and had created a better
understanding of its purpose.

When it became known that the Benedictine sisters would most
probably have to leave China, the Vicar Apostolic of Kaifeng, Most
Reverend Joseph Tacconi, hastened to invite the sisters to staff a
middle school in his diocese. To his plea was added that of the Sisters
of Providence who were conducting both a lower and higher middle
school in Kaifeng. They needed help and were only too glad to offer
their higher middle school to the Benedictines. Eager to accept this
invitation, the sisters begged Mother Louisa and Bishop Busch to
let them remain in China and work in this new field of Kaifeng. To

this prayer Bishop Busch would not listen. They petitioned a second and a third time, and on April 8, 1935, he consented. The missionaries prepared to leave for Kaifeng in Honan Province.[3]

By the time the sisters reached Kaifeng the plans for their taking charge of the higher middle school had to be relinquished because of growing political unrest. Instigated by communists, students throughout China were rioting and striking against their schools and threatening the lives of their teachers. Conducting a school under such conditions was inviting trouble. Instead, a dispensary for the sick poor was opened. Here the sisters also instructed the children of the poor in religion. Such instructions were given only to children whose parents were prospective converts or who attended classes in religion. Soon the sisters were also given charge of adult classes. The 9,000 poor who were treated in the dispensary were thus brought into contact with Christianity. The dying were baptized, and a great number were given instructions with baptism following later. While the poor were waiting for their medical treatment they were told about God and His love for man, and those showing some interest were asked to rest a while in a small adjoining room where further conversation was carried on. Many were the questions asked about "the foreign God." So promising was this field that in 1936 Mother Louisa sent two more sisters to Kaifeng, Sister Ursuline Venne to assist as teacher, and Sister Annelda Wahl, to assist in the dispensary.

In 1937, just as the dispensary was proving most successful, war broke out between Japan and China. As the Japanese troops pushed the Chinese troops south and the fighting came near to Kaifeng, group catechetical instruction was discontinued. The dispensary took on a more public character, for the work was carried on under the aegis of the International Red Cross of which Father Clougherty was the local chairman. The Red Cross also set up refugee camps for the thousands of Chinese fleeing from the Japanese troops. In this emergency the Catholic and Protestant groups worked together to turn school buildings and missions into camps for these unfortunate refugees. The sisters worked in one camp where a group of 1700 women and children were crowded into a compound supposed to care for only 600 persons. Here the sisters found a splendid opportunity for planting the word of God and baptizing the dying.

The sisters were also drafted with other missionaries to care for the thousands of wounded Chinese soldiers who were being brought through Kaifeng from the front to safety further south. Any time of the day or night, when a train of soldiers was expected, a siren would blow to signal the Red Cross nurses and sisters to gather their medical supplies and hurry to the railroad station as best they could. At times official cars flying the United States flag would transport them. At other times they hired rickshaws. Sometimes they walked. On one occasion the call came at 2:30 in the morning. The chaplain offered Holy Mass in the convent at 3 o'clock, and after a hurried breakfast the sisters hastened to the station where two trainloads of sick awaited them. While they were eating their noon lunch, a second call came, and they worked until 9 o'clock that night. Other times they worked all night and returned home at 5:30 in the morning. One trainload alone brought 2,000 wounded packed on the floors of dark boxcars or on the top of flatcars. Those able to be brought out were treated on the dusty station platform, where storm lanterns were tied to the posts to give light to the workers. The mortally wounded were cared for in the unlighted boxcars. One of the sisters in a letter written April 12, 1938, described the nursing care they could give in such surroundings.[4] Only two sisters worked in a car, for the wounded were packed so close together on the floor that the nurses could hardly step between them. Afraid to move lest she step on a body, one sister held a candle for the other who in a crouching position dressed wounds filled with pus and maggots in an indescribable stench.

Day and night work at the railroad station and in the military hospital was unnerving, but the siren warning of the bomb raid was worse. If they were home near their bombproof cellar under the United States flag, they were guaranteed some protection, but the railroad station was a favorite target for the bombers. One day bombers flew over the station three times and the sisters expected bombs to drop any minute and destroy them. But they said a prayer and kept on working. If the warning came in time the nurses hurriedly jumped onto a boxcar and were taken out into the country.[5]

It was zeal for souls that kept the sisters at this work. They spoke to these poor sufferers of the good God and showed by their own actions the meaning of Christianity. Many of the dying asked for baptism and it was administered to them. Many who were not dying but asked for the sacrament had to be told they needed further instruction and must wait. To all, the sisters spoke of God and His goodness and planted in their minds an idea which might later bring fruit. It was still possible to get letters out to the United States and one of the sisters wrote:

I wish you could see these men. They are wonderful. All those who have been baptized have little crosses or Benedictine medals on a string around their necks or arms. And when we come around they show them to us. Some of those who are not baptized beg to be every time the sisters come around. We tell them that they are not in immediate danger of death and we may not baptize them until they have been better instructed. One day after baptizing a very sick man the soldier next to him, a hardboiled soldier, said, 'Now baptize me too. I heard everything you told that fellow and I believe it all.' The other day I went into a boxcar to attend to a soldier who was going to be taken off the train for he was about to die. He had been shot through the lungs from side to side. When asked if he was a Catholic he answered, 'Yes,' and not believing him I asked when he was baptized. Then he answered, 'A little while ago.' A Chinese catechist working with us had reached him before me. We have many chances of sending souls to Heaven. Please do not recall us from China; it would break our hearts, for there are so many chances here of doing good. It is dangerous work but the good God will care for us.[6]

And this was written after they had received the second notice and warning from the American consulate to leave China. They reported that 150 Chinese soldiers were baptized in 1937 and the following year 146.[7] At the dispensary and refugee camp in the course of a few months they baptized 47 dying.

Under these circumstances regular convent life was impossible. Aspirations and short prayers had to replace the formal Choral Office on some days, but living daily in danger of death and seeing God's miracles of grace in the converts kept the missionaries close to Him. One sister wrote that all they could do was to keep on with their daily tasks as serenely as possible, living only for the day and leaving the morrow in the loving hands of God.

One day word came that the Japanese were about to capture the city of Kaifeng. The Chinese people fled and the refugee camps were nearly emptied. The sisters were advised to pack clothing, bedding, and a week's supply of food and to be ready to flee to a larger and more substantial mission house of the Sisters of Providence near the cathedral. For several days the city was given over to pillage by the Japanese soldiers. The stories of murder, rape, and destruction that reached the sisters' ears struck fear in their hearts, but they decided to stay in their own home. Some mission compounds were broken into and the Chinese refugee women abused. Several times soldiers forced their way into the Benedictine compound, "but were tactfully put out by Father Francis Clougherty whom Bishop Tacconi appointed as protector of the convent." [8]

In time order was restored — the order imposed on a conquered people. At least the sisters were safe from the Japanese soldiers. Even though the sisters belonged to a neutral country and were free to leave they could not abandon their Chinese people to their fate. The past few years showed them the rich harvest of souls awaiting them. St. Benedict's Convent agreed, and in August, 1939, not only sent them additional help in the persons of Sister Flora Goebel and Sister Vestina Bursken, but decided to erect a new and larger mission house. The old convent was to be turned into a dispensary and a school for poor children. The new building was to be used as the convent and a school for paying pupils. This work prospered and in the school year ending in July, 1941, the mission had instructed 224 children and 52 adults for baptism.

This success might have lulled them into a feeling of security had not rumors of unrest, of hatred of all foreigners, of communism and banditry seeped into the convent. In the back country not policed by the Japanese soldiers, bandits and communists had free reign. With news of the murder of their bishop-elect, Antoni Barosi, by Chinese bandits, fear possessed the sisters. Sister Francetta recorded the event in a letter written to Mother Rosamond on November 27, 1941, less than two weeks before she herself became a prisoner. She wrote:

Our Bishop left on a mission tour a few weeks ago with his trusted servant, Han. On the way he was joined by another priest and visited the village of Ting-Tsun where there were two Fathers stationed. At noon of the day following their arrival, seventeen men entered the compound and ordered out of the place all of the Christians who had gathered to honor the Bishop. One of the Fathers went to see what was going on and when he did not return the Bishop and the other two Fathers went to investigate. The assassins tied and gagged them. Before this was done the Bishop spoke kind words to them but it availed nothing. They beat him and killed him and his companions. Three were strangled and one was drowned. They then looted the entire mission compound and threw the bodies in the well. Only when they left the compound in the evening did the Christians dare return. They searched and finally found the bodies. All night they worked in retrieving the bodies. Reverently the Christians removed the wet clothing, dried it, and reverently redressed the Bishop and his priests and cleverly bricked the coffins up in the church. It will be some time before the bodies of our dear martyrs can be brought to Kaifeng. They will be buried in the same cemetery where our own dear Sister Rachel lies buried. Fortunately these murderers did not touch the tabernacle. The virgin catechists consumed the Sacred Particles knowing that no priest would dare come to the place for some time. You can imagine how upset we are.[9]

Events now moved rapidly. On December 7, 1941, ten days after the above letter was written, the Japanese attacked Pearl Harbor, and the United States declared a state of war to exist between itself and Japan. But Pearl Harbor did not mean a new enemy to the sisters. They had spent the last four years in supporting their beloved Chinese against the armed aggression of Japan. There was now, however, a difference in their legal status: during the Sino-Japanese War they had been technically neutrals. Now they were classed as enemies and participants and treated as such. Later Sister Flora stated:

Well do I remember the day. Sister Ronayne, Sister Vestina, and I were attending Holy Mass in a church in the city. During the services an Italian Brother came in and called one of the priests out of the church. He returned and called out a Sister of Providence. He returned again and all Americans were asked to leave the church. . . . When we got outside, the Japanese informed us that the U.S. and Japan were at war and we were to be interned as prisoners. Orders were given to rush home and prepare to leave our convent. On the way we stopped at the dispensary and I grabbed the stethoscope and two other expensive instruments. On reaching the convent we found it full of Japanese soldiers. We were given twenty minutes to pack and leave for the Protestant mission compound where we and Protestant missionaries were interned. After a few weeks here we and other American missionaries were moved back to our convent or mission where we were all interned. After fifteen months of living under house arrest we were told on March 21, 1943, "Take your beds, plenty of bedding, books, and all your clothes. Be prepared to stay a long, long time. You are moving to the camp at Wei Hsien to be interned with 2000 other enemies." The Japanese inspected our packing and confiscated certain articles that took their fancy or which they judged to be an aid to the enemy.[10]

The camp at Wei Hsien was a former Presbyterian mission. Among the 2,000 persons held there by the Japanese were 150 priests, 200 sisters and brothers, five bishops, a prefect apostolic, and a number of Protestant missionaries. Here the Americans and other prisoners of war were completely cut off from communication with the rest of the world. The Japanese provided the food and guarded the walls but left the prisoners to organize their own camp life.

The sisters established their own way of life and approximated as closely as possible the community life of Benedictines. They had been allowed to keep their Breviaries and were allotted rooms to themselves in which they could hold community prayers. Prison life was organized by the prisoners themselves who formed committees in charge of the sick. The education committee soon opened classes for the children and classes in Chinese language for the adults. An orchestra and a choral group were formed. Sisters Francetta, Ursuline, and Ronayne sang in the glee club on Friday and Saturday evenings. Sister Ursuline joined the orchestra as did one of the interned bishops who also played the violin. The sisters and the priests also took their share of assignments from the labor committee. Each had at least five hours of camp duty and some had ten hours. Food had to be cooked for 2000 prisoners and water had to be pumped. Thirty men shared the work of pumping by hand the water supply for this immense crowd. One priest was chief baker. Of these days Sister Flora said, "We were served but two meals a day. Sometimes the meat did not arrive in time to be cooked and sometimes it arrived only the next day. It was hard on the men who had to work hard at pumping water or digging ditches to drain the swamp on the premises."

A black market was soon in operation and a Capuchian friar was one of the men who played this game — not for himself however but for the children who suffered greatly. He dug a hole in the wall, wrote out a list of foods wanted, and handed it to a Chinese friend outside with the understanding he would be there at the same time next day for the food. This was done at great risk, for all communication with the outside was forbidden under heavy penalty. One day this friar was caught at the hole talking to a Chinese. He knew the guards could not bring the charge of black marketing against him unless they found the incriminating list on his person. When caught he managed to sneeze and when he pulled his handkerchief out of his pocket he managed to draw out the list too. The next moment he stumbled over a large stone in the path, and as he fell he put the paper under the stone. On rising to his feet he was minus the paper. When the guards brought him before the officers to be inspected, there was no evidence. Although he was imprisoned for talking to an outsider he jokingly said that his Rule called for deep silence and now for the first time since his internment he was able to keep it. Allowed to take his Breviary with him, he chanted the Divine Office aloud in the middle of the night according to his Rule, much to the annoyance of the guards who could not sleep. Finally he was released, and his welcome back to camp was hilarious, because he was popular with the internees — especially with the mothers of the small children whose cause he had sponsored.

One of the most annoying things in camp was the roll call taken just before breakfast. Sister Flora described it:

We all had to stand in front of our own house. If some one had died during the night or a baby was born the number given today would not match with the number counted the day previous and then the camp officer would have to re-count. In the meantime some one, thinking all was finished, had left and he would now be missing for the second roll call. Then the officer would demand that all, in the house and out of it, stand in line to be re-counted. But the man who had sauntered off to duty at another part of the camp was still missing and the count would come out different again. Then the Japanese would get mad and order all of the 2000 internees to march out onto the ball grounds. This would be about ten o'clock when the sun was very hot and would require all of two hours.[11]

But to offset such annoyance there was the joy of having regular church services. One sister declared that Sundays were wonderful. With 150 priests and five bishops it was possible to have solemn pontifical Mass every Sunday. The Dutch priests sang the chant beautifully. Protestants came to hear the chant and some eventually asked to be instructed in the Catholic faith. Living and working with the sisters and priests for five months revealed to the other internees the beauty of the Church.

Finally through the efforts of the apostolic delegate, whose native country was on the side of Japan in the war, the Japanese officials were persuaded to remove the Catholic missionaries from the camp at Wei Hsien and to intern them in Catholic religious houses in

Peking. Both sisters and priests were moved on August 23, 1943. They were placed in convents and monasteries belonging to nations friendly or at least neutral to the axis powers.[12] The Benedictine sisters, with others, were placed in the Spanish Convent of Christ the King. The change of place meant no change in the sisters' status. They were still prisoners confined to the buildings in which they were placed. In addition, this arrangement posed a new problem — that of procuring food. While encamped at Wei Hsien the prisoners were fed by their captors, but at Peking no provision had been made. Like so many other internees, the Benedictines had no means of support. Nor was the Spanish convent able to provide indefinitely for its eighty guests. The mother house, St. Benedict's, through the offices of the Red Cross, finally succeeded in sending aid to them.

During the war Japan started to make an exchange of prisoners. In the fall of 1943 Sister Flora was chosen from among the prisoners at the Convent of Christ the King to be repatriated, and on September 15 she left her Benedictine sisters for Shanghai and there boarded the Japanese ship *Teia Maru*. This boat built to accommodate 900 persons now was to carry 1,500 prisoners. Owing to the overcrowded conditions, Sister Flora and the other prisoners lived on deck as the ship steamed down the China coast and out across the Indian Ocean to Mormugao, India. There, on October 15, the American nationals, including 162 Catholic missionaries, were exchanged for Japanese prisoners and put aboard the famous Gripsholm, which was to bring them to New York. On this ship the Red Cross awaited them with clothing, food and medicine. The cleanliness and service were in such striking contrast to what they had left that the prisoners felt they were already back in the United States.

Finally the war came to an end in 1945, and five days after peace was declared four United States officers visited the internees in Peking and told the Benedictine sisters of their freedom. They were in retreat at the time, but the retreat master allowed them to break silence at this good news. The United States officers gave the internees freedom to go about the city and offered to get their letters out to relatives and superiors. The sisters were then placed on the list to receive aid. They were amused on opening their relief packages to find khaki shirts and several packages of cigarettes. These things they sold and bought much-needed shoes and food.

Anxious as they were to return to their convent and their work in

Kaifeng, they had to wait in Peking for many months. All railroad tracks had been torn up between Peking and Kaifeng, and the only means of travel was by airplane or by cart over impassable roads. As soon as transportation could be had, the sisters returned, one by one. Sister Francetta had to wait a year before she could leave for Kaifeng. Writing on August 28, 1946, she described her trip:

We went by plane from Peiping to Hsinsiang on August 3. Here we waited over Sunday, and on Monday we started out by jeep for Kaifeng. It usually takes from three to four hours, but on account of bad roads and rain we were delayed and were on the road thirty hours instead of four. This entailed great hardships since we had neither adequate food nor water supplies. There were six in the group — two U. S. army lieutenants, who were kind enough to bring us to Kaifeng; Father Gerard, O.S.B.; Mother Biance, an Italian sister Superior; a Chinese girl, and I. When we arrived in Kaifeng we were hungry, tired, and covered from head to foot with mud. Our luggage and boxes were wet from the rain. We drank water from the ditches in which we were stalled, and what filthy water it was! But it was wet. Part of the night we spent in the open on the road, and just before a downpour we managed to get to a small village where we six all crowded into an ox's stall — a space of about 6 by 8 feet. The ox happened to be outside. The roof leaked but here we stayed from three A.M. to eight o'clock. The mud and the water on the roads were knee-deep and the jeep had to be pulled out of mud several times. We sisters were gallantly carried over the water by the two soldiers. We backseat jeepers said many a rosary on that trip.[13]

Several months later the other sisters found their way back to Kaifeng.

Their homecoming was full of disappointment. They found the convent and dispensary nearly ruined, for the Chinese and the Japanese had in turn occupied the place. Weeks were spent in replacing broken windows and doors and fixtures. Despite the fact that their catechetical and dispensary work would again have to be built from the ground up, they started out with all good will rejoicing at the fact that another missionary, Sister Mariette Pitz, would soon arrive from St. Benedict's. Scarcely was the dispensary reopened when disturbing news reached Kaifeng. Communist hordes, taking advantage of the disorganized state of affairs, were seizing control of certain sections of the country, killing missionaries and burning churches. This was followed by news that the bandit and communistic group was heading for Kaifeng. By June of the following year, 1947, refugee sisters and priests from communist-controlled territory were passing through Kaifeng in their flight to safety. They told of horrible experiences with communists and bandits. To protect the city, soldiers poured into the place by the thousands. Though the American consul warned all Americans to leave the city, the Benedictines decided to remain as long as possible with their Chinese converts to help them during this new period of suffering. They had lived through two wars and could with the help of God weather this one. But they failed to see that the enemy forces they had previously faced had been bound by international law; their new foes were a law unto themselves. This the Church authorities knew and, while admiring the zeal and bravery of the sisters, commanded them to be prepared to leave immediately if the Reds besieged the city.

But when in December the communist troops laid siege to the city they did it suddenly and without warning. It was then too late to get out. On December 27, 1947, one sister wrote:

On December 12 when the last UNRRA plane left, the Reds began a siege with no warning whatever. Soldiers and refugees came in droves and swarms and flooded the city. No planes were allowed to land. The Methodist, Baptist, and Mennonite missionaries had already left. We will probably leave but the railroads are torn up and no planes can land. We will have to make it by truck to Shanghai. . . . We hate to leave for here in Kaifeng we have been instrumental in bringing about 600 adult conversions besides hundreds of death-bed baptisms given in private. The city is placed in a state of siege and martial law proclaimed.[14]

They were still in Kaifeng three months later when the American Consul ordered all American citizens to leave at the earliest possible date. If they stayed they would do so at their own risk as the United States government could no longer be responsible for its citizens in the interior of China. The sisters packed their trunks and sent them with the one sister who was able to get a plane the next day. "We do this," Sister Francetta wrote, "so that when we do leave we will not have to take time to pack. In fact we will be on the run. We will do our best to stay for there is so much good to do." Four days after this letter was written they did have to run. They all finally reached Shanghai where they found temporary employment in the Aurora Girls High School conducted by the Religious of the Sacred Heart. Here in this refugee city two of the sisters decided to ask permission to return to the United States. The others decided to remain in the Orient for they were informed of an opening in Formosa. By going to Formosa they would escape the Chinese communists and still remain in the Orient.

The priests of the Society of the Divine Word working in Formosa invited the sisters to come to the island and investigate its possibilities. While on this visit Sister Francetta met the principal of Kuang Hua Girls Middle School at Tainan in the southern part of the island and was induced to have the sisters join her in her work. Sisters Ronayne, Mariette, Regia, Ursuline, Wibora and Francetta left the mainland of China early in the spring of 1949 for their new field of work in Formosa.

The Kuang Hua Girls Middle School at Tainan was a private school and, like other schools on the island, under strict government supervision. The sisters were allowed to teach classes in English and music, but native teachers were employed for the other classes. After school hours or during the day the sisters gave religious instructions in their convent. Shortly after the sisters had begun teaching in Tainan, Sister Ronayne and Sister Mariette accepted an invitation from Mr. T. L. Ying, head of the English department of the National Taiwan University, at Taipeh, to teach English in his institution. When they arrived at Taipeh only seventeen of the 3,000 students in attendance at the University were Catholics. But their work with the students was so successful that many students eager to study English and to speak it asked the sisters to open private classes in their convent. Others asked for instruction in the Catholic faith. During the first year about 270 persons enrolled for one or more courses. Classes were conducted at all hours of the day and evening.[15]

At the close of their first year of work in Formosa, war again threatened the sisters' missionary efforts. In June, 1950, the United States Consul urged all Americans to leave Formosa because the Chinese communists threatened to invade the island. The sisters in the south at Tainan decided to flee to Japan but in the general exodus they found it difficult to get passage on any boat. Passage was finally found for Sisters Francetta and Regia. Sisters Ursuline and Wibora then decided to go north and join the sisters at the university in Taipeh until all could obtain passage for Japan. When the United States sent its Seventh Fleet to protect Formosa, the tension and the fear of invasion lessened. Sisters Wibora, Ronayne and Mariette then decided to stay at Taipeh, for the work there was bearing great fruit.[16] Soon the convent chapel was enlarged and made semipublic so that it could serve as a parish church for that part of the city. Henceforth the sisters worked in conjunction with the pastor in preparation of the catechumens. On December 25, 1951, fifty of those instructed were admitted to baptism. Of these fifty, thirty were university students. Each year the number of conversions has increased until today the number of their catechumens admitted to baptism averages 200 annually. This mission was soon forced to ask for aid and St. Benedict's readily responded. Sister Bernard Marie Liang and Sister Barbara Loe, natives of Peking who had entered St. Benedict's a few years earlier, were chosen because they could speak Japanese and Chinese fluently.

The sisters who had fled to Japan were welcomed by the Benedictine priests from St. John's Abbey in charge of St. Anselm's parish in Tokyo. Before 1950 had come to an end, there were three Benedictine sisters there, Sister Ursuline having decided to join Sisters Francetta and Regia. With no knowledge of the Japanese language, they were handicapped in undertaking educational work or even in conducting a medical dispensary. But they were soon at work instructing the children of the numerous families with the U.S. occupation forces at the Tachikawa Air Base on the outskirts of Tokyo. Under the direction of the Armed Forces' chaplaincy the sisters were asked to spend one day a week at the base with these children. This catechetical work was later transferred to the army base in the suburbs of Tokyo. The work next undertaken, conducting cooking classes, is one not usually thought of in connection with mission work. It was accepted at first as a means of support for the convent, but later it became for the sisters the chief means of contact with all classes of people. It has been approved by the apostolic delegate to Japan and by Archbishop Peter Totsuo Doi of Tokyo.

By chance a few Japanese had asked the sisters to teach American cooking. Requests for similar instruction soon increased. There were also requests for instruction in Chinese cooking; and today the number enrolled for one or more of the ten-week sessions has reached 450. During a ten-week session three morning and three evening classes each meet once a week. In the beginning the Japanese women interested in American food met in the morning. American and Japanese men and women wishing to learn Chinese cooking met in the evening. Among the 140 registered during one session in 1955 there were 25 men, including military officers, embassy personnel, and a minister. The 450 persons registered during one year represented many nations and many religious faiths.[17]

In the meantime the sisters were making every effort to learn the difficult Japanese language. In 1954 Mother Richarda sent a member of the faculty of the College of St. Benedict, Sister Benedice Schulte, to the language school conducted by the Sisters of the Holy Souls at Tokyo to study Japanese and to prepare for organizing a novitiate in Japan. The following year Sister Imelda Deguchi and Sister Renata Mori were sent to Japan. They were natives of Tokyo who had received the Benedictine habit at St. Benedict's a few years earlier.

Though St. Benedict's missions in Peking, Kaifeng, and Tainan had to be abandoned, the missionaries had never given up. In school and dispensary, in concentration camps, in refugee groups, they performed the tasks at hand. At the time of this last evacuation in 1949 one sister undismayed by these events wrote:

A school today does not mean a school tomorrow or next year. A flourishing mission set up today may be a shambles of ruin tomorrow. Missionaries to China more than to all others must keep their eyes on the apparent failure of Good Friday, must cling to the hope of Easter beyond, and remember that only God has the true measure of success and failure. Our story, therefore, is not an isolated one. To American minds, attuned to almost continual success, the attitude of missionaries to these reverses, to these blank walls of failure, is hard to explain. Our only thought is of souls who need our help now more than ever.[18]

The term "foreign mission" usually brings to mind religious work in a foreign land and among a non-Christian people. Work in Puerto Rico would not fall within this definition, for the people on that island in 1847 were under the jurisdiction of the United States, and they have been Christians since the 16th century. Nevertheless, when St. Benedict's Convent was asked to conduct a school at Humacao, Puerto Rico, the sisters looked on the venture as a mission to a foreign people. The call had come from the bishop of San Juan diocese and the Benedictines in charge of Holy Name parish at Humacao.[19] Connected with this parish was a school taught by lay teachers. The bishop desired sisters, and the monks naturally looked to St. Benedict's to supply them.

Because of a centuries-old lack of religious instruction, this district, with a population of 30,000, numbered only 1,000 who were considered more than nominal Catholics, while only 500 were regular practicing Catholics. This was the result not of ill will but of ignorance of the principles of their faith. As one missionary stated, "Holy Week was filled with processions and demonstrations without end. . . . It is all very impressive. But it does fill one with pity to see so many faces in church on Good Friday who never return till the following year. What they need is instruction, and that must begin in school." [20]

But the adults had become set in their negligent ways, and because of their aloofness from the clergy, the priests could not hope to do much to reform their lives. The children were less aloof than their parents and could be reached more easily. Convinced that the best hopes for the Church and the religious life of these people was to work with the children and to raise up a new generation of intelligent, practising Catholics, the bishop and the Benedictine priests looked to the parish school as their hope — but a parish school taught by sisters rather than by lay teachers as was the custom there.

St. Benedict's could not answer the first call for teachers, partly because of the ever growing demand for sisters in the Diocese of St. Cloud itself, partly because there were no Spanish-speaking sisters available. Reluctant to refuse the request, Mother Rosamond suggested that action on it be postponed for a year or more.[21] After two more requests and reminders Mother Rosamond accepted the mission. Sister Jeanette Roesch, Sister Adeline Terhaar, and Sister Agnes Herwers were chosen to staff the Holy Name School at Humacao. They left Minnesota by plane on August 1, 1948, and in a few days they were established in their new field of work.

To these sisters the language, the climate, and the manner of native living were as strange as was China to the sisters laboring in the Orient. Only Sister Jeanette could speak Spanish and was, therefore, the only one of the three able to take charge of a class. Sister Adeline taught English for the lay teachers in the other primary grades until she had acquired mastery of the Spanish when she, too, took charge of a classroom. The people and their manner of living were likewise strange to the Minnesota sisters. It was in a strain of mixed annoyance and amusement with Puerto Rican housekeeping methods that Sister Jeanette wrote:

They thought they had cleaned our house but their idea of clean differs from ours. The older girl fed rice to the birds so that they came into the house, even to breed and feed their young. The lamps were surrounded by ornamental work and this served as a nest building place. One of Father's chickens was petted too, and the hen insisted on laying her egg on top of the cupboard. Imagine the cleaning to be done after bird, hen, cats, and dogs! [22]

Teaching the song-loving, noisy, and volatile children of Puerto Rico was a trial but the sisters soon won their good will and affection. Today five Benedictine teachers aided by nine lay teachers conduct an elementary school of 300 pupils and a junior high school. These children are receiving a better understanding of their faith and a consciousness of their duty to practice that faith. Vocations to the religious life are beginning to blossom and five young Puerto Rican women have within the last two years applied for entrance into St. Benedict's at St. Joseph, Minnesota.

Mother Richarda Peters has worked to build up the missions in Puerto Rico and in the Far East so that they will be able to become priories and establish their own novitiate. For this purpose Mother Richarda visited Formosa and Japan in 1954. It is a truism that the Church in a foreign land never thrives unless the leaders in religious life are natives of that land. With that work accomplished the American Benedictines will have repaid Europe for transplanting Benedictines on American soil.

ECCLESIASTICAL SUPERIORS

BISHOPS

The Most Reverend Thomas L. Grace	1859–1875
The Most Reverend Rupert Seidenbusch, O.S.B.	1875–1888
The Most Reverend Otto Zardetti	1889–1894
The Most Reverend Martin Marty, O.S.B.	1894–1896
The Most Reverend James Trobec	1897–1914
The Most Reverend Joseph Busch	1915–1953
The Most Reverend Peter Bartholome	1953–

RELIGIOUS SUPERIORS

By Episcopal appointment

Mother Willibalda Scherbauer
1857–1868

Mother Antonia Herman
1868–1877

Mother Aloysia Bath
1877–1880

Mother Scholastica Kerst
1880–1889

By election

Mother Aloysia Bath
1889–1901

Mother Cecilia Kapsner
1901–1919

Mother Louisa Walz
1919–1937

Mother Rosamond Pratschner
1937–1949

Mother Richarda Peters
1949–

Sub-Prioresses

Sister Benedict Kump
1880–1881

Sister Cecilia Kapsner
1881–1901

Sister Gonzaga Kevenhoerster
1901–1902

Sister Louisa Walz
1902–1919

Sister Rosamond Pratschner
1919–1921

Sister Secunda Hanson
1921–1925

Sister Emiliana VonDrehle
1925–1929

Sister Leonida Meyers
1929–1937

Sister Andrietta Rohrenbach
1937–1943

Sister Carina Julig
1943–1949

Mistresses of Novices

Sister Placida Heine
1877–1880

Sister Cecilia Kapsner
1880–1892

Sister Hyacinthe Simmer
1892–1902

Sister Placida Heine
1902–1905

Sister Secunda Hansen
1905–1908

Sister Emiliana Von Drehle
1908–1925

Sister Borgia Knelleken
1925–1928

Sister Leona Ryan
1928–1937

Sister Lewine Zimmerman
1937–1940

Sister Alcuin Braun
1940–1943

Sub-Prioress	*Mistress of Novices*
Sister Incarnata Girgen	Sister Henrita Osendorf
1949–1955	1943–
Sister Lewine Zimmerman	
1955–	

PRIORIES FOUNDED BY ST. BENEDICT'S PRIORY

St. Scholastica's Convent, Atchison, Kansas	1863
St. Scholastica's Convent, Duluth, Minnesota	1892
Convent of the Annunciation, Bismarck, North Dakota	1946
St. Bede's Priory, Eau Claire, Wisconsin	1948
St. Paul's Priory, St. Paul, Minnesota	1948
St. Placid's Priory, Olympia, Washington	1952

SCHOOLS AND INSTITUTIONS

served by the Convent of St. Benedict

LIST OF ABBREVIATIONS

C closed
R reopened
W withdrew
MA moved to Altoona, Wis.
MJ moved to St. Joseph, Minn.
MK moved to Kent, Minn.
TB transferred to Convent of the Annunciation, Bismarck, N.D. 1946
TC transferred to Benedictine Sisters, Crookston, Minn. 1928
TD transferred to Villa Sancta, Scholastica, Duluth, Minn. 1892
TE transferred to St. Bede's Priory, Eau Claire, Wis. 1948
TL transferred to Franciscan Sisters, Little Falls, Minn. 1893
TO transferred to St. Placid's Priory, Olympia, Wash. 1952
TP transferred to St. Paul's Priory, St. Paul, Minn. 1948

LOCATION*	NAME	INSTITUTION	DATES
Albany	Seven Dolors	School, W	1884–1887
		School, R	1904–
Altoona, Wis.	St. Mary's Academy	Boarding School, C	1906–1938
	St. Mary's Boys' School	Boarding School, TE	1938–1948
Anaconda, Mont.	St. Paul's	School	1949–
Avon	St. Cloud School for Exceptional Children	School for mentally retarded, C	1945–1948
Barnesville	Assumption	School, TC	1888–1928
Baum, Iowa		School, C	1896–1897
Belle Plaine	Sacred Heart	School, W	1877–1882
	Sts. Peter and Paul	School, TP	1889–1948
Bismarck, N.D.	St. Mary's	School, TB	1878–1946
	St. Alexius	Hospital, TB	1885–1946
Bluffton	St. John the Baptist	School	1916–
Bloomfield		School, W	1900–1901
Brainerd	St. Francis	School, W	1885–1887
Breckenridge	St. Mary's	School, W	1878–1880
		School, R	1925–
Browerville	St. Joseph's	School	1892–
	St. Peter's	School	1902–
Buckman	St. Michael's	School	1887–
Buffalo	King's House	Retreat House	1956–
Carver	St. Nicholas	School, W	1876–1881
Chanhassen	St. Hubert's	School, TP	1895–1948
Colorado Springs, Colo.	Mountain Dale Ranch	Rest Home for Sisters, C	1938–1940
Cherokee, Iowa	Immaculate Conception	School, W	1896–1897
Cold Spring	St. Boniface	School	1916–

* Unless otherwise indicated, all cities are in Minnesota

LOCATION	NAME	INSTITUTION	DATES
Dickinson, N.D.	St. Joseph's	School, TB	1905–1946
	St. Patrick's	School, TB	1929–1946
Duelm	St. Lawrence	School	1955–
Duluth	Sacred Heart	School, W	1881–1883
	St. Mary's	Hospital, TD	1888–1892
	St. Clement's	School, TD	1887–1892
	St. Mary of the Sea	School, TD	1884–1892
Dumont	St. Peter's	School	1918–
Eau Claire, Wis.	St. Patrick's	School, TE	1892–1948
Eden Valley	Assumption	School	1901–
Elrosa	Sts. Peter and Paul	School	1946–
Fairfax	St. Andrew's	School, TP	1906–1948
Farmington	St. Michael	Religion School, C	1938–1947
Freeport	Sacred Heart	School	1912–
Gilman	Sts. Peter and Paul	School	1913–
Gladstone, N.D.	St. Thomas	School, TB	1935–1946
Grande Ronde, Ore.	Indian School	Indian School, W	1881–1882
Greenwald	St. Andrew's	School	1930–
Hastings	St. Boniface	School, TP	1890–1948
Heidelberg	St. Scholastica's	School, W	1903–1921
Hutchinson	St. Anastasia	School	1954–
Kent	St. Thomas	School, C	1902–1908
Lake Henry	St. Margaret's	School, W	1886–1939
Lastrup	St. John Nepomuk	School	1951–
Litchfield	St. Philip's	Religion and Music School, TP	1935–1948
Little Falls	St. Mary's	School, W	1897–1949
	Our Lady of Lourdes	School	1919–
Long Prairie	St. Mary's	School, W	1880–1884
		School, R	1895–
Luxemburg	St. Wendelin	School	1881–
McCauleyville	St. Thomas	School, MK	1900–1902
Mandan, N.D.	St. Joseph's	School, W	1886–1887
		School, TB	1913–1946
Maple Lake	St. Timothy's	School	1951–
Mauston, Wis.	St. Patrick's	School, W	1933–1942
	Mauston Hospital	Hospital, W	1934–1937
Meire Grove	St. John's	School	1916–
Melrose	St. Boniface	School	1882–
	St. Patrick's	School, C	1916–1932
Miesville	St. Joseph's	School	1954–
Millerville	Seven Dolors	School, C	1882–1893
		School, R	1914–
Mille Lacs	Mille Lacs Catholic Indian School (Little Flower mission)	Indian Mission	1941–
Minneapolis	St. Elizabeth's	School, W	1877–1881
	St. Joseph's	School	1876–

LOCATION	NAME	INSTITUTION	DATES
	St. Ann's	School, TP	1925–1948
	Most Holy Trinity	School, TP	1945–1948
Montgomery	Holy Redeemer	School, TP	1891–1948
Montevideo	St. Joseph's	School, W	1928–1935
Moorhead	St. Joseph's	School, TC	1879–1928
Morris	Assumption	School, W	1882–1887
Mound	Our Lady of the Lake	Religion School, W	1938–1939
New Munich	Immaculate Conception	School	1879–
New Prague	Community Memorial Hospital	Hospital	1952–
New Richmond, Wis.	Immaculate Conception	School, W	1926–1928
New Trier	St. Mary's	School, W	1872–1877
North Prairie	Holy Cross	School, W	1889–1913
Ogden, Utah	St. Benedict's Hospital	Hospital	1946–
Onamia	Catechetical School	School, C	1932–1957
Pearl Lake	Holy Cross	School	1916–
Perham	St. Henry's	School	1883–
	St. Joseph's	School, W	1884–1916
Pierz	St. Joseph's	School	1872–
	St. Joseph's Orphanage	Orphanage, MJ	1875–1882
Red Lake	St. Mary's	Indian Mission School	1888–
Richfield	Assumption	School, TP	1900–1948
Richland Center, Wis.	St. Mary's	School, TE	1927–1948
Richmond	Sts. Peter and Paul's	School	1906–
Robbinsdale	Sacred Heart	School, TP	1926–1948
Rush Lake	St. Lawrence	School, W	1886–1889
St. Augusta	St. Mary's	School	1886–
St. Bonifacius	St. Boniface	School, TP	1895–1948
		School, W	1858–1863
St. Cloud	St. Mary's	School, R	1869–
	St. Agnes	Academy, MJ	1876–1880
	Holy Angels	School	1887–
	St. Cloud Hospital (Known at various times under titles of St. Benedict's, St. Raphael's, and St. Cloud Hospital)	Hospital	1886–
	St. Anthony	School	1921–
	St. John Cantius	School	1902–
	St. Joseph's Home	Home for Aged	1900–
	St. Clothild's	Kindergarten and Music School, C	1890–1906
	St. Augustine's	School	1943–
	St. Paul's	School	1947–
	St. Peter's	School	1949–
	St. Raphael's Home	Home for Aged	1928
St. Joseph	St. Joseph's Sanitarium	Rest Home for Sisters	1918–

PARISHES, SCHOOLS, AND INSTITUTIONS

serve by the

Convent of Saint Benedict

Saint Joseph, Minnesota

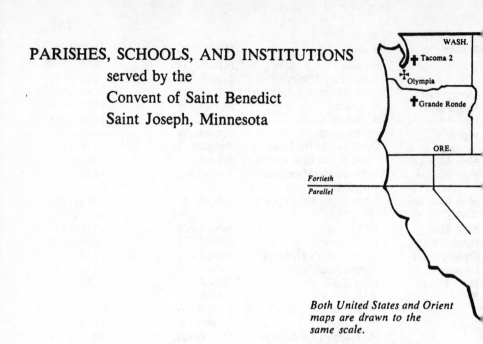

Both United States and Orient maps are drawn to the same scale.

Scale of Miles

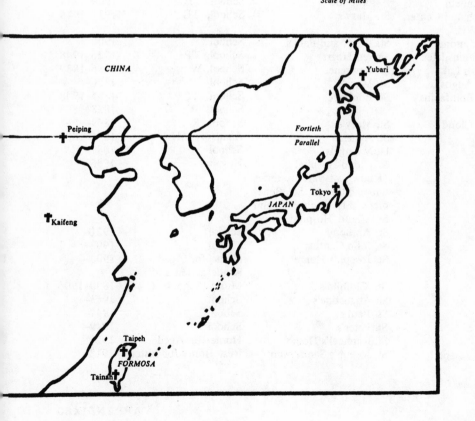

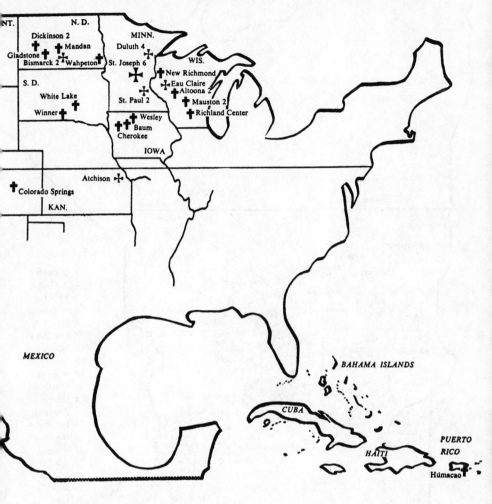

Places outside of Minnesota are complete on this map. Minnesota sites are complete on the following map.

Legend

✝ MISSIONS

✠ FOUNDATIONS
(ATCHISON AND OLYMPIA ARE FOUNDATIONS ONLY. MISSIONS HAVE BEEN LOCATED AT ALL OTHER FOUNDATION SITES.)

A NUMBER FOLLOWS THE PLACE NAME OF SITES WHERE MORE THAN ONE MISSION IS LOCATED.

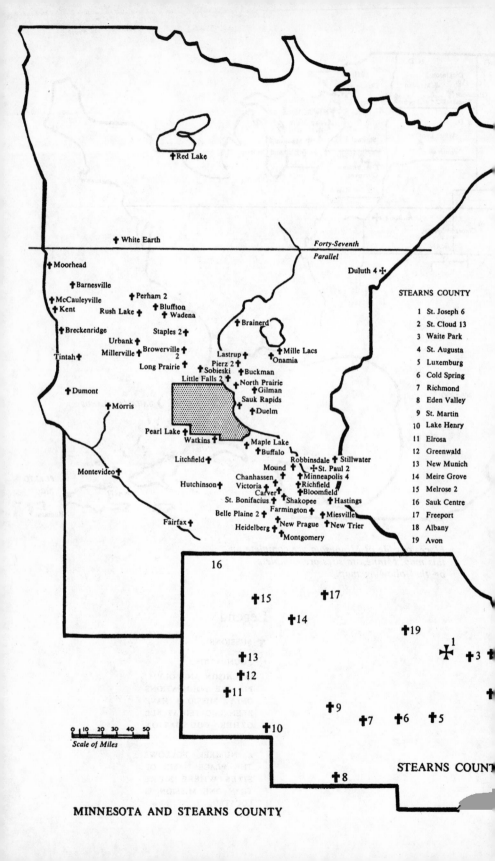

Red Lake

White Earth

Forty-Seventh
Parallel

Moorhead

Barnesville

McCauleyville
Kent   Perham 2   Duluth 4
          Rush Lake   Bluffton
Breckenridge   Wadena
              Staples 2   Brainerd
        Urbank
Millerville Browerville   Mille Lacs
              2   Lastrup   Onamia
Tintah   Long Prairie   Pierz 2
                              Sobieski   Buckman
                    Little Falls 2 North Prairie
Dumont   Gilman
                              Sauk Rapids
              Morris   Duelm
        Pearl Lake   Maple Lake
              Watkins   Buffalo
        Litchfield   Robbinsdale   Stillwater
                              Mound   St. Paul 2
Montevideo   Chanhassen   Minneapolis 4
                    Hutchinson   Victoria   Richfield
                              Carver   Bloomfield
                    St. Bonifacius   Shakopee   Hastings
                    Belle Plaine 2 Farmington   Miesville
        Fairfax   Heidelberg New Prague New Trier
                              Montgomery

STEARNS COUNTY

1   St. Joseph 6
2   St. Cloud 13
3   Waite Park
4   St. Augusta
5   Luxemburg
6   Cold Spring
7   Richmond
8   Eden Valley
9   St. Martin
10 Lake Henry
11 Elrosa
12 Greenwald
13 New Munich
14 Meire Grove
15 Melrose 2
16 Sauk Centre
17 Freeport
18 Albany
19 Avon

16

15   17

14

19

13   1
12   3
11

9
10   7   6   5

8   STEARNS COUNT

Scale of Miles
0 10 20 30 40 50

MINNESOTA AND STEARNS COUNTY

LOCATION	NAME	INSTITUTION	DATES
St. Joseph	St. Joseph's School	School	1862–
(continued)	St. Benedict's Orphanage	Orphanage, TL	1882–1893
	Indian Industrial School	Indian School, C	1884–1896
	St. Benedict's Boys' School	Boys' Boarding School, MA	1897–1938
	St. Benedict's Academy	High School	1881–
	College of St. Benedict	College	1913–
St. Martin	St. Martin's	School, W	1887–1891
		School, R	1955–
St. Paul	St. Joseph's Orphanage	Orphanage, TP	1877–1948
	St. Bernard's	School, TP	1891–1948
Sauk Centre	St. Paul's	School	1896–
Sauk Rapids	Sacred Heart	School	1923–
Sobieski	St. Stanislaus	School	1905–
Staples	Sacred Heart	School	1914–
	The Mary Rondorf Home	Home for Aged	1953–
Stillwater	St. Mary's	School, TP	1882–1948
Shakopee	St. Gertrude's	School, C	1880–1881
Tacoma, Wash.	Visitation	School, TO	1925–1952
	Holy Rosary	School, TO	1892–1952
Tintah	St. Gall's	School, W	1913–1932
Urbank	Sacred Heart	School	1919–
Victoria	St. Victoria	School, TP	1900–1948
Wadena	St. Ann's	School	1903–
Wahpeton, N.D.	St. John's	School, W	1886–1948
Waite Park	St. Joseph's	School, W	1922–1949
Watkins	St. Anthony	School	1907–
Wesley, Iowa		School, W	1895–1897
White Earth	St. Benedict's	Indian Mission	1878–
White Lake, S.D.	St. Peter's	School, W	1885–1886
Winner, S.D.	Immaculate Conception	School, W	1934–1938

STEARNS COUNTY DISTRICT SCHOOLS

DISTRICT
NO.

1 On Cold Spring road
2 On road toward Sauk Rapids
3 Two Rivers Settlement
11 Town of St. Wendel
13 Section 29 town of Le Sauk
47 On Luxemburg road northwest of St. Cloud
56 On road four miles north of Collegeville
72 Near St. Ann
108 Three and one-half miles from St. Joseph, near Five Points
120 Collegeville, Watab Lake
131 Near Lake Henry

LOCATION	NAME	INSTITUTION	DATES
FOREIGN MISSIONS			
Humacao, Puerto Rico	St. Joseph's Academy	School	1948–
Kaifeng, China	St. Benedict's Mission	Dispensary and Catechetical work, C	1935–1948
Peiping, China	Catholic University	Women's College, W	1930–1935
Tainan, Formosa		School, W	1949–1950
Taipeh, Formosa	St. Benedict's	Catechetical Mission School	1949–
Tokyo, Japan	St. Benedict's	chetical work, C	1950–
Yubari, Japan		Kindergarten	1957–

NOTES

1. Rupert Jud, O.S.B., "St. Walburg Benediktinerinnenkloster in Eichstätt," in *Studien und Mitteilungen zur Geschichte des Benediktiner-Ordens und seiner Zweige*, 15:45 (Munich, 1894).
2. Jud, *Studien*, 47; Hildebrand Bihlmeyer, "Die Heilige Walburga," in *St. Benedikte Stimmen*, 27:173 (Prague, 1903).
3. Bihlmeyer, 173.
4. Jud, 49.
5. "Anno 1634, February 6. I, Scholastica Pernezeris, was elected by the venerable convent as unworthy prioress when the gracious late abbess was sick unto death. That night at 7 o'clock the Swedish soldiers with great force entered the city and broke into the convent and into the chamber of the dying abbess like wolves. One of the soldiers jumped on the body of our dying Lady Abbess. . . . Oh God, what fright and heartache did we not endure. Several of the sisters jumped into the waters of the Edelbach and remained therein for twenty-three hours. From Monday to Sunday the invading army swarmed about the place and on Sunday about midnight they set fire to the convent and the town." Quoted in *Die Abtei St. Walburg*, pp. 38–39 (Eichstätt, 1934).
6. Bihlmeyer, p. 175; Jud, p. 49; Reverend John Alzog, *Manual of Universal History*, 3:679 (Cincinnati, 1878).
7. Bihlmeyer, p. 175; Jud, p. 50.
8. Father Boniface Wimmer had a relative in the Holy Cross Convent of the Dominican Sisters in Ratisbon and had thought of applying to that convent for teachers.
9. *Annalen der Verbreitung des Glaubens*, 21:25 (Munich, 1853); Oswald Moosmuller, O.S.B., *Bonifaz Wimmer, Erzabt von St. Vincent in Pennsylvania*, pp. 146–147 (New York, 1891); Willibald Mathäser, O.S.B., *Bonifaz Wimmer, O.S.B. und König Ludwig I von Bayern*, p. 50 (Munich, 1938).
10. Edwarda Schnitzer to the Ludwig-Missionsverein, May 29, 1852 in Bishop Baraga collections. Photostat copies of letters in this collection are in the archives of St. Benedict's Convent in St. Joseph, Minnesota, and will hereafter be referred to as the Baraga Collection. *Annalen der Verbreitung des Glaubens*, 21:237 (1853). This publication will be referred to henceforth as *Annalen*. A file of this publication is in the library of St. John's Abbey, Collegeville, Minnesota. King Ludwig I of Bavaria ascended the throne in 1825. His reforms irritated the liberals and in 1848 he was forced to resign. He lived until 1868.
11. Regina Baska, O.S.B., *The Benedictine Congregation of St. Scholastica*, pp. 32–33 (Washington, D.C., 1935).
12. *Annalen*, 20:470.
13. The bishop's letter is of significance in the bitter controversy that was to develop regarding the status of Benedictine sisters in the United States. From this document of 1853 one can conclude that St. Marys was a diocesan establishment, not a papal institute, nor was it under Father Wimmer's jurisdiction. "I hereby certify that it was with my permission that you took the preparatory measures to establish the community of German Sisters in St. Marytown, Elk Co. — though I expected the matter more formally prepared and the documents accordingly issued containing everything necessary for such a purpose. Feeling confident, however, that no difficulty will rise in framing these so as to be satisfactory on all sides, I have no objection to see the institution commenced; and at the earliest opportunity a proper document can be given. I will remark merely that until the community is incorporated, I will require that the property which the sisters may possess shall be held in trust for them by the bishop of the diocese and that their position here must be such as to enable the bishop to make sure

of the promotion of discipline and to feel satisfied that what is commenced shall not be easily abandoned nor without proper cause." Quoted by Regina Baska in *The Benedictine Congregation*, p. 23.

14. Benedicta Riepp to King Ludwig, 1852. Baraga Collection. O. Moosmuller, p. 147, gives the date July 15 for their arrival. R. Burgemeister, *Historical Development of Catholicity in St. Marys*, p. 13, gives July 22 as the date.

15. *Annalen*, 18:464, *Manuscript Chronicle* of St. Joseph's Convent at St. Marys, Pennsylvania.

CHAPTER TWO

1. Letter of Mother Benedicta Riepp to King Ludwig January 8, 1853, quoted in Willibald Mathäser, "König Ludwig I von Bayern und die Gründung der Ersten Bayerischen Benediktinerabtei in Nordamerika," in *Studien*, 43:165 (1925). Benedicta Riepp to King Ludwig, December 20, 1853. Baraga Collection.

2. Manuscript Chronicle in St. Joseph's Convent at St. Marys, Pennsylvania.

3. Regina Baska, p. 33; Annalen der Verbreitung des Glaubens 23:567.

4. Letter written on high seas. Original in St. John's Abbey Archives. Reference to papers in these archives will be hereafter referred to as S.J.A.A.

5. W. Mathäser, *Bonifaz Wimmer*, p. 50; *Studien* 43:166.

6. Bishop Georg's papers October 29, 1853, in Baraga Collection. These letters all show that the convent at St. Marys was considered by the bishop to have been a dependent convent until the year 1855.

7. Mathäser, p. 119. This author holds that Abbot Wimmer had no sound foundation for his claim of jurisdiction. He writes: "It is true that he [Wimmer] was president of the Benedictine Cassinese Congregation, but that did not give him jurisdiction over the nuns."

8. Mathäser, *Bonifaz Wimmer*, p. 48; Mother Edwarda Schnitzer to the Ludwig-Missionsverein, March 2, 1855. Baraga Collection.

9. Mathäser, p. 120.

10. Bruno Riess to Wimmer April 1, 1857, June 1, 1857. Demetrius to Wimmer March 10, 1857. S.J.A.A.

11. Mother Benedicta to Wimmer May 3, 1857. Copy in S.B.C.A.

12. Mathäser, p. 120. Letter of Wimmer dated July 24, 1857. Copy in S.B.C.A.

13. Demetrius in his letter of June 15, 1857, relates this news to Abbot Wimmer and protests the suddenness of the move.

14. Bishop of Eichstätt to the court chaplain. Baraga Collection. The old tradition held by many of the Minnesota Benedictines that it was Mother Benedicta herself who led the band to Minnesota and that she left for Europe some time later is erroneous. She did not go to Minnesota until after her return from Europe the following year. Mathäser, *Bonifaz Wimmer*, p. 120; Theodore Roemer, *The Ludwig-Missionsverein and the Church in the United States*, p. 129 (Washington, 1933), both make the mistake of crediting Mother Benedicta with leading the group to Minnesota.

15. Mother Edwarda of Eichstätt to the superior in Erie, October 20, 1858. Original in the Convent at Erie.

16. Bishop Georg von Oettl of Eichstätt to the court chaplain at Munich, August 31, 1857. Baraga Collection.

17. Propositions of Mother Benedicta in Baraga Collection.

18. The American Cassinese Congregation was and is a union of Benedictine monasteries in America which were founded by St. Vincent's Abbey from Metten, Bavaria, and follows the statutes and customs of the Bavarian monastery. The American Cassinese Congregation of monks is in turn affiliated with the Benedictine Congregation of Monte Cassino. Hence the term American

Cassinese Congregation. With this grouping they enjoy the privilege of having a general procurator to look out for their interests in Rome.

19. Proposals of July 11, 1858. Original in St. Vincent's Archabbey.
20. Letter of November 11, 1858. Original in St. Vincent's Archabbey. Twelve months were to elapse before this body made its decision .
21. Wimmer to Mother Scholastica of Erie, June 14, 1858. Transcript S.B.C.A.
22. Wimmer to Mother Scholastica of Erie, June 14, 1858. Transcript S.B.C.A.

CHAPTER THREE

1. Sister Willibalda was the daughter of Graf Scherbauer by his second wife, who had been servant of his former wife. The children of his first marriage considered the second marriage a social blunder and refused to recognize Franciska and her brother. For family peace the Graf sent Franciska to the Benedictine school at an early age. It was there she often met King Ludwig I. There is no official paper in St. Benedict's archives listing the names of these founders. The only written record of the names is to be found in a letter of Father Alexius Roetzer to Abbot Wimmer, August 12, 1857. The census of 1857 also records their names and is to be found in the Minnesota Historical Society. Prisca Meier received the name of Amanda when she received the habit. Mary Wolters received the habit and the name of Ehrentrudis in the fall of 1857. In 1863 she left with the group of sisters founding the convent in Atchison and later left the convent for the world. Tradition has it that she later joined with another former nun from the East and taught school in Long Prairie, Minnesota.
2. William Watts Folwell, *A History of Minnesota*, 1:11–28 (St. Paul, 1921).
3. The St. Paul Diocese was created in 1850 and Bishop Cretin took charge in 1851. Father Ravoux was one of the first priests to work in St. Paul and in the Minnesota River Valley.
4. Demetrius to Wimmer July 14, 1857. Transcript in S.J.A.A.
5. Willibalda to Wimmer August 8, 1857. Transcript in S.J.A.A.
6. See the author's article, "Canon Vivaldi's Missionary Activities," in *The Iowa Catholic Historical Review*, 4:32–45 (Dubuque, 1932). Canon Vivaldi of noble Italian family came to this country with Bishop Cretin in 1851 and worked with the Winnebago Indians in Minnesota until 1856 when he left the diocese and later the priesthood and became United States consul in Brazil under President Lincoln's appointment. At Buenos Aires he was reinstated in the priesthood in 1883 and after a year of penance he went to work with the Indians at Chubut. Father Pierz had come from Carniola, Austria, to the United States in 1835 and for seventeen years worked with the Indians of Michigan, Wisconsin, and northeast Minnesota. In 1852 he joined the newly created St. Paul Diocese to work among the Chippewa Indians of the Upper Mississippi River. See Sister Grace McDonald, "Father Francis Pierz, Missionary," in *Minnesota History*, 10:107–125 (June, 1929).
7. Father Pierz had purchased this real estate for a church site in 1855 from Mr. Wilson, often referred to as the "Founder of St. Cloud." The site consisted of one half of block 36 and all of block 37 of the Blake and Wilson survey. Mr. Wilson has long been credited with having donated this land to the Catholic Church, but the records in the Register of Deeds office in St. Cloud show that Father Pierz paid $500 for the property. This is the site of the present Post Office and the Institute and the St. Mary's block.
8. *St. Cloud Democrat*, November 25, 1858, December 9, 1858, and December 15, 1859.
9. *St. Cloud Democrat*, September 26, 1861.
10. Bruno Riess, "First Beginnings of St. John's Abbey," in *St. John's University Record*, 2:62 (June 1889).

NOTES BETWEEN PAGES 1 AND 27

CHAPTER FOUR

1. Clement Staub to Wimmer, July 8, 1857. Bruno Riess to Wimmer, June 1, 1857, April 1, 1857. S.J.A.A.
2. Demetrius di Marogna to Wimmer, March 10, 1857. Transcript in S.J.A.A.
3. Demetrius to Wimmer, August 20, 1857. Transcript in S.J.A.A.
4. Demetrius to Wimmer, July 14, 1857. Transcript in S.J.A.A.
5. His words were: "We are firmly resolved not to tolerate them near us and not to give them any spiritual help unless they acknowledge the jurisdiction of the Praeses of our Congregation which I now happen to be." Mathäser, *Bonifaz Wimmer*, p. 121.
6. Demetrius to Wimmer, August 12, 1857. S.J.A.A. Father Cornelius Wittmann on August 13 wrote to Wimmer that Sister Willibalda could not be dismissed immediately.
7. Demetrius to Wimmer, July 14, 1857. S.J.A.A.
8. Willibalda to Wimmer, August 19, 1857, August 28, 1857. Transcript S.J.A.A. In Father Demetrius's letter to the abbot August 27 he asked the abbot to permit Sister Willibalda to remain in St. Cloud, for her removal would be a great loss to the group. Transcript S.J.A.A.
9. Evangelista to Wimmer, August 22, 1857. Transcript S.J.A.A. She signed her name "M. Evangelista."
10. Demetrius to Wimmer, August 12, 27, 1857. S.J.A.A. Reverend Alexius Roetzer, O.S.B., in making a report to Abbot Wimmer praised the good work of the sisters and remarked that the only adverse criticism would be that the sisters might rise a quarter of an hour earlier and retire a half hour earlier. Likewise, "They might put more time to meditation — the same time as we do." Alexius Roetzer, O.S.B., to Wimmer, August 12, 1857. S.J.A.A.
11. Wimmer to the prioress at Erie, November 15, 1857. Original in Benedictine Convent in Erie.
12. *St. John's University Record*, 2:93 (September 1889)
13. Sister Evangelista to Wimmer, August 22, 1857. *St. John's University Record* 2:93 (September 1889).
14. Demetrius to Wimmer, August 12, 1857. "A piano had to be purchased because the Yankees are especially set on taking up music. The piano cost $330.00 with freight and shipping. It bears the name of a firm in Pittsburgh, 'Charlotte Blum.' Sister Willibalda . . . . praises it highly." See letter of H. Mitchel, November 16, 1856, in the Mitchel Collection in the Minnesota Historical Society, St. Paul, for comment on other pianos in early St. Cloud.
15. Census of 1860. Microfilm copy in Minnesota Historical Society. Original in State Archives. Tradition holds that a vacancy occurred in West Point and Thomas Jackson wanted the place. Within two weeks the appointing power was to be transferred from Colonel Hayes' hands to those of the secretary of war, and Washington was three hundred miles away. Young Jackson borrowed $10 and a horse. The horse gave out and Jackson reached Washington on foot at eleven o'clock at night only to be told by Colonel Hayes on whom he called that his appointive power had already passed on to the secretary. Jackson answered that the day was not yet finished and begged Colonel Hayes to go with him to the secretary of war. The Colonel complied and the future Civil War officer received the appointment.
16. *St. John's Record*, 2:75, (August 1889). For other descriptions of the havoc created by the plague see the *St. Cloud Visitor*, December 10, 1857.
17. *Statuten des Klosters St. Walburg nach der Regel unsers heiligen Vaters Benediktus*. S.B.C.A.
18. Memoirs of Elizabeth Tenvoorde, daughter of John Tenvoorde. An amusing story is told of the efforts of these nuns to adapt the cloistered life to frontier conditions. Since there was no fence surrounding the house and property the

cloister ended at the door sill. The wood for the stove had been placed by the brothers immediately outside of the window and door. As the wood was used the pile receded, and finally it came to a point beyond the reach of the nun with the longest arms. There were no phones by which they could let their neighbors know of their predicament, and they were forced to go for a day and a night without heat before aid came to them. This incident was typical of the uncertainty of the adaptability of their rule of life to their frontier conditions. S.B.C.A.

CHAPTER FIVE

1. *St. John's University Record*, 2:93 (September 1889); *St. Cloud Democrat*, September 26, 1861. In the Announcement Book at St. Mary's Parish, St. Cloud, is found the following announcement: "Today after Mass the contributions for the teacher will be taken up. At our last meeting we decided that the church and school room floors should be tiled. Contributions have already come in and we can begin to buy materials. The rest of the parishioners must contribute money or labor."

2. These names were obtained from newspaper accounts of school programs or entertainments given by the pupils. These family names are still prominent in St. Cloud today.

3. *St. Cloud Visiter*, May 20, June 24, 1858. See also the *St. Cloud Democrat*, December 9, 1858, December 15, 1859.

4. *St. Cloud Visiter*, May 27, July 24, 1858. *St. Cloud Democrat*, December 9, 1858, November 10 and December 15, 1859.

5. *St. Cloud Visiter*, June 24, 1858.

6. *St. Cloud Democrat*, June 30, 1859. It may be said that here started the custom of parishes requiring sisters to put on school entertainments to raise money to enable the parish to pay the teachers' salaries.

7. *St. Cloud Democrat*, July 21, 1859. It is interesting to note here that the "Lady Superior," Mother Willibalda, performed in public by playing a duet with Mrs. Palmer. She was within the cloister since the program was held in the church, but performing before a public audience was an innovation.

8. So, for instance, she wrote in the *St. Cloud Democrat*, October 31, 1858: Reverend Calhoun of the Presbyterian church here had a slave woman whom he said he had brought for the purpose of emancipating. While here she gave birth to a son who according to all international law up to the Dred Scott decision, was to all intent and purpose free. Since that time you have taken that mother and child back to Tennessee and it is understood you have left them there in slavery.

9. *St. Cloud Democrat*, January 10, 1861.

10. *St. Cloud Democrat*, September 26, 1861.

11. *St. Cloud Democrat*, January 23, 1862.

12. Mother McMullen's diary of trip to the Red River. Original is in the convent of the Grey Nuns, Sisters of Charity, in St. Boniface, Manitoba.

13. Father Goiffon's manuscript autobiography is in the possession of St. Paul Seminary, St. Paul, Minnesota. The sad incident is also related in *Annalen*, 29:480–482.

14. *The Dunnigan Catholic Directory for 1860*, p. 209, and the *Metropolitan Catholic Directory for 1861*, p. 181, cite Sister Willibalda as Directress and Abbess. Abbot Wimmer in a letter of April 9, 1859 stated that "the superior *de facto* is Benedicta Riepp; of right it is Sister Willibalda." S.B.C.A. See Mathäser, p. 118.

NOTES BETWEEN PAGES 28 AND 43

CHAPTER SIX

1. Letter of Court Chaplain, Reverend Mueller, March 15, 1859, in W. Mathäser, p. 115–116, n.

2. W. Mathäser, pp. 116–118.

3. This letter continued in the following strain, "The common interests as well as the honor of the Order and the eternal salvation of the sisters themselves along with that of the Faithful obliges me to do all I can to prevent the establishment of such a badly disciplined convent. To have such a group of undisciplined women to support and to care for! No, Your Majesty, that I will not do. . . . If the relations of these nuns is not arranged to our satisfaction by Rome I will give them no money. If Your Majesty will hold back the 3000 florin from my next allotment as you have threatened, and you wish to give that sum directly to the nuns in St. Cloud I am satisfied, for then I have no responsibility. . . . But it is very probable that the money will be spent in unnecessary travel and used badly and to no good purpose. However, I know for certain that Your Majesty will not give funds to a group to encourage them in their disregard of my authority. As Praeses General of our Order in America I have the obligation to prevent individual members of the Order to undertake to establish a convent. That is why I kept the 3000 florin from those runaway nuns and used the money for something better, always forever keeping in mind Your Majesty's approval and the obligation of Prior Benedict to repay the nuns as soon as their status has been settled; that is, as soon as the decision from Rome has been received and there is a moral certainty that a good Benedictine convent can be established in St. Cloud. . . .

"The Court Chaplain in his letter to me seems to hint that I am also keeping back money from the sisters at Newark. . . . They owed me money and it is only just that the sisters pay their debts when they have funds on hand. I took nothing from the sisters that belonged to them." Letter of Abbot Wimmer to King Ludwig April 9, 1859, quoted in Mathäser, p. 119–121. Also see letter of Bishop Fink to Abbot Smith, December 7, 1880. S.J.A.A.

4. The two candidates were Miss Cecilia Mossett and Miss Josephine Leaschell, who were given the names Dominica and Adelaide.

5. Bishop Grace, *Trip to the Red River Valley, 1861*. This diary is written in the third person. Original in St. Paul Seminary. This ceremony of the sisters' investiture took place in the parish church connected with the convent despite their rule of enclosure.

6. Court chaplain to Abbot Wimmer, June 1, 1859, quoted in Mathäsär, p. 124. In the same letter the chaplain warned the abbot against withholding funds sent to the other Benedictine convents.

7. In the following pages the Benedictine nuns will be referred to as sisters. The decree follows.

"His Holiness, having weighed the whole case carefully and judiciously, thought he ought not by any means to grant the aforesaid petitions. But desiring to grant some favors to these same convents, he has especially commended their institution granting to the ordinaries of the places in whose dioceses they are found the faculty of confirming them, provided it be with the profession of simple vows, and under the jurisdiction of the bishops of the same places; they by a special apostolic concession can delegate the abbot president as founder to select their rule of life and even to depute monks of the aforesaid congregation as confessors, nothing to the contrary withstanding. Rome. Given from the office of the Secretary of the Sacred Congregation of Bishops and Regulars.

December 6, 1859

G. Card. della, Genga, Prefect."

Mathäser, p. 134. Photostat copy in Mt. St. Scholastica Convent, Atchison, Kansas.

8. Wimmer to Ludwig, February 22, 1860 in Mathäser, p. 135.
9. The decree sent to the Bishop of Erie stated:
"Your Grace knows . . . the discontent which Sister Benedicta arouses in those convents erected by Abbot Wimmer and the necessity of arranging matters so that no greater evils follow.

"Desiring to offset these, His Holiness, Pope Pius IX, commands that she return to her own monastery of Eichstätt, and so entrusts this command to you, that you with that prudence with which you are eminently endowed, communicate this to the aforesaid abbot as well as to the nun named above, and that you urge the execution of the pontifical request, taking care that due caution be preserved.

December 6, 1859.
G. Card. della Genga"

Mathäser, p. 134.
10. Wimmer to procurator in Rome, May 12, 1861. Original in St. Vincent's Archabbey, Pennsylvania; Bishop Young to Bishop Grace of St. Paul, January 28, 1861.
11. *St. Cloud Democrat*, March 20, 1862. Shortly before her death Mother Benedicta had written to Abbot Wimmer in Pennsylvania asking pardon for the various disagreeable events that she may have caused. Original in St. Vincent's Archives, Pennsylvania.
12. *St. Cloud Democrat*, August 28, September 11, 1862; Bruno Riess, *St. John's University Record*, 3:26–27 (March 1890).
13. George Kulzer, *Life Story of George Kulzer*, manuscript. A translation from the German original was made by Mary Obermiller Kulzer. The original and the translation are in her possession. Father Bruno who was stationed at St. Joseph at this time also gives a good description of the agony of the terrified women and children of the settlement in an article in *St. John's University Record*, 3:27 (March 1890).
14. *Berichte der Leopoldinen-Stiftung in Kaiserthume Oesterreich*, 33:29–34 (Vienna, 1861). This publication consisted of annual reports on the condition of the missions in the various American dioceses and was published by an organization known in Austria as the Leopoldinen-Stiftung. The society was founded in Vienna in 1829. These publications consist mainly of the letters and official reports of the missionary priests and bishops in America to the officers of the society. A nearly complete set of the Berichte is owned by the Minnesota Historical Society; another file is in the library of St. John's University at Collegeville, Minnesota.
15. Bishop Grace to Prior Othmar Wirtz, April 27, 1863. S.J.A.A.
16. Sister Regina Baska, p. 87, places the date of leaving for Kansas on November 1. The date of moving the convent from St. Cloud to St. Joseph is uncertain. Most probably they did not move until the group had left for Atchison and after Bishop Grace's visit to St. Cloud on November 26. See Abbot Alexius' manuscript, *History of the Benedictines in Minnesota*, p. 25.

CHAPTER SEVEN

1. Father Pierz's baptismal register. Photostat copy in St. Benedict's Convent Archives.
2. Register of Deeds office in St. Cloud. The church was to be put under patronage of St. Joseph and the settlement was to take its name from that patron despite the fact that the post office designated it as Clinton.
3. Bruno Riess, "The First Beginnings of St. John's Abbey" in *St. John's University Record*, 2:16 (February 1889).
4. Father Bruno Riess was one of the five Benedictine monks sent to Minnesota

by Abbot Wimmer at the request of Father Pierz and Bishop Cretin. They had arrived in May of the year 1856 and were stationed below St. Cloud on the banks of the Mississippi River. On arrival they took charge of the parish in St. Cloud and Sauk Rapids. A few years later the monastery moved to the present location of St. John's Abbey.

5. *St. John's University Record,* 2:25 (March 1889).

6. *St. John's University Record* 2:74 (August 1889). This beautiful custom was kept by the people of St. Joseph for many years.

7. Alexius Hoffman, O.S.B., Manuscript History of St. John's. This building was thirty feet wide and fifty-six feet long. The string of buildings was located on block three of the town somewhere between the present school building and the chaplain's cottage on the main street. This was the first home the sisters could call their own and yet they did not hold the deed, for the convent was not yet incorporated under the laws of the state. The abbey held the deed in trust for them.

8. Willibalda to King Ludwig, December 4, 1864. Baraga collection. Memoirs of Sister Ida Aschenbrenner in S.B.C.A.

9. Willibalda to King Ludwig, December 4, 1864. Baraga collection.

10. Convent Annals. S.B.C.A.

11. Father Buh had been brought over to this country by Father Pierz to aid him in missionary work among the Chippewa Indians. They both came from Carniola which then belonged to Austria. Sister Scholastica had to change her name in religion to Evangelista some time later when Sister Scholastica Kerst of the Shakopee convent came to St. Joseph. Henceforth we shall refer to sister by her second name, Evangelista. All but one of these new members were foreign born.

12. James Bishop, *The Day Lincoln Died,* p. 145 (New York, 1955). *True Magazine,* February 1953, revived this sensational story.

13. Decrees of 1866. St. Vincent's Archabbey Archives.

14. Wimmer to prioress at Erie, June 24, 1866. Original in St. Benedict's Convent, Erie, Pennsylvania.

15. The Benedictine monks had recently moved their monastery from St. Cloud to a region four miles from St. Joseph. In 1866 this monastery had been raised to the dignity of an abbey and the new name, "St. Louis on the Lake," authorized. Reverend Rupert Seidenbusch of St. Vincent's Abbey was elected the first abbot and arrived in Minnesota the following year, June 13, 1867.

16. Memoirs of Sister Evangelista and Sister Martina. Sister Antonia was born in Krautheim, Baden, December 22, 1835. After coming to the United States she entered the Benedictine Convent in Erie, Pennsylvania, and after three years she was sent with a group to found a new convent in Chicago. See Sister Claudia Duratschek, O.S.B., *The Beginnings of Catholicism in South Dakota,* p. 77 (Washington, D.C., 1943).

17. Annals, S.B.C.A. Claims of apparitions of celestial spirits and disturbances created in the house by the evil one were common. Sister Johanna, the novice mistress, claimed several communications with saints and angels and several brushes with the devil when he disturbed the quiet of the house by throwing things around. There is no doubt that the evil spirits are active in their endeavor to throw obstacles in the way of new communities of religious. On the other hand, there is evidence that many of the experiences of these novices were to be attributed to insufficient nourishment, to spiritual reading beyond their understanding, and to lack of a qualified spiritual director. Bishop Grace gave no support to these visions.

18. When school opened, it was found that the greater number of boarders were Protestants. Among them were Hatty and Gertrude Arnold. Hatty later married Mr. Sartell of Sartell. Gertrude became Mrs. Clement of Rockville. Another pupil was a member of the Metzroth family in St. Cloud. S.B.C.A.

19. Memoirs of Sister Placida Heinen.
20. *Der Wanderer*, July 1, 1871.
21. *Der Nordstern*, January 18, 1877. *St. Cloud Times*, January 5, 1876.
22. Later, Sisters Ida Aschenbrenner, Hildegard Hasler, and Walburga Muelken joined the New Trier group.
23. Mother Willibalda to Abbot Alexius, September 17, 1877. S.J.A.A. At one time she appealed to Abbot Wimmer to apply to Rome for a dispensation from her vows which were solemn. The matter apparently went no further. After the New Trier episode and her return to St. Joseph she acted as organist in the parish church there and in other places such as New Munich, Pierz, and Chanhassen until age compelled her to retire. After that she devoted her time to needle work and prayer until her death, February 12, 1914.
24. This building is still in use at Pierz and the grille in the outside door has been kept as a relic of old days.
25. Mother Antonia to Abbot Alexius, January 1, 1877. She complained to the abbot that the prior no longer supplied the laundry with the fats for soap-making nor with wood for the laundry stoves, pointing out that the small recompense given for the work was insufficient if the above supplies were not donated.
26. Abbot Alexius to Mother Gertrude Flynn of Shakopee, February 15, 1877. S.B.C.A. A few months after Mother Antonia resigned her office she returned to her former convent in Chicago and later joined Abbot Marty in his work among the Indians in Dakota Territory. She became one of the founders of the convent school at Yankton, South Dakota. She died at Pierre, South Dakota, January 30, 1912.
27. Mother Aloysia's manuscript autobiography. S.B.C.A.
28. Abbot Innocent Wolf to Abbot Alexius, March 3, 1879; Bishop Fink to Abbot Smith, December 7, 1880. S.J.A.A.
29. Archives of St. Benedict's Convent, June 4, 1879.
30. Today prayers before breakfast are said silently in the language of each sister's choice. The absence of a set formula may be explained by the fact that breakfast was unheard of in St. Walburga's in Eichstätt and in the Minnesota convent until 1865.
31. The first mentioned opponent received the sacraments before his death and asked the priest to read his retraction aloud to the parish at his funeral. The other man's son was struck by lightning and had to be buried under circumstances horrible to his family. Later on, the father himself was found frozen to death in a swamp. The four sisters sent to face this parish war were Mother Willibalda, Sister Baptista Frederick, Sister Luitgardis Billig, and Sister Thecla Heckmann. Memoirs of Reverend P. Henry, O.S.B., S.B.C.A.
32. Mrs. Wood's scrap book. Wood Papers are in possession of the Minnesota Historical Society. Sister Grace McDonald, "A Catholic Newspaper Woman and Novelist," *Mid-America* 17:30–36 (Chicago, January 1935). Mrs. Julia Wood of Sauk Rapids, Minnesota, wrote many novels under the pseudonym of Minnie Mary Lee. Born at New London, New Hampshire, she received her education there and entered the literary field. She and her husband moved to Minnesota, and after 1851 they published the *New Era*, weekly newspaper in Sauk Rapids. Besides contributing to her husband's newspaper, she wrote a number of novels. In 1870 she became a Catholic. After her conversion to Catholicism her novels were of an apologetic nature.

CHAPTER EIGHT

1. Jessamine Slaughter Bergum, *Zezula: or Pioneer Days in the Smoky Water Country*, p. 71 (Valley City, N. Dakota, 1937).

2. *Bismarck Daily Tribune*, October 21, 1893. *Bismarck Saturday Evening Journal*, April 18, 1885.
3. Abbot Martin Marty of St. Meinrad's in Indiana gave up his position as abbot to work among the Sioux Indians of Dakota. He became the bishop of the Sioux Falls Diocese in 1889 and in 1895 was transferred to the St. Cloud Diocese
4. *Bismarck Tribune*, June 16, 1875; *Bismarck Weekly Tribune*, November 20, 1875.
5. *Bismarck Tri-weekly Tribune*, March 28 and April 6, 1878.
6. Sister Anatolia, memoirs, S.B.C.A. *Bismarck Weekly Tribune*, August 14, 1878.
7. Reverend Chrysostom Foffa to Abbot Alexius, October 24, 1879. S.J.A.A.
8. *Collections of the State Historical Society of North Dakota*, 1:271–272. (Bismarck, 1906). Mrs. Slaughter died in 1911 in St. Joseph's Home in St. Cloud.
9. A letter of Father Paul Rettenmaier, O.S.B., to Abbot Alexius, December 10, 1883, described the attempt of the four robbers. S.J.A.A.
10. Father Chrysostom to Abbot Alexius, March 23, 1880. S.J.A.A. Memoirs of Sister Hilda. S.B.C.A.
11. This letter and memoirs of Sister Anatolia show that he did not understand the crowded condition of the convent and school. Reverend William Eversmann, O.S.B., to Abbot Alexius, May 23, 1881; Reverend Edward Ginther, O.S.B., to Abbot Alexius, September 5, 1881.

CHAPTER NINE

1. Bishop Grace to Prior Othmar Wirtz, April 28, 1864; Alexius Edelbrock's manuscript history, pp. 47–48. S.J.A.A.
2. Sister Scholastica to Abbot Alexius, May 2, 1876. S.J.A.A. "Could not you bring it about so that I and four others who feel the way I do could be allowed to start an independent house in St. Paul? We could get a few more teachers from the East to help us. We do this only on condition that you will be our superior. But everything will have to be arranged and settled in such a way that the convent here will know nothing about it until it is too late to interfere. I am sending this through Father Koering."
3. Bishop Grace to Mother Gertrude Flynn. S.B.C.A.
4. Minutes of chapter meeting. S.B.C.A.
5. Of the sixty sisters at St. Joseph at this date only seven were non-German. The steps taken to amalgamate the Shakopee group were taken by Mother Scholastica while Abbot Alexius was in Europe.
6. Bishop Grace to Prior Othmar Wirtz, April 28, 1864, and October 27, 1865. Alexius Edelbrock's manuscript history, p. 47.
7. Bishop Grace to Mother Gertrude January 24, 1877. S.B.C.A.
8. Abbot Alexius to Mother Gertrude, March 22, 1878. S.B.C.A. Abbot Alexius' manuscript history of St. John's, p. 47. S.J.A.A. Refusing the sisters a place in the parish church was a serious matter, for the sisters had no chaplain and were accustomed to attend Mass at the parish church.
9. Bishop Grace to Mother Gertrude, February 2, 1877. S.B.C.A.
10. Data given at an interview with Sister Anatolia Langford in 1925. Sister Anatolia was one of the members of the Shakopee convent until its merger with that at St. Joseph. This remarkable woman continued in active work up to the year 1945. Mother Gertrude Flynn gave the same testimony in 1920.
11. Abbot Alexius to Bishop Ireland, April 10, 1885. S.J.A.A.
12. Data pertaining to Bishop Ireland is found in Mother Aloysia's memoirs. Sister Anatolia Langford in an interview in 1922 gave the facts relating to Mother Scholastica Kerst.
13. *Der Nordstern*. September 22, 1881, "The following names of donors have

been preserved in the cornerstone: St. John's Abbey $1000.00; Mr. P. J. Kerst, St. Paul, $1000.00; Bishop Seidenbusch, St. Cloud, $455.00; Mr. Ig. Will, St. Paul, $400; Mr. M. Walz, Mr. J. Linneman, Mr. F. Bernick, Mr. J. Philippi, Mr. J. Seifert, Mr. P. Ley, Mrs. Aschenbrener, Mr. Ambrositsch, Mr. Loder-mayer, Mr. H. Prebreuil, Mr. W. Feneis, Mr. H. Nierengarten, and Mrs. M. Loso, all of St. Joseph, each $25.00; Mr. L. Paulissen of Kankakee, $25.00."

14. *St. Cloud Times*, July 5, 1882; Abbot Alexius Diary. It was in keeping that the saint under whose protection the convent was placed should be that of the founder of the Benedictine Order. It does not imply that the sisters had lost their devotion to St. Joseph. The numbers enrolled in the new academy were such that all were convinced that the new building was too small; and when Abbot Alexius in the spring of 1883 offered the sisters Father Gregory Steil as architect and Brother Andrew Unterburger as foreman, together with the magnificent gift of $12,650 the work was started on the east-west wing. When this 1883 wing was completed, the chapel was moved to the second floor of the new wing. Today this area is used as the sisters' infirmary.

15. The following pages are in great part taken from Sister Grace's article, "A Finishing School in the 1880's which appeared in *Minnesota History,* June 1946. Reprinted with the permission of the Minnesota Historical Society.

16. A letter written to his daughters on this occasion tells of his part in the fight: "Mouth of Big Horn on the north side of Yellow Stone.
    July 5th, 1876.
    My dear daughters, you will no doubt see by the papers that General Custer's command had a fight with the Indians on the Little Big Horn, where General Custer and twelve Officers and nigh on to 300 men were killed during the fight. I with 3 others became separated and had to hide in the brush for 2 days and one night and had a narrow escape from drowning. I escaped through the grace of God; many a time then did I think of you and wonder whether I would ever see you again. I write to you now to assure you of my safety. I doubt whether we get back to Lincoln before November."
    Mr. Gerard was a friend of the missionary, Father DeSmet, who had baptized his daughters. These two girls later entered the Benedictine Order and received the names of Anastasia and Adelberta. Sister Adelberta died in 1912; Sister Anastasia is still living. Mr. Gerard died in St. Cloud and was buried at St. Joseph, Minnesota. For accounts of his career, see Linda W. Slaughter, "Leaves from Northwestern History," in the *North Dakota Historical Collections,* 1:223; *Bismarck Tribune,* April 15, April 22, 1874, October 11, 1876; and a record of an interview with one of his daughters. S.B.C.A.

17. *St. Benedict's Academy, Annual Catalogue 1882–1883*, p. 7 (St. Paul, 1883).

18. Martingale's book was published by Elredge Brothers of Philadelphia; Smith's book was published by J. B. Lippincott and Company of the same city. These and other textbooks used in St. Benedict's Academy are now preserved in the convent archives.

19. The quotations are from pages III and IV of the Preface of Barnes' *General History,* which was published by A. S. Barnes and Company of New York and Chicago.

20. Records of student expenses are to be found in the account books of the academy for 1882 and 1887–89, now in the archives of the College of St. Benedict. There, too, are displayed examples of the pioneer students' handiwork. Courses are listed in the *Annual Catalogue, 1882–83,* p. 9.

21. The rules are in the archives of the convent.

22. *Annual Catalogue, 1883–84,* p. 11; *Annual Catalogue, 1889–90,* p. 11.

23. The letters quoted appear under the title "When We Were Very Young," in the *St. Benedict's Quarterly,* 2:34, 36 (February 1928). An introductory note indicates that they are based upon "data gleaned from the archives of St. Benedict's."

NOTES BETWEEN PAGES 81 AND 105

24. *Northwestern Chronicle*, July 3, 1884; *St. John's Record*, 1:55 (May 1888). Mr. Arctander's brother became a convert to Catholicism and in 1896 was ordained a priest for the archdiocese of St. Paul.

25. Bishop Seidenbusch's reaction is recorded in the manuscript chronicle at St. John's Abbey under date of June 22, 1881.

CHAPTER TEN

1. *St. Cloud Times*, August 13, 1884.

2. *Der Nordstern*, August 20, September 3, November 25, 1884 (St. Cloud).

3. Community memoirs, St. Scholastica's Convent, Duluth, Minnesota.

4. Papers in Archives of St. Charles Seminary, Carthagena, Ohio; *Perham Enterprise-Bulletin*, August 1, 1929; *The St. Paul Pioneer Press*, November 20, 1892; *Fergus Falls Weekly Journal*, October 15, 1885; *Leopoldinen-Stiftung* 42:46–47.

5. Six brothers and thirteen sisters of the Society of the Precious Blood and several families joined Father Joseph in his secession. The government census of August, 1870, gives the names of the sisters, brothers, and other members of this group.

6. *The St. Paul Pioneer Press*, November 20, 1892; Documents in Cleveland Chancery office. See also *Berichte der Leopoldinen-Stiftung*, 42:46–47 (Vienna 1872); *Fergus Falls Weekly Journal*, October 15, 1885.

7. Memoirs of Sister Theodora Dunn and Sister Chrysostem Sanz who were stationed at Long Prairie at the time. Memoirs of Reverend Henry Borgerding. S.B.C.A.; *Perham Enterprise*, August 1, 1929.

8. Memoirs. S.B.C.A.

9. Memoirs. S.B.C.A.

10. The Benedictines withdrew from this parish school in 1948 in compliance with Bishop Aloysius Muench's program of giving his diocesan schools to the sisterhoods whose mother houses were in his diocese. The Franciscan Sisters of Hankinson then took charge.

11. Letter of the Hon. Henry Rice to Abbot Alexius February 21, 1884. Original in the U.S. Office of Indian Affairs; Microfilm in S.B.C.A.; Abbot Alexius Diary. S.J.A.A.

12. Agnes Repplier, *Mére Marie of the Ursulines*, p. 21 (New York, 1931).

13. Indian Industrial School register. S.B.C.A.

14. *Der Nordstern*, April 14, 1886.

15. Mother Scholastica to Abbot Alexius, April 13, 1886. S.J.A.A. Later this building was converted into novitiate and since 1939 when a third story was added, it has been known as Marmion Hall.

16. *St. Cloud Journal Press*, July 16 and July 23, 1885. The court decided that Mrs. Stevenson should be given three years to pay her debt. In 1893 Bishop Zardetti transferred the orphans from St. Joseph and Pierz to an institution in Little Falls of which he asked the Franciscan Sisters of the Immaculate Conception to take charge. In July he informed the diocese: "The only motive for inducing us to make the change was the desire to have a separate institution for this purpose and to provide sufficient work for the Franciscan Sisters. . . . The Diocese is indebted to the good sisters in St. Joseph for the care hitherto taken of these little ones." He also felt the caring for orphans was a more homogeneous occupation for the Franciscans. *The Diocese of St. Cloud*, July, September, October, 1893 (St. Cloud). This periodical was the official diocesan paper.

17. Mother Scholastica to Abbot Alexius, April 6, 1881. S.J.A.A. The Bureau of Catholic Indian Missions advanced the money to pay for transportation.

18. Letter of Rev. J. B. Brouillet to Abbot Alexius, November 18, 1880; The Catholic Bureau Indian Missions to Abbot Alexius, February 21, 1881. S.J.A.A.; *Annual Report of Commissioner U.S. Office of Indian Affairs, 1878*, p. 112

(Washington, D.C.). Archbishop Blanchet retired in 1880 and was succeeded by Archbishop Seghers.

19. Abbot Alexius to Reverend Norbert Hofbauer, O.S.B., December 9, 1881; S.J.A.A.

20. Abbot Alexius to Reverend Norbert Hofbauer, O.S.B., December 9, 1881; Abbot Alexius to Bishop Seghers, December 18, 1881. S.J.A.A. It is interesting to note that the abbot tried to get $600.00 remuneration for the sisters' railroad fare but failed. Then the abbot and Mother Scholastica urged this band of sisters to get money from friends to defray the expense of the return trip.

CHAPTER ELEVEN

1. *The Northwest Magazine,* 3:13, October 1885 (St. Paul).

2. The court decided the marquis had acted in self-defense. While this man awaited his trial in Bismarck, his wife lived with the Benedictine sisters at the hospital. He later returned to France where he was directed by the French government to organize an expedition to the Sudan. There he met his death at the hands of native tribesmen. His wife in turn organized an expedition to hunt for the false guide who had betrayed him and did not rest until he was apprehended. *Bismarck Tribune,* June 29, 1883.

3. The water was often so muddy that it was let stand in the barrels for some time in order to allow the sediment to settle to the bottom. A part of a loaf of bread thrown into the barrel was supposed to aid in settling the mud.

4. *Bismarck Tribune,* October 2, October 9, 1884.

5. Mr. McKenzie had a long and checkered career. Those who knew him, whether friend or enemy, agreed in declaring him a genius and a man generous with money and favors. When life became too settled in Dakota he moved to Alaska, at the time of the Nome gold rush, where he held a federal office. In 1884 when still in Bismarck he sent his young wife and two infant daughters to the finishing school or academy at St. Joseph. Lewis Crawford, *History of North Dakota,* 1:420–421.

6. Abbot to the prior at St. John's, April 14, 1885; The Bismarck *Saturday Evening Journal,* April 18, 1885; *Bismarck Tribune,* May 10, 1885; *Bismarck Pioneer,* April 15, 1885; Reverend Bede to the abbot, May 20, 1885. S.J.A.A.

7. On May 3, 1885, the abbot wrote in his diary: "I blessed the ad interim called Lamborn Hospital at Bismarck, D. T., and dedicated it ad honorem St. Alexi. The ceremony took place at 6:30 A.M. on the fourth Sunday after Easter. Sisters Alexia, Gabriel, Juliana, Thomas, and Opportuna were present." S.J.A.A.

8. Community Annals, S.B.C.A.

9. Father Bede to the abbot, December 9, 1885. S.J.A.A.; *Bismarck Tribune,* February 2, 1886.

10. The *Bismarck Daily* carried the following account of the accident which brought him to the hospital. On the Fourth of July, Osborn with several other prisoners made an attempt to escape prison. Osborn asked the jailor to let him go into the hall to his trunk for clothes. The jailor complied but as he did so Osborn turned on the jailor and calling his four comrades to help, they attempted to lock the jailor in the cell. They were frustrated in this and the jailor shot the horse thief in the neck below the collar bone. Osborn the thief screamed out defiance and curses and said, "I did not think you had sense enough to shoot; if I had, I would have got you first. I expect to go to hell in about half an hour and I would rather go to hell than to the penitentiary!" The newspaper concludes: He was brought to the Lamborn Hospital where he is doing well. *Bismarck Daily Tribune,* July 7, 1885; *Weekly Tribune,* July 10, 1885; Records of St. Alexius Hospital. S.B.C.A.

11. Theodore Roosevelt's name cannot be found in the records of the hospital, but

Sister Juliana, one of the founders of the hospital, often related incidents that occurred during his convalescence there.

12. Sister Juliana Memoirs. S.B.C.A.; Father Bede to the abbot, July 13, 1885. S.J.A.A.
13. *Northwestern Lancet,* 8:108 (Minneapolis).
14. Helen Clapsattle, *The Doctors Mayo,* pp. 194, 197, 236 (New York, 1943).
15. Description given by Dr. Charles Mayo in Helen Clapsattle, *The Doctors Mayo,* p. 241.
16. Attempts had been made to install a pump in the basement of the hospital. Water was found but the pump did not work. By 1890 the pump was functioning, but the water had to be carried pail by pail up the stairs to the various rooms.
17. Dr. V. J. LaRose, in an interview in 1942, declared no asepsis was practiced at St. Alexius before 1899. Sister Amalia Eich, one of the earliest Bismarck nurses, gave the facts about the sterilizer.
18. Clapsattle, p. 304.
19. Sister Boniface Tummins was appointed head of the hospital and superior of the sisters in 1892, seven years before Dr. Quaine joined the staff. Sister made the mistake of selling the stoves before the new heating system was in working order. Material and gadgets had to be shipped from the Twin Cities and the delays were so frequent that the contractor did not finish the work until long after cold weather had set in.
20. Data given by Dr. V. J. LaRose and Sister Juliana Venne in 1942.
21. *The Bismarck Capital,* September 12, 1935. At the time of the founding of this hospital it was said to be the only regular hospital between Minnesota's western boundary and the Rocky Mountains. Property for a new hospital site was purchased in 1913 and the new 125-bed hospital was opened two years later with a medical staff of 18 physicians and surgeons.

CHAPTER TWELVE

1. Dom Cuthbert Butler, *Benedictine Monachism,* pp. 29–31 (London, 1924).
2. In line with the indult which Abbot Wimmer had procured from Rome in 1866, the sisters had been substituting the Blessed Virgin Office for the Divine Office on ferial days; but now the small office was substituted on all days.
3. Mother Scholastica to Abbot Alexius, May 7, 1881. S.J.A.A.
4. Minutes of the general chapter. S.B.C.A.; Regina Baska, p. 130.
5. The face veil worn over the regular veil but thrown back from the face was used in public down to the year 1933. The wearing of the large side rosary was abandoned in 1935.
6. Mother Scholastica to Abbot Innocent. S.B.C.A.
7. Mother Scholastica, September 15, 1885. S.B.C.A.
8. Superioress in Chicago to Mother Scholastica, March 20, 1884.
9. Abbot Alexius' directives to a pastor, November 19, 1887. S.J.A.A.
10. Abbot Zilliox to Abbot Alexius, September 27, 1887. S.J.A.A.
11. Document in chancery office of archdiocese of St. Paul.
12. Interview with Mother Cecilia, April 24, 1926. Annals, S.B.C.A.
13. Letter of P. Norbert Hofbauer to Abbot Alexius, August 8, 1889. S.J.A.A.
14. Annals of community.

CHAPTER THIRTEEN

1. Mother Aloysia, it will be recalled, had filled out the unfinished term of Mother Antonia Herman in the 70's by appointment.
2. Upon Dr. Zardetti's arrival in the United States he had taken the position of

professor of theology in St. Francis Seminary, Milwaukee. When Bishop Marty invited him to his diocese in Dakota as vicar general he accepted. He was destined to spend but one year in this mission field, for which he was little fitted by disposition and then was called to head the new diocese of St. Cloud.

3. *The Diocese of St. Cloud*, June 1892.

4. Rev. Henry Borgerding, O.S.B. Memoirs. S.B.C.A.

5. *The Diocese of St. Cloud*, April 1892, June 1893. This was the official organ of the bishop and his clergy.

6. Letter, Bishop Zardetti to Convent. S.B.C.A. Annals of convent. Archbishop Ireland was also responsible for abolishing the lay sisterhood in the convents of the Sisters of St. Joseph in St. Paul.

7. Letter of Abbot Innocent Wolf to Abbot Bernard Locnikar, March 10, 1893. S.J.A.A.

8. John Greer, *The History of Education in Minnesota*, p. 13. (U.S. Bureau of Education, Washington, D.C., 1902); Wm. W. Folwell, *A History of Minnesota* 4:173 (St. Paul, 1924); *Laws of Minnesota Relating to the Public School System*, p. 3 (St. Paul, 1939).

9. Peter Guilday, *History of the Councils*, pp. 238–289 (N.Y. 1932).

10. W. Folwell, 4:174–175.

11. John Greer, *The History of Education in Minnesota*, p. 35.

12. Zardetti papers, S.B.C.A.; *Diocese of St. Cloud*, April 1892.

13. German was still the official language of the convent. All public devotional exercises were conducted in either German or Latin, most of them in German.

14. Mother Scholastica, after relinquishing the office of prioress, had been teaching school at Perham and at Moorhead. Her sister, Sister Alexia, was at this time superior at the hospital in Duluth.

15. Memoirs of Sister Anatolia Langford and Sister Edmund Hilton. S.B.C.A.

16. St. Benedict's had already given the new Duluth convent the title to all its real estate and other property in that city. In July, 1894, one year and three months after the above transfer of property was made, the parents of two of the Duluth sisters began successful negotiations to recover a $20,000 donation given to St. Benedict's while their daughters were members of that convent. See letter of M. P. Roach, attorney, to Mother Aloysia, January 4, 1896. S.B.C.A.

17. *St. Cloud Times*, September 20, 21, 23, 1895; *Journal Press*, May 3, 1898.

18. Bishop Marty was installed as bishop of St. Cloud in March, 1895. He died on September 19, 1896. A story is related illustrating his kindness. Even as vicar apostolic he did the shopping for the sisters at Yankton. On one occasion he purchased shoes for one of the sisters and very humbly returned home with the shoes under his arm. See Idelphonse Betschart, *Der Apostel Der Siouxindianer Bischof Martinus Marty, O.S.B.*, p. 129 (Einsiedeln, 1934).

CHAPTER FOURTEEN

1. Bishop Wehrle to Mother Louisa Walz, August 14, 1931; Mother Cecilia of Garrison to Mother Louisa, November 17, 1931. S.B.C.A.

2. Sister Leonida's memoirs. Sister Rosaria Zenner in a letter to Mother Louisa April 25, 1937 wrote, "The Bishop declares he does not remember what he said and did during his illness this winter. Several corroborated this."

3. Mother Louisa to Bishop Wehrle, June 9, 1937. S.B.C.A.

4. Sister Rosaria to Mother Louisa, May 23, 1937; Bishop Wehrle to Mother Louisa, June 4, 1937; Abbot Alcuin to Bishop Wehrle, June 18, 1937. S.B.C.A.

5. Diary in S.B.C.A. The pipe organ purchased some ten years earlier was moved from the old chapel to the new. The stations of the cross were repainted and installed in the new chapel. The chapel was irrevocably set aside for divine

service by the rite of consecration, performed by the Most Reverend Peter Bartholome on Sunday, October 24, 1943.

6. The students' infirmary up to this time occupied the space on first floor which is now within the enclosure and used as faculty study.

7. This isolation infirmary was, after a few years, remodeled and converted into a guest house.

8. These parochial schools were at Dickinson and Mandan, North Dakota; Bluffton, Browerville, Cold Spring, Dumont, Eden Valley, Fairfax, Freeport, Gilman, Heidelberg, Kent, Melrose, Millerville, Meire Grove, Pearl Lake, Richmond, St. Cloud, Sobieski, Staples, Tintah, Perham, Watkins, Wadena, all in Minnesota. The boarding school was at Altoona, Wisconsin.

9. Reverend Henry Borgerding, O.S.B. Annals. S.B.C.A.

10. Sister Justina, a leader in the movement for the production of liturgically correct church vestments, is author of the book, *Christian Symbols and How to Use Them*, which was published by Bruce in 1935.

11. Bishop Hunt to Mother Rosamond, May 4, 1943; Annals. S.B.C.A. Reverend W. J. Giroux to Mother Rosamond, September 14, 1943.

12. Letter of Samuel C. Powell to Arthur Bunker, vice-chairman of the War Production Board, July 3, 1944. A copy is in the convent archives.

13. *Standard Examiner, Ogden*, September 19, 1946. St. Benedict's Hospital Records, Ogden. Sister Mary Margaret Clifford was appointed hospital administrator and Sister Floretta Schoemer was appointed religious superior of the sisters who staffed the hospital: Sisters Laetitia Griep, Edicta Zierden, Frederica Hens, Daria Duerr, Estelle Nordick, Davora Thielen, Vestina Bursken, Myron McGinley, Benora Gaida, Philomene Lutgen, Samuel Slaughter, Edwardelle Schroeder, Mary Jude Meyer, Herena Mueller, Amos Marie Dickson, Aelred Stang, and LaRose Schwartz.

14. St. Benedict's Hospital Records. One of the outstanding works of this hospital was the establishment of the department for the mentally ill. The neuropsychiatric department was opened March 16, 1949, with a bed capacity of ten.

15. Official Proceedings of the City Council, 1947.

16. Agreement of city council and sisters. Office of city council; *New Prague Times,* December 20, 1951.

17. The first sisters sent to staff this hospital were Sisters Jameen Mape, Ruth Ann Duclos, Ella Schweitzer, Mary Jude Meyer, Cormarie Auer, Mary Afra Guettler, Alverna McGinnis, Martha Schrantz.

CHAPTER F'FTEEN

1. When Right Reverend T. Leo Keaveny, the diocesan superintendent of schools, with the consent of the prioress, appointed Sister Rosetta Jeub to fill the new office of diocesan supervisor of schools the office of community supervisor was more or less merged with that new office. In order not to duplicate Sister Rosetta's work, the community supervisor, Sister Loraine Tracy, withdrew from the schools within the St. Cloud Diocese and gave all of her attention to those schools in other dioceses. Since 1949 both offices have been filled by Sister Aloysius Weber.

2. *Laws of Minnesota Relating to the Public School System,* State of Minnesota Department of Education, p. 3 (St. Paul, 1939).

3. The opinion of Clifford Hilton, assistant attorney general, given March 31, 1915, in the Biennial Report of Attorney General, 1916, pp. 145–146 (Minneapolis, 1916).

4. *Laws of Minnesota Relating to the Public School System,* p. 339; *Der Wanderer,* January 16, 23, 1919, February 20, March 27, 1919.

5. In 1867 the office of county superintendent was created and that officer made

up the examinations for the applicant for a teacher's certificate. This was changed in 1887 when the examinations were made up by the state superintendent of schools and sent out to be administered by the county superintendent. Among the first sisters to receive certificates were Sister Josepha Victor and Sister Cecilia Kapsner who took their examinations in the years 1876 and 1877 respectively.

6. J. Burns and B. Kohlbrenner, *A History of Catholic Education in the United States, pp.* 224–225 (New York, 1937). This year, 1921, the name of state normal schools was changed to state teachers colleges.

7. *Laws of Minnesota Relating to the Public School System,* p. 3.

8. Quoted in a letter of attorney general to the commissioner of education, August 4, 1938. Copy in S.B.C.A. In 1952 the College of St. Benedict instituted a department of elementary education which was accredited by the state department of education. The majority of the convent's primary teachers are now trained there.

9. *Laws Relating to the Minnesota Public School System,* p. 108 (St. Paul, 1946).

10. Gladstone papers, in S.B.C.A.

11. Gerhardt et al vs. Heid et al in *Northwestern Reporter,* pp. 127 and 131.

12. Gerhardt et al vs. Heid et al. p. 135.

13. Gerhardt, p. 132.

14. In the summer of 1946 Bishop Ryan of Bismarck told the sisters to cancel the teaching contracts which they had signed for the school year 1946–1947. He knew that the state legislature was planning to pass a law forbidding the wearing of the religious garb by public school teachers. Rather than have the sisters put out, he forbade them to start classes. But the school board held them to their contracts. In 1948 the sisters were not granted contracts by the school board and they quietly withdrew.

15. Holy Angels High School in St. Cloud had been opened in the fall of 1899; St. Mary's in Altoona, Wisconsin, in 1906; and St. Patrick's High School in Eau Claire, Wisconsin, in 1915.

16. Among those dropped were the incomplete high schools in Millerville, Tintah, Wahpeton, and St. Patrick's in Melrose. The small four-year high school at Altoona was also closed.

17. Unlike many such institutions, St. Benedict's Convent did not abandon its high school when turning to college work. In 1938 St. Benedict's Academy was changed from a boarding school to a day school. It continued to emphasize the classical and scientific curriculum as in the past. The school reverted to a boarding school in 1956.

18. Records in dean's office.

19. *St. Cloud Times,* June 7, 1918; *Catholic Bulletin,* June 8, and June 15, 1918; Lynn and Dora Haines, *The Lindberghs,* p. 293 (New York, 1931). The previous year one degree had been issued to a student who had completed three years of college work elsewhere before registering at St. Benedict's. This student, Caroline Scoblic, was at the time a candidate for entrance to the convent. On receiving the habit she received the name Sister Claudette.

20. If not the first, St. Benedict's was one of the first colleges in the state to organize a separate unit of the Red Cross during World War II. Sisters Irma, Jeanette, Remberta, Estelle, and Grace received the Red Cross silver pin for their donations to the Blood Mobile.

21. The regularly appointed chaplains have been Fathers Herbert Buerschinger, Elmer Eisenschenk, Alexander Korte, Angelo Zankel, Vitus Bucher, Cassian Osendorf, Osmund Jacobs, Odilo Kohler, Harold Fuchs, Roderic Albers, and Michael Marx.

22. These schools were the Catholic University of America, St. Louis University, Marquette University, Columbia, and the universities at Toronto, Ann Arbor, Ames, and Quebec.

NOTES BETWEEN PAGES 169 AND 196

23. Sister Mary Grell was given a Fulbright grant which entitled her to a year of research and study in Germany in the field of biology. Sister Rogatia Sohler received a grant for work on cancer at the Divi Thomae, Sister Luanne Meagher for work in Latin at the University of Chicago, and Sister Marianne Pomerleau received a grant from the French government for study in France. Sister Inez Hilger and Sister Mariella Gable have gained national repute for their work in anthropology and creative writing respectively.

24. Records in the Alumnae office at College of St. Benedict. Sister Jeanette Roesch died in 1955, Sister Adelgundis Bergmann in 1946, Sister Vivia Nangle in 1944, Sister Olivia Egan in 1940, Sister Modesta Wieland in 1939.

25. Shorthand report of sermon. S.B.C.A.

CHAPTER SIXTEEN

1. At the beginning of the century all but 30 of the 292 members were of German parentage and spoke the German language. But in 1925 the number of sisters who were not familiar with the German language had tripled. The reading of German books at table was then dropped and the next year 1926, the night prayers were recited in English. That year also marked the last retreat given in German. Because of the necessity of accommodating both students and sisters to the services of one chaplain it was the custom till 1931 to distribute Holy Communion to the sisters before the Mass. Another innovation made during these years, but one which had no connection with the liturgical movement, was the discarding of the large fifteen-decade rosary as part of the religious dress and the wearing of the extra veil when on the street. See Chapter Books and Annals, 1933.

2. Convent Annals and Business Records. S.B.C.A.

3. Convent Annals.

4. Sister Gemma Gertken has long worked in furthering the chant in schools and children's choirs. In 1945 she prepared the work, *Techniques of Grade School Music,* which appeared in mimeograph form and is used in the schools of the diocese taught by Benedictine sisters. In 1948 she wrote the musical accompaniment for the book published by McLaughlin and Reilly Company of Boston entitled *Chant Melodies for Home, Church, School, and College.* Sister Gemma also worked with Dr. Eugene Lapierre on the book, *A Simplified Modal Accompaniment to First Class and Greater Feasts,* which was published by the Gregorian Institute of America.

5. Rev. Clement Theunte, O.P., letter to Sister Estelle, 1944. S.B.C.A. Sister Estelle Nordick and Sister Ada Nordick are nieces of Father Theunte.

6. In 1930 the Rural Life Conference joined with the Confraternity of Christian Doctrine in promoting this movement but in 1935 it relinquished the work in favor of the Confraternity. The National Council of Catholic Women likewise took an active interest in the work. See *The Catholic Educational Association Bulletin Report of Proceedings,* November, 1921, pp. 273–274 (Columbus, Ohio). Raymond Witte, *Twenty-five Years of Crusading,* p. 182 (Des Moines, 1948).

7. Letter of Abbot Alcuin Deutsch of St. John's to Mother Rosamond, May 25, 1942 and July 15, 1942. S.B.C.A.

8. *The American Benedictine Review,* 4:121 (Newark, New Jersey, Summer, 1953).

9. O. G. Harrison, "The Formulas Ad Virgines sacras. A Study of the Sources" in *Ephemerides Liturgicae,* 66:253–269 (Rome, 1952). The Benedictine Review, 9:16–17 (Atchison, July, 1954); Memorandum from the Most Reverend Abbot Primate Bernard Kaelin, October 24, 1952. Mount St. Scholastica Archives.

1. One bishop had changed the style of head dress; another forbade eating between meals; and a third attempted to have the sisters replace the Little Office by the rosary.
2. Bishop Ullathorne to the prioress of St. Benedict's Convent, Erie, January 4, 1880. Copy in S.B.C.A.
3. Reverend Stanislaus Woywood, *A Practical Commentary on the Code of Canon Law*, p. 207 (New York, 1952). Revised by the Reverend Callistus Smith.
4. Letter of Mother Aloysia Northman of Atchison to Mother Cecilia, February 20, 1918. S.B.C.A.
5. Letter of Mother Cecilia to mother president, February 11, 1918. S.B.C.A.
6. Letter of mother president to Mother Cecilia, February 20, 1918. "Abbot Praeses and Abbot Innocent think it best to wait until the present Declarations are approved; then we will take up your peculiar conditions separately. As Rome is now ready to approve the present declarations as they stand it would delay the matter indefinitely if we were to make or bring in other difficulties. . . . Once they are approved you should make application and then have your works considered. They think you will then have less difficulty in being admitted and still keep the works you are doing."
7. Convent Annals.
8. Regina Baska, pp. 134–135.
9. Abbot Alcuin to Mother Louisa, June 3, 1920, wrote that the abbot primate stated that the petition reached him too late for action. S.J.A.A.
10. Stanislaus Woywood, p. 207; I. Lanslots, O.S.B., *Handbook of Canon Law*, p. 13 (New York, 1909).
11. St. Benedict's Convent Archives.
12. Mother Aloysia Northman of Atchison to Mother Louisa, May 21, 1923. S.B.C.A.
13. Abbot Alcuin to Father Ignatius, March 26, 1931. S.J.A.A.
14. Mother Rosamond to Bishop Busch, April 25, 1939. Copy in S.B.C.A.
15. The document was signed by Mother Rosamond Pratschner, Sisters Carina Julig, Ethelburga Farrell, Myron McGinley, Benedict Kapsner, Cordula Benken, Irma Schumacher, Rosaria Zenner, and Alcuin Braun. S.B.C.A.
16. This demand of Bishop Ryan caused most of the opposition to the petition for papal approval. St. Benedict's was not averse to creating an independent priory of the sisters working in the Bismarck diocese but desired to get the Decree of Praise before establishing it. Bishop Ryan wanted his priory erected immediately and before the papal approval was granted. Letters of Bishop Ryan to Bishop Busch, dated September 23, 1941, and November 29, 1941, are in the St. Cloud Chancery. Bishop Busch to Mother Rosamond, December 17, 1941. S.B.C.A. Bishop Ryan's letter to the papal delegate, May 24, 1943. Chancery office, St. Cloud.
17. Translation as given in the *Declarations and Constitutions of the Congregation of St. Benedict*, 1947, St. Joseph. Notice of Rome's action reached St. Benedict's on April 2. A second document in this dossier provided for the erection of a diocesan Benedictine house in Bismarck, to be known as the Convent of the Annunciation.
18. Official letter dated May 20, 1947. S.B.C.A. Papal delegate to Bishop Busch May 25, 1947.
19. The delegates were Sister Richarda Peters from St. Benedict's, Sister Sylvia Stevens from St. Bede's, and Sister Luanne Meagher from St. Paul's. Sister Luanne acted as secretary of the meeting. In the spring of 1951 the first canonical visitation was held.
20. Copy in S.B.C.A.
21. Sacred Congregation of Religious. S.B.C.A. For other congregations it is usual to have a cardinal protector in case the congregation has no house established in Rome. The cardinal protector acts as a Roman agent for the business trans-

actions of the congregation with the Vatican. He possesses no jurisdiction over the institute; his concern is only to promote the good of the institute by his counsel. In the case of the Benedictines the Holy Father himself retained his office of protector.

CHAPTER EIGHTEEN

1. *Berichte,* 49:8. The ruling permitting only one religious sect to work on a reservation was mitigated in a ruling of Secretary C. Lunn on February 7, 1881.
2. *Berichte,* 49:9.
3. *St. Paul Pioneer Press,* October 2, 5, 1877. The first charge was that he refused to obey the agent's orders. The second was that he had sent the two daughters of Chief Hole-in-the-Day to St. Benedict's Academy at St. Joseph, Minnesota.
4. Interview with Father Aloysius Hermanutz in 1927.
5. *Der Wanderer,* October 6, 1877; *St. Paul Pioneer Press,* October 3, 5, 1877.
6. St. John's Abbey Archives.
7. Abbot Alexius Edelbrock's Diary for 1878. Father Buh, a veteran Indian missionary, joined the party at Perham and spent some days initiating the neophites in their new life.
8. Dr. Herman Zschokke, *Nach Nordamerika u. Canada,* p. 505 (Wurzburg, 1881).
9. *Berichte,* 51:6; Sister Philomena Memoirs. S.B.C.A.
10. Father Aloysius Memoirs and manuscript history. S.J.A.A.
11. Letter of Father Aloysius to abbot, January 2 and 19, 1879.
12. Sister Lioba interview in July, 1928.
13. Class Record of Mission School. S.B.C.A. One of the pupils, Jane Horn, later became a Benedictine and took the name of Sister Marciana. She died on April 1, 1956.
14. Father Aloysius' manuscript history. S.J.A.A.; *The Indian Sentinel, 1911,* pp. 30–31 (Washington). Bishop Grace of St. Paul gave $200 toward the building fund and $465 was begged in the vicinity of the Twin Cities. The Austrian Mission Society contributed $1,080 and St. John's Abbey shouldered the rest of the $20,000 debt.
15. Sister Philomena Memoirs, S.B.C.A. *Der Wanderer,* July 26, 1883; *Northwestern Chronicle,* October 1, 1882.
16. *Der Nordstern,* June 22, 1882.
17. Financial accounts for the years 1885 and 1886 in White Earth Papers. S.B.C.A.
18. Whether the amount of foodstuff was that consumed by the 25 boarders or by only the 10 contracted for is not known.
19. Miss Drexel later founded the Sisters of the Blessed Sacrament for the Education of Negroes and Indians. It was at this time that Bishop Ireland visited White Earth and declared the Benedictine sisters working there were to receive a salary.
20. *Minneapolis Tribune,* October 11, 18, 19, 1898; *Minnesota History Bulletin,* 3:289.
21. *Father Ketcham's statement before the Subcommittee of the Committee on Indian Affairs; United States Senate,* pp. 4, 17, (Washington, 1905).
22. Letter of Father Valerian Thelen, O.S.B., to Mother Rosamond, May 21, 1945. S.B.C.A.
23. Interview with Father Aloysius on July 20, 1927; *St. Paul Globe,* July 10, 1883; Letter of Father Steffen of the Catholic Indian Bureau to the abbot, March 16, 1883. S.J.A.A.
24. Indian Agent Sheehan had in 1885 written to Abbot Seidenbusch informing him there were 700 Catholics at Red Lake in need of a priest and asked that one be sent. Letter of Sheehan to Seidenbusch, April 20, 1885. S.J.A.A.
25. *St. John's University Record,* 1:134 (December, 1888); *Der Nordstern,* November 15, 1888.
26. Letter of Father Thomas to the abbot. December 26, 1888. S.J.A.A. See *Der Nordstern,* January 10, 1889.

CHAPTER NINETEEN

1. Minutes of City Council 1883–1884 in St. Cloud City Hall. *St. Cloud Times,* August 26, 1882.
2. *Der Nordstern,* September 30, 1885.
3. *Der Nordstern,* February 10, 1886. The first group of nurses were Sister Anselma Billig, Sister Valentine Reiling, Sister Thomas Ryan, and Sister Genevieve Byrne. This cream-colored brick building on Ninth Avenue is today used for a music conservatory.
4. *St. Cloud Times,* March 3, 1886.
5. *St. Cloud Times,* April 21, 1886. In addition to the patients taken to the hospital some fifty-four were taken to the school and convent of St. Mary's Church where the teaching sisters served as nurses.
6. For biographical sketches of these pioneer St. Cloud physicians, see William B. Mitchell, *History of Stearns County,* 1:381, 395–397 (Chicago, 1915).
7. Tradition has it that the sign "St. Benedict's Hospital" was already placed above the entrance of the new building when Bishop Zardetti visited it the day before the dedication ceremony. He demanded the sign to be taken down and the name of the hospital be changed to "St. Raphael's Hospital." In his dedicatory sermon of the next day he said, "I have named this hospital St. Raphael's. In calling it St. Raphael's I wished to give the sisters and the doctors an assistant and a patron whose feast shall be annually celebrated." See *St. Cloud Times,* May 31, 1890.
8. Records of St. Raphael's Hospital 1890–1891. The first hospital had cared for 400 patients during the first two years of its existence but this new institution cared for only one-half that number during a like period of years.
9. Smith's Mass in A was sung by this small choir. *The Journal Press* of St. Cloud on August 1, informed its readers that Father Jones delivered the sermon in English, and "Father Gregory of St. Paul delivered a strong sermon in German. For the Offertory the choir sang Ave Maria by Rev. John Katzer, O.S.B., and in conclusion sang a German song to the Virgin Mary."
10. The State of Minnesota in 1907 passed an act making it unlawful to practice professional nursing unless the nurse has obtained a certificate. And a certificate was issued only to those who had attended a school of nursing or who were able to pass the state examination. The first sisters to become registered nurses were Sisters Elizabeth Vondrehle, Cunigunda Kuefler, Theolinda Gottwald and Salome Amschler.
11. Treasurer's Report. S.B.C.A.; *St. Cloud Register,* December 31, 1944.
12. Reverend Emeric Lawrence, O.S.B., "Circle of Mercy" in *Catholic Digest,* 17:53–54 (St. Paul, November 1952). From October 1919 to May 1944, the records show that the sacrament of baptism was administered to 1,212 persons.

CHAPTER TWENTY

1. Records in St. Joseph's Home, St. Cloud. A name found on the register for the year 1911 is of interest to the Sisters of St. Benedict. It is the name of the woman Mrs. Linda Slaughter, who fought for the right of the sisters to open the Catholic school at Bismarck in 1878.
2. St. Benedict's Convent Archives.
3. Records in St. Raphael's Home.
4. Sister Benedict Klein was henceforth called Mother Benedict by all in the St. Paul area because of her position as mother of the orphans. She is not to be confused with Mother Benedicta Riepp.
5. *St. Paul Globe,* October 24, 1887. Ten years later a second addition was built to the original unit.
6. Board of Directors report for the year. St. Joseph's Orphanage.

NOTES BETWEEN PAGES 229 AND 265

7. Sister Juliana's memoirs. S.B.C.A. Sister Juliana Venne was stationed with the orphans from 1909 to 1923 when she retired to the mother house at St. Joseph, Minnesota.
8. The Benedictine sisters in charge of this orphans' home have belonged to three Benedictine convents. During the first three years the sisters came from St. Gertrude's Convent at Shakopee. From 1880 (when St. Gertrude's Convent was closed and its sisters brought to St. Benedict's Convent at St. Joseph) until 1948, the sisters in charge of the orphans belonged to the mother house at St. Joseph. In 1948, when St. Benedict's was divided into three independent priories, the care of the orphans was given to the Benedictine priory erected in St. Paul.

CHAPTER TWENTY-ONE

1. Convent Chronicle. S.B.C.A.
2. Mother Louisa to Sister Francetta, July 4, 1934. Letter of Mother Louisa, December 10, 1933.
3. Sister Donalda Terhaar did not go to Kaifeng but returned to the U. S. because of illness.
4. Sister Francetta to Mother Rosamond April 12, 1938; Sister Wibora to Mother Rosamond March 13, 1938. Sister Rachel had died in 1937 and thus escaped the horrors of the war.
5. Letter of Sister Francetta to Mother Rosamond April 22, 1938. "The other day at the station the danger siren shrieked and we did not know what to do. A policeman came and rushed us to the freight car on the side tracks. We climbed the platform between two cars and thus they took us several miles out into the country where they made us get off and squat in a grain field until the all clear signal was given. On the way back a plane flew over us but did not drop a bomb. God is good."
6. Sister Wibora to Mother Rosamond May 9, 1938.
7. Sister Ronayne to Mother Rosamond March 13, 1938.
8. Sister Francetta to Mother Rosamond August 20, 1938.
9. Letter. S.B.C.A.
10. Sister Flora after the release of prisoners returned to the United States on the *Gripsholm*. The story of prison life in Japanese internment camp was related by her on her return to St. Benedict's.
11. Interview with Sister Flora. Papers and records in S.B.C.A.
12. This was an arrangement made by the Holy Father with Japan in order to safeguard religious discipline.
13. Sister Francetta to Mother Rosamond August 28, 1946. S.B.C.A. Two sisters returned to the United States instead of returning to their mission.
14. Sister Francetta to Mother Rosamond December 27, 1947. S.B.C.A.
15. Convent annals and reports. S.B.C.A.
16. Sister Francetta to Mother Rosamond June 25, 1950, July 31, 1950.
17. Seven young women from China and four from Japan were received into the mother house at St. Joseph, Minnesota, between 1947 and 1955.
18. Sister Wibora to sisters at St. Benedict's. S.B.C.A.
19. Letter to Mother Rosamond December 12, 1947. S.B.C.A. The Benedictine monks from St. John's Abbey in Minnesota had taken charge of this parish in July 1947.
20. Basil Stegman to Mother Rosamond, April 5, 1948.
21. The Congregation of St. Benedict was at this time erecting the St. Paul's and the St. Bede's priories, and under those conditions when the membership of either was in an undecided state no new commitment could be undertaken by St. Benedict's.
22. Sister Jeanette to Mother Rosamond, August 14, 1949.

BIBLIOGRAPHY

I UNPUBLISHED MATERIAL

Sources are located in scattered places. The assortment of documents is so varied that only locations and general descriptions can be given. A detailed listing would serve no practical purpose.

A. St. Cloud, Minnesota

    1. St. Cloud Diocesan Archives. Record of administrations of Bishops Zardetti, Marty, Trobec, Busch. Their papers, official notices and letters.

    2. City Hall. Records of City Council Proceedings.

    3. Cathedral of St. Mary. Papers pertaining to the establishment of this parish school. Sunday announcement books.

    4. St. Cloud Hospital. Records of patients and student nurses.

    5. St. Raphael's and St. Joseph's homes. Records of guests and finances.

B. St. Paul, Minnesota

    1. Archdiocesan Archives in Chancery office and St. Paul Seminary. Collection of Bishop Grace's and Archbishop Ireland's papers. Bishop Grace's diary of a trip to the Red River and Father Goiffon's manuscript autobiography.

    2. Minnesota Historical Society. State and Federal census records, 1859–1880. Mitchel letters, Bishop Whipple's papers and diary, 1876–79. Mrs. Wood's papers and scrapbook.

C. Collegeville, Minnesota

    1. St. John's Abbey. Letters of abbots to Church dignitaries and to individuals of the abbey. Letters to St. Benedict's Convent regarding matters of import to St. Benedict's Convent. Letters of pastors concerning parish schools. Abbot Alexius' manuscript history of St. John's. Rev. Aloysius Hermanutz's manuscript history of the White Earth Indian Mission and Francis de Malissey de Gonzaga's autobiography. Files of the reports of the Ludwig Mission Society of Bavaria and of the Leopoldinen Society of Austria. Microfilm copies of letters, and contracts of the U. S. Government and the Indian schools at White Earth and Red Lake.

D. St. Joseph, Minnesota

    1. St. Benedict's Academy. School records, business records, catalogues.

    2. College of St. Benedict. Account books, day books, ledgers, record books of all descriptions. Official catalogues and bulletins, files of letters and miscellaneous documents.

    3. Convent of St. Benedict.
Correspondence: Official notices of mother superiors to the branch houses. Correspondence with clergy and bishops, and personal letters of some sisters.
Convent Records: Acts and ordinances of the Chapter and of the Council, account books, ledgers, books of constitutions and

customs, 1857–1956. Confirmation and baptism records of members, vows of sisters, obituary records. Photostatic copies of letters of the American founders to King Ludwig and his Mission Society located in the archives of Munich, Bavaria. Microfilm copies of material in the files of the Indian Bureau at Washington, D.C., and a photostatic copy of Father Pierz's baptismal record. Scrapbooks, memoirs, diaries, annals, record of vacation school teaching, a transcript of George Kulzer's diary, and a photostatic copy of Stearns County census of 1860. Early class records, quarterly reports, and contracts of the Indian school at White Earth with the U. S. Government.

E.   St. Boniface, Manitoba, Canada
    1. Convent of Sisters of Charity, St. Boniface. Mother McMullen's diary of trip to the Red River in 1859.

II   PUBLISHED SOURCES

Annalen der Verbreitung des Glaubens, Munich, 1850–1893.
Berichte der Leopoldinen-Stiftung in Kaiserthume Oesterreich zur Unterstützung der Katholichen Missionen in America, Vienna, 1853–1893.
Catalogue of St. Benedict's Industrial School, St. Cloud, 1887.
Congressional Record, Washington, D.C., 1916.
Dunnigan's American Catholic and Laity's Directory of the United States, Baltimore, 1859, 1860.
Hoffman's Catholic Directory, Milwaukee, 1901–1911.
Laws of Minnesota Relating to the Public School System, 1939, 1946, 1949, St. Paul.
Mathäer, Willibald, *Bonifaz Wimmer, O.S.B., und König Ludwig I von Bayern,* Munich, 1938.
Metropolitan Catholic Almanac and Laity's Directory, Baltimore, 1851–1861.
Sadlier's Catholic Almanac and Ordo, New York, 1864–1896.
The Catholic Directory, Milwaukee, 1901–1911.

III   NEWSPAPERS

The writer used the newspaper files at the Minnesota Historical Society, the North Dakota Historical Society, the library of St. John's University in Collegeville, and the library at the Convent of St. Benedict's as well as newspaper clippings at St. John's University and at St. Benedict's.

Bismarck Weekly Tribune, 1875, 1876.
Bismarck Tri-weekly Tribune, 1878.
Bismarck Tribune, 1874–1878, 1883–1885, 1893.
Bismarck Capitol, 1935.
Bismarck Saturday Evening Journal, 1885.
Bad Lands Cow Boy, Medora, D. T., October 2, 1884.

Catholic Bulletin, St. Paul, 1912, 1918.
Der Wanderer, St. Paul, 1867, 1889, 1915, 1919, 1951, 1953.
Der Wahrheitsfreund, Cincinnati, 1855, 1861.
Der Nordstern, St. Cloud, 1877–1886, 1890, 1896, 1900, 1918.
Fergus Falls Weekly Journal, 1885.
Katholische Kirchen Zeitung, Baltimore, 1854–1858.
Minneapolis Star, Minneapolis, 1953.
Minneapolis Tribune, Minneapolis, 1898, 1952.
Northwestern Chronicle, St. Paul, 1867, 1869, 1882–1885, 1889.
St. Cloud Visiter, 1857, 1858.
St. Cloud Democrat, 1858–1862.
St. Cloud Times, 1878–1888, 1890, 1895, 1899, 1900, 1918, 1851–1852.
St. Cloud Journal Press, 1885–1887, 1890, 1898.
St. Cloud Register, 1944, 1953.
St. Paul Pioneer Press, 1871–1872, 1877, 1892.
Salt Lake Tribune, 1946.
The Ogden Standard-Examiner, 1945, 1946.
The Western Banner, 1859.

IV BOOKS

Alzog, J., *Manual of Universal History*, Vol. 3, Cincinnati, 1878.
Baska, Regina, O.S.B., *The Benedictine Congregation of St. Scholastica: Its Foundation and Development*, Washington, D.C., 1935.
Betschart, Ildephonse, *Der Apostel Der Siouxindianer, Bischof Martinus Marty, O.S.B., 1834–1896*. Einsiedeln, 1934.
Burns, J. A. and Kohlbrenner, *A History of Catholic Education in the United States*, New York, 1937.
Burgemeister, Remegius, *Historical Development of Catholicity in St. Marys, Pennsylvania*, 1919.
Bergman, Jessamine Slaughter, *Zezula: or Pioneer Days in the Smoky Water Country*, Valley City, 1937.
Butler, Dom Cuthbert, *Benedictine Monachism*, London, 1924.
Bishop, James, *The Day Lincoln Died*, New York, 1955.
Catalog of Nuns and Convents of the Holy Order of St. Benedict in the United States, Latrobe, 1879.
Catalogue of Nuns and Convents of the Order of St. Benedict, St. Mary's, Pa., 1903.
Clapsattle, Helen, *The Doctors Mayo*, New York, 1943.
Crawford, Lewis, *History of North Dakota* 3 vols., Am. Historical Society, Inc., Chicago, 1931.
Die Abtei Walburg, Augsburg, 1934.
Duratschek, Sister Claudia, O.S.B., *The Beginnings of Catholicism in South Dakota*, Washington, 1943.
Duratschek, Sister Claudia, O.S.B., *Crusading Along Sioux Trails, A History of the Catholic Indian Missions of South Dakota*, Yankton, 1947.
Delatte, Dom Paul, *The Rule of St. Benedict*, trans. by Dom Justin McCann, New York, 1921.
Folwell, Wm. W., *A History of Minnesota*, Minnesota Historical Society, Vol. 1 (1921), Vol. 4 (1924), St. Paul.
Guilday, Peter, *A History of the Councils of Baltimore*, New York, 1932.
Greer, J., *The History of Education in Minnesota*, Washington, 1902.

Haines, Lynn and Dora, *The Lindberghs*, New York, 1931.
Kleinschmidt, Beda, O.F.M., *Auslanddeutschtum und Kirche*, 2 vols., Münster, 1930.
Ketcham, Rev. W. H.,*Father Ketcham's Report before the Subcommittee on Indian Affairs*. 1905, Washington.
Ketcham, Rev. W. H., *The Religious Garb and Insignia in Government Schools*, 1912.
Lanslots, D., O.S.B., *Handbook of Canon Law for Congregations of Women under Simple Vows*, New York, 1909.
Long, Theodore K., *Forty Letters to Carson Long*, New Bloomfield, 1931.
Mitchel, Wm. B., *History of Stearns County*, Vol. 1, Chicago, 1915.
Moosmüller, Oswald, *Bonifaz Wimmer, Erzabt von St. Vincent in Pennsylvania*, New York, 1891.
Moosmüller, Oswald, *St. Vincenz in Pennsylvanien*, New York, 1873.
900 Yahre Abtei St. Walburg, Augsburg, 1934.
Papers Read Before the Historical and Scientific Society of Manitoba, 1944–1945, Winnipeg, 1945.
Pierz, Franz, *Die Indianer in Nord-Amerika ihre Lebensweise, Sitten, Gebräuche u.s.w.*, St. Louis, 1855.
Roemer, Theodore, *Ludwig Missionsverein and the Church in the United States 1838–1918*, Washington, 1933.
Schmeckebier, L. F., *Office of Indian Affairs: its history, activities and organization*. New York, 1927.
Winchell, Neil, William, *History of the Upper Mississippi Valley*, Minneapolis, 1881.
Witte, Raymond, *Twenty-five Years of Crusading*, Des Moines, 1948.
Woywood, S., *A Practical Commentary on the Code of Canon Law*, Revised. New York, 1952.
Zschokke, Herman, *Nach Nordamerica und Canada*, Wurzburg, 1881.

V MAGAZINES AND ANNUALS

Acta et Dicta, St. Paul, 1933.
American Benedictine Review, Newark, Summer 1953.
Annual Report of the Commissioner of U.S. Office of Indian Affairs to the Secretary of the Interior 1878, Washington, D.C., 1878.
Annual Report of the Indian School Superintendent to the Secretary of the Interior, Washington, D.C., 1881.
Biennial Report of the Attorney General, Minneapolis, 1916.
Catholic Digest, St. Paul, November, 1952.
Collections of the State Historical Society of North Dakota, Bismarck, 1906.
Collections of the State Historical Society of South Dakota, Aberdeen, 1940.
Collections of the State Historical Society of Minnesota, Vol. 1, St. Paul, 1872.
Ephemerides Liturgicae, Rome, 1852.
Fu Jen News Letter, Peking, 1931, 1932.
Gelb Hefte: historische und politische zeitschrift für das Katholische Deutschland, Munich, 1924, 1927.
Iowa Catholic Historical Review, Dubuque, April, 1932.
Mid-America, Chicago, January, 1935.
Minnesota History, St. Paul, 1929, 1946, 1953.
Northwest Magazine, St. Paul, October and December, 1885.
Northwestern Lancet, Minneapolis, April, 1888.
Northwestern Reporter, St. Paul, June, 1936.

Report of the Proceedings and Addresses of the Eighteenth Annual Meeting of the Catholic Educational Association, Columbus, 1921.

St. Benedict's Academy Annual Catalog, St. Paul, 1883, 1884.

St. Benedicts Stimmen, Prague, 1903.

St. John's University Record, Collegeville, Minnesota, January, May, 1888, March, August, September, 1889, March, 1890.

Studien und Mitteilungen zur Geschichte des Benediktiner-Ordens und Seiner Zweige, Munich, 1882, 1894, 1926, 1931.

The Diocese of St. Cloud, St. Cloud, 1891, 1892, 1893.

The Benedictine Review, Atchison, July, 1954.

The Indian Sentinel, Washington, D.C., 1911.

The Scriptorium, Collegeville, 1948.